Paul.

LIVES AND LETTERS

LIVES
AND
LETTERS

A History of Literary Biography

in England and America

by

RICHARD D. ALTICK

New York : Alfred·A·Knopf

1 9 6 9

Grateful acknowledgment is made to the following persons and firms who have allowed the use of copyrighted material in this book:

Clarendon Press, Oxford, for a quotation from *The Creation of Character in Literature*, by John Galsworthy.

Columbia University Press, for a quotation from *Hardy of Wessex*, by Carl J. Weber.

Doubleday & Company, Inc., for quotations from *Cakes and Ale*, by W. Somerset Maugham. Copyright 1930 by W. Somerset Maugham. Reprinted by permission of Doubleday & Company, Inc.

Leslie Fiedler and the *Sewanee Review* for a quotation from Mr. Fiedler's "Archetype and Signature." Copyright 1952 by the University of the South.

Harcourt, Brace & World, Inc., for quotations from *Eminent Victorians*, by Lytton Strachey.

Houghton Mifflin Company, for quotations from *Amy Lowell: A Chronicle*, by S. Foster Damon.

John Murray, for a quotation from *Sir Walter*, by Donald Carswell.

Charles Scribner's Sons, for a quotation from *The Letters of Henry James*, edited by Percy Lubbock.

University of Illinois Press, for a quotation from *Henry James and H. G. Wells*, edited by Leon Edel and Gordon N. Ray.

L. C. catalog card number: 64-17699

THIS IS A BORZOI BOOK,
PUBLISHED BY ALFRED A. KNOPF, INC.

PUBLISHED OCTOBER 18, 1965
SECOND PRINTING, July 1966
THIRD PRINTING, DECEMBER 1969

TO

Alice and Robert Estrich

PREFACE

❧

My FIRST thanks must go to the American Council of Learned Societies for the award of a fellowship in 1959–60 which enabled me to begin accumulating systematic notes on biographies and what has been written about them. The Ohio State University, through the ever-sympathetic agency of its Department of English and College of Arts and Sciences, subsequently made further periods of time available for reading and writing by transferring me from the classroom to "research duty." The same administrative friends of scholarship provided me with the services of two hard-working assistants, Samuel Jones and David Young, and with typing aid.

Portions of the manuscript, in earlier drafts, were read by Professors William Charvat, Robert C. Elliott, Robert M. Estrich, John Harold Wilson, and Andrew Wright, all of whom lent their funds of specialized knowledge and their keen eyes for stylistic lapses to the betterment of my pages. My former colleague, Professor Francis Russell Hart, allowed me to read his valuable Harvard dissertation on one aspect of the history of biography; for this privilege, as well as for many stimulating talks, I am grateful. To Professor James L. Clifford, who could have written a much better book on biography but who generously abandoned his own plan when I announced mine, I owe both the gift of an extensive bibliography, prepared for his students at Columbia University, which saved me many hours of work, and the benefit of conversation and correspondence on a topic to which we are both partial. A number of other friends, by their interest and practical assistance, sustained me when the going was rough. My wife and daughters, having long since become reconciled to the manufacture of books on the premises as a necessary evil somehow inseparable from the academic life, tolerated the production of this one with exemplary good humor. As I send it off to the printer, I have more reason than ever to regret the convention that allows only the author's name to appear on the title page.

INTRODUCTION

❧

"BE THERE a thousand lives, My great curiosity has stomach for 'em all": so, paraphrasing Othello, wrote James Boswell in his journal for April 8, 1775. It is easy to understand his voracity, at the very moment when biography was about to cease being a not very important relation of journalism, history, and the literature of moral instruction and achieve a dignity of its own. (Almost precisely two years later, Dr. Johnson would contract with a group of London publishers to write his epoch-making *Lives of the Poets*.) Already the unique interest of true narratives of people's lives had become evident; and it was to increase without pause down to our own day.

Until Boswell's time, most biographies, in the English tongue at least, had been written about saints, divines, monarchs, statesmen, soldiers, retired courtesans, and highwaymen. But ever since, steadily edging out the pious, the powerful, and the perverse, one class has claimed the center of the biographical stage: the men and women who have created our literature. The life of the poet, as Lionel Trilling has remarked, nowadays is "the paradigm of all biography." For reasons that lie deep in social and cultural history, as well as in homely human preference, people have liked, and continue to like, to read the lives of authors. The demand for literary biography (a term that in this book will always refer to subject, not treatment: "biography of men of letters," not "biography with specifically literary quality") has in fact been insatiable, so that all the examples that have been produced in England and America alone would fill a good-sized library.

Why has literary biography been so popular over the years, not only among the cultivated but among readers whose interest in history, sociology, or psychology, let alone literature itself, is but casual? The most obvious answer is that it is an incomparably diversified gallery in which to behold the human comedy —and the human tragedy. Since literature has always been an intensely personal pursuit, the people who have engaged in it, far from merging into any cloudy similarity, have been as various as the limits of human personality allow. "What a miscellaneous world!" exclaimed the ex-bluestocking and evangelical tract writer Hannah More, heroine of one of the worst biographies ever written. What a gloriously miscellaneous world indeed, the inveterate reader of literary biography affirms. Henry James gazes down a Boston vista and stammers: "Do you feel that Marlborough Street—is precisely—*passionate?*" Virginia Woolf, sick at heart, leaves her cottage and finds the death she seeks in the cold waters of a nearby stream. Wordsworth solemnly reads "The Leech Gatherer" aloud to his barber as the shears snip the poet's locks. Hart Crane, aged twenty, crouches cross-legged on the floor behind the counter in one of his father's chain of candy stores in Akron, Ohio, smoking a Cinco cigar and reading Pound's *Pavannes and Divisions.* John Ruskin, still obsessed with his passion for young girls but now, in his senility, afflicted in addition with a compulsion to utter monotonous curses, is puzzled when maidens scurry from his lawn as he greets them: "Bow-wow, bow-wow! Damn!" Keats, chilled to the bone after riding outside a coach in bad weather, coughs up bright red blood and recognizes his death warrant. Arnold Bennett, attending a *Daily Mail* celebrity dinner, encounters the Prince of Wales in the lavatory and is somewhat shaken to hear His Royal Highness say: "I don't know you very well, but may I tell you a story?" William Blake, at the request of a friend, conjures up the devil, who politely sits in a chair and then as amiably disappears. Amy Lowell, touring the headwaters of the Nile and faced by an imminent Arab insurrection, cows the restless natives by brandishing a fountain pen. Sir Walter Scott, returning home from welcoming George IV to Edinburgh in 1822, sits down, screams, and remembers he had stowed in his tail pocket the precious glass from which he had drunk the monarch's health. Longfellow, already once widowed, finds his wife in panic, her summer dress aflame, and is himself burned in futilely trying to save her life. The gigantic Thomas Wolfe fights his long-suffering editor and father substitute, Maxwell Perkins, on the floor of a New York restaurant, crying, as he pummels the recumbent Perkins, "Let me alone, you damned old woman!"

But there are other, more subtle, motives behind the reading of literary lives than the well-nigh universal relish of character and drama. Literary biography has shared in, and profited by, the general shift of literary interest from external action to the inner spectacle of the mind and feelings. However well supplied with *res gestae* the lives of some men of letters are, the chief appeal of literary biography resides in its recital not of adventures in the world but of the experience of a sensitive and self-aware human spirit. The peculiar attraction of literary biography is essentially that of the psychological novel and the confessional lyric. Like them, it opens the windows of the soul.

And it opens, in particular, the windows of an artist's soul, thus gratifying a curiosity—to describe the phenomenon in its lowest terms—that has marked every generation since romanticism began in earnest the quest for the creator behind the creation. All books about artists imply an attempt to shed light on the mystery of the artistic process, but literary biographies as a class are more successful than others because they are couched in the language of the art with which they deal. The biographer and his writer-subject, especially if, in addition to his formal literary works, the latter has left abundant personal records upon which the biographer can draw, share a common tongue: they use words to describe a congeries of life experiences whose ultimate product is an art composed, likewise, of words. To view, with a biographer's aid, the processes of artistic development and fruition in a writer is ordinarily easier and more satisfying than in a composer, painter, or sculptor, who use nonverbal languages which are as distant from the printed word as the sounds of a symphony are from the program notes which purport to describe them.

Literary biography draws its appeal also from the seeming remoteness of the literary life from everyday experience. War and politics—other familiar settings of biography—come relatively close to us all. Artistic creation seldom does; it exists in a world foreign and strangely attractive to us. We all have some sort of yearning to express ourselves as artists do. Even when we are faced with the brutal facts of some writers' disappointments and tragedies—their suffering and privation, their struggle for recognition, the sheer cost of creativity to body and mind—we persist in regarding literary people as fortunate. In our reasonable moments we would not wish to be in their shoes, but we cannot help envying their accomplishment of self-realization and expression to a degree that is impossible to us. Literary biography, then, like fiction, serves sometimes as a kind of escape literature, a form of wish-fulfilment. Vicariously it makes authors of us all.

It is no accident that the popularity of literary biography has increased most notably in the past century and a half, a period which has also been marked by a growing sense that the artist as a person is detached from society, indeed is a special kind of being quite apart from the common run of men. This powerful notion, which reaches back to classical antiquity but received its modern impetus from the romantics at the beginning of the nineteenth century, was further publicized, in both theory and personal practice, by the so-called esthetes and decadents of the period stretching from Rossetti to Oscar Wilde and Yeats. In their fiction, Henry James and Willa Cather probed the figure of the Artist as a Special Case. Whether we regard it as a profound social truth or merely as an occupational neurosis, the idea of the artist as alien has been one of the predominant themes—even platitudes—of recent criticism. Thus literary biography has acquired additional interest as a collection of studies in departures from the norm—portraits of people apart. The biographies themselves may not necessarily prove that artists are really a separate race; some literary people, in fact, on close inspection turn out to be disconcertingly normal and at home in their society. For all we know to the contrary, Chaucer and Shakespeare were perfectly well adjusted to themselves and the world about them. Nevertheless, the very existence of the myth (to use a handily ambiguous term) has unquestionably done much to stimulate both the writing and the reading of literary biography.

If the artist, in our inherited conception, is an outsider, he is also a rebel. He symbolizes resistance to the pressures which induce us lesser men to think and act in sheeplike unison; he is among the heroes Western society celebrates as it laments the disappearance of individualism. To be sure, our dramatic mid-twentieth-century habit of pacing up and down behind the bars of conformity is nothing new; the sense of captivity was strong in such diverse spokesmen of past generations as Wordsworth, Emerson, and John Stuart Mill. But we seem to feel it more poignantly nowadays, and we are perhaps more inclined than any previous age to attribute to the artist the defiant freedoms we consider ourselves as being too timid or weak to claim as our own. We may recklessly romanticize in the process, but the urge to do so is genuine and intense; if we look in the right places, we can find in literary biography numerous chronicles of steadfast nonconformity. It is no little thing, Yeats once said, "to achieve anything in art, to stand alone perhaps for many years, to go a path no other man has gone, to accept one's own thought when the thought of others has the authority of the world behind it, . . . to give one's life as well as one's words which are so much nearer to one's soul to the criticism of the world." The very word *artist* connotes personal independence won, perhaps at high cost but nevertheless won, against all the repressive forces of society. And, though we may sometimes credit the poet with more emancipation than he in fact enjoys, in most cases our instinct is right.

From its very birth as an English literary form until well past the middle of the nineteenth century, the universal justification of biography was its didactic usefulness. Because this moral preoccupation hampered biography's development as a candid report of life, its eventual jettisoning was an event over which we never cease to rejoice. It is ironic, then, that one should again be led in the 1960's to mention the instructive, inspirational function of literary biography; yet it does exist, and it is valuable. The biographies of artists who had the courage of their higher instincts were never more immediately pertinent than they are today, and as we read them, a modicum of that courage may rub off on us. No one can accuse Sir Osbert Sitwell of copybook philistinism, yet it was he who remarked, not many years ago, that "even apart from its productions, the spectacle of genius or of exceptional talent or personality, of lives spent happily or unhappily in the service of an ideal, and of the application of the rare, yet essential, *common sense* of art towards life may possess its own practical, no less than moral or semi-historical, value."

These are among the reasons why people, including myself in my nonprofessional hours, read literary biography. But to the historian of literature and culture, the role I have assumed for the purpose of this book, biography is much more than the sum of the separate stories it tells. It is, for one thing, a narrative art with a fairly long history and a large set of technical problems which writers, ever since the days of Izaak Walton, have tried to solve. For another, both as an art and as a form of historiography, it is a product of general culture. Its conventions and modes, its emphases and suppressions, are determined by the manifold pressures, interests, aspirations, and anxieties of each successive era in which it is produced. It rewards study, therefore, both as a form of literature and as a social institution.

Since the expansion and illustration of this last point is the business of the present book itself, it need not be dwelt upon here. I should perhaps remark that, though my concern is with literary biography in particular, much of what I have to say is applicable to biography in general, irrespective of subject matter. In some places it has been necessary to suspend my narrative of specifically literary biography in order to explain certain forces and tendencies that have affected all life writing at given times. My special intention, however, has been to show how the biographies of writers have been the product of prevailing cultural conditions. I have touched upon a cognate topic—the way in which they have both mirrored and affected the critical thought of their times—but I have not dealt with it as thoroughly as its importance deserves. Its full exploration I leave to other hands.

Although my appetite, or power of endurance, has not matched Boswell's, as the grist for this study I have read several hundred literary biographies, a total which may seem modest enough until it is realized that a considerable number of them were in two or more volumes. I have not read all the good books in the field; I am sure I have read my share of the bad ones. Because my purpose was to cover, systematically and analytically, a tract of literary history which for the most part had previously been the subject only of impressionistic discussion, I endeavored to spread my net so widely with respect to date of publication, scale of treatment, scholarly and literary quality, and level of presumptive audience as to have a sound basis for the many generalizations the historian is expected to make. My statements about the tendencies of critical opinion on biography in various eras are derived from a reading of several thousand reviews in nineteenth-century periodicals and of every general discussion of biography, in books and magazines, that I could locate.

The special nature of the story told in these pages has made it desirable to employ a substitute for the conventional chronological narrative whose progress is measured by an orderly series of titles and dates. The history of literary biography before the last half-century is not primarily one of masterpieces and near-masterpieces, nor did it witness a steady refinement of form and technique. It is true that the genre had its great moments, now and again, from the seventeenth century onward, and in our time the incidence of well-wrought biographies has markedly increased. But in the long view it seems to me that it is the genre as a whole, along with the literary and extra-literary forces which affected it, that deserves the closest examination, rather than the parts—the individual books—of which it is composed. The predominant interest of the history of the form, particularly in the century and more between Boswell's *Johnson* (1791) and Strachey's *Eminent Victorians* (1918), resides not so much in events as in slow-moving tendencies and in conditions, such as the reign of reticence, which changed little over long periods of time. It has therefore seemed legitimate to use a broadly topical rather than a narrative approach in dealing with the nineteenth century. Similarly, the discussion of the ideals and techniques of contemporary literary biography to which the final chapters are devoted is descriptive and critical in its conception.

Though I have departed from the usual procedure adopted by the historian of a literary form, I have not, I hope, sacrificed my perspective or my fidelity to the facts. I think often of the epitaph in Peterborough Cathedral of Mandell Creighton, bishop of London and historian of the Papacy, which concludes with six pregnant words that imply both the loftiness of the historian's ambition and the mortal odds against its full achievement: HE TRIED TO WRITE TRUE HISTORY. I too have tried.

CONTENTS

((*x v i i*

CONTENTS

I

The Beginnings

CHAPTER I

Literary Biography
Before Its Time

✳

Iɴ the year 1598 a thick folio volume called *The Workes of
Our Antient and lerned English Poet, Geffrey Chaucer* appeared
on the London bookstalls. It was not the first collected edition of
Chaucer, but what distinguished it from its predecessors was an
introduction headed thus:

THE LIFE OF OVR LEARNED
English Poet, Geffrey Chaucer

So much as we can find by Herauldes, Chronicles, & Records, of his	Countrey. Parentage. Education. Mariage. Children, With their Reuenues. Seruice. Reward. Friends. Bookes. Death.	Mariage. Lands. Seruice. Reward. Issue. Death.

In the following dozen or so pages the editor, a schoolmaster
named Thomas Speght, gathered all the facts then known, or
what purported to be the facts, about Chaucer the man. This
was the first "life," in the English language, of a great English

poet. It makes 1598 as good a year as any from which to date the beginnings of English literary biography.

Nobody reads Speght today, for his biographical introduction is only a heap of unrelated and fragmentary statements on the topics listed. Nor does anybody now go to him for dependable facts, because apart from such meager data on Chaucer's life as were found in the authentic public records of Chaucer's age, his "facts" came from earlier collectors, who were, to put it mildly, of uneven reliability. These men were John Leland and John Bale, and as compilers who defiled the stream of English biographical tradition at its source, they deserve a special word or two.

Between 1534 and 1543 John Leland, bearing a warrant as "the king's antiquary," ransacked the country's religious houses for early English historical documents, in which, of course, lay a certain amount of information on writers. It was well that he did so, because, even as he worked, a great many of those documents perished or were scattered when the monasteries and abbeys were expropriated and in many cases ravaged by the forces of Henry VIII. Had it not been for Leland's making numerous extracts from them, their contents would now be utterly lost. On the other hand, modern students, bred in a more fastidious scholarship, have had hard things to say about him. A pioneer American authority on Chaucer, Thomas R. Lounsbury, wrote, with somewhat excessive but understandable exasperation, that "Leland was an antiquary who was not content with recording history; he manufactured it, and the products of his invention, accepted as statements of fact, have stood for centuries in the way of investigation. . . . Wherever it was possible for Leland to make a mistake of fact he made it; wherever it was possible for him to draw an erroneous inference, he drew it; wherever it was possible for him to give a wrong impression, he gave it. . . . As an antiquary he was privileged to be dull, to be interested in matters no one else cared about; the one thing that was forbidden him was to be inaccurate. Unfortunately, in the biography of Chaucer this is the only thing which he was."

Leland lost his mind in 1547, and his large collections went unprinted until 1710–15. But the manuscripts were available for quarrying by other scholars, among whom the first was John Bale, playwright, bishop of Ossory, and ferocious Protestant controversialist, who in such time as he could spare from helping stir the religious turbulence of the mid-sixteenth century put together the first dictionary of English writers. His *Scriptorum Illustrium Maioris Brytanniae* [Celebrated Writers of Great Britain], a massive folio printed in Basel in 1557–59, is composed of several hundred entries relating to chroniclers, theologians, monks, monarchs, and others who wrote books in the earlier English centuries. Everything is in Latin, the biographical information as well as the extensive lists of books. Caxton is there, and Langland, the supposed author of *Piers Plowman,* and the interminably garrulous John Lydgate; along with such figures, whose names if not their works recommend them to remembrance, as Iohannes Skuish and the bearers of sonorities like Robertus Perscrutator and Sulcardus Westmonasteriensis. Chaucer is allotted one paragraph of biographical information, plus a bibliography which includes a number of works that we now know he did not write. Among them is *The Testament of Love,* which, from Leland and Bale until no more than a century ago, was assumed to be Chaucer's and to contain valuable fragments of the poet's autobiography. In such a manner, during those early stirrings of interest in literary men's biographies, was fancy hopelessly intermingled with fact. Leland averred something, and Bale printed it; Speght duly added it to the sum of information on Chaucer as of 1598; succeeding editors of Chaucer picked it up and surrounded it with newly acquired myths—and so, fed by man's zestful credulity, error flourished through the centuries.

When Thomas Speght compiled the first English life of an English poet in 1598, literature contained, strictly speaking, no such genre as biography. The word itself came into the language only in the 1660's. But the writing of lives had already occupied English pens for hundreds of years, to commemorate the pious and the powerful. The medieval ancestor of biography was the saint's life or, to be more accurate about it, the saint's legend. From the Anglo-Saxon era down to the fifteenth century, in prose and verse, for the most part in Latin but sometimes in the vernac-

ular English tongue, biographies of saints and martyrs had provided nutrition for Christian souls. Their purpose was a simple
and obvious one: to inspire mortals to emulate the saintly spirit
and selfless deeds of other mortals, whom the Church had canonized.

To read very extensively in medieval saints' lives requires a
special taste that few modern people have or would care to cultivate. Apart from an occasional picturesque or humanizing touch,
such as an anecdote, there was no attempt to draw individualized
portraits or to examine psychology. To the authors of these lives
—anonymous for the most part—a saint was a saint, the value of
whose story lay not in who he was, and specifically where and
when he lived and what he actually did, but rather in the edification a reader could derive from what he was *said* to have done.
For their narratives the hagiographers drew freely from the great
stockpile of heroic qualities and supernatural deeds that had
accumulated since the beginning of the Christian era and attributed the same ones, with generous impartiality, to saint after
saint. They even, by some innocent accident such as misreading a
document or mistaking a name, invented purely fictitious saints
and then proceeded to endow the new creations with an ample
roster of miraculous accomplishments.

It was upon these miracles, rather than the everyday circumstances of their saints' existence, that the hagiographers concentrated, with a single-mindedness that is testimony both to their
devout credulity and to their human appetite for thrilling events.
The abiding interest of saints' lives lay in the variety, splendor,
and (in crass earthly terms) the impossibility of the deeds that
Saint So-and-so performed and the trials he underwent; not what
he looked like, or what sort of family he came from, or when he
died.

Thus the saints' lives are only a most primitive form of biography, lacking at least two of the prime qualities that a modern
life narrative must have before it can be called a biography. They
are composed of the materials of legend, not of sober, docu-
mentable history; and although legend has not been wholly expunged from biography even in our day, its presence is usually
disapproved of. True biography, again, is characterized by a

strong sense of individuality. But the men and women who populate the saints' lives are as stylized as the images of them made by medieval sculptors and manuscript illuminators and workers in stained glass (hagiographers themselves, in other media). The portrayals often are moving, thus fulfilling their religious purpose, but they are neither individual nor realistic. Their relevance is to the life of the spirit in a timeless world, not to the life of a flesh-and-blood human being with a habitation and a name.

One unmistakable heritage the saints' lives did leave: the idea, ineffaceable until quite recent times, that no matter under what auspices it was written, ecclesiastical or secular, biography should be an instrument of inspiration and instruction. Without this spiritual or utilitarian *raison d'être* biography could not have survived through centuries when the spirit of delight was, of itself, an insufficient apology for a book's existence. At the same time, however, the implicit denial that biography should provide entertainment or satisfy curiosity militated against the collection and preservation of the very kind of data that men in later centuries were to find most revealing. Early biographers, from the hagiographers on down until Boswell changed everything, for the most part disdained the concrete particularities, the significant trivia that are indispensable to modern biographical portraiture. Haloes and homely details did not go well together, nor did crowns and crotchets.

Custom did not change much when, in the Tudor era, life writing shifted its emphasis from the "commendation of virtue" to the "detestation of vice." Now it was not the pious who were the center of interest—though, of course, they were far from forgotten—but the powerful; or, at least, the once powerful. The theme was secular and gloomy: the higher proud (and therefore sinful) men rise, the harder they fall. Boccaccio, composing *De Casibus Virorum Illustrium,* had ransacked history for examples; in turn, the fifteenth-century English writer Lydgate had spun out Boccaccio's lugubrious tales to a mortal 36,300 lines. But the cosmic sigh "Vanity, vanity, all is vanity" was most immediately audible to the Elizabethans in *A Mirror for Magistrates,* a series of royal biographies by various authors, "Wherein may be seen by

((7

example of other, with howe grevous plages vices are punished:
and howe frayle and vnstable worldly prosperitie is founde, even
of those, whom Fortune seemeth most highly to favour."

The postmedieval shift of interest from miraculous and martyred saints to the catastrophes of temporal princes was progress
in the sense that biography was on the way to becoming secu-
larized in subject matter as well as auspices. Otherwise, such
books as *A Mirror for Magistrates* and the few sustained individual biographies the sixteenth century produced marked little
artistic advance over the saints' lives.[1] It was their didactic
theme, cautionary or commemorative as the case might be, rather
than their fidelity to the experienced facts of a particular human
life, that commanded the attention of their authors; not the individual man as such, but the universally applicable lessons that
could be drawn from his story.

It is odd that the art of biography did not share in the splendid surge of creative energy during the Elizabethan era. Bacon
was puzzled by it, even as we are today. "For lives," he wrote in
The Advancement of Learning (1605), "I do find strange that
these times have so little esteemed the virtues of the times, as that
the writings of lives should be no more frequent. For although
there be not many sovereign princes or absolute commanders, . . .
yet there are many worthy personages that deserve better than
dispersed report or barren elogies." In the five years before
Speght's life of Chaucer appeared, Spenser had published his
Amoretti and *The Faerie Queene;* Bacon had printed the first
version of his *Essays;* and some ten of Shakespeare's plays had
been performed, including *A Midsummer Night's Dream, Richard
II, Romeo and Juliet, The Merchant of Venice,* and the two parts
of *Henry IV.* One would think that life writing would inevitably
have been caught up in the general excitement. Certainly the

---

[1] One noteworthy exception is George Cavendish's life of Cardinal Wolsey,
written in 1557. As Richard S. Sylvester demonstrated ("Cavendish's *Life of
Wolsey:* The Artistry of a Tudor Biographer," *Studies in Philology,* LVII [1960],
44–71), Cavendish carefully delineated Wolsey as a tragic hero, and by his deft
handling of structure, episodes, and point of view strikingly anticipated some of
the techniques of modern biographers. The book, however, went unprinted until
1641, and was known only in condensed and garbled form until the early nineteenth century; it therefore had no effect upon the standards of biography at a
time when such models of artistry were much needed.

sheer logic of humanism, the governing spirit of the Renaissance, favored the swift burgeoning of biography as an art form. With the fading of medieval assumptions, which had denied the importance and significance of the individual human being and dwelt upon the illusory and penitential qualities of life on this earth, sixteenth-century English humanism focused joyously upon the substantiality, the positive value, of human existence. The endless delight of this brave new world, which had so many *different* people in it, gave biography, in theory, infinitely greater justification than it could possibly have had in the otherworldly Middle Ages. Psychological analysis, the differentiation of personality through significant physical detail and distinctive speech, the painting in of recognizable circumstantial background—such techniques, the essence of mature biography, had ample warrant in the new artistic spirit, to say nothing of their actual exemplification, occasionally in realistic prose fiction and more extensively in the plays of Shakespeare.

Furthermore, the rediscovery of classical literature brought with it translations of Latin and Greek biography: Tacitus' life of Agricola, Suetonius' lives of the Caesars, above all Plutarch's *Lives* as made into English by Sir Thomas North. In an age that venerated everything produced in antiquity and, on the other hand, increasingly regarded medieval literature as a relic of centuries of ignorance and superstition, the fact that biography had engaged the cultivated talents of a Plutarch gave it much greater cachet than it derived from its native sources in the now-closed monasteries. Nevertheless, the Elizabethans chose to realize their delight in the newly discovered complexities of human behavior by imaginative exercise, in drama and poetry, rather than by expanding the still narrow limits of life writing. Biography was to prove one of the very last harvests from the seed of English Renaissance humanism.

· 2 ·

If the development of English biography as a whole was slow, the development of literary biography in particular was even slower. In the sixteenth century and the greater part of the seventeenth, the term "literary biography" as it is used in this book would have been meaningless, simply because no one as yet conceived of authorship as a distinct, or at least a respectable, occupation. No single one of the several hundred "celebrated writers" listed in Bale's dictionary was, in the usual sense, a man of letters; all were men of various learned callings, though predominantly ecclesiastics—monks, friars, bishops who happened to write books—and in Bale's entries the biographical material was less important than the bibliographical. It was the books, not the men behind them, that counted.

In Elizabeth's later years there were, it is true, men who tried to live by the pen, but they had no social status whatsoever. They were, in fact, despised. Grub Street had already come into existence, and its denizens were quickly stereotyped in the upper-class imagination as penniless, bibulous hacks, striking humiliating bargains with booksellers or licking the boots of titled potential patrons. That any of them would be judged worthy of a biography in an age when biography was devoted to monarchs and Protestant martyrs and ecclesiastics was incredible, except insofar as their debauched and godless lives could be used as awful warnings by Puritan moralists.

As for the rest of the men who belong to the history of Tudor literature, it was their social position or their eminence in church or state, not their literary accomplishments, that measured their eligibility for biographical notice. There were several sixteenth-century biographies of Sir Thomas More—one by his son-in-law William Roper; a second, much fuller, by Roper's friend Nicholas Harpsfield; and a third, by More's nephew William Rastell, which survives only in fragments—but in all of these the subject is More the commanding historical figure, in the very center of public life and close to the court, and the participant in a great conflict between monarchy and church, rather than the author of *Utopia*. Sir Philip Sidney would be remembered in the same manner as a truly perfect English knight—a member of an aristocratic family, a courtier and an accomplished gentleman—and not specifically as a writer. Fulke Greville's early memoir of Sidney, written about 1610–12 and first published in 1652, says nothing whatever of his hero's writings except for a brief discussion of the *Arcadia* from the point of view of a political philosopher.

Hence the emergence of literary biography had to await the emergence of the man of letters as a distinct type of social being. It was no accident that with the exception of Speght's *Chaucer*, the first separate, nondictionary biographies of men of letters appeared about the time (roughly the period of Dryden and Pope) that authorship was developing into a profession. But something more had to happen before a firmly established institution of literary biography could come into being. There had to be a revolution in critical doctrine.

The basic postulate of modern literary biography is that there is an essential connection between person and artist, that the personality of the writer and the events of his life have a demonstrable relevance to the psychic forces, however defined, that produce his art. Individual traits and circumstances, in other words, are the key to art. As we shall see, this concept of the inseparability of the creator and the creation, as well as the corollary principle that to understand one is to illuminate the other, was first formulated in the romantic esthetic of the early nineteenth century; and its full implications could not be explored and illustrated until the advent of twentieth-century depth psychology.

In the Middle Ages there was no such belief. As René Wellek has said: "The very conception of the aims of the poet, who was usually pictured as a humble craftsman in the service of his Maker, the widespread anonymity of literary creation, the prevalent 'communism' both of subjects and forms, which shows that originality and individuality were not valued, the absence of any regard for the historicity of events: all these parallel symptoms of the medieval mentality explain the absence of any literary history"—and, we can add, any literary biography. The interest manifested in the lives of writers in the past two centuries would have been incomprehensible to medieval man, because he could not possibly have grasped the assumptions that underlie it. Above all, perhaps, he could not have understood the veneration the men of the Renaissance and later ages lavished upon art itself. Art to him meant, essentially, a cluster of crafts devoted to didactic and inspirational aims; in it there resided no intrinsic greatness but only a certain salutary power over men's souls. It was a means, not an end. To envision the gorgeous palaces of prelates and merchants filled with paintings and statuary and furniture and objects of virtu assembled for the sheer love of beauty was beyond the ability of medieval man.

Although the Renaissance valued art, including literature, as a supreme expression of man's delight in worldly experience, and at the same time rediscovered the dignity of the individual person, its critical thought failed to make the all-vital connection between the two; it did virtually nothing to establish the significance of the individual person as a literary artist. To be sure, Sidney and other Elizabethan critics praised "the poet"—but as a type, an abstraction, rather than a specific, identifiable human being. It was not the poet's personal characteristics that were significant; they were, in fact, irrelevant. The sole quality that distinguished him was his possession of a "genius," an indescribable, nonrational faculty whence sprang his song. The poet created not by any conscious exercise of the will or the intellect but by "inspiration"—a command and a gift from some greater force outside him. What that force was depended on the time when the critical theory that defined it was being expounded. To the classical pagan, it had been the Muse; to the Renaissance Christian, it was God; to the eighteenth-century deist, it was to be the impersonal, metaphysical force called Nature. In any case, inspiration, the begetter of poetry, had nothing to do with any explainable human activity. It came unbidden, it was utterly mysterious in its operation. The poet was a mouthpiece, not an originator. The sort of man he was, the nature of his personal experiences, had no pertinence whatsoever to his gift of art. What conceivable critical pertinence, then, could his biography have?

Nor was this all. Renaissance literary theory heavily stressed rhetoric, the elaborate set of stylistic devices by which the writer obtained his effects, rather than individuality of utterance. It was the skill with which the poet handled various classes of metaphors, for example, and the order in which he arranged his materials, that engaged the attention of critics—not the degree to which his style was flavored by his personality. Though there was some disagreement from epoch to epoch and from one school of thought to another, English critical opinion from the Elizabethan age down past the middle of the eighteenth century generally deprecated, if it did not actually condemn, the twin offenses of egotism and excessive originality. These got in the way of the Muse, substituting personal preoccupation for inspiration. Matters of primarily individual concern, those that did not have a readily apparent universal application, were not fit subjects for poetry. And although mere slavish imitation of models was not desirable, neither was defiance of the accepted norms of style in favor of some more distinctly personal, and therefore eccentric, manner. The whole tenor of critical theory, until the great "romantic revolution," was strongly anti-individualistic and therefore anti-biographical. The man and the artist had yet to be seen in a single glass.

Thus, although it is hard to explain why the art of biography in general developed so slowly down to the eighteenth century, there are reasons enough why, among the several hundred lives that were written, there were few lives of writers in particular. And when an age is itself indifferent to men of letters as subjects of life narratives, it can hardly be expected to lay down well-filled biographical time capsules about them for the instruction of future centuries. The Elizabethans were avid for news of the past, and among them were some great historians and antiquarians, bent on recovering everything that could be learned of earlier centuries. But, to our immeasurable loss, they seldom reflected, except when they fell into that melancholy frame of mind in which they wrote their haunting poems on mutability, that the inexorable process of time would soon turn their present into yet another chapter of the past. They were so busy living—and writing and reading history—that they neglected to provide for posterity. "One cannot help wishing," a modern biographer of Spenser has commented, "that a man like Thomas Heywood, instead of industriously compiling an encyclopedic history of women that contains hardly a reference to the ladies of his own

((13

day, had chronicled the stirring lives of some of his fellow dramatists, and that Ralegh had written during his tedious years of
confinement in the Tower, not a history of the world, but a narrative of his own life and times." Even so, more information survives on Ralegh than on Shakespeare or Spenser.

Lacking well-arranged and efficiently indexed contemporary
chronicles, modern biographers of sixteenth- and seventeenth-
century writers must piece together, with great labor, such tiny
and widely scattered fragments of information as survive. The
Elizabethans had no *Who's Who,* no newspapers, no magazines
containing interviews with the Queen's civil administrator in
Ireland, Mr. Edmund Spenser, or picture stories on life at the
Penshurst estate of Sir Philip Sidney. Because of the high cost of
materials and postage, relatively few letters were written, and
few of them escaped destruction; and those that perished first
were the kind most precious to biography—the intimate personal
missives that bring the reader closest to the writer. Over 180
letters of John Donne remain, but they are for the most part so
formal and ceremonial that they reveal little of the man. Only a
handful of diaries and other kinds of personal memoranda still
exists. And only with the utmost rarity, as when a Scots laird, the
poet William Drummond, entertained Ben Jonson for a couple of
weeks at his estate at Hawthornden and set down his guest's
freely expressed opinions and numerous anecdotes about him, did
it happen that someone deliberately recorded the sort of personal
data for which the literary biographer hungers.

Since, apart from one or two inspired efforts like Drummond's,
nobody ever singled out writers as being particularly worth describing in detail, all we can hope to know of Elizabethan and
seventeenth-century authors is the little that can be assembled
from scattered documents and read, or at greater or less peril
inferred, from their writings. Fortunately, the English have always had a tendency toward bureaucratic *paperasserie,* so that
since the Middle Ages every man above the laboring class has had
a fairly wide variety of opportunities to get his name in the official records. Information about Shakespeare and his family, for
example, has been found in documents connected with land

transfer and ownership, parish registers of births, marriages, and deaths, the municipal archives of Stratford-on-Avon, the records of the Queen's court and of her administrative departments, various kinds of legal instruments, and wills. In Shakespeare's case, moreover, some information can be derived from the documents associated with the London theatrical world and from the records of the booksellers' guild, the Worshipful Company of Stationers, which was the quasi-official copyright office. There are a few references to him in the extant writings of other Elizabethans who knew, or at least had heard of, him. There are also a number of stories about him that were first written down from oral report in the middle or later seventeenth century, after his death; but these are of such shaky authenticity as to be worth very little. All the available solid facts about Shakespeare the man—a prosperous middle-class citizen who happened to be connected with the theater—could be adequately set out in half a dozen pages of this book, and they tell us nothing of what we would most wish to have information about, his character and personality.

Little more, and in most cases less, is known about Shakespeare's fellow writers. Occasionally, to be sure, the biographer is fortunate. The preservation of the Sidney papers permits us some vivid glimpses of the family's fairest flower, the poet-soldier Sir Philip. Spenser comes alive, for a brief period, in the personal letters he wrote to the poet and controversialist Gabriel Harvey; but very few such correspondences between Elizabethan literary men survive. Thanks to two unbroken series of college records, we know exactly when Christopher Marlowe was in residence during his years at Cambridge. But no document yet discovered reveals where he was, and what he was doing, during his several mysterious periods of absence from the university. Was he, as scholars suspect, engaged in cloak-and-dagger espionage, at home or abroad?

In this dismaying account of the darkness in which biographers of earlier English men of letters must grope, Milton's life provides the only bright spot. He left, in his poems, prose "defenses," and private letters, a body of autobiographical data far greater than that which survives from any other pre-eighteenth-century man of letters. But that is only partly because he was a poet. Because he was deeply involved in the political events of the era, spending eleven years in high government office, and was also a scholar of international reputation, he figures prominently in the pamphlet literature and the official archives of his time, as well as in the reminiscences of his contemporaries, who made special efforts to collect and record as much as could be known of his personality and character.

Even in his case, however, much of the information that comes down to us is prejudiced. As a controversial figure in an age of fierce partisanship he was both reviled and defended in print, and most of what he wrote about himself sprang from a natural desire for self-justification. So also of many of the literary figures of the Restoration, whose biographies must be fashioned from sources that provide us with but a single certainty, namely, that they are contaminated by the seething political and religious hostilities, scandalmongering, and personal vendettas of an age extraordinarily given to feuding and character-blackening.

Grateful though we must be for such knowledge as we possess, we shall never cease regretting that we know so little about the lives and personalities of the English authors of every century before the eighteenth. Except for Milton, we can glimpse them only at a great distance, and at that, only intermittently. They appear for brief moments and then disappear again into the impenetrable mists of time. To be able to see them at all, considering how little record they left in the first place and how much of that meager ration has disappeared in the interval, is a privilege for which we must thank generations of diligent scholars. But to seize and hold them in view, as we are able to gaze at length on more recent figures, is forever an impossibility.

Shortly after the middle of the seventeenth century, the practice was begun of prefixing a short biographical sketch to the collected works of an author, as Speght had done with Chaucer, and in this form the fragmentary life stories of certain well-regarded authors were transmitted from generation to generation. But the principal chain of biographical tradition was the series of biographical dictionaries which Bale had inaugurated, in Latin, at the very beginning of the reign of Elizabeth I.

A formal history of these encyclopedias of English authors would have to be constructed on the sequential principle of an Old Testament chapter of begats, and would make equally dull reading. But each book has a character, if not a flavor, of its own. Thomas Fuller's *History of the Worthies of England* (1662) was one of Charles Lamb's favorite books, and understandably, because it is quaint and whimsical and full of oddities. In the midst of much information on each county's architectural monuments, proverbs, folklore, battles, "natural commodities," and medicinal waters, the amiable Fuller inserts entries dealing with the county's "worthies," some of whom were literary men. These are not systematic biographical sketches but merely casual assemblages of data or speculations; the passage on Chaucer, for example, is devoted to reviewing the conflicting claims of previous authorities as to where the poet was born. Occasionally there is a character vignette drawn in vinegar, as when Fuller says of the poet Edmund Campion: "A man of excellent parts; though he who rode post to tell him so, might come too late to bring him tidings thereof, being such a valuer of himself that he swelled every drop of his ability into a bubble by his vain ostentation. And indeed few who were reputed scholars had more of Latin, or less of Greek, than he had."

Unfortunately Fuller's ingratiating qualities were not inherited by his successors. Edward Phillips' *Theatrum Poetarum, or a Compleat Collection of the Poets, Especially the Most Eminent, of All Ages* (1675), a pocket-sized volume divided into sections on the ancients and the moderns, mingles names that every schoolboy used to know with far more names—Latin, Greek, French, Spanish, Italian, as well as English—that none but the most erudite literary specialist has ever heard of. It is critical rather than biographical in emphasis. Most of the entries are only a sentence or two in length, and they are so vague as to be virtually meaningless. Once in a while, however, even this most pedestrian of compilers shows spirit, as in his forthright comment on "*John Skelton,* a jolly English Rimer, and I warrant ye accounted a notable Poet, as Poetry went in those daies, namely King *Edward* the fourth's Reign, when doubtless good Poets were scarce; for however he had the good fortune to be chosen Poet Laureat: methinks he hath a miserable loos, rambling style, and galloping measure of Verse; so that no wonder he is so utterly forgotten at this present, when so many better Poets of not much later a date, are wholly laid aside."

Phillips' successor, William Winstanley (*The Lives of the Most Famous English Poets, or the Honour of Parnassus* [1687]), is reputed to have begun life as a barber. According to his contemporary Anthony Wood, he gave up the razor but retained the scissors, to clip lavishly from the work of his predecessors. It is certainly true that, even in a time when in literary matters the distinction between what is thine and what is mine was blurred, the renegade barber was too free with the shears. He cut whole swatches from Phillips and Fuller without the slightest acknowledgment. At least one entry, however, if not Winstanley's own, certainly is not Phillips'. Of Milton, his uncle, Phillips had commented: "it will better become a person less related then [*sic*] my self, to deliver his judgement." Winstanley had no such delicacy. "*John Milton,*" he wrote, "was one, whose natural parts might deservedly give him a place amongst the principal of our English Poets. . . . But his Fame is gone out like a Candle in a Snuff, and his Memory will always stink, which might have ever lived in honourable Repute, had not he been a notorious Traytor, and most impiously and villanously bely'd that blessed Martyr King *Charles* the First." Even Dr. Johnson, Milton's most formidable detractor, would not have gone that far.

And Leland-Bale-Fuller-Phillips-Winstanley begat Gerard Langbaine's *An Account of the English Dramatick Poets* (1691), in which the "lives and characters" are almost totally eclipsed by lists of plays, critical comments, and copious quotations; and Langbaine begat the two-volume *Poetical Register* (1719–20) of Giles Jacob, who was not overnice either about borrowing from his predecessors; and so the family tree grew, generation after generation. In 1753 appeared *The Lives of the Poets of Great Britain and Ireland to the Time of Dean Swift,* a five-volume work that bore on its title page the name "Cibber," the implication being that the author was the famous actor-dramatist Colley Cibber. (The true compiler was a Scottish hack named Robert Shiels, who had helped Dr. Johnson with his dictionary. For the use of his more illustrious family name and his services as a reviser, Colley Cibber's son Theophilus, then in debtors' prison, received twenty guineas.) The chief importance of this work is that it was the direct ancestor of Dr. Johnson's own *Lives of the Poets.*

These books, slapdash or industrious, modest or ambitious (Thomas Birch's *General Dictionary* [1734–41] ran to ten huge folio volumes, and William Oldys' and Joseph Towers' *Biographia Britannica* [1747–66], to six), were the chief repositories of biographical knowledge concerning virtually all English authors who lived before 1700. As such, along with a certain hard residue of unassailable facts they transmitted a farrago of misinformation and legend that has taken two hundred years to straighten out. It would not have been so bad if each compiler had copied verbatim from his sources; at least the original error would have been preserved in its pristine purity. However, as happened perhaps most notoriously but by no means solely in Chaucer's case, what an earlier compiler suggested (no doubt erroneously) as a possibility, a later one set forth as a certainty. Qualifications usually fell by the wayside, and from the acorns of hesitant speculation grew the oaks of confident affirmation. Stories were twisted, or merged, or transferred to another period, or grossly misinterpreted. Whether the compilers were merely careless, or whether they strove to ensure the originality of their work despite their lack of anything new to say, the result was the same: error multiplied in book after book.

· 3 ·

In order to complete the pedigree of collective biography as far as Dr. Johnson's *Lives of the Poets* it has been necessary to run slightly ahead of our story. As a consequence, the two most significant figures in seventeenth-century biographical activity have been passed over, an omission that must now be rectified. One of these figures, a very deliberate and accomplished artist, gazed backward, toward the saint's-life tradition; the other, a busy fact collector, all unconsciously proclaimed the future. Izaak Walton produced the first biographies (apart from Cavendish's *Wolsey*) that were works of literary art, and in so doing he revealed the limitations of the prevailing biographical mode. John Aubrey, thirty-three years his junior, left only sheaves of disorderly notes, but they abundantly show that his biographical instincts were far ahead of his age.

Walton was a London ironmonger by trade and a fervent partisan of King and Church in the age of the Puritan revolution. Unlike his predecessors, who wrote biographical sketches with their left hands, he worked with care and devotion, spending many years preparing a series of short lives and, what is equally important, revising and polishing them after their first publication. He took the occupation of biographer at least as seriously as he took his fishing, which is saying a good deal. Walton set out to show how the lives of five men of his time, four of them ordained Anglican priests, the fifth a deacon, exemplified "the ideal character produced by the Christian humanism of the Church of England, the combination of gentleman, scholar, and saint, as opposed to what he considered to be the narrower and harsher type encouraged by Puritanism."

All five of Walton's subjects were writers; two of them, John Donne and George Herbert, were great poets. But it is not as men of letters that Walton treats them. The *Lives* belong to the school of ecclesiastical biography that had sprung up as a result of the seventeenth-century's passionate concern with religious men and the quality of the religious life. The literary accomplishments of the Dean of St. Paul's and the rector of Bemerton are only incidental to what Walton considers the truly memorable aspect of their lives, their saintliness.

And these are, in essence, saints' lives. They have, admittedly, an intimacy and a degree of authenticity that the medieval hagiographers did not even aspire to, let alone achieve. Walton either knew his subjects personally or got his material from men who did. He was able to portray them as men of their time, which was close to his own, and he had access to a fair amount of concrete information about them, including anecdotes and letters. There was no need to repair to the storehouse of adaptable incident from which the hagiographers had constructed their fresh legends.

But Walton's purpose was not so much to write narratives as to paint portraits in words; and the portraits he set out to write were not realistic but idealized. Oliver Cromwell, Walton's contemporary, commanded his portrait painter to depict him as he was, warts and all. Walton differed from the Puritan leader on this essential criterion of biography as thoroughly as he opposed him on matters of political and ecclesiastical organization. He used the facts at his disposal with artistic freedom, to re-create Donne, Hooker, Herbert, Wotton, and Sanderson not as they had been in life but as he wished them to be remembered. The result is that all five men, who actually differed greatly from one another in character and personality, tend to merge into a single image: a placid, devout, essentially passive man, irreproachable perhaps but more than a little dull, such as Walton himself seems to have been. These are not five men as they lived but five men transfigured by Walton's pious purpose and stylizing technique.

Walton's *Lives* are works of literary art, but as factual narratives and character sketches they are decidedly imperfect. They owe their fully deserved reputation not to their historical substance or their biographical technique but to their style. Walton's grave, cadenced prose has that unmistakable but somehow indescribable flavor that is uniquely seventeenth century: an effect of innocence and artlessness achieved through what one can be certain is the exercise of conscious and painstaking art. It is an instrument of well-wrought simplicity.

In these "obituary poems," as Sir Walter Raleigh (the early twentieth-century man of letters, not the Elizabethan) called them, literary historians have found Walton anticipating various devices and interests of modern biography. They are there, but Walton did not invent them. Perhaps most prophetic of a certain kind of biography three centuries later is Walton's occasional imaginative excursion into the mind of his subject, to report what Donne or Herbert was presumably thinking at a given juncture in his life. Similarly, to a greater extent than any preceding biographer, Walton dramatizes his material by inventing elaborate conversations. And he anticipates the technique, though fortunately not the length, of the modern "life and times" biography; in the life of Hooker, for example, he drops the man for many pages while describing the religious events of Elizabethan times. In all five of his narrative sketches, indeed, but most often in the "Sanderson," Walton is given to suspending the story for the sake of introducing collateral material, such as a survey of the political-ecclesiastical situation at the time spoken of or a miniature portrait of one of his subject's friends. He does so, always, with disarming apologies, prefacing a new digression with some such phrase as "the next imployment of my Readers patience." He ends one, also, in this fashion: "I should now return to Boothby Pannel, where we left Dr. Hammond and Dr. Sanderson together, but neither can be found there" (Hammond having gone to London and Sanderson been carried prisoner to Lincoln). It is not often that a biographer, whether of the seventeenth or the twentieth century, proposes to return to his *locus quo ante*, after an excursion, only to blandly confess that his birds have flown the coop. But Walton, with his dry charm, carries it off.

The realism for which Walton is often praised is not very marked. He merely uses more circumstantial details than most of his predecessors did. He lightens the prevailing marmoreal quality of his pages with occasional incidents and vignettes designed to illustrate the essential humanity of his saints; and these, taken as a whole, are enough to save the five men from being cold sculptured effigies on a tomb. The breath of life, although never robust—the grave Dean Donne is not credited with a gay youth or with more than one or two of the great love poems that have won him his twentieth-century fame—is at least sufficient to keep some blood in their cheeks. A few of Walton's anecdotal interludes, decorous and gentle as befits their context, would be prized by the most discriminating of modern biographers. This one, for instance, from the life of Herbert:

In another walk to *Salisbury*, he saw a poor man, with a poorer horse, that was fall'n under his Load; they were both in distress, and needed present help; which Mr. *Herbert* perceiving, put off his Canonical Coat, and help'd the poor man to unload, and after, to load his horse: The poor man blest him for it: and he blest the poor man; and was so like the *good Samaritan*, that he gave him money to refresh both himself and his horse; and told him, *That if he lov'd himself, he should be merciful to his Beast.* –Thus he left the poor man, and at his coming to his musical friends at *Salisbury*, they began to wonder that Mr. *George Herbert* which us'd to be so trim and clean, came into that company so soyl'd and discompos'd; but he told them the occasion: And when one of the company told him, *He had disparag'd himself by so dirty an employment;* his answer was, *That the thought of what he had done, would prove Musick to him at Midnight; and that the omission of it, would have upbraided and made discord in his Conscience, whensoever he should pass by that place; for, if I be bound to pray for all that be in distress, I am sure that I am bound so far as it is in my power to practise what I pray for. And though I do not wish for the like occasion every day, yet let me tell you, I would not willingly pass one day of my life without comforting a sad soul, or shewing mercy; and I praise God for this occasion:* And now let's tune our Instruments.

At such moments, Izaak Walton's characters live. But in general, one's faith that they were real human beings, in distinction to the somewhat improbable saints of medieval legend, rests upon one's assent to the spirit in which Walton works, rather than upon any convincing body of realistic detail. Despite the small touches that suggest their humanity, their images are nevertheless as stylized as if executed in stained glass.

In contrast, the glimpses John Aubrey offers of all sorts of people, the profane as well as the devout, have the deliciously shocking verisimilitude of a high-speed candid photograph. If this book were to be limited to the men and women who actually wrote biographies, Aubrey's name would not even appear. But the history of biography reserves an honorable alcove for those who gathered and preserved the raw materials from which formal biographies are later constructed—a function that has its own temperamental requirements of inquisitiveness, pertinacity, and a

shrewd sense of what constitutes good copy. In these respects
Aubrey was Boswell's worthy ancestor; he had the keen percep-
tions of a journalist, the alert sensitivity of a free-hand sketcher.
Unfortunately, the Boswellian strain in him was mixed with
Samuel Taylor Coleridge's constitutional inability to bring anything to a satisfactory conclusion, so that he bequeathed to posterity no biography, but a large, chaotic, and utterly beguiling
collection of rough notes, now known as Aubrey's *Brief Lives*.

Aubrey was a specimen of that numerous breed of lettered
Englishmen, the tireless, insatiably curious antiquarian. Among
his other activities by way of snapping up unconsidered trifles, he
was a field agent for Anthony Wood, himself an antiquarian but a
most unpleasant and rancorous man, whose magnum opus was
Athenae Oxonienses (1691–92), a weighty biographical dictionary of the worthies associated with Oxford throughout its already
long history. In behalf of this enterprise, Aubrey followed his
nose here and there throughout the country, wherever the scent
of prospective gossip led him. He sent the results of his investiga-
tions and interviews to Wood, who absorbed many of them into
his ponderous volumes. (The notes were not published separately, under Aubrey's own name, until 1813.) Having benefited
enormously from Aubrey's labors, Wood nevertheless confided to
his journal that he was "a shiftless person, roving and magotie-
headed, and sometimes little better than crased."

Magotie-headed or not, Aubrey had a superb instinctive sense
of the revealing detail of appearance, manner, or speech whose
presence marks the difference between flat generalized portraiture and incisive individual characterization. He cared little or
nothing for the philosophical significance of his data; he was not
concerned, as Walton was, to assemble the materials that would
prove a man to have been as pious as he was reputed to have
been. Aubrey collected lively anecdotes and personal details for
their own sake. Of the jurist Sir Edward Coke he wrote: "His
second wife, Elizabeth, the relickt of Sir William Hatton, was
with Child when he married her: laying his hand on her belly
(when he came to bed) and finding a Child to stirre, What, sayd
he, Flesh in the Pott. Yea, quoth she, or els I would not have

maried a Cooke." Nothing could be farther removed from Walton's extended eulogies than Aubrey's brisk summary of Lady Venetia Digby, "a most beautifull desireable Creature" of distinctly tarnished chastity: "when her head was opened there was found but little braine." Of another Digby, who was executed for his part in the Gunpowder Plot, he records: "When his heart was pluct out by the Executioner (who, *secundum formam*, cryed, Here is the heart of a Traytor!) it is credibly reported, he replied, Thou liest!" As a student at Christ Church, a certain mathematician, Aubrey reports, preached "the Passion Sermon, which some old divines that I knew did heare, but 'twas sayd of him then in the University that our Saviour never suffered so much since his Passion as in that sermon."

But Aubrey was much more than a connoisseur of flavorsome stories. He had a zeal to record what Boswell would later call "characteristical circumstances" of men and women. In a—for him—lengthy profile of Thomas Hobbes, he includes this evidence of the philosopher's wise habits of body:

> 'Tis not consistent with an harmonicall soule to be a woman-hater, neither had he an Abhorrescence to good wine but he was, even in his youth (generally) temperate, both as to wine and women. I have heard him say that he did beleeve he had been in excesse in his life, a hundred times; which, considering his great age, did not amount to above once a yeare. When he did drinke, he would drinke to excesse to have the benefitt of Vomiting, which he did easily; by which benefit neither his witt was disturbt longer then he was spuing nor his stomach oppressed; but he never was, nor could not endure to be, habitually a good fellow, i.e. to drinke every day wine with company, which, though not to drunkennesse, spoiles the Braine.

He had, in addition, the gift of capturing the whole essence of a character in a few telling phrases. He describes the theologian John Hales as "a prettie little man, sanguine, of a cheerfull countenance, very gentile, and courteous; I was recieved by him with much humanity: he was in a kind of violet-coloured cloath Gowne, with buttons and loopes (he wore not a black gowne) and was reading Thomas à Kempis; it was within a yeare before he deceased. He loved Canarie; but moderately, to refresh his spirits."

In Aubrey's disorderly notes, physicians rub shoulders with countesses, and soldiers with dons; and among the throng are some literary people. It was Aubrey who first set afloat the famous, if dubious, attribution of Francis Bacon's death to a cold contracted while experimentally deep-freezing a fowl. It is in Aubrey that we first encounter the startling, and entirely fictitious, statement that Ben Jonson "killed Mr. Marlow, the Poet, on Bunhill, comeing from the Green-curtain play-house." Of the playwriting team of Beaumont and Fletcher, he conveys the pleasing information that they were "both batchelors; lay together, had one Wench in the house betweene them, which they did so admire; the same cloathes and cloake, &c.; betweene them." Andrew Marvell he describes as "of middling stature, pretty strong sett, roundish faced, cherry cheek't, hazell eie, browne haire." On Milton, Aubrey, who interviewed his widow, brother, and nephew, was able to collect several pages, including the facts that while he was composing *Paradise Lost* his inspiration "began at the Autumnall Aequinoctiall, and ceased at the Vernall or thereabouts" (which was why he took four or five years to complete the poem) and that "he would be chearfull even in his Gowte-fitts, and sing." Aubrey's few paragraphs on Shakespeare are the authority for a number of familiar but porous assertions, such as that when he killed a calf in his father's butcher shop (actually, his father was a glover) "he would doe it in a high style, and make a Speech," and that he modeled the constable in *A Midsummer Night's Dream* on one he saw in a village in Buckinghamshire (there is no constable in *A Midsummer Night's Dream*).

The most severe charge that can be laid against Aubrey is that of credulousness. It is true that he believed more than he should have. But those who have examined his notes, their margins crammed with questions, the spaces between the lines black with additions and corrections, come away with a healthy respect for Aubrey's genuine concern for finding out the truth. The accents of a true scholar are heard in his despairing cry when confronted with two discrepant estimates of the amount of Sir Edward

Coke's landed wealth: "What shall one beleeve?" And while he was never loath to set down hearsay evidence (as, indeed, no scholar should be, for even the most doubtful story may turn out to contain a germ of truth), he spent at least as much energy seeking out the most reliable sources of information and trying his best to establish dates and names. It is hardly fair to assume, as some have done, that his notes were written in the wake of nightlong carouses, so that the numerous gaps represent "drunken hiccups." In reality they represent the genuine scholar's hope that fortune sooner or later will favor him with the information to fill the empty spaces. Systematic he was not; busy, eager, and, according to his lights, zealous for the truth he certainly was. We owe him a great deal, for, as he wrote, "How these curiosities would be quite forgott, did not such idle fellowes as I am putt them downe."

Aubrey, however, had no effect on the biographical art of his time. From his unorganized notes an ungrateful Anthony Wood chose what he wanted for his *Athenae Oxonienses*, but the talents that might under happier conditions have revolutionized English biography toward the end of the seventeenth century had to await reincarnation in the more methodical person of James Boswell.

Meanwhile, certain other forces helped prepare the way for the more sophisticated and comprehensive kind of biography that was to begin to develop a century later. The same seventeenth-century interest in psychology that had borne literary fruit in the character essays of Overbury and Earle (short sketches, inspired by those of the Greek Theophrastus, of type characters who exemplified various human qualities) and, in another sphere, stimulated the speculations of Hobbes and Locke, tempted some men to look deeper into their own selves. This philosophical bent toward introspection was assisted by the religious nonconformism of the period, which transferred man's quest for spiritual truth from dogma to the promptings of the individual soul. In this Puritan century people grew self-conscious as they had never been before. They looked into the mirror of self, and what they saw engrossed them. From Samuel Pepys, Londoner, civil servant, man of taste, and compulsive lecher, to John Bunyan, humble tinker and visionary, people put down their intimate experiences of flesh and spirit. Such diaries as those of Pepys and his friend John Evelyn remained hidden until well into the nineteenth century. Spiritual autobiographies like Bunyan's *Grace Abounding*, on the other hand, loaded the bookstalls as the seventeenth century turned into the eighteenth. Exultant or anguished, learned or semiliterate, starkly authentic or obviously concocted for the market, the flood of confessional literature had a powerful, though indirect, effect on the art of biography. It helped erode the tradition of reticence, or at best indifference to psychological phenomena, which had inhibited biography from being a record of more than activity and external personality. Once the fashion had been established of recording and even publishing the secrets of one's mental experience, it was only a step—though, as events proved, a long-delayed one—to the examination of other people's inner lives. Imaginative literature, of course, had never shirked the task. But to find the materials of psychological truth in real life, in documentary form as it were, was something new.

A corollary development, also leading eventually toward greater intimacy with the subject, was the increase in the number of lives written by relatives of memorable men and women. Lady Anne Fanshawe's tribute to her diplomatist husband, Sir Richard —a combination of memoir, reminiscence, and diary; Lucy Hutchinson's life of her Puritan soldier-husband, John; the Duchess of Newcastle's biography of her husband, born William Cavendish; and Richard Baxter's *Breviate of the Life of Margaret Baxter*, a Puritan-era saint: all are the products of the commemorative urge that was so strong in the later seventeenth century. All, it must be said, with the exception of John Evelyn's tribute to his chaste and lovely mistress, Margaret Godolphin, are more creditable in intention than in execution. However justly they may be praised for their sincerity, their simplicity, their moving evidence of a widow's or a widower's attachment to the memory of a noble-hearted spouse, they are not works of art. None of these writers was an artist except unintentionally and casually. Their books did nothing to advance the art of biography (and three of them, Lucy Hutchinson's, Lady Anne Fanshawe's, and Evelyn's, were not printed until 1806, 1829, and 1847, respectively). But they were among the first biographers to demonstrate the gain in immediacy and authenticity that personal acquaintance with the subject could afford. They also inadvertently proved the axiom that the intimate effect which it is possible for a near relative to achieve as a biographer is usually counterbalanced by his emotional involvement. The eulogistic mood does not normally lead to biographical success.

· 4 ·

In the eighteenth century biography was more talked about, more practiced, and more read than in the preceding hundred years. Yet with the development of new literary tastes and cultural assumptions, which sometimes existed side by side with, or were themselves modifications of, the older ones at which we have just glanced, biography's position was no less ambiguous. Its curious hesitation between encouragement and neglect was, if anything, more marked. If certain characteristic forces in the eighteenth-century air theoretically hastened biography's coming of age, other forces effectively retarded it.

The eighteenth was the most secular of all English centuries to date. "Know then thyself, presume not God to scan," urged Pope; "the proper study of mankind is man." The religious preoccupation that heretofore had led biography to focus on the lives of saints, martyrs, and churchmen as the best means of fulfilling its moralistic purpose diminished. More and more, the spirit that governed both writers and readers was an unabashed curiosity, inherited from the Renaissance and now much enlarged, regarding every aspect of the human spectacle. The strength of that curiosity was manifest both in the popularity of the new genre of journalistic biography, written to the taste of the bourgeois reading public that flourished alongside the old-established cultivated one, and in the biographical cast of much of the fiction produced for both audiences.

The requirements of the men and women who constituted the

steadily enlarging popular audience were both simple and pronounced. They wanted reading matter that was full of personality and incident; and they wanted to read about people of, preferably, the middle or artisan class (therefore people like themselves), who did exciting things or had exciting things happen to them. At the same time, many of these new readers, indifferently educated but eager for the unsophisticated delights of print, had qualms about letting their eyes rest on what was palpably untrue. The Puritan horror of imaginative literature as compact of lies was still strong in the eighteenth century. The conscientious reader, therefore—typically a member of one of the nonconformist sects—needed, like his Elizabethan forebear, to believe that he was reading the truth.

Here was biography's golden opportunity; for, in shrewd if not always scrupulous hands, it could satisfy all these requirements. A London publisher, early in the century, found the Grub Street hands to do the work. He was Edmund Curll, to whose name the epithet "unspeakable" is stuck forever. Avaricious and litigious, a liar, controversialist, and issuer of dirty books, he probably enjoys the most diversified notoriety in the history of English publishing. Curll was also a very acute analyst of popular taste.

> It occurred to him that, in a world governed by the law of mortality, men might be handsomely entertained on one another's remains. He lost no time in putting his theory into action. During the years of his activity he published some forty or fifty separate Lives, intimate, anecdotal, scurrilous sometimes, of famous and notorious persons who had the ill-fortune to die during his life-time. He had learned the wisdom of the grave-digger in *Hamlet,* and knew that there are many rotten corpses nowadays, that will scarce hold the laying in. So he seized on them before they were cold, and commemorated them in batches. . . . His books commanded a large sale, and modern biography was established.

Under such unsavory conditions did biography first become a popular genre in England. In Elizabethan times, it is true, there had been a few scattered pamphlet lives of pious citizens or executed highwaymen. But these had been mere chapbooks, foam on the sea of contemporary literature, and well-received though some of them may have been, they had touched off no sustained fashion. The case was different when Curll set his hacks to work in the first decades of the eighteenth century. He mass-produced full-length biographies. And he destroyed, for good, the lingering assumption that biography should deal only with the highly placed, whether prelate or prince, saint or sinner. The subjects of the new catchpenny biographies were actors, antiquarians, merchants, tradesmen, criminals, travelers, soldiers of fortune, eccentrics, scientists, reformers, adventuresses, preachers, valets, reformed rakes, gamblers, slave traders, intellectual women—the variety was as broad as the spectrum of eighteenth-century English society itself. Witness some of the people whose lives Daniel Defoe—not a Curll author, but writing at the same time—narrated in a mere eight years, in the midst of a great deal of other journalistic activity: a "learned and reverend divine," English and Scottish officers with records of long service and amazing adventures in half a dozen countries, a castaway mariner, "the present Czar of Muscovy," a "dumb philosopher" (a Cornish tinner's son who first spoke a few days before his death at the age of fifty-eight), several pirates, including one who was the "Mock King of Madagascar," eminent highwaymen, and female virtuosos of sin.

Though purporting to be "real life narratives," these books hovered in the dim disputed territory between fact and fiction. Some were relatively veracious accounts of actual events, though probably none could survive intact the tests of modern historical scholarship. The majority, however, were free fictional embroideries on what may or may not have been an original modicum of fact. All were designed to entertain the reader while simultaneously assuring him that he was not wasting his time. The authors' frequent assertion of truthfulness, and more important, their use of specific dates and places and of realistic circumstantial detail, guaranteed that this was not fiction and therefore was wholesome literature. But the narratives themselves support the inverted adage that fiction is stranger than truth.

As literature, these popular biographies (except for a few of

Defoe's) were almost worthless. Lively but crude products of the dawn of journalism, they were written by hacks who had no more interest in the artistic potentialities of the genre than they had in the dependability of their facts. Only insofar as they adopted the techniques of fictional narrative—use of concrete physical detail for verisimilitude, dialogue, portrayal of dramatic scenes— did they foreshadow eventual developments in serious biography.

When "veracious" biography borrowed devices from fiction, fiction was not long in returning the compliment. The shape many novels took in the period beginning with Richardson was evidence of the growing taste for biography and its influence on the fictional art. Their very titles are significant: *Clarissa, or the History of a Young Lady; The History of Tom Jones, a Foundling; The Life of Mr. Jonathan Wild the Great; The Life and Opinions of Tristram Shandy, Gentleman.* Such novelists as Fielding, hoping to dissociate themselves from the stigma attached to the old-fashioned romancers, and at the same time revealing both the literary frame of reference in which they saw their art and their own awareness of the popular demand for life narratives, explicitly referred to themselves as biographers.

The strength of interest in matters especially related to biography is discernible too in the frequent fictional concern with psychological analysis. The surge of tearful introspection that constituted the literary fashion of *sensibilité*—the cultivation of feeling for its own sake—was the secular counterpart of the mood behind the spiritual biography and autobiography, with their descriptions of the emotional turmoil attending sin and illumination.

In other forms and on other levels of literature the same inward turning was to be noticed. Journals were kept not only by men like John Wesley, who continued his own for some fifty-five years, but by such antithetical figures as Boswell and Fanny Burney. Gibbon wrote no fewer than six drafts of an intimate autobiography. This also was a great age of letter writing; Pope, Walpole, Gray, Lady Mary Wortley Montagu, Shenstone, Cowper, and scores of other men and women conducted extensive correspondences, a leading subject of which was themselves. The degree of self-revelation involved in these various kinds of personal documents differed greatly from writer to writer, and for contemporary publication much of the original intimacy was left out; but in the aggregate they marked an important shift in direction, toward the eventual exploration and exposure of the private consciousness.

If, in one regard, the spirit of the age was introspective, in another it was notably social. People not only gazed within themselves: they loved to contemplate one another. In the comfortable warmth of a gregarious society, layer after layer of character unfolded, in its amiability or its severity, its wisdom or its foolishness, its dull normality or its riotous eccentricity. Peculiarities of dress, personal habits, gestures, speech—all were clues to the inner man; and so, above all, were "table talk" and the anecdotes that proliferated in a gossipy age. With pens as sharp as their eyes, Addison and Steele and their successors conveyed the fruits of their observation to tens of thousands of readers who perhaps never frequented a salon or coffeehouse but whose curiosity about their fellow men was unquenchable. Swept-together anecdotes and conversation fragments attributed to the age's leading poets and wits—"Swiftiana," "Walpoliana," "Hogarthiana," and so on—enjoyed wide popularity. The contents of the most famous collection, Joseph Spence's anecdotes of Pope, though first printed only in 1820, were publicized by Dr. Johnson and others, who had access to the manuscript. So diligently did the mills of literary gossip grind that early in the nineteenth century the highly diversified product occupied, along with other matter, no fewer than seventeen big volumes of John Nichols' *Literary Anecdotes of the Eighteenth Century* and *Illustrations of the Literary History of the Eighteenth Century*. In one sense, Boswell's *Life of Johnson* is simply a compilation of "Johnsoniana" on a grand scale. But biographical materials do not make biographies, and this flood of personal literature, though a direct response to the period's swelling interest in the attitudes and subject matter associated with biography, had the actual effect of diverting the biographical impulse into a side channel. The compilation of "ana" relating to identified individuals occupied energies that might otherwise have been devoted to the writing of formal lives.

Still other forces in the social and intellectual climate encouraged the biographical spirit. The eighteenth century was an age of induction and empiricism that sought to discover the grand universal laws of human as well as physical nature through the accumulation and analysis of data. To find the forces that determine the aptitudes, inclinations, motives, and choices of the individual man, the records of human conduct had to be studied. "We must," said Hume in the introduction to his *Treatise of Human Nature*, "glean up our experiments in this science [of psychology] from a cautious observation of human life, and take them as they appear in the common course of the world, by men's behaviour in company, in affairs, and in their pleasures." The last words explain well the philosophical significance of compilations of table talk and anecdotes; and here, indeed, eighteenth-century psychological inquiry provided a very acceptable rationale for biography. In addition, the age, subscribing to Locke's theory that the infant mind was a clean slate upon which experience proceeded to write its intricate inscription, wanted to know how people grew from the nullities they were at birth, how external circumstances pummeled and buffeted and smoothed them into their mature selves. Biography, by describing the social and intellectual events of individual lives, could help it learn.

But the gain from such study was not exclusively intellectual —description for the sake of arriving at general principles. The ethical-minded eighteenth century found at least equal value in biography's services to morality. As Goldsmith put it when introducing his abridgment of Plutarch (1762):

> Biography has ever since the days of Plutarch been considered as the most useful manner of writing, not only from the pleasure it affords the imagination, but from the instruction it artfully and unexpectedly conveys to the understanding. It furnishes us with an opportunity of giving advice freely, and without offence. It not only removes the dryness and dogmatical air of precept, but sets persons, actions, and their consequences before us in their most striking manner, and by that means turns even precept into example. . . . Counsels, therefore, as well as compliments, are best

conveyed in an indirect and oblique manner; and this renders biography, as well as fable, a most convenient vehicle for instruction.

And talking with Lord Monboddo, during his journey through the Hebrides in 1773, of the high value of the "history of manners" in illuminating human nature, Dr. Johnson concluded: "I esteem biography, as giving us what comes near to ourselves, what we can turn to use." It was this utilitarian function of biography which accounted for much of its prestige at the end of the eighteenth century and the beginning of the nineteenth.

But as a serious art form, worthy of the talents of accomplished writers and the attention of the best critics, the status of biography remained uncertain at least until the latter years of Dr. Johnson's life. If the raw material of biography was itself valuable for various philosophical and didactic purposes, there was no compelling reason why it should be reshaped in an artistic spirit: to the inquiring mind, a case history or an unedited collection of table talk was as useful as a work of literature. Moreover, an important, though by no means universal, tendency of eighteenth-century opinion on the nature of human behavior ran directly contrary to the assumption on which biography flourishes, that of the genuineness and importance of human differences. In an intellectual context where the fixed and invariable phenomena of existence were stressed, the kind of human material that constitutes the subject matter of biography was regarded as being merely eccentric and irrational—the superficial diversity that obscures the real unity which is truth. From this viewpoint, biography had nothing of great moment to say to a philosophical mind. The predominant aim of literature was to portray men gathered into groups, either through institutions or through their sharing of those fundamental traits which, taken together, comprised "human nature." It was the general, the typical, the normal, the ideal—the great stratum of likeness beneath all superficial differences in human character and experience—that preoccupied the neoclassic art of the period. The proper study of mankind was man, to be sure, but man as a social animal, not *a* man.

This aversion to the accidental and atypical as the subject

matter of art was reflected in technique. Perhaps the most solid and unswerving principle of the neoclassical esthetic was that the artist, in Dr. Johnson's famous image, should not number the streaks of the tulip, but instead should devote himself to depicting an ideal tulip, the grand synthesis or Platonic construct of all individual tulips. Portraiture consisted not in the faithful reproduction of a man's tiewig and kneebreeches, the furrowed lines of his face and the dirt under his nails, his habits at table and his hesitations in speech; these were accidental and irrelevant details, the sort of distractions that critical parlance condemned as "vulgar." Rather, the true business of the artist was to sandpaper down these individualities and reveal the essential man—the member of a class—who lay concealed beneath the surface peculiarities.[2]

In its portrayal of human beings, therefore, the eighteenth century still clung to formula. The Theophrastan character sketch had a late revival in the gallery of miniature portraits Addison and Steele painted of the men assembled in the Spectator Club: Sir Roger de Coverley, the type of country gentleman; Sir Andrew Freeport, the type of city merchant; Captain Sentry, the type of soldier; Will Honeycomb, the type of man about town; and so on. In the novel too, as it developed after Richardson's success in the 1740's, the aim, in contrast to that of the old romance, was to represent universals under the transparent guise of specifics. "I describe not men, but manners," asserted Fielding in the third book of *Joseph Andrews;* "not an individual, but a species." His portrayal of the lawyer in the stage coach, for example, was designed not to "mimick some little obscure fellow" who actually existed but, instead, to represent every man of his kind from the "first mean selfish creature [who] appeared on the human stage, who made self the centre of the whole creation."

---

[2] In writing of eighteenth-century thought there is the constant peril of oversimplification and unqualified generalization. Although it is true that the esthetics of the age were strongly uniformitarian, one must hasten to add that, as M. H. Abrams puts it (*The Mirror and the Lamp* [New York, 1953], p. 40), "taken in its full context, the recommendation of the typical, general, and familiar as basic requirements of art usually turns out to be accompanied by a statement of the need for the leavening qualities of individuality, particularity, and novelty as well." It cannot be assumed, then, that *all* individualizing details were frowned upon. The question was one of emphasis.

Such intention, typical of the age's theory, was of course opposed to the differentiating realism that lies at the heart of true biography, and it had much to do with the general eighteenth-century failure to proceed with the refinement of the biographical art. But, just as nature is said always to geometrize, so artists tend inescapably to individualize. The central fact in the development of the eighteenth-century novel is that at its best it contravened both the precepts and the practice of orthodox neoclassicism. Like Hogarth, who filled his type figures with so much realistic detail that they ceased being types and turned into intensely individual human beings, at the peak of their artistry Fielding and Smollett and Sterne left generalization far behind. Their great accomplishment, sabotaging all the theory of the age, lay in their achievement of likenesses which had a vitality and a validity far transcending their type. And it was precisely this that was to be Boswell's contribution to the eventual progress of the biographical art.

· 5 ·

Of the many hundreds of "lives" published during the eighteenth century, only a small percentage dealt with authors. Those that did were usually biographies only to limited extent, for the word "life," with its attractive connotations, was often used in the titles of books or of prefatory essays that were, in fact, much more critical than biographical.

As in preceding centuries, the weight of critical thought discouraged biographical interest in authors. In neoclassical criticism the individual writer, the person behind the poem, was of little significance. He was to be praised, of course; a decent gratitude for the treasures he left behind demanded as much. But the specific events of his life or the characteristics of his personality had nothing to do with what he wrote. The poet was simply a mouthpiece of "common sense"—"what oft was thought, but ne'er so well express'd"—and the value of his work lay in its statement of universal truths rather than in any revelation of individual taste or original ideas.

It was the product that mattered, not the producer or the

circumstances of production. Contemporary criticism, like the criticism of the Elizabethan age and the age of Dryden, talked much of the faculty whose fortunate possession set the poet apart from ordinary people. "Genius," "invention," "inspiration," "judgment"—such terms were bandied about to the accompaniment of subtle metaphysical distinctions, but they were never authoritatively defined. Whatever the qualities of mind and the talents that enabled a man to be a poet, critics in the earlier eighteenth century generally were uninterested in speculating how they were acquired or developed. The etiology of literary genius, which now is one of the principal concerns of biography, was still a closed book.

Gradually, however, opinion changed. Against the standard neoclassic doctrine that "originality" is a poor substitute for skillful imitation of classical models and obedience to the hallowed rules of art, such men as the poet Edward Young asserted that originality was a positive virtue. Ideas like these were sufficiently in the air by 1759, when Young read his *Conjectures on Original Composition* to Dr. Johnson, to impel Johnson to remark afterward that he "was surprized to find Young receive as novelties what he thought very common maxims." It was a long step forward, but an even longer one would be required before the new critical respect for originality—that is, emancipation from the rules and the necessity of imitating one's betters—could lead to awareness that each poet had a personality of his own, and that it was in the cultivation and free expression of the differences which lay between him and all other men that true originality lay. This romantic conception of the poet as a spokesman, not for the Muse or Nature but for himself as an individual human being, gifted with extraordinary perception and wisdom, was as yet hardly even foreshadowed. Only by dim implication, seldom if ever by explicit practice, did the critics of the eighteenth century recognize the pertinence of biography to their studies.[3]

Might there not, however, be other reasons, apart from a still

---

[3] Instead, the slowly developing recognition of the relationship between the individual creator and his creation manifested itself in the attempt to find biographical clues in the poet's works. See the quotation from Dr. Johnson, page 100 below, note 9.

unrecognized critical relevance, why the lives of authors were particularly worth recounting? The customary eighteenth-century answer was No. "The deep or extensive learning of a man of letters," wrote Horace Walpole in 1778 with his characteristic witty pessimism,

> is but a barren field for biography. His notions are speculation; his adventures, enquiry. If his studies fermented or consolidated into compositions, the history of his life commonly proves but a register of the squabbles occasioned by his works, of the patrons he flattered, of the preferments he obtained or missed. The date of his publications and their editions form the outlines of his story; and frequently the plans or projects of works he meditated are taken to aid the account; the day of his death is scrupulously ascertained; —and thus, to compose the life of a man who did very little, his biographer acquaints us with what he did not do, and when he ceased to do any thing.

Opposed to this negative view, however, was a minority report that proved to be the voice of the future. It had been expressed as long ago as 1668, when Thomas Sprat, conscious of the novelty of his short biography of the poet Cowley, had gone to some pains to defend his writing about a mere author:

> Perhaps it may be judged, that I have spent too many words on a private man, and a Scholar: whose life was not remarkable for such a variety of Events, as are wont to be the Ornaments of this kind of Relations. I know it is the custom of the World to prefer the pompous Histories of great Men, before the greatest Virtues of others, whose lives have been led in a course less illustrious. This indeed is the general humour. But I believe it to be an errour in mens judgments. For certainly that is a more profitable instruction, which may be taken from the eminent goodness of men of lower rank, than that which we learn from the splendid representations of the Battels, and Victories, and Buildings, and Sayings of great Commanders and Princes. Such specious matters, as they are seldom delivered with fidelity, so they serve but for the imitation of a very few, and rather make for the ostentation than the true information of humane life. Whereas it is from the practise of men equal to our selves, that we are more naturally taught how to command our Passions, to direct our Knowledge, and to govern our Actions.

In this early declaration of biographical principle, two points, apart from Sprat's conventional insistence on the moral usefulness of biography, are of special interest. One is Sprat's utter silence on the possibility of a "Scholar's" life throwing light on his works. (For "Scholar" one may legitimately read "Poet" here, for Sprat was, of course, thinking of Cowley.) The other is that in 1668 there was no hint of the eventual romantic reverence for the man of letters as being apart from, and far above, the common run of humanity. On the contrary: it was still "Commanders and Princes" who were "great Men," and the peculiar value of the sayings and doings of "Scholars" was that they were "men equal to our selves."

Sprat's voice, in any case, was little heard and less heeded. But many years later (1760) his simple argument was repeated and amplified by Samuel Johnson, the century's most advanced thinker on matters biographical, who in an *Idler* essay forthrightly described the delights that literary lives might contain:

> It is commonly supposed that the uniformity of a studious life affords no matter for a narration: but the truth is, that of the most studious life a great part passes without study. An author partakes of the common condition of humanity; he is born and married like another man; he has hopes and fears, expectations and disappointments, griefs and joys, and friends and enemies, like a courtier or a statesman; nor can I conceive why his affairs should not excite curiosity as much as the whisper of a drawing-room or the factions of a camp.
>
> Nothing detains the reader's attention more powerfully than deep involutions of distress, or sudden vicissitudes of fortune; and these might be abundantly afforded by memoirs of the sons of literature. They are entangled by contracts which they know not how to fulfill, and obliged to write on subjects which they do not understand. Every publication is a new period of time, from which some increase or declension of fame is to be reckoned. The gradations of a hero's life are from battle to battle, and of a author's from book to book.
>
> All this, modified and varied by accident and custom, would form very amusing scenes of biography, and might recreate many a mind which is very little delighted with conspiracies of battles, intrigues of a court, or debates of a parliament. . . .

A better statement of the special pleasures of literary biography has not been written in the two hundred years since Johnson set this one down. But note the operative words *curiosity* and *amusing*. Though Johnson was far from underestimating the moral usefulness of biography, here he stressed simply its value as entertainment. Thus he touched unerringly on the quality which was responsible, more than any other, for the popular appeal that biography already had, and that literary biography in particular would achieve once he and Boswell had done their work.

It was with curiosity and amusement, chiefly, that people in the eighteenth century looked upon living authors—emotions complicated, under special circumstances, by admiration or loathing. Writers were becoming more numerous and conspicuous members of society. The inky wars in which men like Pope and Swift won so many battle ribbons, and the increasing practice of politicians' hiring literary mercenaries to fight their campaigns for them, brought authors into the public consciousness as never before.

This greater popular interest in literary affairs and those who participated in them gratified itself, for the most part, by following the progress of current letters—polite as well as polemic—in the pamphlets, newspapers, and magazines. Due space was given to authors in the ponderous general biographical dictionaries, and there were even a few catchpenny guides to living writers. Particularly after the middle of the century, the various magazines and periodical miscellanies devoted considerable space to biographical articles on contemporary novelists and, to a lesser extent, poets and dramatists. Public curiosity about older men of letters was catered to by the more or less biographical prefaces to their collected works—"memoirs" which in due course were copied, *in toto* or in excerpts, into the magazines.

There seemingly was little demand for full-dress biographies of authors, although, in the case of the less recent ones, much information of use to such books was being accumulated as a by-product of the century's antiquarian zeal. But two events in the decade immediately following Dr. Johnson's remarks quoted above indicate that the popular curiosity and desire for amusement, in connection with authors both living and dead, were mounting. In their symbolism they cast long prophetic shadows over the whole subsequent history of literary biography.

The *Idler* number containing Johnson on literary biography was dated March 29, 1760. At that very time an untidy, eccentric, poverty-stricken parson named Laurence Sterne printed, at York, the first two volumes of *Tristram Shandy*. The book made its way to London, where it caused a sensation; its author followed it—and three months later returned to York in a splendid carriage drawn by the best horses money could buy. In the interval he had become a national celebrity. His book had been treated to the ultimate flattery: a whole *Shandy* literature of imitations, travesties, and spurious "continuations" began to flow from the presses, with every penny-hungry London writer trying to get into the act. Fashionable hostesses vied to engage the whimsical country clergyman for their salons and dinners; failing that, they sought to keep up with the fad by serving a new dish called a "Shandy salad." And, fateful omen, Sterne autographed his books. Beginning with volumes five and six, no copy of *Tristram Shandy*, like a certain familiar American remedy, was genuine without the originator's signature. This was a practical necessity, to protect Sterne's publisher, and incidentally the public, from the competition of books falsely alleged to be from his pen. The practice itself, however, did not begin with Sterne, having been used, as malicious reviewers delighted in pointing out, by Mrs. Theresia Constantia Phillips, a memoir-writing, blackmailing courtesan of recent notoriety.

Between *Tristram Shandy* itself and salads and signatures, in the England of the 1760's public attention centered on the lanky figure of Laurence Sterne as it had on no previous man whose sole distinction was that he had written a highly original work of literature. It was fitting that he was probably the first writer to whom, it was said, the most unsatisfactorily addressed letter would be delivered without delay. "Tristram Shandy, Europe" presented no more difficulty to the post office than Bernard Barton's later missive addressed

TO

> *Sir Walter Scott, in London, or elsewhere!*
> He needs not ask, whose far extended fame
> Is spread abroad o'er Earth, like light, or air,
> A local habitation for his Name

or the letters confidently directed, in the 1890's, to "Mark Twain, God Knows Where." And, just as people had made special trips to Hampstead to look for the Flask Walk that figures in *Clarissa Harlow*, after Sterne's *Sentimental Journey* appeared in 1768, Dessein's inn at Calais, where the book's first scenes are laid, became a standard port of call for pilgrims who paid well for the privilege of viewing, or even sleeping in, "Sterne's Chamber." How much of the inn actually was the one Sterne described (there had been a serious fire), and how far "Sterne's Chamber" resembled the one he had occupied, mattered little. There was satisfaction enough in fancying oneself so close to so famous an author.[4]

In 1769 the nation's enthusiasm for another writer—this time one who had been dead for a century and a half—resulted in another kind of display that was both a seriocomic episode, amply and facetiously covered by the press, and a portent. At Stratford-on-Avon, late that summer, David Garrick produced what was, in one sense, his masterpiece: the Grand Shakespeare Jubilee, a festival orgy of panegyrics, processions, dinners, fireworks, oratorio, illuminations, exorbitant prices, and rain, from which English poet worship can conveniently be dated. These ceremonies simply made official and gave widespread publicity to what was already a *fait accompli*. Ever since the end of the seventeenth century, when Shakespeare's plays were restored to the stage, interest in the man behind the plays had been drawing more and more pilgrims to Stratford. Those with serious purpose,

---

[4] Two years after Sterne's death, the suicide of the "marvelous child" Thomas Chatterton, an adolescent poet and forger, fed in another way the growing public interest in literary people as human beings. The furor over the true quality of his inventive genius, the motives that led him to forge the "Rowley poems," and the assignment of blame for his death called forth innumerable articles in newspapers and magazines and scores of pamphlets and books. Shops even sold printed handkerchiefs representing him as "The Distressed Poet" facing starvation in a garret, the picture being surrounded by lachrymose prose and verse.

such as the actor Betterton, came to collect whatever stray wisps of biographical tradition might still linger in ancient Stratford recollections. The rest came to see the dramatist's grave and memorial bust in Trinity Church, New Place (a Queen Anne house on the site of the half-timbered structure Shakespeare had occupied after he retired from the stage), and, in New Place's garden, the mulberry tree Shakespeare was reputed to have planted. The tourists' demands to be shown through the house and their insistence on helping themselves to the sacred wood led the owner, an irascible clergyman, to raze the house and chop down the tree. The remains of the latter he sold to a sagacious buyer, appropriately named Thomas Sharp, who for the next forty-three years busied himself with converting it into an inexhaustible stock of small boxes, goblets, toothpick cases and other mementos of Shakespeare. Although the more reflective of the tourists who bought them must have found it wonderful that the old tree had had so much wood in it, a more powerful impulse overruled their skepticism: a desire to feel a little closer—if only to the degree made possible by the possession of a souvenir—to an author whom they venerated.

For the fact is that as early as the 1760's, however indifferent critical orthodoxy may have been to such matters, people were becoming unashamedly sentimental over books and their authors, quick or dead. In 1769 the young Orientalist William Jones, unable to attend the Stratford ceremonies, made a pilgrimage instead to Forest Hill, near Oxford, where Milton was thought to have written some of his poems. The excursion inspired him with the ambition, apparently never realized, of holding a solemn Milton jubilee in some future year. "Such an honor," he wrote, "will be less splendid, but more sincere and respectful, than all the pomp and ceremony on the banks of the Avon." Three years later a Welsh knight in Pembrokeshire undertook a counterjubilee in honor of Addison and left funds for a repeat performance every seven years, but this movement too got nowhere.

By the closing decades of the century, therefore, various motives—genuine reverence for literary genius, sentimentality, curiosity, appetite for entertainment—were combining to form an eager audience for the kind of literary biography that would satisfy at least most of these impulses. Whatever the ways in which the formal philosophical and critical opinions of the age either encouraged or inhibited the prosperity of biography as a form of literature, the sharpened desire to look over the walls of another man's life—even if he was discovered merely sitting in a chair, thinking—was enough to guarantee its popularity. The mixture of interests that stimulated readers' desire to know more about authors *as men* outweighed any amount of literary theory that dissociated the man from his work—as the triumph of Boswell's book in 1791 dramatically proved.

CHAPTER II

Johnson and Boswell

✻

S AMUEL JOHNSON was the most fortunate event in English literary biography. In three major roles, as the first important theorist and an able practitioner of the art and then as the subject of the greatest biography, he is the giant who bestrides our story.[1] Not until the coming of the long-legged, cadaverous, ironic Lytton Strachey, Dr. Johnson's antithesis in virtually every respect, would a single man have a comparable effect on the progress of biography.

The day before Easter, 1777, Johnson was interrupted at his customary pre-Easter spiritual stocktaking by a delegation representing a syndicate of some forty London booksellers, who had a proposal to make. A many-volumed edition of the English poets, printed in eye-straining type and abounding in misprints, had recently been issued at Edinburgh and was being sold in London,

---

[1] As a serious student and practitioner of biography, however, Johnson was anticipated by Roger North (1653-1734), a lawyer whose lives of his three brothers, the Lord Keeper of the Great Seal under Charles II, a Turkey merchant and Commissioner of the Treasury in the same reign, and a stiff-necked divine, were published in 1742-44. The enormous quantity of manuscripts North left has never been thoroughly examined, but among them are earlier drafts of his biographies, showing how deliberate was his craftsmanship, and, most important of all, a "General Preface" to his life of the Lord Keeper, which is the fullest theoretical discussion of biography before Johnson. Excerpts from this preface, the manuscript of which is at St. John's College, Cambridge, were first printed in *Biography as an Art*, ed. James L. Clifford (New York, 1962), pp. 27-37. An estimate of North's place in the history of English biography is found in Clifford's essay, "Roger North and the Art of Biography," *Restoration and Eighteenth-Century Literature* (Rice University Semicentennial Publications, Chicago, 1963), pp. 275-285.

and the organized booksellers proposed to issue a superior competitive edition. One of the standard features of such collections was a biographical and critical essay prefixed to the works of each poet. Hence the proposal. Almost sixty-eight years old, Johnson was the most famous living man of letters; if his name could be associated with the London booksellers' project, its success was assured. Would he, for a fee he could name, write the essays? Johnson named the reasonable sum of two hundred guineas (to which the booksellers added a further hundred), and in due time got, reluctantly, to work.

The accidents of publishers' rivalry had given him a magnificent chance to climax his already distinguished career by writing in a genre to which his tastes had always strongly inclined him. It was the "biographical part of literature," he told the company at the Mitre Tavern on July 6, 1763, that he loved most. Before that date he had already contributed several biographical sketches to the *Gentleman's Magazine* and others to collected works of such authors as Roger Ascham and Sir Thomas Browne, and in several papers in the *Rambler* and the *Idler* he had laid the groundwork for a literary theory of the form. Apart from Dryden, who had discussed it briefly and somewhat pedantically in his life of Plutarch, Johnson was the first important English critic to take biography seriously. Repeatedly, in the years Boswell was recording his talk, he brought the conversation around to the topic.

He was, of course, above all a moralist; to him the value of any form of literature was to be measured by its service to man in quest of a better life. "No species of writing," he asserted, "seems more worthy of cultivation than biography, since none can be more delightful or more useful, none can more certainly enchain the heart by irresistible interest, or more widely diffuse instruction to every diversity of condition." Far more than history or fiction, biography contained examples that were not only easily intelligible to the common run of readers but, more important, were immediately applicable to their private ethical needs. Everywhere we look in biography, said Johnson, we find lessons that come home to us. If well told, with an abundance of incident, the life of any man or woman, no matter how exalted or humble, how wise or foolish, has a wealth of moral meaning. "We are all prompted by the same motives, all deceived by the same fallacies, all animated by hope, obstructed by danger, entangled by desire, and seduced by pleasure."

Johnson was the first great advocate of personal, as opposed to public, biography. "The business of a biographer," he wrote in 1750, "is often to pass slightly over those performances and incidents, which produce vulgar greatness, to lead the thoughts into domestick privacies, and display the minute details of daily life, where exterior appendages are cast aside, and men excel each other only by prudence and by virtue. . . . There are many invisible circumstances which, whether we read as inquirers after natural and moral knowledge, whether we intend to enlarge our science, or increase our virtue, are more important than publick occurrences." He had no patience with biographers who thought their obligation discharged when they gave a perfunctory narrative, drawn from other books, of their subject's career in the world. It was the essential person, not external events, that was the true subject matter of biography; and the biographer should prize, not scorn, the humble fragments of data which throw light on character and motive. "More knowledge," said Johnson, "may be gained of a man's real character, by a short conversation with one of his servants, than from a formal and studied narrative, begun with his pedigree, and ended with his funeral."

Therefore, he maintained, "nobody can write the life of a man, but those who have eat and drunk and lived in social intercourse with him"—a dictum which, if true, would invalidate 95 per cent of all biographies, and which, as a matter of fact, Johnson himself had to overlook in writing the lives of the many poets he had not known personally. However insupportable the flat generalization was, it nevertheless put Johnson's critical authority behind a revolutionary principle of biography. Boswell seized upon it as evidence of Johnson's own approval of the candor he adopted in writing Johnson's life. Unluckily, many of Boswell's imitators interpreted Johnson's dictum and Boswell's practice as licensing candor for mere gossip's sake. Nothing was further from either man's intention. The biographer's attention to what Boswell called "minute particulars" had always to be in the service of the reader's moral aspirations. By a realistic portrayal of character he could make the reader comprehend that the subject of the biography was a human being like himself, living in the same moral world, and thus could dramatize the direct applicability of the story to the reader's own problems and strivings.

Frankness demanded not only the inclusion of many presumably "insignificant" details; it required as well a fearless account of the subject's weaknesses and vices. To Johnson, who knew better than most people the sadly mixed nature of the human creature, a biography that was nothing but panegyric was next to useless. "If nothing but the bright side of characters should be shewn," he told Edmond Malone, the future biographer of Shakespeare and Dryden, "we should sit down in despondency, and think it utterly impossible to imitate them in *any thing*. The sacred writers . . . related the vicious as well as the virtuous actions of men; which had this moral effect, that it kept mankind from *despair*, into which otherwise they would naturally fall, were they not supported by the recollection that others had offended like themselves, and by penitence and amendment of life had been restored to the favour of Heaven." Such lessons, Johnson said, must not be left to the reader to infer. The biographer must be not only a chronicler but a moralist as well, describing vice only to condemn it, and everywhere pointing out the ethical implications of his story.

We have already noticed Johnson's enthusiasm for the lives of literary men, a class whom biographers had, he thought, most unjustly neglected. Relaxing before a peat fire in a Hebridean farmhouse in September, 1773, Johnson "said he did not know any literary man's life in England well-written. It should tell us his studies, his manner of life, the means by which he attained to excellence, his opinion of his own works, and such particulars." Six years earlier, King George III, coming to him as he read in the royal library, had "expressed a desire to have the literary biography of this country ably executed, and proposed to Dr. Johnson to undertake it."

((49

Now, in 1777, the booksellers seconded the King's appeal, and Johnson agreed. The task to which he addressed himself was to occupy four years, and on the whole it was not enjoyable. Johnson was growing old, and much of what he had to do was sheer drudgery. He wrote the *Lives of the Poets* "in my usual way, dilatorily and hastily, unwilling to work, and working with vigour and haste." But hard writing, the saying goes, makes easy reading, and Boswell's prediction that "this is the work which of all Dr. Johnson's writings will perhaps be read most generally, and with most pleasure" has proved accurate. After the passage of almost two centuries this collection of biographical and critical essays on fifty-two seventeenth- and eighteenth-century poets still belongs to that select library of books which can be read and reread with undiminished delight.

It is, for one thing, written with that special laconic, aphoristic crispness whose secret died with Johnson. The style is not "Johnsonese," but "Johnsonian": there is considerable difference. People assume that Johnson *always* wrote in elephantine sentences, with massively balanced clauses and antitheses, the whole burdened down with semicolons and ponderous Latinical vocabulary. He did not. Although there are in the *Lives* occasional traces of Johnson's notorious manner, as a rule he writes with marvelous succinctness. He has a magical gift for turning a phrase. There are literally hundreds of sentences which embrace a world of moral meaning within a dozen simple words. He performs miracles with an abstract vocabulary. Though he makes only very sparing use of metaphorical concretions, he never leaves the earth; his comments are never merely theoretical or metaphysical, but seem inevitably to be prompted and documented by the careers he writes about.

The book is full of the richness of Johnson's mature thought. He had, as he said of Addison, "read with critical eyes the important volume of human life, and knew the heart of man from the depths of stratagem to the surface of affectation," and this hard-won knowledge of life is embedded in every page. Johnson's wit and wisdom (because they are seldom separated, the cliché may stand) are seemingly inexhaustible. His manner is dry, often tart, always bracing. Listen to him:

It has not been discovered that [Waller's] wife was won by his poetry; nor is anything told of her, but that she brought him many children. He doubtless praised some whom he would have been afraid to marry, and perhaps married one whom he would have been ashamed to praise. Many qualities contribute to domestick happiness upon which poetry has no colours to bestow, and many airs and sallies may delight imagination which he who flatters them never can approve. There are charms made only for distant admiration. No spectacle is nobler than a blaze.

. . . the liberty of the press is a blessing when we are inclined to write against others, and a calamity when we find ourselves overborne by the multitude of our assailants; as the power of the crown is always thought too great by those who suffer by its influence, and too little by those in whose favour it is exerted; and a standing army is generally accounted necessary by those who command, and dangerous and oppressive by those who support it. ("Savage.")

[Collins] designed many works, but his great fault was irresolution, or the frequent calls of immediate necessity broke his schemes, and suffered him to pursue no settled purpose. A man, doubtful of his dinner, or trembling at a creditor, is not much disposed to abstracted meditation or remote inquiries.

A grotto is not often the wish or pleasure of an Englishman, who has more frequent need to solicit than exclude the sun; but Pope's excavation was requisite as an entrance to his garden, and, as some men try to be proud of their defects, he extracted an ornament from an inconvenience, and vanity produced a grotto where necessity enforced a passage.

Because in his hands the art of biography was dedicated to the service of practical morality, Johnson never hesitates to offer his positive interpretation and judgment of a character or a deed. The biographer is at least as prominent as the men whose lives and personalities he describes. In his doughty, prejudiced, sometimes wrong-headed, but more often crushingly sensible way, he applies his great battery of moral judgments to the human materials he has assembled. Since he habitually saw men as they really are, there was no danger that he would succumb to the temptation, still strong in his age, to be merely encomiastic. The opening paragraph of the first of the *Lives,* that of Cowley, sets the tone of the whole collection. Of Sprat's earlier sketch of the poet, he says: "His zeal of friendship, or ambition of eloquence, has produced a funeral oration rather than a history: he has given the character, not the life of Cowley: for he writes with so little detail that scarcely any thing is distinctly known, but all is shewn confused and enlarged through the mist of panegyrick." There would be no "panegyrick" in Johnson's *Lives* if he could help it; only justice.

Thus Johnson, far from paying undue deference to the deceased, treated them with exactly the same blunt forthrightness for which his remarks on his living contemporaries are so famous. This is the habit most responsible for the remarkable illusion he manages to provide that the poets of whom he writes are alive, and the subject of brisk disagreement around the tavern fire: he talks about them as if they were. The question of whether Addison, say, or Swift or Pope was a scoundrel or a charlatan, or whether he knew how to write, is just as urgent to Johnson as the same question applied to a living (but absent) Smart or Goldsmith. Such judgments as these, in the *Lives*, have a quality indistinguishable from Johnson's ex cathedra comments, as reported by Boswell, on the men he knew in the flesh:

> . . . let it be remembered for [Blackmore's] honour that to have been once a school-master is the only reproach which all the perspicacity of malice, animated by wit, has ever fixed upon his private life.

> The reader of Swift's *Letter to a Lady on her Marriage* may be allowed to doubt whether his opinion of female excellence ought implicitly to be admitted; for if his general thoughts on women were such as he exhibits, a very little sense in a Lady would enrapture and a very little virtue would astonish him.

Johnson's conviction that a biographer's first allegiance is to truth is nowhere better exemplified than in his life of Richard Savage. This was a biography Johnson had first written in 1744, when he, like Savage, was a booksellers' hack. Savage's life and character were, from any conceivable point of view, not to be envied. Allegedly the illegitimate son of a countess (an assumption he tirelessly exploited, even to writing an autobiographical poem called *The Bastard*), he was often a penniless derelict in the London streets, a shameless parasite clinging to whatever acquaintances could be depended on to give him a meal and shelter for the night. Johnson's Hogarthian drawing of him is sympathetic, as befits a friend, yet severe, as befits a moralist. A lesser biographer would have turned Savage's story into a cruel farce or a sentimental debauch (and several contemporary writers did one or the other). Johnson took a squalid subject and treated it with unfailing, though often acidulous, dignity.

> He had not often a friend long, without obliging him to become a stranger.

> For the acquisition of knowledge he was indeed far better qualified than for that of riches, for he was naturally inquisitive and desirous of the conversation of those from whom any information was to be obtained, but by no means solicitous to improve these opportunities that were sometimes offered of raising his fortune: and he was remarkably retentive of his ideas, which, when once he was in possession of them, rarely forsook him; a quality which could never be communicated to his money.

> The reigning error of his life was, that he mistook the love for the practice of virtue, and was indeed not so much a good man as the friend of goodness.

> He continued to resent neglect without attempting to force himself into regard.

> Surely the fortitude of this man deserves, at least, to be mentioned with applause; and, whatever faults may be imputed to him, the virtue of suffering well cannot be denied him. The two powers which, in the opinion of Epictetus, constituted a wise man are those of bearing and forbearing, which cannot indeed be affirmed to have been equally possessed by Savage; and indeed the want of one obliged him very frequently to practise the other.

Johnson was not always right, of course. There are many instances in the *Lives* where his incomplete information, or his misreading of a date, or his political and religious prejudices (most notoriously in the case of Milton) betrayed him into a palpably unfair interpretation of events and motives. But even after modern biographers have corrected his distortions, Johnson's achievement remains undiminished. He was the first biographer

((53

to set up, and to practice according to his lights, an ideal toward which all good biography should aspire: the ideal of the judicious, candid, three-dimensional portrait.

Johnson was sixty-nine years old when the first four volumes of the *Lives* were published. He can be forgiven, therefore, for having been somewhat less than indefatigable in his pursuit of fresh facts. The frustrations that try the scholarly flesh were never more affectingly epitomized than in his remark in the life of Dryden: "To adjust the minute events of literary history is tedious and troublesome; it requires indeed no great force of understanding, but often depends upon enquiries which there is no opportunity of making, or is to be fetched from books and pamphlets not always at hand." He did a certain amount of original research. From his friend John Nichols, the proprietor of the *Gentleman's Magazine,* he borrowed books, and from the Duke of Newcastle the manuscript of Spence's anecdotes of Pope, Addison, and others; he made a trip to Oxford in quest of information; and he received data from certain friendly antiquarians. But most of his material he got where every other eighteenth-century biographer found it: in the biographical encyclopedias and the prefaces to editions of various authors' works.

If he infrequently went out of his way to discover, by fresh inquiry, the actual truth of a disputed matter, he refused to be taken in by what purported to be the truth. He was the first great man of letters to insist that biographical tradition be put to the trial of Common Sense. Johnson's greatest advantage as a scholar was his profound sense of human frailty. No one was more aware than he of the multifarious sources of error in human report, and the ineradicable tendency men have to stray away from the truth, or even invent it. "Thus it is that characters are written," he says in the life of Roscommon: "we know somewhat, and we imagine the rest."

Throughout the *Lives* the confounder of "Ossian" Macpherson is seen disposing of smaller pretenders in the form of unsupported or improbable biographical tradition. One of his favorite devices was to discredit a hand-me-down "fact" simply by applying the homely test of likelihood. Reporting the old story that Milton's daughter, who knew neither Latin nor Greek, repeated portions of Homer, Ovid, and Euripides to her father from memory, he observed: "Yet here incredulity is ready to make a stand. Many repetitions are necessary to fix in the memory lines not understood; and why should Milton wish or want to hear them so often!" Confronted with the statement of Samuel Butler's brother that the author of *Hudibras,* despite the silence of the official records on the point, went to Cambridge, he remarked: "The brother's seems the best authority, till, by confessing his inability to tell his hall or college, he gives reason to suspect that he was resolved to bestow on him an academical education; but durst not name a college for fear of detection." With his fine instinct for the common varieties of error, he could identify a specimen at a hundred paces. After recounting the story that Milton was offered the chance to continue in the Latin Secretaryship despite the defeat of his party, Johnson concluded: "But this tale has too little evidence to deserve a disquisition; large offers and sturdy rejections are among the most common topicks of falsehood."

Comments like these, so swiftly incisive, so destructive of pretension, are possible to any intelligent person: they require no special training whatsoever, but a wide experience of life and an unillusioned knowledge of men. Nevertheless, they are surprisingly rare in all subsequent biography. No biographer, not even the most (technically) sophisticated product of twentieth-century graduate schools, has approached Johnson's shrewdness in such matters—perhaps because none has attained his wisdom. Dr. Johnson could, in fact, have written a brilliant chapter, entitled "The Supreme Importance of Common Sense," for a modern manual of critical scholarship. Though common sense was his chief weapon against biographical myth, he also illustrated the practical uses of historical knowledge, as when he discredited the story that Otway's *Don Carlos* had run for thirty nights in 1675 because "so long a continuance of one play upon the stage is a very wide deviation from the practice of that time."

In addition, Johnson knew the importance of assessing the relative authority of various witnesses and of not rejecting a certain story out of hand simply because it comes from a suspect source. He recognized the possible evidential value of even the most dubious data. After quoting Aubrey in the "Roscommon," he observed: "The present age is very little inclined to favour any accounts of this kind, nor will the name of Aubrey much recommend it to credit; it ought not however to be omitted because better evidence of a fact cannot easily be found than is here offered, and it must be by preserving such relations that we may at last judge how much they are to be regarded." And he subscribed to the modern principle of what might be called biographical propinquity—the axiom that, other things being equal, the evidence provided by the man nearest the event is more dependable than that from later, more distant sources.

Despite everything that Johnson said about skepticism, however, and his frequent exercise of that admirable trait, he did, on occasion, suspend his better judgment and accept error as fact; and once in a while the weary old scholar lapsed into carelessness and forgetfulness. A more serious criticism that can be made of the *Lives* is that his narratives often lack balance. This was partly due, as the same defect may be in a modern biography, to the unequal distribution of the available data. On some important events in his subjects' lives he had little information, hence was able to give them much less attention than they deserved; conversely, the relative abundance of data on less important events led him to allot them an unwarranted amount of space. But the imbalance seems sometimes to have been a matter of Johnson's own choice. On Dryden, for example, he said much about the prolific writer but almost nothing of the man, even though a considerable amount of personal information was already in print.

Johnson usually was content to offer a loosely arranged miscellany of facts rather than a coherent portrait. He moved restlessly from point to point, lingering only over a character trait or an episode that happened to engage his interest, arousing his indignation or pity or sense of irony. There is little evidence anywhere in the *Lives* that Johnson had any interest in formal structure. He simply hung his data together in chronological sequence, without any nice proportioning of part to part. But so did every other biographer of his age. There was, as yet, no sense that biography should have a certain structural logic, a symmetry as satisfying as the canons of neoclassical esthetics demanded of buildings and gardens and music. In this very important respect, the idea of biography as a form of literary art had not yet even begun to take shape.

It would be unfair, also, to reproach him for failing to do another thing that would have occurred to nobody else in his age to do: that is, to bring the biography of a man to bear on the criticism of his works. To praise him, as Joseph Wood Krutch has done, for being a pioneer in the integration of biography and criticism is to give credit where credit is not owing. Johnson's innovation, such as it was, lay in his juxtaposing the man and the poet. He places them side by side, and inevitably there is some reciprocal coloration. But the two do not coalesce into a single image. Seldom does Johnson state or even imply connections between the poet's personality and his art. But neither did anyone else in his time.

These reservations help to define more accurately the place of the *Lives of the Poets* in the emergence of English literary biography. The parts are greater than the whole. The qualities that distinguish the book are all qualities of first-rate biography: ceaseless quest for the essence of the subject's character, the application of the biographer's experience of the world to the moral and psychological problems his narrative raises, the spirit of skepticism governed by common sense. All these even now are uncommon enough to make us wonder at Johnson's easy command of them. Still, they are indispensable ingredients rather than a totality. The *Lives* are a masterpiece because of their wealth of *aperçus* rather than their sustained illumination. And although several of them, above all the studies of Savage, Swift, and Pope, are extended and systematic enough to be virtually exempt from this criticism, it remains true that in general Johnson lacked the integrating, shaping talents that the very greatest artists in biography should possess. He showed his age what a biography should contain; he did not demonstrate how it should be built.

((57

· 2 ·

"To write the Life of him who excelled all mankind in writing the lives of others," began Boswell, "is an arduous, and may be reckoned in me a presumptuous task." Boswell shrank neither from arduous industry nor from the allegation of presumptuousness that he all too accurately foresaw, and so, for these among other reasons, he wrote a great book. "In biography there can be no question that he excelled, beyond all who have attempted that species of composition; upon which, indeed, he set the highest value. To the minute selection of characteristical circumstances, for which the ancients were remarkable, he added a philosophical research, and the most perspicuous and energetick language." These too are Boswell's words, speaking of Dr. Johnson; but they can equally well be applied to him, as it is certainly conceivable he wished them to be. There is no need to decide who excelled whom. Each biographer had a quite different purpose; the two books are not rivals but complements. Johnson had been satisfied to write a long series of biographical sketches, in the usual eighteenth-century mode. From the beginning, however, Boswell had something much more ambitious in mind. His plans, to be sure, were nebulous. From the time he first met Johnson, in 1763, he had stored up Johnsoniana more or less in the way in which he accumulated notes on other subjects; Boswell's highly developed collector's instinct assured him that everything he wrote down was worth preserving, no matter whom or what it dealt with. But slowly the idea grew of extracting from his ever-swelling private journals those passages that related to Dr. Johnson and fashioning from them a biography on a scale previously unattempted.

Though toward the end of Johnson's life Boswell made no secret of his project, the outlook for its successful execution was not good. He had had little experience as the author of lengthy works; most of his writing had taken the form of ephemeral squibs and pamphlets and contributions to newspapers and magazines. Could such a man, disappointed for the most part in his personal ambitions, drinking more heavily than ever, leading a

58))

more and more disorderly life, possibly accomplish anything more worthy of Dr. Johnson than one of those common biographical trifles that, Johnson himself once growled, the dogs of Grub Street did not know how to write with dignity?

Johnson died in 1784. His death was a public event. A measure of his celebrity, as well as of the increased popular interest in the professional man of letters, was the unprecedented shower of magazine articles, pamphlets, and books about him that fell from the presses in the next seven years. Johnson dead served the booksellers as faithfully as had Johnson living. There was a spate of hastily assembled biographies, by men whose very identities are obscure; there was Sir John Hawkins' work, more substantial, but destined to be the subject of many tart remarks in Boswell's text and footnotes; there was Mrs. Piozzi's *Anecdotes*, about which, also, Boswell would have unflattering things to say; and there was a whole assortment of biographical and critical fragments, as well as elegies and odes in Johnson's memory. Preoccupied as he was throughout life with morbid imaginings of the grave, Johnson mercifully did not foresee this posthumous scramble for cash and notoriety on the part of people who knew, or claimed to have known, him. It would, as Dr. Arbuthnot had said of Curll's biographies many years before, have added a new terror to death.

Meanwhile, Boswell busied himself with his bundles of manuscript notes, which had piled up over the years. From them he first drew the journal of the three-month tour he and Johnson had taken through the Hebrides in 1773. This presented few problems: it had a natural unity, and Johnson had read the manuscript and approved it. Having revised it with the constant assistance of Edmond Malone, Boswell published it the year following Johnson's death. But by far the greater task remained, to extract from his informal chronicles spanning the twenty-one years of their friendship all the materials relating to Johnson. The labor of separating the pertinent from the irrelevant was itself tremendous: "*Sorted till I was stupified*," he recorded in his diary in June, 1786. In addition, Boswell committed himself to obtaining all the reminiscences he could from Johnson's surviving friends, and these notes too had to be organized and integrated with the narrative whose main substance was provided by Boswell's private journals.

The task clearly would have defeated an Aubrey, but somehow Boswell was equal to it. Perhaps the presence of Malone spelled the difference. His contribution to the shaping of the *Life of Johnson* was not so much advice on specific points of selection and method—these Boswell decided for himself—as moral support. Had he not constantly assured Boswell that his project was important, and his chosen approach valid and exciting, it is quite possible that the biography would have gone down, unrealized, in the shipwreck of Boswell's own life.

As it was, Malone gave him the courage he needed to devote seven distracted, yet uniquely satisfying, years to the breaking of new ground in biography. For the scale, the comprehensiveness, the intimacy of the *Life of Johnson* there was no model; nor, in the scanty theoretical writings on biography apart from Johnson's, was there approval. Boswell was thoroughly conscious of the novelty of his book, no less than of its worth: "I am absolutely certain," he wrote his friend William Temple, "that *my* mode of biography, which gives not only a *history* of Johnson's *visible* progress through the world, and of his publications, but a *view* of his mind, in his letters and conversations is the most perfect that can be conceived, and will be *more* of a *Life* than any work that has ever yet appeared."

The admirable fullness of portraiture which is one of the book's greatest qualities was the result partly of chance and partly of Boswell's intelligence and industry. It was chance that its subject was a man who had expressed himself so copiously and quotably on so many subjects, and thus left his biographer ample materials for the delineation of his mind. It was either chance or remarkable foresight that led Boswell to keep voluminous journals long before his biographical purpose had crystallized. But it was no accident that Boswell, far from being swamped by his data, knew how to go about making a book out of them. He had a clearly formulated ideal of biography, and he saw how he could realize it. Instead of the flatness that inevitably results from use of a single vantage point, he aimed for a three-dimensional effect by, as he said, "an accumulation of intelligence from various points, by which [Johnson's] character is more fully understood and illustrated." Wherever possible, he quoted from Johnson's "own minutes [private diaries], letters, or conversation, being convinced that this mode is more lively, and will make my readers better acquainted with him, than even most of those were who actually knew him, but could know him only partially." To Johnson's own words, Boswell added the constant testimony of an eyewitness—himself—whose powers of observation and retention, cultivated over many years, were never more acute than when in Johnson's presence. The third indispensable element was the recollections of the many persons who had known Johnson before Boswell came on the scene, or who were present on occasions when Boswell was absent, or who could provide additional details of scenes that he did describe first-hand. "I will venture to say," Boswell wrote with no exaggeration whatsoever, "that [Johnson] will be seen in this work more completely than any man who has ever yet lived."

No previous biographer had been a tithe as assiduous as Boswell was in pursuit of the hitherto uncollected fact. Dr. Johnson himself had been an armchair researcher whose sources were, for the most part, limited to the books within reach. Boswell, persuaded that the authenticity and lifelikeness of a biographical portrait are directly proportional to the amount of material drawn upon and the variety of sources from which it is obtained, cast as wide a net as humanly possible. He was as expert as any modern biographer in reconstructing single episodes from several sources. His description of Johnson's conversation with George III, for example, was synthesized from information obtained from Johnson himself; from Bennet Langton, who heard Johnson tell about it one day at Sir Joshua Reynolds'; from a letter Johnson's printer-friend, William Strahan, wrote to Bishop Warburton; and from other private documents and oral reminiscences.

Eighteenth-century biographers habitually praised the accuracy of their own accounts, but few had much reason to do so. Boswell was the first to back up a claim of "scrupulous authenticity" with a record of extensive and painstaking inquiry. Johnson was eager enough to destroy a biographical myth if he could do so by use of information at hand or by simple reliance on his native shrewdness, but not if it required much exertion. Boswell on the other hand was tireless in his anxiety to establish the exact fact. He would run half over London, as he said, in order to fix a date correctly. And though many of the unkind remarks he dropped regarding the books by Sir John Hawkins and Mrs. Piozzi undoubtedly were motivated by personal jealousy—their authors were, after all, his rivals for the limelight—they also sprang from his honest intolerance of inaccuracy and bias and his desire to root out the considerable amount of legend from the Johnsonian story before it could burgeon any further. Boswell's zeal for accuracy was worth the pains it cost him. Modern scholarship, which has examined his every page with the most minute care, has found very little to correct.

If Boswell paid far more than lip service to the ideal of biographical accuracy, he also differed from his predecessors in actually avoiding the uncritically eulogistic mood which they repudiated, *pro forma,* and then adopted. "I profess," he announced, "to write, not his panegyrick, which must be all praise, but his Life; which, great and good as he was, must not be supposed to be entirely perfect. To be as he was, is indeed subject of panegyrick enough to any man in this state of being; but in every picture there should be shade as well as light." Hannah More, Johnson's pet in the days when she frequented London literary circles, had begged Boswell to "mitigate" some of the "asperities" of "our virtuous and most revered departed friend." Boswell retorted that "he would not cut off his claws, nor make a tiger a cat, to please anybody." His utter frankness in delineation was the main reason why the *Life of Johnson* made such a stir, and it remains today one of the book's most remarkable qualities. Once in a while, to be sure, Boswell toned down a few details, such as the bawdy talk in which Johnson occasionally indulged, especially when Garrick goaded him on. Nevertheless, the immense amount of research that has been done on Johnson's life and character has exposed no significant respect in which Boswell suppressed or modified the truth. No discreditable episode in Johnson's life, no disagreeable trait of behavior, went unmentioned in his pages.

Some of Boswell's contemporary critics maintained that in portraying Johnson's less statuesque side he had destroyed a hero. No dispassionate reader of the *Life* would agree. Johnson is not a whit less great, is, some would say, all the more admirable a man, for the way Boswell depicts him. His very weaknesses, which were serious, make his strengths heroic. Actually, what the critics complained of was Boswell's insistence on the revealing, private detail rather than what tradition considered the proper concern of biography, the great and memorable act. Johnson's greatness was so evident to him that Boswell assumed it would be obvious to everybody else. What he wanted to present to his own age, and to posterity, was not a walking set of principles but a human being: not a posed figure who could be admired from a reverential distance, but a puffing, muttering, grimacing, shambling, pocked, untidy, half-blind, rude, contentious, dogmatic, superstitious, intolerant man whom any number of people not only admired but unaffectedly loved.

Boswell chose to make Johnson come alive in his pages through the use of lavish but controlled detail: each detail significant and revealing in itself, and the total cumulative in effect. He mingled the material of Flemish realism (an analogy he himself was aware of) with what was to be, a century later, the method of French neoimpressionism. His raw material was the individually minute data of the senses—sharply observed particulars of personal appearance, dress, conduct, peculiarities of speech, locale. From these thousands upon thousands of small details, carefully arranged on the broadest canvas a biographer had ever commanded, Boswell produced the vivid portrait—or whole set of portraits—which makes the *Life of Johnson* a masterpiece.

Boswell gives us incomparably more to see and hear than any preceding biographer. When Boswell and Johnson encounter Johnson's old schoolfellow, Oliver Edwards, we recognize the prosy bore as the very model of the person most of us discover our own schoolmates to have turned into at the interval of several decades; Boswell places him, once and for all, by a sensitive reproduction of his conversation. When an episode occurs in a street, the street is duly named, so that everyone who knows eighteenth-century London can envision the exact locale—

buildings, sidewalks, gutters, street cries, smells, and all. When a boy in a water taxi pleases Johnson and Boswell, they reward him not with a (generalized) coin but with a (specified) shilling. Above all, the manifold physical eccentricities and compulsive mannerisms of Johnson are described with an unflinching particularity that has engraved them in the memory of readers for over a century and a half.

How novel this kind of reporting was in Boswell's time is suggested by the frequency with which he calls attention to it in order to defend it. He is almost oppressively conscious of the disapproval that hangs in the critical atmosphere of an age still anxious for the avoidance of "vulgar" particulars and the achievement of general (and therefore philosophically significant) effects. "I cannot," he says on one occasion, "allow any fragment whatever that floats in my memory concerning the great subject of this work to be lost. Though a small particular may appear trifling to some, it will be relished by others; while every little spark adds something to the general blaze: and to please the true, candid, warm admirers of Johnson, and in any degree increase the splendour of his reputation, I bid defiance to the shafts of ridicule, or even of malignity." With which magnificent gesture— Boswell against the critics—he proceeds to increase the splendor of Johnson's reputation by a rather circuitous route; for the following scene is in the country, where Johnson, on a visit to a friend, is trying to clear an artificial waterfall of accumulated débris. "He worked till he was quite out of breath; and having found a large dead cat so heavy that he could not move it after several efforts, 'Come,' he said, (throwing down the pole,) *you shall take it now;'* which I accordingly did, and being a fresh man, soon made the cat tumble over the cascade." Johnson the great moralist and man of letters is not immediately evident in the scene, but Johnson sweating to dislodge a dead cat from a waterfall nevertheless is the man who wrote *The Vanity of Human Wishes,* and Boswell's great achievement is that he leaves no doubt in our minds of their identity.

In addition to being a supremely gifted portraitist, Boswell was a born dramatist. The time being what it was, an age of intense sociability; and Dr. Johnson being the man he was, loving nothing more than to sit with chosen company and talk away the evening; and Boswell being the man *he* was, a constant playgoer whenever he was in London, it was almost inevitable that the book should have been deliberately planned as a series of scenes. Boswell had the priceless advantage of having been present on hundreds of occasions when there was free discourse between Johnson and one or more interlocutors, many of them men of high intellect whose conversation put him on his mettle, others being fools, lightning rods to bring down the bolt of his devastating wit. Boswell had made full records of those scenes, as well as of the equally numerous times when he and Johnson were alone, in Johnson's rooms or strolling through the streets. The book's strong dramatic element, in fact, was already in existence when Boswell transferred the Johnsonian passages of his private journals into the manuscript of the *Life*. It took no such labor as is usually the lot of the modern biographer who seeks to dramatize his pages by a painstaking assembling of facts, but the effect of this spontaneous staging, so to speak, is all that the serious biographical artist could wish. The man who is the subject of the biography is constantly placed in a social milieu. He is surrounded by others, and their interaction, as mirrored by their conversation, provides an unexcelled immediacy of impression, both of him and of them.

Few of the scenes in Boswell mark crucial episodes in Johnson's life. But Boswell was always less interested in the strictly narrative side of his study than in portraiture. And Johnson could be most accurately and extensively portrayed in the midst of a company, talking and, in the process, unfolding his mind. Hence Boswell uses scenes (many of which he adroitly stage-managed with such results in view) for the sake of character revelation. With the assistance of the people present at the Mitre or the Thrales', Johnson from 1763 to 1784 literally talked himself into his own biography. The constant conversation in the book, whether Johnson is responding to Boswell's inquisitive prodding as they sit alone or is participating in a free-for-all in a drawing room whose air is pungent with dispute, accounts for as much of its vividness as does Boswell's evocation of physical appearances. Though the immediate interest is in the juxtaposition of personalities and the collision of ideas, in the end the effect is what Boswell strove for above all: the reader has learned to know a man.

· 3 ·

Along with its gigantic merits, however, the *Life of Johnson* has certain qualities which, to a modern critic, make it less than a perfect example of biographical art. Nowadays, thanks to the recovery of the fabled Malahide papers, it is possible to study how Boswell transformed his jottings into a printed masterpiece; and as a result nobody subscribes to Macaulay's once widely shared view of him as a sottish fool who somehow blundered into writing a work of genius. Boswell was an artist, and he knew what he was doing. But his artistry was, in some ways, limited, though less by any personal deficiencies than by the conditions of his age and the special circumstances that led to the writing of his book.

Those circumstances, to be sure, probably enabled Boswell to make a better book than he otherwise could have, because they were such as to encourage the exercise of his special talents. He was an artist who was best fitted for small-scale operations: the management of individual scenes, the writing of descriptive passages—detail work rather than architecture. His genius was less adapted to solving the larger problems of structure and proportion. The materials he possessed and the particular nature of his own experience with the subject of his biography required, for best utilization, precisely the sort of creative gift he brought to the task.

Nevertheless, it must not be forgotten that the *Life of Johnson* was written principally from notes made during, and dealing with, a relatively limited period of its subject's life. Johnson was born in 1709; Boswell first met him in 1763, when he was a few months short of fifty-four; Johnson died in 1784. Yet the whole first half of Johnson's life is condensed into barely one tenth of the biography, whereas the final eight years of Johnson's seventy-five spread over no less than half the pages.

The heart of the book is Boswell's first-hand reporting of Johnson as he knew him. But not only were the two men acquainted only in the last twenty-one years (considerably less than a third) of Johnson's life; during that period they were in the same vicinity for a total of less than two years and two months, and when they were apart, there were long lapses in their correspondence. So, even despite Boswell's praiseworthy attempts to make up for this limitation by tapping the memories of Johnson's other associates, by far the major part of the *Life* is devoted to a small group of segments of Johnson's whole career. The book is decidedly out of balance. It is essentially a report of the older Johnson as Boswell happened, from time to time, to see him.

Again, the fact that Boswell's journals formed the basis of the book from 1763 onward had, along with its manifest advantages, certain disadvantages. As we have noted, the nature of those memoranda, with their great emphasis on conversation, virtually required that the biography be cast as a long series of scenes. Even after making all allowance for Boswell's efforts to fill in from other sources, it remains true that the majority of these scenes are presented from the viewpoint of James Boswell. Boswell may not unfairly dominate the picture, as he used to be accused of doing, but his presence is obvious enough. Johnson is seen chiefly through his eyes and ears, simply because it was through them that the raw stuff of the *Life*, the contents of the journals, was acquired.

Though one would not for a moment wish Boswell to have sacrificed his scenes, they did put him in something of a straitjacket. Down to 1763, his story of Johnson's career had to be synthesized from second-hand materials. Boswell was able, therefore, to construct a smooth-running narrative, interweaving the events of Johnson's private life with the progress of his literary career. He was free to rearrange and organize, in any way that seemed proper, the assorted facts he had gathered from Johnson and others. It was a fairly simple job of retrospective reconstruction. But abruptly, in 1763, the whole character of his source material changed. Henceforth the journals would, in effect, determine the form the biography would take. Extended scenes,

((67

hitherto very infrequent, would predominate, and the summary narrative would accordingly diminish in importance. When Boswell takes up his role of first-hand observer, the whole technique of the book shifts from the essentially narrative to the dramatic mode.

The primacy of the journals as source material had one other regrettable effect. Their structure was, of course, rigidly chronological; they were a day-by-day record of Boswell's life. An orderly narrative of events is desirable, indeed requisite, in any biography. But where the calendar arbitrarily dictates the biographer's direction, there is bound to be a miscellaneity of effect. The straighter the chronological course, the more rapid and abrupt the tacking from one subject to another. Within the framework of a single year, and profusely interspersed with one another, occur discussions of Johnson's external life, literary activities, domestic events, travels, emotional and intellectual tendencies as expressed by letters and conversations dating from that year, and whatever else the records assign to the stated period.

The predominance of scenes in Boswell intensifies this disorderliness. Reporting each conversation as it happened, Boswell had little choice but to follow the stream of discussion wherever it led—to the views of Johnson and others on religion, philosophy, politics, on the vagaries of human behavior, on individual personalities, on Johnson himself. Because Johnson returned to the same subject—death or his love of good eating—and gave instances of his kindness or his irritability a score of times over the years Boswell records, the separate bits of data normally are scattered throughout the book. Admittedly, life is like that, and the fidelity with which Boswell reflects the shifting interests of Johnson and his conversational circle contributes its substantial share to the pervasive verisimilitude. But one of the purposes of art is to reduce the disorderliness of life.

The enduring fame of the *Life of Johnson* as a browsing book, to be opened at random, is itself an indication of its lack of taut organization. The very circumstance that Boswell chose to transfer his journal entries more or less *en bloc* to the book, concentrating his energies on the touching up of detail rather than on a

sweeping reordering and reassessment of material, suggests a deficiency in his equipment as an artist. He was somewhat lacking in
a sense of relative values. His anxiety not to neglect the apparently
trivial which actually had relevance led him to include, also, the
genuinely trivial. Between the familiar peaks of interest, from
which no one would wish a single word to be subtracted, are long
level stretches which Boswell could have drastically shortened. He
was so engrossed in his wealth of source material that he could not
see it in perspective. A greater artist would have taken more care
to distinguish among the various gradations of importance and interest that his raw data contained.

Partly because his materials were inadequate and partly because he was not much interested in the topic, Boswell pays little
attention to Johnson's development from childhood to old age.
His overriding concern is not with what Johnson once was but
with what he became. He collected everything he could discover
about Johnson as a sickly child in Lichfield and a poverty-
stricken misfit at Oxford, but he does not succeed in picturing the
youth on the same scale or with the same closeness of effect that
were possible for the later years. Boswell's Johnson seems to have
been born into the hulking body presented in Reynolds' portrait;
for all Boswell suggests to the contrary, as an infant he was already equipped with the mind that would produce the *Lives of
the Poets*. It remained for a modern biographer, James L. Clifford
in *Young Sam Johnson*, to atone for the lack of genetic sense in
Boswell's early pages by tracing the development of Johnson's
ideas and the probable course of his emotional life from childhood into his middle years.

If Boswell's interest in Johnson's growth was limited, so was
his insight into his mature mind. For its time, of course, the
degree of psychological revelation the *Life* afforded was unprecedented. Johnson had been unusually candid in discussing his
private opinions and some selected aspects of his emotional history, such as the "amorous propensities" he suffered when confronted with the white bosoms of the actresses backstage at Garrick's theater. But apart from quoting from Johnson's spiritual
diary, published after his death as *Prayers and Meditations*, Bos-

well was confined to what Johnson chose to divulge, either in his presence or in letters to others to which he subsequently had access. Here once more the scene technique has its limiting effect: the Johnson who appears in Boswell is, above all, a man of strong social proclivities. So brilliantly does he shine in conversation, so confident is he in his relations with others, that the reader tends to forget that he was also a lonely and haunted man. Boswell knew it, and from time to time cites what Johnson wrote in solitude. But, though the spectacle of troubled spirits (most of all, his own) held a lifelong attraction for him, Boswell did not —of course, could not—explore Johnson's with the fullness and penetration to which modern psychological techniques have accustomed us. It did not occur to him, any more than it would have to anyone else in his time, to analyze the important evidence found in Johnson's published writings, especially the *Idler* and *Rambler* papers, for clues to his often tormented moral and spiritual condition. That too was a task reserved for such modern scholars as Bertrand Bronson and Walter J. Bate, who by ranging beyond Boswell's materials into Johnson's own have added considerable psychological depth to the portrait he painted.

If one uses present-day criteria, therefore, Boswell's *Life of Johnson* is in some respects unsatisfying. Both in structural technique and in psychological insight it has been surpassed by biographies of other figures. Yet the old saying persists: there could be only one Johnson, and only one Boswell.

Its very uniqueness gave it an ambiguous, indeed a doubly ironical, role in the subsequent history of English life writing. For one thing, this undisputed classic of biography came virtually at the beginning of the form's major phase of development rather than as a climax to a long period of growth. The *Life of Johnson* was not evolved; it just suddenly happened. And so there was no broad foundation for the genre, such as it would have had if Boswell, as an exponent of large-scale biography, had been preceded and surrounded by fellow practitioners of merit.

Boswell's book was, in the strict sense, inimitable. Since his materials were as unique as his subject, it was the special nature of the book, as well as its lonely eminence, which unfitted it to stand at the beginning of a new literary tradition. Readers delighted in it, critics admired it—but how far could subsequent biographers learn their art in its pages? In some ways they simply could not, because they had at their disposal no documents comparable to those amazing Boswellian journals. If the *Life of Johnson* had not been quite so fortunate in its subject, the character of its sources, and the special genius of its author—if it had, on the other hand, been more nearly associated with the normal stream of development instead of being a massive sport—it might have exercised a more positive and salutary effect on the biographical writing of the next hundred years. Had nineteenth-century biographers possessed a model somewhat easier to follow, they might have produced better work.

One or two other characteristics of the *Life*, its scale and its attention to the revealing detail, were more readily imitated—a mixed blessing. The amplitude of Boswell's treatment ended, once and for all, the notion that literary biographies should take the form of portraits in miniature like Walton's or Johnson's *Lives*. Henceforth a biography's size was limited only by the availability of data, the energy of the biographer, the tolerance of the publisher, and the pocketbook of the purchaser. Nineteenth-century biographical practice, acquiesced in if not actively encouraged by publishers and circulating-library proprietors who made larger profits from multi-volumed works, turned bulk from a virtue into a lamentable defect. The bigger the book, the greater the likelihood of dullness, and the smaller the chance that the materials would be worked over in an artistic spirit. In art, excessive quantity is usually a fatal enemy of form.

The large scale of treatment Boswell adopted was due to his belief in the supreme artistic value of "suggestive traits and vivid detail." The danger, as critics of biography in the next generations never tired of pointing out, was that in less gifted hands the same recipe could produce not a soufflé but a leaden pudding. And it did. Invoking Boswell's illustrious precedent without appreciating the subtle craftsmanship it involved, biographers loaded their books with copious unsifted detail, much of which was trivial, irrelevant, and dull.

((71

But it was not merely this practical consequence of Boswell's example—adoption of his method by biographers who lacked his peculiar gifts—that worried critics. The bigger question was: Should Boswell's method be used at all? The *Life of Johnson* was caught in the middle of the timeless tug-of-war between realism and idealization. Unless they were mortally upset by the sight of the revered Dr. Johnson in his soiled nightcap and slippers, most readers found the book "entertaining" and "amusing" and accepted it on that relaxed basis. But if they applied to it the serious canons of art, they had, to say the least, their doubts. Realism in depiction of character and scene was the forte of a certain kind of novelist, Fielding and Smollett, for instance, or, to reach back to the beginning of the century, Defoe. To conjure up a host of concrete details of physical appearance and behavior for the purpose of fiction—that is, of a kind of writing which passed the time for readers but had little claim to the title of true art—was one thing; to use similar details to make a subject of biography as unmistakably alive as a vividly realized character in a novel was another. As a realistic artist, Boswell had much in common with Fielding and Smollett. But the persisting strength of the neoclassic tradition, which deplored the intrusion of the "vulgar" detail in art, made that, in many people's eyes, a dubious distinction.[2]

The esthetic issue here was inseparable from the moral: they both involved the problem of decorum. Although it had resulted in an endlessly pleasurable book, Boswell's penchant for verisimilitude and the significant detail was not in good taste. Concentration on a great man's gross table manners and unbuttoned speech was not only artistically indefensible, it was morally wrong. The proper function of biography was to inspire the reader by recording the noble conduct and wise words of men who were worthy of emulation. This purpose, it was widely thought, was defeated by the candor of which Boswell made such a complacent virtue. If a man could not be a hero to his biographer (and what heroism was

---

[2] "The biographer of Cowper," Lady Hesketh told William Hayley about 1802, as he worked on his life of the poet, "should not consider himself as the writer of a *Novel*, and indeed I am firmly of opinion that you should deal only in *generals*, and by no means give a particular account of the life of our friend." (Thomas Wright, *The Life of William Cowper* [London, 1892], p. 9.)

there in grotesque physical appearance, eccentric conduct, and bludgeoning tactics in conversation?), he could be a hero to no one else.

To describe a man by the use of Boswell's unsparing realism, far from providing a model for moral imitation, simply catered to impertinent curiosity; it amounted to stripping off the toga to discover the condition of the underwear. This was a serious charge indeed, in an epoch when eighteenth-century ideals of decorum were being reformulated and coarsened into nineteenth-century notions of decency. The *Life of Johnson* appeared just at a time when the English were valuing privacy more and more highly, in response to forces, such as the Boswells abroad in the world, that were bent on violating it. There were many aspects of a man's life—the list seemed to grow longer every year—which were none of the world's business, and such privacy was a right as applicable to the grave as to the houses of the living. Dr. Johnson, it is true, was himself on record with some wholesomely corrective views on the flight from frankness, biographical and otherwise, but the age was not disposed to listen.

Thus, as the early nineteenth century's moral prison house closed about biography, people continued to admire and read the *Life of Johnson*. They were glad Boswell had written it, because, as they said—it is not easy to resolve the inconsistencies here—he had not only made Johnson more vivid as a man but increased his stature as a moral hero. Nevertheless, they feared and discouraged the repetition of the Boswellian process in the case of anyone else. In the moral and social climate of the many decades following 1791, nobody cared, or dared, to imitate Boswell's frankness.

All subsequent English biography was written, and read, in the shadow of Boswell. But far from advancing the art of biography, the *Life of Johnson* actually retarded it, by providing a model incapable of imitation in an era when the very qualities that made it great were themselves being devalued. The book's historical importance lies, rather, in Boswell's having elevated large-scale biography to a place of dignity in the hierarchy of literary forms. He rescued it from the squalid associations that still clung to it from the days of Curll and the Grub Streeters, and made the composition of biographies a literary activity in which the most respectable writers could unapologetically engage. He revealed possibilities in biography that no one had ever dreamed of, and by his own performance showed that the art required peculiar talents of no mean order and, indeed, of positive rarity. And Boswell vindicated forever the claim of literary men to be subjects of biography. In 1781, during an unusually happy gathering at the home of Garrick's widow in the Adelphi, "Somebody said the life of a mere literary man could not be very entertaining. JOHNSON. 'But it certainly may. This is a remark which has been made, and repeated, without justice; why should the life of a literary man be less entertaining than the life of any other man? Are there not as interesting varieties in such a life? As *a literary life* it may be very entertaining.'" After Boswell wrote Johnson's own life, there was no longer any question on that score.

II

From Boswell to Strachey

The Uses of Biography

✳

THIS is an age of biography!"
Never was a cliché more faithful to fact than this one, which echoed all the way down the long corridors of the nineteenth century. The century after Boswell was, in truth, an age of biography; in its later decades some writers went so far in their enthusiasm as to assert that biography was the most popular of all forms of current literature, though that honor actually went to fiction. Biographies ranged in size from tiny chapbooks to the occasional life-and-letters in six or eight volumes, a work as massive as a Victorian sideboard. There were whole series, or "libraries," of book-length biographies: Eminent Women, English Men of Action, Military Biographies, Great Artists, Great Musicians, English Worthies, Men Worth Remembering, Lives Worth Living. . . . Nor was the era's outpouring confined to books. From the very beginning, in the 1830's, of the miscellaneous weekly papers addressed to the purposeful rather than the frivolous reader, the condensed biographical narrative was a journalistic staple. The *Penny Magazine* and *Chambers's Journal* and their many imitators abounded with earnestly written capsule lives. Then too, there were the biographical dictionaries—for this was also an age of reference books. Scores of general biographical encyclopedias, adapted to the needs of every class of book user from the savant to the self-teaching workman, loaded the shelves. And publishers' lists were filled with a broad and curious array of specialized compilations devoted to the biographical annals of a

certain class: painters, architects, engravers, violinmakers, fiddlers, eccentrics, Welshmen, Irishmen, saintly women, philosophers, divines, actors, brave men, boy princes, royal servants, freethinkers, ecclesiastics, physicians, "earnest men," good wives, booksellers.

By a pleasantly symbolic accident, the year that marked the century's end saw the completion of the monumental *Dictionary of National Biography*, a fitting climax to a hundred years of incessant biographical writing. The *DNB* summarized the dignity biography had acquired as a national literary institution, a panoramic reflection of the British spirit and accomplishments over a thousand years.[1] Despite the impetus provided by Boswell, that dignity had been attained only slowly, by the acquisition of new uses—and the reaffirmation of old ones—which recommended the form to an age that applied a utilitarian yardstick to all its arts.

As the century opened, biography was only beginning to at-

[1] The *DNB* was undertaken in 1882 by George Smith, a public-spirited publisher who had made a fortune with the novels of Thackeray and Charlotte Brontë, the essays of Matthew Arnold, Browning's later poetry, the *Cornhill Magazine,* and the proprietorship of Apollinaris mineral water. It was edited by Leslie Stephen and, after his health broke down, by his assistant Sidney Lee, both of whom were knighted for their services. The dictionary was published with a punctuality almost unmatched in book-trade history, a volume appearing every three months from January, 1885, to July, 1900. When the original alphabet was complete in sixty-three volumes (there have since been several large supplements), 29,120 men and women associated with British history, the famous and infamous, the stately and the eccentric, had been commemorated by a staff of 653 contributors, the longest articles being devoted to Shakespeare (forty-nine double-columned pages), Wellington, Bacon, Cromwell, Queen Elizabeth I, Sir Robert Walpole, the first Duke of Marlborough, and Sir Walter Scott.

The enterprise required an investment variously reported as £100,000 and £150,000, and Smith, who from the outset had intended the *DNB* as his monument, cheerfully assumed a loss of half that amount. His noblest expectations were fulfilled. Though it is not infallible, and facts that have come to light with the passing of seventy and more years require occasional revision of its articles, the dictionary is a scholarly achievement of which any country could be proud, and not merely for the reason given by one of Smith's eulogists: "There is something peculiarly English, we may please ourselves by thinking, about the steady progress of this private enterprise, unhasting, unresting, so that it is the first finished, though Germany and Belgium had State aid and nearly thirty years start." (See the "Statistical Account" at the end of the final volume of the original issue and W. E. Garrett Fisher, "Mr. George Murray Smith and 'National Biography,'" *Fortnightly Review,* new ser., LXIX [1901], 880–893.) Walter Pater is reported to have read "religiously" each volume of the *Dictionary* as it appeared. (Thomas Wright, *The Life of Walter Pater* [London, 1907], II, 117.)

tain independent status as a literary genre. Officially, insofar as encyclopedias reflect standard current opinion, it remained for many years "only a branch of history," as the *Penny Cyclopædia* (1835) called it, though many people would have quarreled with the implications of "only" and hastened to add, in the words of another reference work, that it was certainly "a very entertaining and instructive species of history."[2]

"Instructive" in what ways? For one thing, as a rich source of information on the way people lived in other ages. Just before Macaulay was to initiate the writing of social history, Carlyle praised Boswell's *Life of Johnson* because it

> will give us more real insight into the *History of England* during those days than twenty other Books, falsely entitled "Histories," which take to themselves that special aim. . . . The thing I want to see is not Redbook Lists, and Court Calendars, and Parliamentary Registers, but the LIFE OF MAN in England: what men did, thought, suffered, enjoyed; the form, especially the spirit, of their terrestrial existence, its outward environment, its inward principle; *how* and *what* it was; whence it proceeded, whither it was tending. . . . History . . . will tell us, question it as we like, less than one genuine Biography may do, pleasantly and of its own accord!

Revelation of the small but meaningful details of ordinary life in some past era—domestic routine, dress, the aspects of streets, social behavior, the sort of material too commonplace and un-dramatic for the chronicler of battles and ministries: this service

[2] In 1800 a periodical called *The Juvenile Library* invited its readers to submit their views on the question "Is History or Biography the more improving Study?" Among those who did so was "Master T. L. Peacock, age 14," whose contribution included this passage:
> With bright examples the young mind to fire,
> And Emulation's gen'rous flame inspire,
> Biography her modest page displays,
> And follows one alone thro' life's uncertain ways.
> 'Tis her's, alike, with faithful pen t'impart
> The virtues, or the failing, of his heart;
> She tells of all the talents he possest,
> She makes us Virtue love, or Vice detest;
> She makes our hearts espouse the former's cause,
> And 'twixt the two a glowing contrast draws.

Nevertheless, young Master Peacock awarded to History, rather than Biography, "the golden crown of Victory." (William E. A. Axon, "The Juvenile Library," *The Library*, new ser., II [1901], 69–70.)

of biography accounted in part for both the respect in which it was held and the avidity with which ordinary readers consumed it. It was on this ground that biographers and their reviewers defended what some people looked upon as a gratuitous preoccupation with the minute external circumstances of a man's life. If these "trivialities," as unsympathetic observers called them, had little specifically biographical significance, they were invaluable illuminants of an age's general color and tone. That was why Pepys's diary, first published (with many excisions) from the manuscript in 1825 and more fully in 1848–49, quickly won so delighted an audience. It was as an intimate evocation of Pepys's age, not as a document of personality—the character of Mr. Pepys, after all, severely disturbed nineteenth-century moral sensibilities—that the diary first was established as a classic.

This nonbiographical function of early nineteenth-century biography complicated the problem of artistic technique, since it seemed to justify the inclusion of multitudinous details that had little or no bearing either on the narrative or on the character portrayal. Fortunately, the rise of social history as an important branch of historiography met the demands of Carlyle and many of his contemporaries and took the pressure off biography, which became free to devote itself to a man's life rather than his times— even though it did not always do so. Today the situation is reversed: the biographer borrows from works on social history the sort of material the historian once drew from biography.

In the generation after Boswell biography continued to be prized also as raw material for the study of psychology. The facts it gathered concerning the histories of individual minds made possible, according to James Stanfield, the pioneer systematic theorist of the biographical art, "a more attentive examination of the principles of the human character" that could be "actively applied to the improveable points of education and conduct."[3] In particular, biographical data provided grist to the busy mills of the associationist psychologists, who stressed the supreme impor-

[3] It worked the other way, too. Stanfield (on whom, see below, pages 184–185) asserted that the already-established principles of human behavior could be used to explain various obscure passages in the individual lives that were subjects of biography.

tance of environment—the character of the objects a person contemplated—in shaping the habits and quality of the individual mind. Stanfield defined the assumption of associationism which formed one particular focus of early nineteenth-century biographical interest, in passages such as these:

> . . . there is no object, physical or moral, that can be presented to the conception at this susceptible period of life [i.e., childhood] but will produce correspondent emotions; and according to the nature, force, and duration of the excitement, and the aptitude, sensibility, and steadiness of the disposition, permanent habits, manners, and opinions, will be formed, affecting every aspect of the future conduct and character.

> . . . the constitutional and moral circumstances of early youth have the chief influence in the formation of character; . . . the impressions then received do, by situation, incline or strengthen the disposition to be peculiarly excited by circumstances of a similar nature; and . . . in the continuance of this process of action and reaction, a cast of permanency is given to the character, modified by the strength and duration of the impressions, the susceptibility of the disposition, and the power of resisting the influence of contravening occurrences.

Associationist psychology and the contemporary theory and practice of art were closely linked. Associationism supplied numerous estheticians with the postulates on which they built their theories of creativity; furthermore, as we shall see in a little while, the biographies of artists in particular, and of literary artists above all, were precious because they seemed to offer the most intimate, detailed, and transparent histories of the development of individual minds.

Its reflection of social history, therefore, gave biography a journalistic function, and its fund of data on the development of the individual mind made it a valued casebook of "mental science." But biography in these early days had an even more exalted role, for it was also made the key to the new romantic interpretation of history. By and large, preoccupied as it was with the universal and changeless principles that were held to govern all human affairs, the eighteenth century had written history in terms of laws and institutions. As that century gave way to the nineteenth, however, the most advanced and original thinkers in England, following an example imported from Germany and France, proclaimed the supreme role of the individual man in shaping human events. The rationalistic analysis of historical causation now seemed pedantic and futile; the uniformity and predictability that had been assumed in human affairs savored of mere scholastic theorizing. It was men, not impersonal forces—or at least men acting decisively as the agents of those forces—that shaped destiny from epoch to epoch. In England, this biographical emphasis in history was most influentially proclaimed and practiced by Carlyle, whose dicta ("History is the essence of innumerable Biographies"; "The History of the world is but the Biography of great men") became high-ranking Victorian platitudes. So, for a while, it seemed as if the fledgling would swallow the mother; biography, far from being "only a branch of history," was history itself. History, in this extreme view, was hardly more than the stories of heroic men writ large.

The important word here is "heroic"; because the unbroken prosperity of biography in the nineteenth century, to say nothing of its intellectual significance, cannot be explained without reference to the fashion—one might indeed say institution—of hero worship. At the beginning of the century, coincident with the new emphasis on men rather than laws as the makers of human destiny, appeared the romantic theory of the genius—a demigod, distinguished from ordinary men by his extraordinary powers of insight and expression or action and impatient of control by secular institutions. This concept filled, and would continue to fill for the better part of the century, an urgent need in English emotional life. For, as Matthew Arnold, brooding at the monastery of the Grande Chartreuse, and countless other spiritually homeless children of the Victorian age knew, the old Christianity was dead. The eighteenth century's confident rationalism had fatally eroded the foundations of supernatural religion. The energies that had once been devoted to the veneration of saints and martyrs, the original subjects of English biography, now were redirected. A new race of heroes was in the making. The war against Napoleon gave the country Nelson, who, even as he lay dying in Hardy's arms in the *Victory*'s blood-slippery cockpit, was transformed from a national hero into a national legend. His co-hero, the Duke of Wellington, survived the war and the floodtide of political liberalism (he being the very definition of unreconstructed Toryism) to become eventually the recipient of the costliest funeral England had yet known and, simultaneously, the subject of the best poem (Tennyson's "Ode") that Victorian hero worship added to the nation's literature. And even before Waterloo, two glamorous but nonmilitary heroes had appeared, to inhabit a wing of the British pantheon on which construction had only just begun: Walter Scott and Lord Byron.

By the middle of the century, hero worship had become so important in some quarters of contemporary thought as to be elaborately systematized. Its rationale and operation were best illustrated by positivism, an up-to-date brand of rationalism, devised by the French philosopher Auguste Comte, which had a pronounced effect on such English intellectuals as John Stuart Mill, Harriet Martineau, George Eliot, George Henry Lewes, John Morley, and Frederic Harrison. Committed to the old idea that the workings of society are ruled by immutable natural laws and yet recognizing mankind's persistent need to color with emotion the affairs of the intellect, positivism sought to provide a surrogate for traditional Christianity in what it called a "religion of humanity," a kind of racial narcissism—mankind adoring mankind. This "Catholicism without Christianity," or "Catholicism-*cum*-science," as it was known to the irreverent, involved, among other things, a list of 538 heroes and benefactors of mankind, which was the positivist equivalent of the Roman Catholic calendar of saints. The year was divided into thirteen months, each celebrating some triumph of *homo sapiens* and each presided over by a representative deity in human form. Ancient poetry month was the special dominion of Homer, and modern epic poetry month was sacred to Dante, modern drama month to Shakespeare, and modern industry month (true to the era's veneration of the printing press as the most powerful weapon of advancing civilization) to Gutenberg. In each month's program of worship, furthermore, was assembled a regiment of subsidiary saints, who often made highly incongruous company. The enforced association of Thomas à Kempis, Byron, Shelley, Klopstock, and Madame de Staël could hardly have been as harmonious—or as intelligible—as the positivists, in their rationalistic innocence, imagined.[4]

The making of secular saints' calendars was very much in the air. In London's Bohemia, a lively coterie of budding artists, headed by Dante Gabriel Rossetti, issued in 1848 the Pre-Raphaelite Brotherhood's own rating chart. It was portentously headed: "We, the undersigned, declare that the following list of Immortals constitutes the whole of our Creed, and that there exists no other Immortality than what is centred in their names and in the names of their contemporaries, in whom this list is reflected." The hierarchy was a curious one:

**** Jesus Christ
*** Shakespeare, the author of the Book of Job
** Homer, Dante, Chaucer, Leonardo da Vinci, Goethe, Keats, Shelley, Alfred the Great, Landor, Thackeray, Washington, Browning
* Boccaccio, Fra Angelico, Mrs. Browning, P. G. Patmore, Raphael, Longfellow, Tennyson

The Pre-Raphaelites also crowned with laurel, but not with stars, a large group of minor geniuses that included Spenser, Byron, Wordsworth, Joan of Arc, Michelangelo, Titian, Milton, Cromwell, Bacon, Newton, Poe, Hood, Emerson, Leigh Hunt, and Columbus. Apart from other peculiarities, it is notable that this list, representing the enthusiasms of a group of high-spirited, and in their own field blithely iconoclastic, young painters, contains more men of letters than representatives of any other field of endeavor.

---

[4] The thirteenth month, dedicated to modern science, was something of an anticlimax. Its presiding genius was Marie François Xavier Bichât (1771–1802), an anatomist and physiologist at whose feet such inferior luminaries as Galileo, Newton, and Lamarck were assigned to sit. It is not often noted, incidentally, that an authentic, however inadvertent, witness to the power of positivist thinking over Englishmen's minds in the sixties and seventies is found on the podium of the Albert Memorial, which contains 169 portrait sculptures of benefactors of mankind.

However constituted, the new order of heroes, as Walter Houghton has pointed out in *The Victorian Frame of Mind,* served many needs. The people of the nineteenth century, growing more aware every year that simultaneous revolutions in technology and society were confronting them with problems well-nigh insoluble by ordinary means, looked not to the heavens but in the streets around them for messiahs. These hero-messiahs might be, by profession, statesmen, engineers, or poets—but whoever they were, they would have the answers for which society was groping.

It was not alone what heroes said that mattered: it was what they did. Carlyle in his middle years insisted that it was in great men's actions, fully as much as in their pronouncements, that lessons of great wisdom could be read. Hence, obviously, the usefulness of biography, which could be interpreted as parable, not only for the guidance of men in society but for inspiration in their private lives. Their consciences troubled by the grimy compromises and capitulations seemingly required by the mounting fierceness of commercial rivalry, the people of the time needed moral guidance of the kind the Bible and its ministers seemed no longer able to supply.

Most important of all the reasons for this great surge of hero worship was the Victorians' desire for reassurance. The conditions of industrial and commercial life tended more and more to erase individuality and feed a fatalistic conviction that a man's personal destiny lay totally beyond his control, in, for example, the inexorable laws of economics that determined whether he would eat or starve tomorrow. At the same time, after the middle of the century the pendulum that had swung so far toward an interpretation of history as the record of powerful men's decisive deeds swung back toward a renewed emphasis on impersonal law. As sensitive spirits like Tennyson recognized, evolution, taken at its face value and swallowed whole, reduced the importance of the individual human being to virtually nil. Viewed against the ruthless workings of natural law, as formulated by Darwin, an individual person seemed almost a cosmic irrelevance.

At this point the paths of history and biography sharply diverged. As the historians followed the philosophers and formulated new theories of laws and institutions, conceived of as evolving in time—Darwinism applied to society—their biographical preoccupation faded. Logically one would assume that, in such an intellectual atmosphere, the writing and reading of biography should have entered on lean times; for what do individuals matter in a universe ruled by impersonal forces of change? The Victorians' answer was that, all the same, they mattered very much. So biography continued to flourish under the Carlylean sanction, heedless of the Darwinian discreditation. Its popularity was, in effect, the Victorians' most defiant reply to the depersonalizing implications of contemporary thought. The examples of great men, past and present, counteracted to a certain extent the leaden feeling of frustration, of impotence, that oppressed many people and found voice in the bitter lines of such poems as "The Scholar-Gypsy":

> Light half-believers of our casual creeds,
>   Who never deeply felt, nor clearly will'd,
> Whose insight never has borne fruit in deeds,
>   Whose vague resolves never have been fulfill'd;
>   For whom each year we see
> Breeds new beginnings, disappointments new;
>   Who hesitate and falter life away,
>   And lose to-morrow the ground won to-day . . .

Stories of heroes gave the Victorians the comforting assurance that the individual can, after all, prove the master of brute circumstance, that he does have freedom to make of his life what he will, despite the alleged tyranny of universal law.

In the perspective of a century, this was probably the supreme value biography possessed in the doubt-ridden Victorian age. "Lives of great men," wrote a poet then as celebrated in England as he was in his own America, "oft remind us, We can make *our* lives sublime." Biography earned its way by being on the side of virtue against vice, by providing examples of honest, wise, generous, prudential, or profitably inventive conduct. Everyone who had anything to say about biography as a form of literature stressed its didactic duty. James Stanfield asserted in

1813 that the biographer was "intrusted with the sword of justice, as well as with the pen of truth. What he describes as a faithful narrator, he may celebrate or stigmatize as an authorized moralist." The critic Francis Jeffrey in 1835 spoke of biography as

> the most instructive and interesting of all writing,—embodying truth and wisdom in the vivid distinctness of a personal present- ment,—enabling us to look on genius in its first elementary stir- rings, and in its weakness as well as its strength,—and teaching us at the same time great moral lessons, both as to the value of labour and industry, and the necessity of *virtues*, as well as intellectual endowments, for the attainment of lasting excellence.

One can read the same refrain in the innumerable articles on the pleasure and profit of good reading that were published in Vic- torian mass-circulation periodicals and the lectures that politi- cians and clergymen delivered at the opening of mechanics' insti- tute reading rooms and public libraries.

In the higher reaches of the genre (the level on which most literary biography existed), inspirational purpose ordinarily was present by implication rather than expressly avowed. Neverthe- less the concept of biography as an instrument of edification was all-pervasive, and in the books designed for the mass audience— the subliterature of biography—it was carefully spelled out. The age aspired to personal enrichment, whether in the soul, the pocketbook, or the intellect, and popular biography provided copious examples of how this could be achieved. Faithfully and inexhaustibly it catered to the era's hunger for "useful knowl- edge."

Earlier in the century especially, the dissenting sects printed a great number of pious biographies in their denominational maga- zines and in books and tracts for children and adults. Many of the subjects of these religious narratives—missionaries, for example, some of whom were martyred in the cannibals' pot—can be lo- cated in no standard biographical dictionary, but to the habitual consumer of such literature their names were as familiar, and revered, as those of Nelson and Wellington. Church reformers, silver-tongued preachers, and godly philanthropists were other favorite subjects; so that, in effect, this sprawling sector of nineteenth-century popular literature represented a sort of low-brow Protestant *Acta Sanctorum.*

Besides the specifically religious biography, there was the prudential. Secular in its choice of topics and its didactic design, it appealed to a portion of the reading audience less preoccupied with religion. The goal here was the attainment not of the Kingdom of Heaven, but of a villa in a fashionable London suburb—a man's deserved reward for industry, financial sagacity (thrift and shrewd investments), and, if many authors' silence on the matter is any guide, not too fastidious a social conscience. These biographies, typical of a somewhat later epoch of the century than the religious ones (which, however, kept their popularity decade after decade), were part of the Victorian period's "literature of success": biography with a frankly avowed utilitarian purpose, devoid of artistic value and, to a modern reader, repellent in its ethical assumptions. Its great master was Samuel Smiles, sometime physician and for a dozen years official of the South Eastern Railway, whose best-selling collections of anecdotes and thumbnail biographies (*Self-Help, Character, Duty, Thrift, Lives of the Engineers, Industrial Biography, Men of Invention and Industry*) focused attention on the class whom Carlyle called the Captains of Industry: the canal builders, inventors, and mill owners who, if their solid utilitarian virtues could only be matched by spiritual illumination, were the great hope of modern England. These books served as a powerful propaganda machine for Victorian middle-class principles; they were as much the mouthpiece of the ethos of the industrial age as the saints' lives were of the medieval church's precepts.

> Biographies of great, but especially of good men [wrote Smiles], are ... most instructive and useful, as helps, guides, and incentives to others. Some of the best are almost equivalent to Gospels— teaching high living, high thinking, and energetic action for their own and the world's good. British biography is studded over, as "with patines of bright gold," with illustrious examples of the power of self-help, of patient purpose, resolute working, and steadfast integrity, issuing in the formation of truly noble and manly character; exhibiting in language not to be misunderstood, what it is in the power of each to accomplish for himself; and illustrating

the efficacy of self-respect and self-reliance in enabling men of even the humblest rank to work out for themselves an honourable competency and a solid reputation.

Here, once more, biography was harnessed to the purposes of an age.[5]

Less specifically connected with the aims of religious parties or social classes was a third kind of popular biography, which was inspirational in a somewhat different way. Relatively indifferent to the materialism that dominated books of the Samuel Smiles tradition, Robert Southey's "Essay on Uneducated Poets" and George Lillie Craik's *The Pursuit of Knowledge under Difficulties* stressed the heroism of overcoming handicaps rather than the actual attainment of fame or fortune. This being the case, it was natural that they paid more attention to such ordinarily nonlucrative occupations as art, belles lettres, and learning.

In the publishers' and journalists' formula for popular biography, instruction had to be coupled with amusement. In hundreds of thousands of English (and, for that matter, American) homes, biography served as a substitute for the forbidden novel. Populous nonconformist sects, as well as the Evangelical party of the Church of England itself, looked upon fiction with the censorious eyes of their Puritan forebears—as a seductive device straight from the devil's workshop. It takes some exercise of the historical imagination to realize that the novel in the age of the irreproachable Jane Austen and Walter Scott was widely regarded as immoral, but it was. Not until after mid-century, when religious scruples concerning imaginative literature were gradually relaxed, and the matchless attraction of Dickens' novels brought more and more people into the fold of fiction readers, did the novel become almost universally respectable. Meanwhile, biography was acceptable to the strictest consciences. Its purpose was the same as the one attributed to novels by the apologists of fiction: "catching morality as it flies." Dispensing with abstract principles and theory, it brought morality down to specific cases,

[5] Blatant overemphasis on a theme often breeds a wry reaction, but presumably it was only a publisher's need for a novelty that led to the striking of a sour note in W. H. Davenport Adams' *Wrecked Lives; or, Men Who Have Failed,* one of whose chapters was devoted to Robert Burns.

((89

making it intelligible to the most literal, unspeculative sort of mind. It told a story, which is exactly what novels did. At its best it had suspense, dramatic scenes and episodes, psychological interest, vivid backgrounds, all the charms of fiction without fiction's damning evil of untruthfulness. Not that, if soberly examined, all popular biographies, whether of explorers or engine makers, proved to be veracious in every detail. But the nineteenth-century common reader was no more disposed to look a gift horse in the mouth than was his Elizabethan ancestor, who devoured the most improbable fictions untroubled by scruple so long as a phrase like "True History" appeared on the title page. Biography gave him what he wanted: escape from the deadening monotony of day-to-day living in a narrow and dreary physical environment, escape from the evident certainty, despite the heartening case histories laid before him, that he would never be rich or famous or even really comfortable, that even the most modest of his dreams would never come true. In reading the lives of great generals and statesmen and bridge builders—and poets—he could find at least temporary, vicarious fulfillment. Put yourself in his place, as the title of a once-famous novel of Charles Reade urged. He did, and in so doing, made his own life more bearable.[6]

[6] Although the great preponderance of nineteenth-century opinion favored biography, now and again a dissentient voice was heard. "Biographies generally," George Eliot told Mrs. Thomas Adolphus Trollope in 1879, "are a disease of English literature"; and William Morris confided to Georgiana Burne-Jones that he found biographies "dull to extremity, I suppose because they are generally a mass of insincerities and platitudes." (*The George Eliot Letters*, ed. Gordon S. Haight [New Haven, 1954–55], VII, 230; J. W. Mackail, *The Life of William Morris* [London, 1911], II, 76.) From time to time throughout the century fear was expressed that candid biography would, for various reasons, prove a pernicious force, adversely affecting men's behavior. "I am apprehensive," wrote the Tonbridge schoolmaster Vicesimus Knox, "that the custom of exposing the nakedness of eminent men to every eye, will have an unfavourable influence on virtue. It may teach men to fear celebrity; and, by extinguishing the desire of fame and posthumous glory, destroy one powerful motive to excellence." ("On the Character of Doctor Johnson and the Abuse of Biography," *Works* [London, 1824], II, 350.) Another anxiety was that the prospect of being the subject of biography, and more immediately the presence of Boswells taking notes, would deter men from the kind of "frank," unaffected behavior upon which the Victorians set much store. "I very much question," Dickens remarked to John Forster in 1848, "whether it would have been a good thing for every great man to have had his Boswell, inasmuch that I think that two Boswells, or three at most, would have made great men extraordinarily false, and would have set them on always playing a part, and would have made distinguished people about them for ever restless

· 2 ·

These, then, were among the motives which led to the writing and reading of biography in general and therefore determined the environment in which literary biography itself took shape. Literary biography served some of the same purposes, most notably the moral, and in addition, as we shall see, had several important functions of its own.

"From the lives of some poets," wrote Walter Scott when he began his autobiography in 1808, "a most important moral lesson may . . . be derived, and few sermons can be read with so much profit as the Memoirs of Burns, of Chatterton, or of Savage." But, he added, his own history could not be turned to such purposes: "it is hardly to be expected that much information can be derived from minutely investigating frailties, follies, or vices, not very different in number or degree from those of other men in my situation." Scott reckoned, however, without John Gibson Lockhart, who some thirty years later was to prove as adept as any other man of his age at extracting homilies from biography. Introducing a letter Scott wrote to the Duke of Buccleuch, for example, Lockhart wrote:

> I am not ashamed to confess, that I embrace with satisfaction the opportunity of thus offering to the readers of the present time a most instructive moral lesson. They will here see what pure and simple virtues and humble piety may be cultivated as the only sources of real comfort in this world and consolation in the pros-

and distrustful. I can imagine a succession of Boswells bringing about a tremendous state of falsehood in society, and playing the very devil with confidence and friendship." (*Letters of Charles Dickens,* ed. Walter Dexter [Bloomsbury, 1938], II, 83.) The same worry, with variations, was expressed by a writer in *Blackwood's Magazine* (LXV [1849], 220–223), Charles Allston Collins in *Macmillan's Magazine* (X [1864], 161), and a reviewer in the *Athenaeum* (No. 2786 [March 19, 1881], p. 389). They agreed that once a living man appeared likely to be written about after his death, his friends could not depend on his being his natural self either in company or in letters that were possibly destined for print; nor could either he or they rely on their letters being held in confidence. The fears persist today: Stephen Spender observed in the *Saturday Review* (January 25, 1964, p. 19) that the new custom of "instantaneous research"—collecting documents and data about living writers—has made it hazardous for any author to write a private letter. Shakespeare, he said, would not have dared write his sonnets under modern conditions.

pect of futurity,—among circles which the giddy and envious mob
are apt to regard as intoxicated with the pomps and vanities of
wealth and rank; which so many of our popular writers represent
systematically as sunk in selfish indulgence—as viewing all below
them with apathy and indifference—and last, not least, as uphold-
ing, when they do uphold, the religious institutions of their country, merely because they have been taught to believe that their
own hereditary privileges and possessions derive security from the
prevalence of Christian maxims and feelings among the mass of
the people.

Frederick Lawrence, in his life of Fielding (1855), observed
that "many instructive lessons may be drawn from his chequered
and wayward life; since, at every stage of it, it will be seen how
surely retributive sorrow and suffering follow in the track of mis-
spent hours, and how little good principles and the best intentions
avail, without the habit and practice of 'prudent, cautious self-
control.'" "Barry Cornwall," writing in 1866, while disclaiming
the necessity or the possibility of finding any "formidable moral"
in Lamb's life, went on to find one or two. Lamb's history, he said,
showed "what one poor man of genius under grievous misfortune,
may do, if he be courageous and faithful to the end"; he "never
preached or prescribed; but let his own actions tell their tale and
produce their natural effects"; he was a man of broad sympathies;
"he was made stronger by trouble; made wiser by grief."

Some literary figures offered irresistible pretexts for moralizing: most conspicuously, perhaps, Burns, Chatterton, and Savage,
whom Scott mentioned, and Cowper, Goldsmith, and Lamb.
From the assortment of eulogy, delicate apology, and significant
omission that make up the obligatory concluding chapters on the
subject's personality and character in early nineteenth-century
literary biography, the student of contemporary moral attitudes
can reap a rich harvest. And Thackeray's famous lectures on *The
English Humourists of the Eighteenth Century* are pervaded by
the spirit exemplified in his observation that "as his [the humor-
ist's] business is to mark other people's lives and peculiarities, we
moralise upon *his* life when he is gone—and yesterday's preacher
becomes the text for to-day's sermon." Thackeray's eighteenth-
century authors are less biographical subjects drawn from history
than figures in a mid-Victorian morality play. Swift is reprehensi-

ble not only because he made savage fun of the idea of eating children, but because in his relations with women he exhibited none of the chivalric grace of Dick Steele, who, with all his weaknesses, was a gentleman. Addison was a noble hero, "kind, just, serene, impartial, . . . admirably wiser, wittier, calmer, and more instructed than almost every man with whom he met. . . . He could scarcely ever have had a degraded thought. . . . When this man looks from the world whose weaknesses he describes so benevolently, up to the Heaven which shines over us all, I can hardly fancy a human face lighted up with a more serene rapture: a human intellect thrilling with a purer love and adoration than Joseph Addison's." Smollett, whatever his shortcomings, was "manly, kindly, honest . . . still brave and full of heart, after a long struggle against a hard fortune." Pope's "frailties and meannesses" were canceled out by the fact that he loved his mother. But Thackeray refused to conceal Fielding's moral weaknesses "in a cloud of periphrasis," and Sterne, to him, was a charlatan who made capital of false sensibility: "he used to blubber perpetually in his study, and finding his tears infectious, and that they brought him a great popularity, he exercised the lucrative gift of weeping."

Yet on the whole, literary biography was less committed to overt moralizing than one would assume from its nineteenth-century context. Homilies were present, but, except in cases like Burns's, whose every biographer seems to have felt duty-bound to spell out the lessons his story implied, they were not oppressively lengthy or numerous. Instead, the special subject matter of literary biography raised at least the possibility of another purpose. Might it not, as the history of individual creators of literature, throw light on literature itself, and so serve the ends of criticism? The answer, as delivered by the biographers themselves and, more explicitly, by their reviewers, was mixed, contradictory, and (with whatever show of assurance the individual dicta were laid down) at base uncertain. For every school of thought on the various aspects of the topic there was a counterbalancing body of opinion. All one can confidently say is that the relevance of biography to criticism—however "criticism" was defined in the period—was never fully clarified.

《 93

As M. H. Abrams has said: "So long as the poet was regarded primarily as an agent who holds a mirror up to nature, or as the maker of a work of art according to universal standards of excellence, there was limited theoretical room for the intrusion of personal traits into his product." But toward the end of the eighteenth century this orthodox neoclassical attitude slowly faded, and a work of art came to be seen less as the product of an impersonal creator, obedient to rules and models, than as that of an individual human being. Literature, ceasing to be simply a library of writings, became the sum of the living images of the authors who had created it—a landscape now populated with figures. For better or worse, biography and criticism became inseparable.

This critical insistence on the work of art as above all a manifestation of human individuality—that quality which nineteenth-century thinkers, reacting against the previous age's preoccupation with the general, the universal, and the uniform, prized so highly—coincided with a dramatic change in the character of literature itself as it was produced in the romantic and Victorian ages. Poetry and essays in particular drew less of their substance from books and more from the writer's experience and sensibility. If critics increasingly addressed themselves to the individual creative intelligence behind the literary work, it was in great part because so much contemporary writing was itself intensely and avowedly personal.

Thus both in criticism and in the actual practice of the nineteenth century, the person behind the poem became the center of interest. The conjunction of criticism and biography that began under such circumstances in the romantic era took three main forms. First, biography could be used to help explain the work of art. Second, evidence found in the work of art could be made to throw light on the artist's life and character. Finally, as an extension of the same process, the work could be interpreted as an embodiment of the essential personality of the artist, the discovery of which was, in this view, the highest purpose of criticism.

If, as was axiomatic in romantic theory, the potter left his thumbprints on the vase, then a knowledge of his life, his personality, and the conditions of the age that affected them could help define the special qualities of the works to which his name was attached. Hitherto the signature had meant little as a guide to deeper comprehension; now it meant a great deal, provided the critic was enabled to visualize the figure who held the pen. The amount of profit to be gained from such application of biographical knowledge to the work of art varied from writer to writer. It was agreed that some literary artists put more of themselves into their works than did others. Much was made of a facile antithesis between the "objective" and the "subjective" poet. The former was basically impersonal, a representationalist who looked at an object rather than through it and who was primarily concerned with the world around him. Although biographical evidence was often relevant in his case, it was far more significant when it dealt with a "subjective" poet, such as one of the English romantics, who filled his poems with his moods, his sensuous impressions, the discoveries his gift of supersensuous vision made possible of the essences behind surfaces. The best-known statement of this view of the critical use of biography, as of the middle of the century, is Browning's, in his prefatory essay to a volume of Shelley's (spurious) letters. Instancing Shakespeare as an exemplar of the objective poet and Shelley of the subjective, Browning asserted that the work of all poets can be understood better through a knowledge of their biography. But while the work of an objective poet ("a fashioner") speaks more or less for itself, describing objects and experiences that are familiar to us, though seen through another consciousness, that of a subjective poet ("a seer"), because it is so intensely personal and aspires toward the absolute, is written in a kind of spiritual shorthand which it is the biographer's privilege to explicate.[7]

Belief in the relevance of biographical information to the critical act was, however, by no means universal. The school of mid-twentieth-century criticism which denies such relevance had a doughty precursor in Wordsworth, who asserted in 1816 that "if [a poet's] works be good, they contain within themselves all that

[7] Browning's essay provides one of the best rationales we have of the mid-nineteenth-century enthusiasm for literary biography. It is probably inappropriate to note that he recanted, almost ferociously, when it was his turn to become the object of biographical curiosity; see below, pages 158–159.

is necessary to their being comprehended and relished." Almost seventy years later a writer in the *Cornhill Magazine* said: "As a general rule we are not required to know anything of the private life of an artist or a poet to appreciate his works fully and get all the good from them we can which they are capable of yielding to anybody." Throughout the century there was, in fact, a persistent current of critical opinion that anticipated the modern doctrine of the autonomy of a work of art. Leigh Hunt, though in a certain mood he could indulge in the worst excesses of sentimental life writing masked as criticism, was nevertheless capable of interpreting and criticizing a poem without reference to its signature. In a later generation Matthew Arnold, the magistrate of Victorian criticism, discharged his office with little use of biography, and in the same Arnoldian epoch Walter Pater and his school, using a very different set of esthetic criteria, were equally chary of muddying the waters of criticism with biographical débris, unless it was their own.

Despite these noteworthy exceptions, however, the steady drift of nineteenth-century critical attention was away from the work and toward the writer. "The widespread use of literature as an index—as the most reliable index—to personality" was, as Professor Abrams puts it with only moderate exaggeration, an "innovation, which swept everything before it in applied criticism for more than a century." The critic tended to become the biographer, or at least to invade the biographer's territory. And so, in effect, the critic and the literary biographer sought the same end by different routes. Both had for their goal the discovery of personality, partly for its own sake, partly for enhanced understanding of the work of art. Whereas the critic achieved his vision of the man-behind-the-work primarily through a reading of the work itself, the biographer employed, for the most part, nonliterary—that is, historical, personal—data. Sometimes, of course, they traded material, the critic seizing upon the external evidence provided by the biographer, the biographer in turn adopting insights afforded by a reading of the literary texts themselves. In brief, the ordinary relationship between author, biographer, and critic was this:

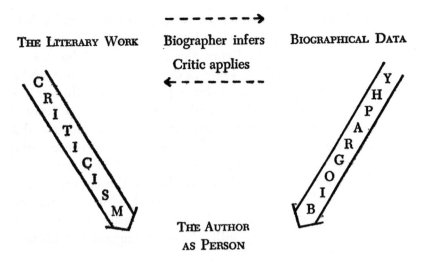

THE LITERARY WORK · Biographer infers · BIOGRAPHICAL DATA

Critic applies

CRITICISM

YHPARGOIB

THE AUTHOR
AS PERSON

One of the century's most characteristic and familiar literary exercises, indulged in impartially by both critics and biographers, was to read a poem, novel, tragedy, or what not, as a quasi-autobiographical document and thus to "illustrate" the author's life narrative. Biographers of Byron and Shelley, for example, regularly quoted, at appropriate junctures, passages from the poets' more or less confessedly autobiographical poems which seemed to spring from, or bear upon, the experiences described. Lamb's biographers constantly used lengthy quotations from the Elia essays as authentic evidence of what Charles Lamb was like; Percy Fitzgerald drew upon *Tristram Shandy* as a presumably reliable reflection of its author's experiences; Edmund Gosse used Donne's poems to fill in the otherwise shadowy outline of the poet's early life.

But the most intensive, protracted, and imaginative ransacking of an author's works for autobiographical clues was the one conducted by the Shakespeare commentators. On the assumption that from Shakespeare's poems and plays could be extracted a well-rounded conception of the author that was as authentic as one derived from personal letters, eyewitness accounts, and other such documents, every line was searched for hidden biography. To many critics, the sonnets were the chief key to the mystery, and an incalculable amount of time and labor was spent on elucidating their enigmatic statements, which, a century and a half after the industry began, still defy interpretation that is generally acceptable.[8] To others the living Shakespeare could be discovered in the plays instead. And he was discovered: as a Tory and a Radical, a Protestant and a Catholic (or else a freethinker), a widely traveled cosmopolitan and a stay-at-home, a heavily learned savant and a fresh-cheeked countryman, a soldier and a seaman, a shrewd businessman and a musician, a sportsman and a naturalist. Whatever one's preference, it could be documented from Shakespeare's works. However sharply the commentators' versions of Shakespeare the man conflicted with one another, taken altogether they represent "the largest mass of conjectural biography under which any author has ever staggered on his way to immortality."

The quest of the historical Shakespeare was both the most extravagant manifestation and the most fitting symbol of the century's urge to translate literature into a series of biographical documents. As the long adventure's seriocomic history illustrates, from regarding a literary work as a convenient means of annotating its author's biography the Victorians had to move only a step farther along the same premise to the conclusion that the whole work of art—not its scattered statements but its totality of form and language—contained what, at the time, was regularly called the "soul" of the poet. A poet's production, according to Browning, was "less a work than an effluence. That effluence cannot be easily considered in abstraction from his personality,—being indeed the very radiance and aroma of his personality, projected from it but not separated. Therefore, in our approach to the poetry, we necessarily approach the personality of the poet; in apprehending it we apprehend him, and certainly we cannot love it without loving him. Both for love's and for understanding's sake we desire to know him, and, as readers of his poetry, must be readers of his biography also."

[8] This poetic dialogue admirably summed up the century's debate on the point: WORDSWORTH (sonnet on the sonnet, 1827): "With this key Shakespeare unlocked his heart."
BROWNING ("House," 1876): "Did Shakespeare? If so, the less Shakespeare he!"

This was the ultimate extension (or, as some would say, *reductio ad absurdum*) of the biographical-critical relationship. The esthetic interest became indistinguishable from the biographical, or, put another way, the literary work ceased to be an artistic object and was transformed into the person of its creator. The final goal of criticism was not a reading of the poem as a poem but what, in the ultraromantic view, was infinitely more desirable, a vision of the precious human spirit behind it. This was what Carlyle meant when he dwelt, with variations, on the theme that "no Poem is equal to its Poet" and "the life of every man . . . is a Poem," and Emerson when he echoed, "the true poem is the poet's mind." The poem itself was simply a nimbus of words behind which the devout reader could discover a man.

This confidence, which was widely shared, rested on the assumption that the man and the artist were the same person. But there were those who were convinced that authors had double personalities and that it was therefore perilous to infer the nature of the man from the self-created image of the artist. The scholarly Edmond Malone, at the very beginning of the century, had warned of the caution with which evidence found in a literary work had to be applied to the writer: "To deduce an author's character from sentiments expressed in his writings, when they are at variance with the tenour and actions of his life . . . can afford no gratification to lovers of truth. His works, however, may be safely appealed to, when they strongly enforce the practice of those virtues for which the writer, through life, was eminently distinguished." A writer in the *Edinburgh Review* in 1820—it may have been Hazlitt—pointed out that writers formed an exception to the general biographical rule: "In passing from the public to the private life of kings, of statesmen and warriors, we have, for the most part, the same qualities and personal character brought into action, and displayed on a larger or a smaller scale, —and can, at all events, make a pretty tolerable guess from one to the other. But we have no means to discover whether the moral Addison was the same scrupulous character in his writings and in his daily habits, but in the anecdotes recorded of him." Often, in fact, the biographical data directly contradicted inferences drawn from a man's writing. It was tempting, for example, to read back and forth between Byron's poetry and Byron's biography. But Thomas Moore cautioned against any facile identification of the two. "In one so imaginative as Lord Byron," he wrote, "who, while he infused so much of his life into his poetry, mingled also not a little of poetry with his life, it is difficult, in unravelling the texture of his feelings, to distinguish at all times between the fanciful and the real." A wholesome admonition to nineteenth-century readers intent on discovering the real man in his poetry might have been found in the story told of Hippolyte Taine, the French critic, who in discussing Tennyson with the poet's friend Sir Francis Palgrave cried: "Was he not in early youth rich, luxurious, fond of pleasure, self-indulgent? I see it in his early poems —his riot, his adoration of physical beauty, his delight in jewels, in the abandonment of all to pleasure, in wine and—" "Stop, stop!" Palgrave said. "As a young man Tennyson was poor. His habits were as they still are, simple and reserved. He has never known luxury in your sense; and if his early poems are luxurious in tone, if they are full of beautiful women and pearls and gold, it is because he is a poet and gifted with a poet's imagination." In the face of this assurance, Taine made a choice thoroughly typical of his time: clinging to his intuitive preference, in his book he portrayed Tennyson as "a young voluptuary, a rich profligate." However erroneous it may have been, Taine's eagerness to identify the artistic personality and the man-as-he-lived exemplified a habit which was then well over a century old[9] and still flourishes in the present age.

Taken by itself, Carlyle's declaration that "it is Biography that first gives us both Poet and Poem, by the significance of the one elucidating and completing that of the other," suggests a conception of the purpose of literary biography that could hardly be improved upon today. The biographer would be the mediator, the

---

[9] As Dr. Johnson proves in his *Lives of the Poets* ("Thomson"): "The biographer of Thomson has remarked that an author's life is best read in his works: his observation was not well-timed. Savage, who lived much with Thomson, once told me how he heard a lady remarking that she could gather from his works three parts of his character: that he was a 'great lover, a great swimmer, and rigorously abstinent'; but, said Savage, he knows not any love but that of the sex; he was perhaps never in cold water in his life; and he indulges himself in all the luxury that comes within his reach."

interpreter, between the creation and its maker; he would constantly work back and forth between the two, so that our understanding of both poem and poet would benefit. But Carlyle's next sentence immediately reveals that he had no such reciprocal illumination in mind:

> That ideal outline of himself, which a man unconsciously shadows forth in his writings, and which, rightly deciphered, will be truer than any other representation of him, it is the task of the Biographer to fill-up into an actual coherent figure, and bring home to our experience, or at least our clear undoubting admiration, thereby to instruct and edify us in many ways. Conducted on such principles, the Biography of great men, especially of great Poets, that is, of men in the highest degree noble-minded and wise, might become one of the most dignified and valuable species of composition.

In Carlyle's view, therefore, it was solely the poet, not the poem as well, which it was the function of biography to "elucidate."[1]

Carlyle at least conceded the usefulness of biography in clarifying and perhaps adding to the image of the writer which was found initially, and principally, in his work. Others, however, refused to go even so far, holding (as a corollary to the opinion that biography was irrelevant to criticism) that the whole life and character of the poet were to be read in his poems. Protesting against Currie's scandalous life of Burns, Wordsworth asserted that to revive the Burns of historical record was an act of impertinence; the only Burns worth thinking about was the one embodied in the poems. Wordsworth's nephew Christopher was oppressively faithful to his uncle's conviction when he announced, in introducing his *Memoirs of William Wordsworth,* that "His Works . . . are his Life. And it would be a superfluous and presumptuous enterprise to encroach upon this their province, and to invade the biographical eminence on which his Poems stand. Let them retain their supremacy in this respect; and let no other Life of Wordsworth be composed beside what has thus been written

---

[1] His indifference or outright hostility toward everything that smacked of the merely esthetic is well known. Dante Gabriel Rossetti told of Carlyle's walking with William Allingham, the poet, and announcing that he planned to write a life of Michelangelo. "But, mind ye," he quickly added, "I'll no' say much about his *art.*" (Hall Caine, *My Story* [London, 1908], p. 179.)

with his own hand." As anyone can infer from the two lamentable volumes Christopher Wordsworth produced on this premise, to maintain that a poet's works *are* his life, no more and no less, would mean the death of literary biography. Life writing would become simply the construction of a montage of all the avowedly or implicitly autobiographical passages in the author's work, together with what could be deduced from his style, his choice of subject, and other kinds of internal evidence.

This extreme view was, fortunately, not widely held, though it provided a convenient and lofty rationale for the biographical reticence of families who, like the Wordsworths, were dedicated to guarding their poet's posthumous privacy. Literary biography flourished in the face of this and similar obstacles, all of which, however, tended to minimize the critical usefulness of biographical information. When biographers of the period did venture upon pages of criticism and interpretation, they seldom attempted to establish a vital link between the writer's personality or experience and his work. When he paused to consider his subject's writing, the biographer ordinarily removed his historian's hat before donning the critic's cap; he did not lay the one atop the other. Indeed, whether or not it was rooted in biographical facts, criticism sometimes was held to be scarcely within the biographer's province. Jeffrey, writing in the *Edinburgh Review* in 1835, asserted that "last and lowest" among the materials of which literary biography consists are "the biographer's own (generally most partial) description and estimate of his author's merits, or . . . elucidations and critical summaries of his most remarkable productions."

Hence when biographical information was occasionally used to illuminate literary works as objects of art, the spotlight was in the hands of the critic rather than of the biographer. The biographer supplied the facts, but it was the critic, if anyone, who applied them. But if the nineteenth century never managed to convince itself that biography had a direct and constant bearing on critical interpretation, literary biography was valued for other reasons. Its figures were more articulate observers of life than were those of other classes who provided subjects for biography. Apart from whatever philosophical guidance was to be found in their formal works, their private diaries and letters often had great interest in their record of the impact that nature and the human scene had upon men who were both sensitive and gifted in the use of language. Biographies that printed these private documents added to the race's store of wisdom.[2]

· 3 ·

Even more important, however, notably in the first third of the century, was the contribution literary biography made to man's understanding of himself: the light it threw on the development and workings of the mind in general and of the artistic mind in particular. One could not, as a rule, hope to learn much of importance concerning the subtler operations of the intellect and the feelings from the memoirs of generals, politicians, explorers, or other men of action. But literary men, by their very nature, thought and felt; in recent generations they watched themselves thinking and feeling; and they set down on paper what they saw, thus piling up case histories for later students of the mind.

Now, for the first time, there was an ample supply of documents relating to the inner lives of men of genius. The introspective and subsequently confessional urge typified by Rousseau's and Goethe's turning their souls inside out became epidemic. The private letters and journals of literary people were filled less with epigrams, gossip of the political and fashionable worlds, or general philosophical and social comment than with subject matter that persistently clustered about the capital letter *I*. Variable though the moods were, passionate, facetious, cynical, sentimental, stoic, self-pitying, the countless pages written, for private information alone, by Cowper, Burns, Byron, Shelley, Lamb,

[2] One further value of literary biography—and in a time of a rapidly expanding audience an important one—lay in its ability to enlist the interest of the ordinary reader by its enlivening and sugar-coating of criticism. "The truth is," observed John Dennis in 1882, "that while the mere criticism of books often proves a barren task, necessary perhaps but seldom altogether acceptable, every booklover likes to hear of the men whose works have made his joyous moments more joyful, and the hours of solitude and sadness more serene." ("Literary Criticism and Biography," *Fraser's Magazine*, new ser., XXVI [1882], 520.)

Keats, Wordsworth, and other men of the age marked a genuine revolution in human habit. To the extent that they were published (as many of Cowper's, Burns's, Byron's, Keats's and Lamb's were before mid-century; the rest followed at various intervals) they had an inexhaustible allure to readers who shared the current enthusiasm for psychological speculation.

Nor were correspondences and diaries the only self-revelatory documents that came to swell the biographer's fund of intimate information and enhance the interest literary biography had for the reader. Men of letters, recognizing both the scientific value and the popular interest that attached to their experience, began to write more or less formal autobiographies. The most monumental evidence of a contemporary poet's retrospective absorption in his psychological development is Wordsworth's unfinished *Prelude*, which was explicitly conceived and executed as an account of the "Growth of a Poet's Mind." Sir Walter Scott's fragmentary narrative of his early years, which Lockhart printed in his first volume, John Stuart Mill's *Autobiography*, Carlyle's *Reminiscences*, and numerous other memoirs of literary men (including, presumably, Byron's, which perished in his publisher's fireplace) testify to this growing interest in the development of the artistic or philosophical character viewed both from without and within. Before 1800, only nine English poets wrote autobiographies that survive; between 1800 and 1900 at least forty-two wrote such accounts. In fact, the total of autobiographies written by British literary men of all sorts before 1800 is only about twenty-three, whereas during the next hundred years at least 175 were produced.

For many years one of the principal topics of English critical discussion had been the psychology of artistic experience. How does an artist differ from other men? What conditions of heredity and environment affect the development of artistic genius? What, psychologically speaking, is the nature of the imagination: how is it nurtured, how does it make its presence felt? These and kindred topics were endlessly debated by the critics and estheticians. At the same time that poets like Keats began to keep charts of their emotional pulse rates, the day-to-day atmosphere of their spirits as they composed or reflected, biographers assembled similar data on other writers wherever they could find it. It is significant that one of the earliest definitions of the function of the literary biographer—James Stanfield's, in 1813—ran: ". . . the principal duty of the [biographical] artist is—to gain, and give, if possible, a comprehensive view of the circumstances and associations that first brought inclination to the [literary man's] pursuit; the materials of operation, the studies, the exemplars, the connection of design, the modes of proceeding, and the adopted means of advancement and completion."

To describe and analyze the influences that set a youth's feet on the road to poethood was one of the most rewarding tasks the literary biographer faced. He seized upon all the information he could find about his subject's early reading, the circumstances of his formal education, and (a topic of much importance in this age of nature worship) the presumable influence that natural scenery had upon his sensibilities. Byron's biographers, beginning with Thomas Moore, offered long lists of the books the poet had read as a child and adolescent, and so did Burns's and Shelley's. Future poets' experiences at school—Shelley's at Sion House and Eton, Byron's at Aberdeen and Harrow—were dwelt on in detail, mainly to prove that their unhappiness as sensitive youths ground between the upper and nether millstones of birch-swinging masters and cruel schoolmates was the source of their later rebelliousness against all forms of authority. As for the influence of landscape on exquisitely receptive sensibilities, Wordsworth's *Prelude,* which appeared after his death in 1850, reflected an interest that had been manifested in the biographies so far published of all poets of his generation. The early biographies of Burns, and above all those of Byron, are documents by which we can reconstruct the period's commitment to associationist psychology, in particular the idea that the poetic temperament is profoundly affected by sensuous impressions of natural beauty as they interact with the observer's feelings.

To modern readers, these confident attempts to trace the genesis and development of the poetic genius are for the most part inconclusive. Having recited in profusion the titles of the books Burns and Shelley and Byron read, biographers seldom paused to consider what specific effects the individual books had upon the youths' temperament, opinions, or artistic habits. The careful kind of analysis of early reading experiences which in more recent times has assisted the solution of such biographical and critical problems had to await the coming of another epoch of psychological inquiry. We now find only historical interest in the inferences the early biographers drew from their data. But we are grateful that the period's conviction, following the precepts of Locke, Rousseau, and Hartley, that the first two decades of life are the crucial ones, led to the gathering and preservation of so much valuable raw material to which modern analytic techniques can be applied.

Another lively intellectual topic in the decades immediately after Boswell was the peculiarities of different kinds of temperament. The so-called "literary character" won its full share of attention. In 1795 Isaac Disraeli published *An Essay on the Manners and Genius of the Literary Character,* subsequently enlarged several times and published under its more familiar title, *The Literary Character; or, the History of Men of Genius, Drawn from Their Own Feelings and Confessions.* In this lengthy hodge-podge drawn from his incredible store of erudition, Disraeli sought to anatomize the literary temperament: its "irritability," its enthusiasm, vanity, jealousy, preference for solitude and meditation, tendency toward improvidence and domestic unrest, and a host of kindred traits that were thought to be characteristic of *homo scribens.* Disraeli's book, supplemented by his companion treasuries, *Calamities of Authors* and *Quarrels of Authors,* typified the age's inclination, seen also in the critical remarks of such men as Wordsworth, Coleridge, and Mill, to view writers as a distinct breed. Numerous literary biographies reflected this fashion, treating their respective subjects as exemplifying the preformulated traits of the literary character. They subscribed to the commonplaces that, as Burns's biographer, Dr. Currie, put it, "philosophic melancholy . . . generally forms the poetical temperament" and that the normal condition of a poet's mind is excitement. Moore, in his life of Sheridan, likened poetic genius to "those seas, that become more luminous the more they are agitated." In domestic surroundings inspired authors usually were unhappy, though whether they were more sinned against than sinning was a matter of some uncertainty. Moore, writing of Byron, spent several pages elaborating on "the truth . . . that rarely, if ever, have men of the higher order of genius shown themselves fitted for the calm affections and comforts that form the cement of domestic life." But it was usually admitted that a codicil to Eve's curse was the necessity for woman to suffer in the interests of literature. Scott showed little compassion for Mrs. Dryden, a woman in any case of "a violent temper and weak intellects," who failed to endure "the apparently causeless fluctuation of spirits incident to one doomed to labour incessantly in the feverish exercise of the imagination. Unintentional neglect, and the inevitable relaxation, or rather sinking of spirit, which follows violent mental exertion, are easily misconstrued into capricious rudeness, or intentional offence."

Whatever the psychological interest of such passages, their bearing on criticism is tangential at best. But one other result of the age's absorption in the habits of the mind occasionally gave literary biography the closest potential relevance to critical inquiry it was to achieve until the coming of modern psychological methods. This was the curiosity, generated by the shift of critical emphasis from art as a product of inspiration to art as a product of conscious craft, about the way individual literary works came into being: their author's habits of composition and revision, the evidence offered by successive drafts and proof sheets of a poem's progress from first conception to publication. Scott told of Goldsmith's method of compiling his *Letters on the History of England* and his manner of writing poetry. Moore paid occasional attention to Byron's revisions of his poems, and quoted many passages from his letters describing the progress of his current poems. Lockhart likewise traced the growth of Scott's successive novels and gave samples of his proof corrections. And John Forster, many years later, provided what was probably the most intimate and detailed view yet given of a writer at work when he quoted numerous passages from Dickens' letters expressing his alternate frustrations, perplexities, and exultations as chapter after chapter of a novel flowed from his pen.[3]

To reconstruct in this fashion the making of a work of art was looked upon simply as an "interesting" exercise, a "satisfaction of curiosity." That such evidence might have deep critical significance, as helping to define the very quality of the work and the special nature of its creator's literary gift, seldom occurred to the biographers or critics of the time. The rewards of modern studies such as John Livingston Lowes's *The Road to Xanadu* or M. R. Ridley's *Keats's Craftsmanship* were not conceived of. Indeed, in some quarters there was, instead of "curiosity," forthright opposition to a biographer's exhibiting the chips and shavings from a writer's workshop. When Thomas Moore did so in his life of Sheridan, a reviewer wrote testily: "We . . . doubt the utility of filling many sheets with mere school-boy sketches of scenes which never were followed up, of thoughts which were never matured, of poetic exercises which not one in five hundred will think of examining, and which, indeed, will not repay the trouble of perusal . . . these 'curiosities' are really of no sort of value. They do not afford any tangible traces of the progress of Sheridan's mind."[4] Such a reviewer was hardly prepared to approve even of Moore's careful re-creation, from the mass of drafts and odd papers Sheridan left, of the way he wrote *The School for Scandal*—a critical exercise far in advance of its time, analyzing as it did the successive revisions for style, characterization, and dramatic effect and reconstructing Sheridan's probable criticism of his own work.

The choice of word that Moore's reviewer made is significant: "Mind" not "art." The simple fact is that though literary

---

[3] Meanwhile, recognizing the value that attached to such information, some writers took pains to leave records of the circumstances under which their various poems were composed. Late in life Wordsworth dictated such annotations to an amanuensis (the so-called "Fenwick notes"), and so, in turn, did Tennyson.

[4] Similarly, one of the grievances George Eliot had against the literary biography of her time was that "a great poet's trash, written when he was a schoolboy, trash which, if he had remembered it, he would have burnt, is brought into quite mortifying publicity at the end of half a century." Which poet she is referring to is not clear, but the complaint occurs in the course of a letter in which she attacks Forster for printing "poor Dickens's small scraps of memoranda certainly meant for no eyes but his own." (*The George Eliot Letters,* VI, 67–68.)

biographies in the nineteenth century contained a great deal of information we prize today for the aid it gives us in our critical studies, it was not used for that purpose by the biographers themselves. Instead, literary biography, like much of the criticism of the time, was concerned with human—personal—values, not esthetic ones. If it failed to realize the value its documentary material had for critical explication and assessment, that was because the bent of contemporary criticism itself, preoccupied with the psychology of artistic production rather than with the anatomy of the finished product, did not encourage it to do so.

In any event, this manysided curiosity about the processes of the mind that determined the interests and emphases of early nineteenth-century literary biography was not universally shared, nor did it endure. Carlyle came to maintain that all mental activity that really mattered was both unconscious and undescribable. Poetry simply was extruded, mysteriously and miraculously, from a great soul that differed from other great souls (warriors, religious leaders, statesmen) only in the particular medium it selected to express its wisdom. Any attempt to explain the nature of the poetic temperament or the inner events that led to a work of literature was futile—and, because it presumed to apply the dissecting scalpel of intellect to so delicate an organism as art, undesirable.[5] In reaching this position of nescience, extreme romanticism, as personified by Carlyle, was biting the hand that had fed it. Its absorption in the phenomena of the mind had been nourished initially by the confident empiricism of the psychologists; now, soaring in the transcendental empyrean, it rejected their formulations as pedantic pipe dreams. Even men whose

---

[5] Compare a writer in the *Quarterly Review* many years later (1872): "Now, in the case of the poet or the painter, the first, the natural (though the mistaken) impression is that, in order to 'live with him,' we must penetrate into the secret of his soul, unlock the innermost enchanted chamber of his genius, and know, in short, what he never knew himself,—why he thought of that phrase, or laid on that colour. This desire, of course, cannot be gratified by any biographer. The artist, probably, could not have satisfied it for his nearest friends,—not even for himself. Nor, could the secret of genius be laid bare, would this be a desirable revelation. The poet, as such, expresses himself in the finished work: he has said in it all that he could say, or desired to say, in relation to poetry. It would destroy the charm, could he analyse the fine processes of creation; it would seem to him perfectly ludicrous that any one should trouble himself about the sketch and the scaffolding." (CXXXII, 394.)

temperaments were as far removed from Carlyle's as it is convenient to imagine shared the same skepticism. Speaking of the countless anecdotes of childhood that biographers accumulated to illustrate how infallibly the child was father to the man, Sir James Prior, who though a dry-as-dust researcher was no fool, commented: "Such circumstances are not otherwise worthy of notice, than merely for the gratification of curiosity; they indicate nothing. He is a bold speculator who draws decided inferences of what the man is to be, from the casual peculiarities of the mere child."

This attitude was symptomatic of the time. By the 1840's, zeal for inferring the laws of artistic or any other kind of human activity from the biographical records had faded. The brilliant speculations of the Coleridges and the Hazlitts on the psychology of creativity had no counterpart in the next generation, so that literary biography was left without the background of vigorous contemporary thought which might have stimulated some biographers, at least, to probe more intently into the psychological and critical implications of their subject. Though biographers were no less assiduous in collecting information, they tended more and more to spread it on the table noncommittally, for whatever it was worth. For the rest of the century, down to the 1920's in fact, when Freudianism rushed into the vacuum, the questions embedded in literary biography were referable to no system of psychological theory, simply because none had been developed to which Englishmen could subscribe with the confidence they had once placed in associationism.

When interest in "the history of the mind" as a branch of empirical inquiry waned, the prosperity of literary biography was unaffected: it no longer needed the justification supplied by an extrinsic intellectual concern. Instead, the lives of men of letters came to attract more and more readers solely because they *were* lives of men of letters. Partly because the drama of the mind, as exemplified in authors' lives, had proved as deeply absorbing as the drama of outward incident, and partly because literary biography turned out to contain plenty of external excitement after all, the old cry that it was "devoid of incident" gradually ceased to be heard. Even had this ancient error not been exposed, however, there is every reason to assume that biographies of authors would have been written and read in ever-growing numbers. After denying that biography could throw light on the mysterious genesis of a work of art, the *Quarterly Review* writer quoted above (page 109, note 5) had nevertheless to concede that "no craving could be more inevitable, or connected with higher impulses of the soul, than that which leads us to ask what manner of man he was, who has moved us to our best tears and our most poignant admiration, and how far his own nature was the true reflex or mould of his creations." However sentimental, however irrelevant to the central issues of art was the biographical bias of Victorian criticism, it flourished mightily, sustained and strengthened by a dramatic new social and cultural phenomenon, the spread of public interest in literary figures. Emerging from the study, the garret, or a lonely vigil among the lakes and hills, the poet took his place in the newspaper headlines, if not on a pedestal. The steady climb of the man of letters to a prominent and enduring place in the popular consciousness assured an eager audience for everything that was written about him—as we shall now see.

CHAPTER IV

Poet and Public

✳

HERE is an axiom—amply illustrated in the history of the world's religions: one need only remember Chaucer's Pardoner—that veneration carries within itself the seeds of ultimate vulgarization. Not only does the one breed the other; both can exist simultaneously, creating an almost irresolvable tension of attitudes. This simple fact, exemplified for our purposes by the manner in which the nineteenth-century English man of letters came into the public eye, provides the key to the nature of the age's literary biography.

Public interest converged on men of letters simultaneously from two very different angles. On the one hand, a celebrated writer was looked upon as belonging to a new race of heroes—with the result that biographies were expected to be reverential in tone and discreet in the selection of detail. On the other, he was an object of curiosity—with the result that many readers, their tastes conditioned by the interests of the new popular journalism, demanded candid, confidential portraiture, intimate revelations of private habits and domestic arrangements. The cultural milieu which determined the extent and quality of an author's fame in the nineteenth century thus was also part of the matrix of literary biography; and in it may be read the conflicting desires and expectations with which readers opened a newly published life of an author and the forces that decided how many should be satisfied and how many left unfulfilled.

Belief in the superhumanity of poets—men among men, yet somehow not of them—and of their divinely appointed role in lighting the race to a paradisiacal tomorrow was a principal article of the romantic creed, announced by Wordsworth in the preface to the 1802 edition of *Lyrical Ballads*. The poet, averred Wordsworth, was "a man speaking to men: a man, it is true, endued with more lively sensibility, more enthusiasm and tenderness, who has a greater knowledge of human nature, and a more comprehensive soul, than are supposed to be common among mankind. . . . In spite of difference of soil and climate, of language and manners, of laws and customs, in spite of things silently gone out of mind and things violently destroyed, the Poet binds together by passion and knowledge the vast empire of human society. . . ."

Seventeen years later Shelley wrote his *Defence of Poetry*. Of all romantic panegyrics of the poet, that in the essay's last lines is the best known. Poets, Shelley said, not only are "the author[s] to others of the highest wisdom, pleasure, virtue and glory" but are themselves "the happiest, the best, the wisest, and the most illustrious of men . . . men of the most spotless virtue, of the most consummate prudence . . . the hierophants of an unapprehended inspiration; the mirrors of the gigantic shadows which futurity casts upon the present; the words which express what they understand not; the trumpets which sing to battle, and feel not what they inspire; the influence which is moved not, but moves. Poets are the unacknowledged legislators of the world."

The *Defence of Poetry* was not published, however, until 1840. In that same year the notion of the poet as hero received its greatest single impetus when Carlyle devoted two of his six lectures on "Heroes and Hero-Worship" to exalting the literary genius as a seer and a minister to the profoundest needs of the human spirit. "Of all Priesthoods, Aristocracies, Governing Classes at present extant in the world," he declared, "there is no class comparable for importance to that Priesthood of the Writers of Books." The literary man "is the light of the world; the world's Priest:—guiding it, like a sacred Pillar of Fire, in its dark pilgrimage through the waste of Time." Carlyle implied that a greater attention to literary biography is indispensable if modern society is correctly to understand and cherish its own major race of prophets:

((113

The Writer of a Book, is not he a Preacher preaching not to this parish or that, on this day or that, but to all men in all times and places? Surely it is of the last importance that *he* do his work right, whoever do it wrong;—that the *eye* report not falsely, for then all other members are astray! Well; how he may do his work, whether he do it right or wrong, or do it at all, is a point which no man in the world has taken the pains to think of. . . . Whence he came, whither he is bound, by what ways he arrived, by what he might be furthered on his course, no one asks. He is an accident in society. He wanders like a wild Ishmaelite, in a world of which he is as the spiritual light, either the guidance or the misguidance!

The age in which Wordsworth, Shelley, and Carlyle exalted the poet into a demigod and *vates* was committed to a dual quest. It sought a new race of divinities, suited to the needs of an increasingly secular society: figures whose moral characters and the uses to which they put their genius could provide constant guidance to ordinary mortals. And it sought, equally, the inspiration of words. Now that Scripture was widely discredited as an instrument of divine revelation, a substitute had to be found. Some professed to discover comfort in rationalism, and in rationalism's handmaid, natural science; but to men like Wordsworth, Shelley, and Carlyle these were bleak refuges indeed. Some found the true answer in art; above all, the art of literature. In literature was preserved the wisdom of all the ages, the surest key both to reality and to that ultimate ideal essence which lay beyond. In literature a society depressed and bewildered by the progress of materialism and doubt found a new gospel, which could soothe anxiety and provide an inspiring program for social amelioration. "Poetry," said Wordsworth, "is the first and last of all knowledge —it is as immortal as the heart of man." "Poetry," elaborated Shelley, "is indeed something divine. It is at once the centre and circumference of knowledge. . . . What were virtue, love, patriotism, friendship—what were the scenery of this beautiful universe which we inhabit; what were our consolations on this side of the grave—and what were our aspirations beyond it, if poetry did not ascend to bring light and fire from those eternal regions where the owl-winged faculty of calculation dare not ever soar?"

More practically, Carlyle saw literature as the most powerful social force in modern civilization:

He that can write a true Book, to persuade England, is not he the Bishop and Archbishop, the Primate of England and of All England? I many a time say, the writers of Newspapers, Pamphlets, Poems, Books, these *are* the real working effective Church of a modern country. . . . Literature is our Parliament too. Printing, which comes necessarily out of Writing, I say often, is equivalent to Democracy: invent Writing, Democracy is inevitable. . . . On all sides, are we not driven to the conclusion that, of the things which man can do or make here below, by far the most momentous, wonderful and worthy are the things we call Books!

The institution of literature took on a quasi-religious importance it had never had before. Among all the heroes before whom the nineteenth-century Englishman knelt, men of letters as a group were most prominent; of the sixteen longest articles in the *Dictionary of National Biography,* no fewer than six were devoted to writers. The idealized figure of the literary man represented an intellectual and imaginative fulfillment to which the average man could but aspire; and he was the message-giver, the author of the literature that served the nineteenth century as both pulpit and Parliament.

These grandiloquent affirmations of the " 'superior reality' of art, as the seat of imaginative truth" and of "the idea of the independent creative writer, the autonomous genius" came, as Raymond Williams notes, just at the moment when the new industrial society was drastically devaluating both art and the artist. Mammon was elbowing Apollo aside, and to millions of ears there was sweeter music in the steam engine's roar and the cash drawer's clink than ever fell from the poet's lyre. Paradoxically, the values represented by imaginative literature and its makers were being depreciated at the very time the other lobe of contemporary consciousness asserted their supreme importance. It was a remarkable case of cultural schizophrenia, and one might suggest, without unduly straining the psychiatric analogy, that the superstitious reverence in which literature and the literary man were then held was a form of compensation, a way of quieting the guilt stirred by the age's indulgence in the worst excesses of materialism and predatory capitalism and its exploitation of human misery.

At the shrine of Shakespeare, the contemporary penchant for hero worship reached its highest pitch, revealing itself in all its earnestness, pathos, and absurdity. Shortly before his death, James Boswell knelt before the "miraculously discovered" manuscripts of two Shakespearean plays (actually forged by William Ireland) and kissed them; fifty years later his fellow Scotsman Carlyle canonized Shakespeare as "a Saint of Poetry . . . the greatest intellect who, in our recorded world, has left record of himself in the way of Literature . . . a Prophet, in his way; of a strain analogous to the Prophetic, though he took it up in another strain . . . a blessed heaven-sent Bringer of Light." A sentimental cult, promoted by (among others) Leigh Hunt and his disciples, deified Shakespeare, adopting all the paraphernalia of religion—icons, relics, and so on—to signify his divinity. At Stratford-on-Avon, the process of reducing the poet-god to a commercial commodity quickened. Shakespeare's dilapidated, unauthentic birthplace was operated by a rapacious widow whose services to the credulous and devout, especially by way of supplying spurious relics of the poet, knew no bounds. By the 1820's, a half-century after Garrick's grand jubilee, the "bardolators' bazaar" in Warwickshire had won nationwide notoriety.

Stratford was the first of what became in time a chain of literary holy places, objects of the pilgrimages that were a favorite and characteristic nineteenth-century recreation, combining as they did the pleasures of holiday-making with the more sober aim of self-improvement through (presumably) a closer understanding of great authors and their works.[1] From Scott's time onward, booklovers found inspiration in the Trossachs and especially at Loch Katrine, where they used *The Lady of the Lake* as a poetical guidebook; according to Lockhart, Scottish revenue from the duty on post horses rose sharply as a result. Other locales associated with Scott were transformed from sleepy villages to prosperous tourist centers. Melrose owed several new inns to the popularity of *The Lay of the Last Minstrel,* and following Scott's

[1] The positivists for many years made such pilgrimages a regular feature of their ritual: "truly a religious act," as Frederic Harrison said, "and . . . also an educational instrument." They journeyed to the homes or tombs of such literary celebrities as Milton, Bacon, Bunyan, Defoe, Goldsmith, and Shakespeare. At Milton's Horton, they listened to a reading of parts of *Comus;* at Stratford, they enjoyed a lecture and a recital of some of Shakespeare's songs. (Harrison, "Modern Pilgrimages," *Realities and Ideals* [New York, 1908], pp. 175–179.)

death Abbotsford itself became one of Britain's most popular shrines.

The Lake District too attracted more tourists every summer. Their chief objective, no doubt, was the scenery, for romantic poetry and painting had made the English landscape-conscious as never before. But these "loungers at the lakes," as De Quincey called them, were almost as avid for glimpses of the men, pre-eminently Wordsworth, who had made the region famous in literature. It was the same story at Farringford, on the Isle of Wight, after the popularity of *In Memoriam* and *The Idylls of the King* had won Wordsworth's successor in the laureateship a personal fame that exceeded Wordsworth's own. By the sixties the excursionists were arriving in droves, hoping to behold Tennyson in the very act of composing an immortal lyric. Within a few years the vicinity of Farringford became so overrun with literary-minded trippers as to become intolerable, and Tennyson, sacrificing his pleasant proximity to the Queen's summer residence, built a house in an isolated spot on the Surrey downs.

Though cheapened transportation enabled thousands of British families to visit the locales associated with literature, and even, if they were lucky, to glimpse the celebrities themselves, other families had to be content with vicarious excursions, in fireside armchairs. "Tours," "itineraries," and "travels" of all sorts had been a bookshop staple since the seventeenth century, but not until the nineteenth did writers address themselves to the literary topography of Britain, in books about sites made famous by classics or associated with literary biography: *Rambles Through the Land of Burns, The Country of Sir Walter Scott, The Carlyle Country, The Homes of Tennyson, In Kent with Dickens, The Home and Early Haunts of Robert Louis Stevenson.* Such books touched the Victorian purchaser at several vulnerable points—his love for tasteful steel engravings (or, later, reproductions of photographs), his veneration of the native heath and family hearth, his insular pride, and, above all, his growing interest in the personal lives of authors.

The most famous of these books—virtually their prototype—was the 1,100-page *Homes and Haunts of the Most Eminent Brit-*

ish Poets (1847), by William Howitt, Quaker, political radical, spiritualist, and one of the most prolific of early Victorian writers. His sentimental journeying took him from well-kept country houses to tenements like Burns's home at Dumfries, in the stenchy midst of a tanyard. Sometimes the sought-for edifice turned out to have been reduced to a mere pile of stones, the weed-grown outlines of a foundation; almost as often (Howitt offered no explanation for the fact) poets' domiciles had been converted into pothouses, or, as he called them, Tom-and-Jerry shops. Howitt also discovered that localities varied greatly in both their knowledge and their valuations of the poets who had once resided there. In Alloway, not unexpectedly, the cottager who left his potato patch to show Howitt every spot associated with Burns spoke as all Scotsmen evidently did at mention of the sacred name: "The poor man's face kindled with instant animation. . . . 'He was all heart and all man,' he said; 'and there's nothing, at least in a poor man's experience, either bitter or sweet, which can happen to him, but a line of Burns springs into his mouth, and gives him courage and comfort if he needs it. It is like a second Bible.'" At Marlow, on the other hand, apart from general agreement that Shelley had been a bad man who did not believe in the devil, Howitt found little interest in him, and even less information. Told that Shelley had died by drowning, a woman remarked: "Lud-a-mercy! ay, just what we might ha' said he'd come to. He was always on the water, always boating, boating—never easy but when he was in that boat." But almost the only solid piece of data Howitt could unearth—from a pompous man who huffed and puffed like a squire and turned out to be an ordinary tradesman—was that when Shelley left the town, he had paid all his outstanding bills, except the one he owed Howitt's still outraged informant.

· 2 ·

"Art indeed," observed Henry James, looking back after the literary phase of Victorian hero worship had passed its peak, "has in our day taken on so many honours and emoluments that the recognition of its importance is more than a custom, has become on occasion almost a fury: the line is drawn—especially in the English world—only at the importance of heeding what it may mean." Such cynicism could have been applied equally well to certain other institutions and rituals which, by more explicitly identifying the man of letters as the modern counterpart of the old-fashioned saint, helped determine the spirit in which the age's literary biographies were written. Cults, for example: the sodalities dedicated to the study and adoration of the literary great, from Chaucer to Browning. Some of them were scholarly groups, whose primary interest was the establishment and printing of correct texts, the discovery of sources, and the other business of literary learning. In the England of their day they did the kind of work that would later be undertaken by German and American scholars. Others, however, were communal exercises in poet worship.

Most of these were founded and directed by F. J. Furnivall, a merry, extroverted philologist who brought to the late Victorian world of literary scholarship an extraordinary talent for both organization and controversy. Of Furnivall's societies the best publicized was that dedicated to the study of Browning's works and, unofficially but not incidentally, to the adoration of its patron poet-philosopher. The society's solemn deliberations, its anxiety to find lofty moral and spiritual meaning in every line Browning wrote, its ingenuity in casting darkness into corners of his verse where previously there had been only light, made it the subject of perennial facetiousness in the press. Though Browning was flattered by its attentions, the absurdities committed by the foolish virgins and literary-minded clergymen who assembled to praise him proved an embarrassment to his fame in his own lifetime; and though the society perished in 1893, a victim of theological squabbles within the ranks, its dead hand, operating through a succession of biographies as well as innumerable shorter studies, has to a large extent controlled the conception of Browning the man which, however mistaken, remains popular today.

Less solemn, less scholarly, in many cases longer lived, certainly not to be outdone in enthusiasm, and beyond question more convivial than any of Furnivall's corporate ventures in literary veneration were the numerous Burns societies—local brotherhoods, concentrated, naturally, in Scotland, but occurring wherever Scotsmen settled, from Newcastle to New Zealand. They were symptomatic of the same grass-roots phase of literary hero worship which produced the century's harvest of biographical books and articles about the self-styled ploughboy. They twice conducted elaborate celebrations that spread Burns's name across the pages of every English-language newspaper and magazine: in 1859, the centenary of his birth, and in 1896, the centenary of his death. In 1859, according to a voluminous report published soon after the speeches ceased to echo, no fewer than 872 meetings were held to commemorate the poet's birth—676 in Scotland (many in hamlets so small as to be overlooked by the gazetteers), 76 in England, 10 in Ireland, and 110 overseas.

The energy the societies expended in collecting the last atom of information on Burns's habits and friends, while people were alive who claimed to have known him, was enormous. Every moment of the man's life, every spot his eyes lighted on, every woman he ever paid his decent respects to or seduced, every hand he clasped, was investigated, recorded, interpreted, perpetuated in paintings and engravings. At the Glasgow exhibition in 1896 one could view over six hundred pictures of Burns, his relatives and acquaintances, biographical locales, and scenes associated with his poems. But even more amazing was the array of relics on display at the same time. From the Queen downward, hundreds of Burns adorers lent their mementos. There were reverently arranged fragments of construction material: alleged portions of the rafters from Gavin Hamilton's house, the inn of Nanse Tinnock, the roof of Alloway Kirk, the barn at Mossgiel; doors, windows, mantelpieces, pulpit desks, locks from other "edifices the Poet rendered famous." There were branches of trees, the most sacred being that from the hawthorn beneath which the poet bade farewell to Highland Mary. There was enough Burns clothing and household linen to stock a jumble sale: "skirts, caps, hats, pillow-cases, chemises, handkerchiefs, scarfs, gloves, stockings, boots, shoes," as well as brooches, rings, pins, lockets, and masonic jewels. As for furniture and household articles: there were "chairs, tables, cupboards, stools, trays, trunks, drawers, mallets, tongs, pokers, quaichs, cups, ladles, mugs, jugs, bickers, glasses, decanters, bottles of all shapes and sizes, gill-stoups, mutchkin-stoups, tappit-hens, tumblers [the high incidence of drinking apparatus is noticeable], knives, forks, teapots, tea-cups, teaspoons, plates, bowls, pots, pans, mirrors, whips, spurs, walking sticks, knives, scissors, razors, swords, guns, pistols, dirks, spectacles, inkhorns, candlesticks, snuff-boxes, and tobacco pipes." Thus the catalogue of the 1896 exhibition itself; the wonder is not so much that all of these articles survived for a century as that Burns was so plentifully supplied in the first place.

South of the border, relic worship was just as prevalent. One of Leigh Hunt's most treasured possessions was a collection of locks of hair from literary heads: Milton's, Swift's, Johnson's, Keats's, Shelley's, Mary Shelley's, Lamb's, Hazlitt's, Coleridge's, Carlyle's, Wordsworth's, Maria Edgeworth's, the two Brownings', G. P. R. James's. It was fitting indeed that Hunt should have owned such a collection, because through his long career as writer for newspapers and magazines, he did more than any other single literary commentator to encourage the veneration of poets.

It was fitting too that after his death a framed lock of Hunt's own hair should have found its way to the wall of the shrine sacred to one of his friends. At Boscombe Manor, near Bournemouth, Shelley's daughter-in-law kept vigil as the curator of the poet's earthly renown. In a curtained recess in her boudoir were laid out priceless relics of Shelley: his manuscripts, the books he carried to his death in the Italian bay, a miniature (unauthenticated) of him as a child, his rattle. Visitors, gentlemen and ladies alike, were requested to remove their hats when viewing the shrine, although the wife of Thomas Jefferson Hogg —formerly Jane Williams, one of Shelley's friends in his later years—objected with unwelcome logic that in church women kept them on.[2]

---

[2] We shall meet Lady Shelley again in the next chapter. It should be added at this point, however, that the climax of her adoration of her father-in-law

Just as prized as objects associated with dead poets, and ordinarily more available, were those connected with celebrated living men of letters. "Souvenir" or "memento" was the word used, but "sacred relic" would have been more faithful to the impulse behind the request. When Dickens concluded a program of readings, cultivated women would clamber to the platform to pick up the petals fallen from his buttonhole flower. The most grotesque sought-after relic of a poet, however, was the one described by Thomas Moore, whose own castoff clothing, such as old gloves, was treasured by his adorers. After Byron's death, two ladies called on his old Harrow schoolmaster, Joseph Drury, to ask for a souvenir. It was not a sample of Byron's handwriting that they wanted, nor a lock of his hair; instead, they yearned for a bit of hair from one of the dogs Byron had left in Drury's charge. "The dog being brought forward the ladies observed a *clot* on his back, which had evidently resisted any efforts at ablution that might have been exerted on the animal, and immediately selected this as the most precious part to cut off; 'the probability,' they said, 'being that Lord B. might have patted that clot.'"

· 3 ·

As the role of Wordsworth and Tennyson as animate tourist attractions, Browning's as the patron saint of a study group, and Moore's and Dickens' as a source of souvenirs indicates, the process of interlocked deification and debasement extended as much

---

(whom she had never seen), and in many respects the symbolic climax of poet worship itself, came when she commissioned a monument designed after Michelangelo's "Pietà" in St. Peter's: a marble representation of Shelley's almost naked corpse, retrieved, not from the cross, but from the Bay of Spezzia, and held by a sorrowing Mary—not the Virgin, but the daughter of the atheist William Godwin. The monument was duly carved, but the vicar of the church Lady Shelley patronized, who was a man of taste, declined to receive it, and it wound up instead at nearby Christchurch, Hampshire. (Sylva Norman, *Flight of the Skylark* [Norman, Okla., 1954], p. 214.) This was not the end of the Shelleyans' campaign to rehabilitate their theologically recalcitrant hero through the somewhat free use of iconography. In Buxton Forman's edition of Shelley's notebooks (1911) and again in his edition of Medwin's life of Shelley, the frontispiece, captioned "Portrait of Shelley, from a drawing by Alfred Soord," is actually a copy of Leonardo da Vinci's head of Christ, with hair and costume adjusted to early nineteenth-century fashion. (Newman I. White, *Shelley* [New York, 1940], II, 522–523.)

to the nineteenth century's living men of letters as to those of earlier eras. Until this time, living authors, regarded simply as authors, had seldom been highly regarded in Britain. In Boswell's day, if a writer was a public figure, it was usually because he was also in politics or the church or had other activities and connections which by long custom thrust a man into general notice; Sterne and Dr. Johnson were among the few exceptions to the rule. But beginning with Byron and Scott, and assisted by a rapidly changing cultural situation, literature provided Britain with as many current celebrities—and potential subjects for biographies—as did any other profession.[3] Scott with his solid dignity, his sense of *noblesse oblige*; Byron with his never-to-be-fully-analyzed mixture of pose and passionate candor, raffishness and nobility—the two together engaged the public eye and exercised the public emotions as no previous writers had done.

Scott's fame was, of the two, the more quietly developed, the more decorous and cultivated. The British public knew and revered him first as a literary genius in two currently popular forms, the romantic poem and the historical novel, and then as a gentleman embodying the highest virtues of responsible citizenship: a combination of talents that especially recommended him to those who clung to the Augustan ideal of the harmonious balance of humane private accomplishments and service to society. By 1820, as John Buchan pointed out a century later, "He had become a figure of national importance, not only a kind of consul-general for the republic of letters, but a man whose advice and help were sought on the most diverse public affairs. . . . I do not think that there is a parallel in the whole history of letters to the position which Scott filled among his countrymen in the years between 1820 and 1825." When catastrophe came, and the Laird of Abbotsford, his health and literary powers already failing, dedicated the rest of his life to paying off his creditors in full, he

---

[3] Burns, it is true, had become a literary idol before either Byron or Scott; but his fame was not comparable in kind to that of the others. He was a hero principally in Scotland, and among "the people," whereas Scott and Byron found their admirers for the most part in the middle and upper classes. At least, the passion that went into Burns worship gave the Scott and Byron enthusiasts a mark to shoot at.

earned universal sympathy and admiration. When a cruise to the Mediterranean was decided on as a last desperate attempt to save his life, it was a Whig government which placed a frigate at the disposal of Scotland's proudest Tory. At his death in 1832 he was lamented as a national hero.

With Byron it was different. Until March 10, 1812, he had been little known outside the circles to which his aristocratic blood, modest literary accomplishments, and taste for swimming, boxing, gambling, and low life naturally gained him access. But with the appearance of the first two cantos of *Childe Harold* its author, just turned twenty-four, became England's idol. In *Childe Harold* he had created a legend and a hero for, as it turned out, his own use. If he had not been Childe Harold to begin with, he was now, simply because the British reading public, having made the identification, insisted on his living up to it. But that was merely the beginning of his fame; subsequent events transformed him, in the eyes of a national audience, from a melancholy, world-weary adventurer into an *homme fatal,* a demonic hero of un-fathomed powers and unspeakable appetites. It is not often that a handsome young poet and peer, cursed with a limp, parts from his wife amid rumors that the cause, far from being a common-place adultery, had to do with his criminal love for his half-sister; or that, the rumors getting uglier and more credible as they spread, he is hounded out of England, never to return. Was he actually insane, as his wife alleged? Was he an incestuous beast, as wagging tongues implied in the drawing rooms which he had once ornamented and where he was now cut dead? Whatever the truth, it was a magnificent drama such as England had never before owed to the sins of a poet. The young lord, whose poems and person had ruled the fantasies of countless girls and women, and not a few young men, had turned out to be a satyr. A large, scurrilous, and not infrequently obscene pamphlet literature spread broadcast the gossip, the fantastic inventions, and to a small extent the facts; brutal caricatures in the shopwindows ad-vertised Byron's sins to all who could read. In his years of exile, traveling Englishmen gaped at him everywhere he went, hung about the streets outside his successive palazzi; some tramped inside to catch a glimpse of the fallen demigod. The day of the camera had not yet arrived, but Byron, even when boating in the middle of a Swiss lake, was the target of every tourist's spyglass.

After Scott and Byron, no man or woman who made a mark in literature would be immune from public attention. Scott's life, lived in the spotlight with vigor and dignity but never the slightest breath of scandal, proved that men of letters could, as easily as any other breed, provide the flesh-and-blood examples of moral substance and worldly success for which this hero-hungry epoch yearned. The notoriety that succeeded the first radiance of Byron's fame was, of course, another matter; right-thinking people could only deprecate the blatantly self-proclaimed immorality that permeated his career. But his death in the cause of Greek independence went far toward repairing his reputation; and in any case there were plenty of valuable moral lessons to be inferred from his life. To a considerably larger body of readers, however—the forebears of the millions who would later make the fortunes of the illustrated weeklies—the Byron story as it unfolded had few didactic implications: it simply proved that the private lives of literary people made absorbing reading. A steady diet either of Byrons or of Scotts no doubt would pall. But as the press took increasing interest in the affairs of living poets and novelists, and more and more biographies were written, it became clear that in the literary life resided endless variety.

The enthusiasm that went into Scott- and Byron-worship was assisted by the fact that the idols were men of quality; and not least among the attractions the books written about them held for ordinary readers was their setting, in an exalted realm of society to which most English men and women could gain admittance— however much they hungered for it—only through books. As more and more contemporary authors' lives passed, at their conclusion, into books, literary biography was often able to continue to appeal to the taste which throughout the century preferred that circulating-library fiction be laid in Mayfair and populated with ladies and gentlemen of title and substance. For under the radically changing conditions of authorship, and notwithstanding the depressive effect of philistinism, men of indifferent family origin could win both fame and social position solely on account of their writings. Major Pendennis was faithful to the contemporary situation, though not to the strict history of Byron's career, when he observed: "in my time, begad, poetry and genius and that sort of thing were devilish disreputable. There was poor Byron, for instance, who ruined himself, and contracted the worst habits by living with poets and newspaper-writers, and people of that kind. But the times are changed now—there's a run upon literature—clever fellows get into the best houses in town, begad!" In 1838 Charles Dickens, son of a navy clerk, was elected to the Athenaeum Club, the nation's most exclusive assemblage of intellectual and social dignitaries. Carlyle, a peasant by birth and invincible habit—it is said, for example, that he never learned the use of a handkerchief—spent his later years in the frequent company of titled men and women. In the seventies and eighties, there was no more familiar face at the most select London dinner tables, private views of galleries, and other events of the season than that of Robert Browning, son of a clerk in the Bank of England. And so the roster went. From the golden days of the salons at Gore House and Holland House onward, successful poets, novelists, and essayists were sought after, petted, deferred to. They had access even to great country houses from which millionaire financiers and industrialists, those other *arriviste* products of a changing society, were excluded. In such a fashion did high society, sometimes to the embarrassment or positive irritation of the writers it lionized, acknowledge the equally high estate of literature.[4]

Two other indexes of status, the academic and official, con-

[4] As Harriet Martineau, herself a victim, pointed out in a perceptive and indignant article on the phenomenon, Victoria's England was not the first nation to lionize its writers; on a fourteenth-century Easter day, "Petrarch mounted the stairs of the Capitol, crowned with laurel, and preceded by twelve noble youths, reciting passages of his poetry," and four centuries later "Voltaire was overpowered with acclamations in the theatre at Paris, and conveyed home in triumph, crying feebly, 'You suffocate me with roses.'" But this was not the same thing at all. Literary lions had become so numerous as to form a class by themselves, and so had the hunters; and lionism had turned into a veritable, and vulgar, institution. "It is somewhat new," Miss Martineau sardonically remarked, "to see the place of cards, music, masks, my lord's fool, and my lady's monkey, supplied by authors in virtue of their authorship." ("Literary Lionism," *London and Westminster Review*, XXXII [1839], 263–265.)

firmed society's judgment. Scott was offered doctor's degrees simultaneously by both English universities and was made a baronet on the strength of his poems and novels. Browning became the first man of letters since Dr. Johnson to receive an honorary Oxford M.A.; Matthew Arnold received Oxford's D.C.L. Carlyle was elected rector of Edinburgh University and, like Meredith later, was offered, but declined, a knighthood. Tennyson became the first Englishman to be awarded a peerage solely because he was a poet. Thomas Hardy collected five honorary degrees and was made honorary fellow of two Oxford colleges. In 1907 Swinburne was offered, but declined, an honorary degree from Oxford, which he had left, half a century earlier, degreeless and under circumstances that nobody in authority at the time cared to discuss. In the interim he, like his profession over a longer space of time, had become respectable even in the most censorious eyes.

Most symptomatic of the heightened place of literature in the national consciousness was the rehabilitation of the laureateship. By the beginning of the century the post had become, almost by definition, a sinecure-for sycophants. On Southey's death in 1843 there understandably was some talk of abolishing it. Instead, it was given to Wordsworth, who had earned it but who was too old to do more than wear the wreath with weary dignity. Seven years later, following Wordsworth's own death, the choice fell on Tennyson, who in the ensuing forty-two years made the laureateship second only to the prime ministership—indeed, many would have said equal—in national prestige. The man was admirably suited to the office. His invincible personal dignity (amounting in public almost to unstudied grandeur), his obvious consecration to that ideal of the poet's mission which was an article of Victorian faith, raised the institution of literature to the highest peak of public esteem it had ever enjoyed in England. If the man of letters ranked near the top of the hierarchy of mid-Victorian society, he owed his new prestige in large part to the man who held the laureateship. Tennyson made the poet-as-hero official.

Lionization in the fashionable spheres of society, university honors, knighthoods, baronetcies, and peerages had their more democratic counterpart in the attention popular authors received in the press. The editors of the literary weeklies and monthly magazines, sensing the new, seemingly inappeasable public interest in living writers as persons, devoted generous space to them. As early as 1814 the *Champion,* a Sunday paper, ran a series of "Portraits of Authors." Portions of William Hazlitt's *The Spirit of the Age* appeared in the *New Monthly Magazine* in 1824; "Sketches of Contemporary Authors," by the future theologian F. D. Maurice, ran in the *Athenaeum* in 1828; the Scottish miscellaneous writer Allan Cunningham, who made a specialty of this sort of thing, contributed "Living Literary Characters" to the *New Monthly* in 1831. A new generation of literary celebrities was dealt with in Richard Henry Horne's *The New Spirit of the Age* (1844). These are only a few better-known examples of what, from Regency days onward, constituted a busy literary industry. Their ostensible purpose was appreciation and evaluation of the writers' work; but everywhere one turns, the biographical camel is thrusting his nose under the critical tent.

The proportion between the critical and personal elements varied, of course, from article to article. But as this new form of literary journalism evolved, critical comments were kept at a minimum—thrown in to lend a factitious air of instruction to a kind of writing which, if the truth were faced, catered to the growing public appetite for gossip. In 1830–38 *Fraser's Magazine,* an impudent, fearless, effervescent monthly, printed "The Maclise Portrait Gallery of Illustrious Literary Characters," a series of eighty-one drawings by Daniel Maclise with accompanying text by a *Fraser* stalwart, the gifted and alcoholic William Maginn. The latter, no respecter of persons, was anecdotal, humorous, sometimes forthrightly satirical. Maginn's subjects often winced, but *Fraser's* readers devoured what he wrote, and the "Portrait Gallery" became one of the magazine's most popular features.

Like the "homes and haunts" books with their copious engravings, the Victorian collections of literary profiles exploited the age's passion for illustrated books. The "Maclise Gallery," William Jerdan's five-volume *National Portrait Gallery of Illustrious and Eminent Personages of the Nineteenth Century* (1830–34),

Poet and Public •

Henry Fothergill Chorley's *The Authors of England: A Series of Medallion Portraits* (1838), and other such collections, whether composed of respectful likenesses or malicious caricatures, made the faces and figures of eminent writers familiar to many thousands of readers. Engravings of such popular favorites as Moore, Byron, and Scott were available in shops, and as illustrated comic papers proliferated in the wake of *Punch*, Dickens, Carlyle, Disraeli, Bulwer-Lytton, and other literary notables turned up in topical cartoons. Some of the most famous *Vanity Fair* caricatures by "Spy" (Leslie Ward) were of literary men. And in 1868, when Swinburne had his photograph taken with Adah Menken, the fabled mistress of kings and actress-star of *Mazeppa*, his friends saw to it that copies were offered for sale in the shops—the only recorded attempt to promote a poet to fame aboard a horse ridden by an American adventuress in pink tights.

Besides collections of journalistic profiles and "graphic representations" of famous writers, Victorian readers eager for a closer acquaintance with the literary life had at their command scores of book-length reminiscences. These were usually produced *in extremis*, financial or physical, by veteran journalists and frequenters of literary circles like William Jerdan (four volumes, 1852–53), Peter George Patmore, Coventry's father (three volumes, 1855), Cyrus Redding (eight volumes, 1858 and 1863), and S. C. Hall (three volumes, 1871 and 1883). These wandering, pointlessly anecdotal, and often unindexed garrulities of men whose memories had become treacherous and inventive were infuriating and tedious in approximately equal parts, and in general they deserved the bad press they usually got. But their very existence showed how eager the public was thought to be for every detail that could be told about the habits, appearance, and professional and personal life of the hundreds of writers—hacks and geniuses, composers of epics and column-end fillers—who had kept the presses busy in the preceding generation.[5]

Three years before Scott died, a gift book annual called *The*

---

[5] Not quite all of these name-dropping memory books are unreadable, however. To the same genre, but on a much higher literary level, belong Hazlitt's classic essay on "My First Acquaintance with Poets," first printed in the *Liberal* in 1823, and De Quincey's recollections of the Lake poets and other writers in *Tait's Edinburgh Magazine* between 1834 and 1840.

((129

Anniversary printed an extensive description of Abbotsford written, as Lockhart says, "in the character of an imaginary American, supposed to visit Scotland in the summer of 1825, and to examine the place, when Sir Walter was absent, under the guidance of one of the neighboring gentlemen, tolerably familiar with its history." Lockhart himself, it is now known, wrote the piece. But the attribution to the "imaginary American" has its own significance. Already the presence of energetic, inquisitive Americans was making itself felt in the literary holy places of Britain. Washington Irving came, saw, and wrote a book, *Abbotsford and Newstead Abbey*. Yankees were turning up at Wordsworth's doorstep, to emerge either enchanted by his benignity and wisdom or disillusioned, as Emerson was in 1833, by his green goggles and tiresome harping on his prejudices.

Some Americans were effusively welcomed, especially when they brought impressive recommendations. But the arrival of others had the effect of chilling the hands symbolically clasped across the sea. In 1834 came the dandiacal Nathaniel Parker Willis, already a journalist of some note who would later become America's best-paid, best-known, and most vociferously abused "magazinist." (A commercial gentleman, breaking silence at a Boston literary tea, was said to have observed that "he guessed Go-ēthe was the N. P. Willis of Germany.") Armed with introductions from Landor and others, Willis was readily absorbed into the best London society. At Lady Blessington's salon he met Bulwer, Moore, Disraeli, and a host of other stars, about whom he wrote in a long series of letters to the *New York Mirror*, which were copied, it was later claimed, by five hundred other American papers.

A selection from *Pencillings by the Way*, as these dispatches were called, was published in London in November, 1835. Before the book appeared, Lockhart, who had seen the originals as they were printed in the American press, lashed out at Willis in the *Quarterly Review*. "This," he said, "is the first example of a man creeping into your home, and forthwith printing—accurately or inaccurately, no matter which—before your claret is dry on his lips—unrestrained *table-talk on delicate subjects, and capable of compromising individuals.*" Willis' disrespectful references to Lockhart himself may have had something to do with the latter's indignation (though Lockhart, the feared "scorpion" of contemporary criticism, was hardly in a position to throw stones), but, whatever his personal grievance, Lockhart spoke for many of his contemporaries when he attacked the upstart American for his violation of the confidence implied in hospitality. A few months later Maginn, trumping Lockhart's comparatively restrained prose, reviewed Willis' book in *Fraser's* as "chambermaid gabble" and "penny-trumpet eloquence," and branded its author as a "lickspittle," "jackass," "fifty-fifth rate scribbler of gripe-visited sonnets," "windy-gutted visitor," and "namby-pamby writer in twaddling albums, kept by the mustachoed and strong-smelling widows or bony matrons of Portland Place or Curry Row."

Obviously some quarters of British opinion disapproved of Willis and his breezy, indiscreet journalism. Captain Marryat challenged him to a duel, which did not come off. Dickens was annoyed by Willis' describing Furnival's Inn, where Dickens lived, as a run-down tenement; actually it was the residence of well-to-do solicitors. Thackeray, after a brief engagement as contributor to Willis' new paper, named with disarming candor *The Corsair*, caricatured him in *Fraser's* as "Napoleon Putnam Wiggins, of Passamaquoddy" and later, in *Vanity Fair*, as "Mr. John Paul Jefferson Jones."

Of small consequence in itself, the Willis affair nevertheless brought to a head an issue that had been troubling people's minds ever since the private habits and conversation of literary celebrities had first found their way into the newspapers and magazines. It was a question which, as we shall see in the following chapter, cast its agitation across the path of all literary biography. How much should a journalist—or, by logical extension, a biographer— tell? Was it, in fact, a breach of the amenities to print the wine-stimulated confidences of one's dinner companions? This was a subject on which feelings would have run high in any event, but extra heat was generated by the fact that an American journalist had caused the whole uproar. In a period when American manners (or lack of them) seemed to represent social democracy at its worst, it was most convenient, even if erroneous, to look upon the growing inquisitiveness and indiscretion of literary journalism as an importation from General Jackson's raw republic.

· 4 ·

Nonetheless, the new journalism was permanently established, without any necessary help or example from across the sea, and its prosperity depended on an audience which, far from sharing or even comprehending the intellectual concerns of the critical quarterlies, wanted to know what sort of clothes this author wore, and when, in the midst of domestic or social distractions, that authoress managed to find time to turn out her entertaining tales. They wanted to know what bon mots went crackling from one famous wit to another across the table at Holland House and whether it was true that a certain popular magazine writer no longer lived with his wife and children. Now that literary people were as celebrated as statesmen and generals, the man in the street was entitled to ask such questions; and no amount of indignation in higher places could prevent journalists from doing their enterprising best to satisfy his curiosity. Literary gossip, in unabashed print, had become a fact of contemporary life.

Down to about the middle of the century, or slightly thereafter, the information the public received on the private lives and habits of its favorite authors ordinarily was but a report, touched up as desired, of hearsay, to which was added whatever knowledge the journalist happened, or claimed, to have acquired as a personal acquaintance of his subject. Writers for the papers and magazines were less and less given to suppressing what they knew, even though it came to them by way of friendship. Most of the information they published, to be sure, was relatively innocuous. They exposed, or even hinted at the existence of, few of the skeletons that are now known to have populated Victorian closets. But this random way of assembling inside stories on literary people proved inadequate and inefficient, and by the seventies, Victorian literary homes were haunted by journalists, out on assignment. The age of the interview had begun.

Although they soon became a feature of the popular press at large, interviews at first were a specialty of the society-and-gossip papers, led by Edmund Yates's *The World*. Yates, who had won his journalistic reputation with his "Lounger at the Clubs" articles for the *Illustrated Times* in the mid-fifties, made "Celebrities at Home" the *World's* most popular feature. He visited several hundred eminent men and women, from archbishops to jockeys, and confided to an eager audience what his hosts looked like, what they said, how their parlors were furnished, what their working habits were, and how they entertained their friends. Compared with the visit-and-interview pieces that were to come in a decade or two, the "Celebrities at Home" series was discreet to the point of dullness, yet Yates records that its "impertinence" was criticized—a full generation after N. P. Willis—as "an importation of the worst principles of American journalism into this country; . . . it was, in a word, un-English."[6]

From then on, press relations, as they are now called, were a normal complication of the English literary life, as well as an ever-present sign of the new relation between author and audience. Certain flamboyant members of the literary profession sought the limelight and invited sensational treatment in the press. There was the fantastic "Ouida," for instance, whose *Strathmore* and *Under Two Flags*, three-volume romances derided by the critics and extravagantly admired by ordinary readers, made her the best-selling authoress of the late sixties, and who populated her lavish parties with cigar-smoking, free-talking Guardsmen and other pillars of the military establishment. Her well-publicized activities added an extra touch of spice to the Victorian reader's reassuring discovery that authors were people. Conspicuous vulgarity and ostentatious social climbing were traits which could readily be understood, however much disapproved of.

[6] The notion died hard. Many decades later, when someone appealed to A. E. Housman for an interview, that unreconstructed Victorian growled: "Tell him that the wish to include a glimpse of my personality . . . is low, unworthy and American." (George Watson, *A. E. Housman: A Divided Life* [London, 1957], p. 206.)

Meanwhile, prompted both by the unedifying spectacle the Ouidas of the literary world presented and by their personal aversion to publicity, other writers did all they could to discourage the attentions of the interviewer and the gossip columnist. Tennyson was always inaccessible. Not the least of the virtues of Hardy's second wife was her competence as—to use his word—a "chucker-out" of reporters desirous of his opinions and details of his private life. When he did admit newspapermen to Max Gate, it was with the amiably sadistic proviso that they print nothing of their visit.

By the nineties, publishers and authors' agents were beginning to arrange personal publicity for their writers; the pioneer agent A. P. Watt, for example, saw to it that his client Bret Harte, then resident in Britain, broke his long-standing rule against interviews in favor of magazines which were buying his stories. Some authors, especially those who had themselves been working journalists, cooperated with the press. In his later years George Meredith, formerly of the *Ipswich Journal,* was always accessible at his home near Dorking to reporters seeking good headlinable radical opinions. As his latest biographer has pointed out, it was Meredith who first wore the mantle of daily-paper oracle that later descended on Shaw. Shaw, of course, did his bit to tug the mantle down upon himself; early in his career he seems to have written anonymous interviews with *himself* (for example, "Bernard Shaw: Interviewed About His Play Soon to be Seen"—a promotion for *Widowers' Houses,* in the *Star* in 1892).

As new writers won a large popular audience or earned so much critical acclaim that no foresighted editor could risk neglecting them, they were propelled before the public in all their human roles, from abstemious eaters to deep thinkers. The proud resistance of the Hardys become passé, stuffy; the Bennetts and the Wellses of the new century were to find it more humane, convenient, and, in the end, profitable to capitulate to press and public.

But the house of publicity has many chambers, and interviews —news events arranged by the journalists themselves—were only one of the numerous means by which writers entered the nation's consciousness. As professional authors became men to be reckoned with, both in theory (as hero-prophets of the new society) and in practice (as persons who demonstrably wielded power over the sympathies of millions of readers), they were constantly invited to join politicians, ecclesiastics, and peers in petitions, statements to the press, committees, and public meetings. They met and wrote to improve the lot of sweated workers, to open museums and art galleries on Sundays, to prevent cruelty to animals, and to save the natural beauty of Richmond Hill. In the headlines of 1866 writer was ranged against writer—Carlyle, Tennyson, Kingsley, and Ruskin on one side, Mill, Herbert Spencer, Thomas Hughes, and Huxley on the other—in the controversy over Edward Eyre's alleged cruelty to natives when he was governor of Jamaica. Innumerable dinners in support of orphanages, "ragged schools," and homes for repentant or unsuccessful prostitutes, grand openings and prize-givings at mechanics' institutes and evening literary and philosophical institutions required their presence, as the correspondences of men like Dickens amply show.

Then there were the testimonials and birthday celebrations— the most immediately newsworthy proof of the regard in which a nation held its literary heroes. In 1841 Dickens, in the fifth year of his fame, received the freedom of the city of Edinburgh in the presence of 270 diners and 200 "feminine spectators." Henceforth his career was studded with such events, the last being the farewell dinner he was given in 1867 on the eve of his departure for the United States; practically the whole of the "literary, dramatic, and artistic world" was present, along with the band of Her Majesty's Grenadier Guards. When the guest of honor rose to speak, "shouts stormed upon him. Men leaped on chairs, tossed up napkins, waved glasses and decanters above their heads. The ladies' gallery was a flag of waving fans and handkerchiefs," and outside a vast crowd waited to view the celebrities as they left.

When George Meredith turned eighty in 1908, he was given the full treatment as the "Grand Old Man of English Letters." Every paper printed leaders and columns of personal details; a corps of pressmen kept watch over Meredith's cottage at Box Hill

to note every congratulatory arrival and departure, and photographers snapped the crippled sage as he was drawn in his donkey
chair. It was the greatest journalistic tribute to an author since
the young Kipling and the aged Leo XIII had simultaneously
hovered between life and death nine years before. While crowds
gathered outside the New York hotel where Kipling lay desperately ill, the papers headlined every bulletin on his condition, and
the *Pall Mall Gazette,* showing a nice sense of relative values,
gave him pride of place in its news vendors' posters: KIPLING AND
POPE, they read.

· 5 ·

Year by year, then, the distance that had once existed between
an author and his readers steadily narrowed, and though respect
remained—hero worship being an attitude not easy to dissipate—
it characteristically softened, in not a few cases, into something
more homely and affectionate. Dickens throve upon what he
called with justice "the personal (I may almost say affectionate)
relations which subsist between me and the public and make my
standing with them very peculiar." It was a high compliment, to
many minds in fact there could be none higher, to assure a Victorian literary eminence that one felt he belonged to the family.
Even Shakespeare was not immune from such well-meant familiarity: "We don't say Mr. Shakespeare," wrote Mary Cowden
Clarke, who made a concordance to his plays, "but—darling
Willie, dear William, beloved Will." Any writer, ancient or
modern, who populated the book-loving home with cherished
characters was himself an honorary member of the household.
"Mr. Dickens," said a lady in a York street one day, "will you let
me touch the hand that has filled my house with many friends?"

If this companionable spirit, which found its way into printed
criticism as well as personal contacts, strikes us as being a doubtful form of homage, we must remember that many nineteenth-
century authors invited it. From Charles Lamb's genial opening
"Reader—" to the professional colloquialism of journalists like the
bulbous-nosed *bon vivant* George Augustus Sala, the confidential
tone was one of the hallmarks of nineteenth-century popular

prose style. Its adoption, not only by the smaller fry but by such masters of the journalistic essay and the novel as Dickens and Thackeray, probably did as much as column-miles of press coverage to give readers a sense of friendly rapport with their favorite entertainers. As a rule the magisterial elevation of old-fashioned formal prose survived only in books written for a small audience, the intellectual élite. The truly popular writers, of fiction and nonfiction alike, tended to lay their hands on their readers' shoulders and address them in language appropriate to the fireside.

The widespread practice of serializing fiction in monthly numbers and magazines contributed further toward the public's consciousness of the author as a person. As they awaited each installment of *The Pickwick Papers* or *Nicholas Nickleby* with almost unbearable impatience, prospective readers naturally thought of Mr. Dickens, hard at work at that very moment: what was he going to have happen to his characters next? (Sometimes Mr. Dickens did not know either.) The sustained, month-by-month excitement of serial publication intensified the public's sense of participation in the creative act. When a reader borrowed a three-volume novel from the circulating library, he had no such fancy of being present as the manuscript pages piled up on the author's desk. The finished book was a work of art, perhaps, but one whose gestation had not been a constant subject of public anxiety and delight and whose birth, therefore, so far as the audience was concerned, was merely an isolated event, not the culmination of a long process.

Thus even the circumstances of publication tended to keep authors in the public eye; and the knowledge that they, like ordinary beings, had inescapable tasks to perform and deadlines to meet helped make them seem all the more human. At the same time, the wide distribution of their pictures and the publication of their addresses made them more approachable, either in person or by letter. Biographies of the era's famous writers have numerous recognition scenes occurring in public places. A London workman stops Charles Lamb, to point in awe to Sir Walter Scott as he crosses the street. In the rain, a loiterer calls a cab for Tom Moore ("Sure, ain't *I* the man that patronizes your Melodies?") but refuses a tip, in honor of Literature. On Westminster Bridge a workman and two young clerks successively doff their hats to a tall, bespectacled pedestrian and murmur, "Mr. Thackeray." Coming out of a concert, an elderly lady approaches George Eliot and begs to be allowed to kiss her hand; she is followed by a younger lady who requests the same privilege, declaring herself to be "one of the many thousands." Near the Liverpool docks, a cooper with a "fearful stutter" impresses Dickens with his modesty and natural politeness as he tries heroically to articulate his admiration.

All of this is not to say that the nineteenth-century English public united to sing, in one strong clear voice, the praises of its poets and collect, where feasible, their off-hand wisdom or locks of their dogs' hair. William Howitt, visiting Coleridge's cottage at Nether Stowey—then converted into a pothouse—had to explain to the landlord's wife what a poet was. And though he walked the earth as a demigod, even Dickens' celebrity was incomplete. There is something engaging in the cautious statement of the Aberdeen impresario to Dickens' advance agent for his reading tours: "I'm no prapared t' state positively what yewr actiel receats 'll be, *for ye see, sir, amangst ma ain freends there are vairy few wha ha' iver haird o' Charles Dickens.*" If, indeed, we are ever tempted to assume that the fame of certain authors reached to every household in Britain, it is salutary to remember that when George Bernard Shaw, already famous, first settled at Ayot St. Lawrence, some of his neighbors did not know who he was. "I dunno, sir," said a tradesman. "He does something in Lunnon, I think, sir. But it isn't for *me* to ahsk him about his trade—now is it, sir?" But one day a paper printed a picture of a bobby holding up London traffic to allow the village's new resident to cross the street, and he suddenly became a celebrity even in rural Hertfordshire.

Ignorance, however, did less to set limits to poet worship than, in the end, the extravagances of poet worship itself—as the rise of Baconianism and allied heresies illustrates. The sensation of the bogus Tichborne Claimant eventually ceased to reverberate through the English consciousness, but this other alleged imposture, this most grandiose of all (supposed) hoaxes—that of one William Shakespeare's claim to having written the plays printed under his name—continues to stir people up. It is a classic example of what happens when ordinarily sane men and women are torn between two incompatible impulses: on the one hand, the necessity of attaching a body of literature to the name and fully conceived person of an author, and on the other, refusal to believe that the man who received all the honor really deserved it.

In this instance, poet worship overreached itself by making manifest the painful discrepancy between the idol (as constructed from a reading of the plays) and the real man (so far as he could be seen in the historical records). The trouble could be corrected simply by deciding that they were two different persons and transferring credit to where credit was really due. In the case of contemporary literary figures, however, no such easy solution was available. When they tottered on their pedestals, disillusionment could not be cured by reassigning their works bodily to a more acceptable author. The Victorians had to face the fact that though it was all very well to idealize the poet-nature, as Wordsworth, Shelley, and Carlyle had done, the actuality often betrayed the ideal. Shelley himself, arch-apologist for the poet as the wisest, most sublime of mortals, was best known to the newspaper-reading public of his day as a young man of radical notions whom the Court of Chancery had declared unfit to care for his own children. The shock wave that began with the Byrons' separation and the attendant sinister rumors ended in the nation's driving its hero into exile. Hell hath no fury like that of a people whose current idol turns out to have feet of clay, and England's historic wrath when it realized that Byron was, in his own words, "a most profligate sinner," has stimulated connoisseurs of mass hypocrisy to mordant commentary ever since.[7]

"What a set!" exclaimed a disgusted Matthew Arnold many

[7] A generation later (1869–70) Harriet Beecher Stowe's revelation of the story of Byron's incest, as confided to her by his widow, touched off another and even fiercer storm. Mrs. Stowe was excoriated by virtually the whole British press in some of the most furious language employed during the Victorian era. The sensation dominated the headlines for months, and so great was the popular interest that street hawkers sold penny books with a portrait on the cover of "Lord Byron's half-sister, Augusta." Purchasers with retentive memories may have recognized the picture: on earlier occasions it had served as that of Manon Lescaut, Lola Montez, and the lovely poisoner Madeleine Smith. (Ethel Colburn Mayne, *Byron* [London, 1912], II, 320.)

years later, reviewing the manifold marital and extramarital complications of the Byron-Shelley circle. But had he chosen to see things as they really were, he would have been equally shocked by the frequent and well-known moral irregularities that blotted the literary life of his own time. A best-selling novelist and female intellectual, George Eliot, lived without benefit of clergy with George Henry Lewes, a leading journalist and critic whose legal wife, while still under his roof, had had two children by Leigh Hunt's son Thornton. In 1858 Dickens announced his separation from his wife by running a statement, boldly headed PERSONAL, on the front page of his popular weekly, *Household Words*, and requesting all papers to copy it; he was furious when his friend Mark Lemon would not give it space in *Punch*. A few weeks later, English papers copied from the New York *Tribune* a private letter in which Dickens denounced rumormongers for implicating a certain (unnamed) young lady in the scandal. "Upon my soul and honour," he wrote, "there is not on this earth a more virtuous and spotless creature than this young lady. I know her to be as innocent and pure, and as good as my own dear daughters." Even readers who bore Dickens the best will in the world might have been forgiven for suspecting—as was long afterward shown to be true—that behind so much exculpatory smoke lay, *in posse* if not as yet *in esse*, a bit of adulterous fire.

The doings of the Rossetti-Swinburne circle were in the best style of early Bohemianism, and, associated as they were with certain scathing critical attacks on their poetry—notably John Morley's characterization of Swinburne as "an unclean fiery imp from the pit" and "the libidinous laureate of a pack of satyrs," and Robert Buchanan's indictment of the alleged indecencies of "the Fleshly School of Poetry"—they soon became semipublic knowledge. Dante Gabriel Rossetti's untidy domestic affairs, climaxed tragically by the suicide of his wife; his drug addiction, his paranoia, all the physical and mental tortures of his later life: these were not the materials of which true Victorian hero legends could be made. Nor was Algernon Swinburne any better qualified for a niche in the contemporary pantheon: Swinburne with the tiny body and large head, the fluttering hands and orange hair, the penchant for abnormal sexual practices, the shrill-voiced enthusiasms and rages, the incapacity for liquor which resulted in his—not Tennyson's—personifying Poetry to many a London cabman assigned to convey him home.

Much of this was known, of course, only to the specially informed; but the less scandalous eccentricities of the Pre-Raphaelites and the Esthetes were amply publicized, by George du Maurier in *Punch*, by Gilbert and Sullivan in *Patience*. Oscar Wilde appeared at evening parties in knee breeches and shoulder-length hair, and if in reality he did not inhale vaguely indecent perfume from a lily held in his hand, people willingly believed that he did. Seldom had the personality of an English *littérateur*, in all its careless flamboyance and disregard of convention, given the press more scope for satire and jocosity. To the newspapers and magazines of the eighties and early nineties, Oscar Wilde was precious in more than one sense.

On October 12, 1892, Alfred, Lord Tennyson was laid to rest in Westminster Abbey. For days the world had been kept informed of his decline, a gradual, painless weakening, the great soul preparing to cross the bar. Tennyson died as a romantic poet-hero should, almost as if the event had been stage-managed: the moonlight streaming in upon his bed, his Shakespeare open to *Cymbeline*. His funeral was an event of national mourning which recalled to the elderly the funeral of Wellington, just forty years before; recalled, also, the words the Laureate had then written, now freshly applicable: the last great Englishman was dead.

On April 26, 1895, Oscar Wilde went on trial at the Old Bailey, charged with sodomy. Gossip of his unfortunate inclinations had been rampant in London clubland and literary circles for some time; now the sordid details were aired in court, with the press in full and rapt attendance. *Le Byron de nos jours*, to borrow a phrase from Browning, was in the dock. By the time the trial ended and Wilde, flabby and haggard, was sentenced to two years' penal servitude, the Victorian myth of the poet-hero was past revival. The Abbey organ, sounding forth the postlude at Tennyson's funeral—the Dead March from *Saul*—had marked the end of an era in more ways than the mourners then realized.

Now, less than three years later, London dock hands and ditch-diggers, readers of the sensational penny press, instead of using among themselves the genial, unprintable words of abuse that had been standard for centuries, were à la mode: "You bloody Oscar," they shouted at one another. The name of a man of letters had become a public obscenity.

These two events, so utterly diverse, so perfectly symbolic, dramatized a process that had actually begun decades earlier. Even as the tide of poet worship was rising, in the years just following Carlyle's lectures, there remained an obstinate under-tow of antiheroic feeling. The Presbyterian minister and lecturer George Gilfillan, introducing the first of his *Galleries of Literary Portraits* in 1845, felt obliged to defend his panegyric tone, assert-ing that "he is not afraid, once for all, to avow himself, even in this late age, a 'Hero Worshipper,' and to avow his conviction that, even now, there are many heroes." The high-water mark of poet idolatry coincided with the high-water mark of Tennyson's critical reputation. It was an ominous sign when a popular paper, the *Weekly Despatch*, courted additional circulation time and again by offering prizes for the best parodies of the Laureate's poems; reverence for poem—and poet—is in danger when men are tempted to convert an anthem into a comic song.

The fate of poet worship was, in essence, the fate of the con-cept of poetry which Tennyson had embraced ever since he turned his back on "The Palace of Art" in 1832: poetry as a public art, an instrument of social enlightenment and improvement. More and more, as the century drew toward its end, poetry, in the hands of a new generation, closed in upon itself, like a sea anemone. The Tennyson of "Locksley Hall Sixty Years After," trenchantly, prophetically commenting on the march of public events in 1886, was an anachronism—as, indeed, he consciously portrayed himself in that poem. Poetry was only for the few: the exquisitely sensitive, the withdrawn, the alienated. Such was the conclusion that Pater and his follower Wilde, and the many disciples they acquired between them, were forced to reach. The brave confidence of Shelley and Carlyle, that the poet could redeem mankind, had proved unfounded. Even Tennyson, however boundless the comfort his poems had given privately to humble individual men and women, had not reformed his age. Nor had Dickens, despite the occasional success of his many campaigns against specific cruelties, injustices, and abuses of power, brought England any nearer the social millennium. The poet-as-hero had failed, and fallen.

This turn of fortune's wheel, far from diminishing the popularity of literary biography, served only to increase it. Eulogy, it is true, rang increasingly false; whatever affinities literary biography had had with old-time hagiography gradually disappeared. Events, assisting and assisted by the normal evolution of cultural attitudes, had revealed that writers are, for better or worse, human beings. "What art most prizes in the hero," wrote the critic E. S. Dallas in 1866—obviously meaning "audience" as well as "art"—"is the human side of his character, the little touches of nature by which he is more particularly felt to be kin to the whole world, the very points about him which are not exceptional, and which, therefore, are not heroic, but common. If individuals fail as heroes, still they flourish and are of more account than ever as men."

At first, as we have seen in the course of this chapter, this swelling interest in the private personalities and everyday affairs of the great was respectful; later it became impertinent. The venerative distance that traditionally had separated the poet-hero from the public narrowed, and eventually was closed. The whole quality of a writer's celebrity, in fact, was transformed. The public still was hungry for news of him, but it preferred to watch him as an actor in the human comedy rather than as a figure standing statuesquely on a cloud-surrounded eminence, lost in contemplation. This desire was satisfied by the interviews, the confidential personal sketches, and the other devices of mass journalism, which recognized that the literary celebrity had become an object of permanent interest to the man in the street, not because he was an artist but simply because his private affairs, described with the requisite liveliness, made absorbing reading. It was a sign of the times that in 1870, within a month or two of Dickens' death, three "lives" of the novelist were issued by publishers who specialized in supplying what was, in the literal sense, the street trade. One was called *The Life and Times of Charles Dickens. Being the complete Life, both Public and Private, of that Great Novelist: Police News Edition* (sixteen pages!); another was entitled *Charles Dickens. With Anecdotes and Recollections of His Life* (a product of the London Newsvendors' Publishing Company: sixty-four pages). Eleven years later, Carlyle's death was marked by the issue of two hastily produced "biographies" that sold for a penny each. That biographies of contemporary writers should be cooked up for the same audience which normally devoured the adventures of such penny-thriller heroes as Spring Heeled Jack and Sweeney Todd was a cultural phenomenon of no mean significance. It was as if Edmund Curll had resumed business at the old stand.

In Curll's day biography had been a profitable sideline of popular journalism. Now, under the new conditions of the nineteenth century, the demarcation line between journalism and biography was equally uncertain; every fresh development suggested that the two had a virtually inherent affinity for each other. But there was this profound complication: since Boswell's time, biography had achieved dignity as a serious literary genre, and the conflict between the claims and purposes of biographical journalism and those of dignified biographical art became ever sharper.

The age's literary temper and the imperatives of social decorum insisted that biography, dedicated as it traditionally was to the ends of hero worship and wholesome morality, should be discreet, selective, striving toward idealized portraiture. But the age's social temper, impatient of class distinctions, unashamedly curious about the private affairs of the celebrated, demanded more and more in the way of revelations, an expectation that was supported by Boswell's admired example and by such few subsequent biographers as ventured to disclose some of the "intimacies" of their subjects.

What did the readers of serious biography really want? One suspects that they wanted to eat their cake and have it too. Consciously they subscribed to all the prevailing platitudes about biographical restraint and applauded biographers who refashioned their subjects into images more consonant with contemporary ethical ideals; subconsciously many of them, affected even against their will by the spread of "democratic" and "vulgar" interest in lives as they actually were lived, personalities as they really were judged by others, wanted to know more than the typically cautious full-dress biographer was inclined, or allowed, to tell. But this latter desire went counter to the orthodoxy of the age, and dread of it never ceased to shadow the writing of literary biography. The great fear was that where the journalists led, the formal biographers were bound, or at least sorely tempted, to follow.

CHAPTER V

How Much Should a Biographer Tell?

WHILE William Blake was entertaining angels in his cottage at Felpham, his friend and near neighbor was William Hayley, a country gentleman then engaged on a life of the poet Cowper, for which Blake was providing the engravings. For various reasons—in addition to his literary absurdities, the most notorious of which was a grotesquely ornate style, he indulged such personal eccentricities as carrying a raised umbrella while riding horseback—Hayley was the most laughed-at British man of letters of his time. The praise he heaped on Cowper in 1803–4 was typical of his predilection for extremes. To be sure, his defense of eulogy, set forth in his life of Milton a decade earlier, was reasonable enough, according to the tastes of the old century:

> Biographers are frequently accused of being influenced by affection for their subject; to a certain degree it is right that they should be so; for what is biography in its fairest point of view? a tribute paid by justice and esteem to genius and to virtue; and never is this tribute more pleasing or more profitable to mankind, than when it is liberally paid, with all the fervor and all the fidelity of friendship: the chief delight and the chief utility that arises from this attractive branch of literature consists in the affectionate interest, which it displays and communicates in favour of the talents and probity that it aspires to celebrate. . . .

But Hayley's hagiography offended many readers' palates. "Such sugar and treacle praise!!" exclaimed Anna Seward, the poetic

Swan of Lichfield, to Walter Scott; "such lavish iteration of ap-
plausive epithets!! '*great* and *glorious,*' 'revered, sublime, unriv-
alled, matchless!' —such labour to buckram out that unhappy
Enthusiast, that ingenious, interesting and often elevated, but not
first-rate Poet . . ." Scott agreed. "Biography," he replied, "the
most interesting perhaps of every species of composition, loses all
its interest with me when the shades and lights of the principal
character are not accurately & faithfully detaild nor have I much
patience with such exaggerated daubing as Mr. Hayley has be-
stowd upon poor Cowper. I can no more sympathise with a mere
eulogist than I can with a ranting hero upon the stage."

Thanks both to the excesses of Hayley and a few other
practitioners and to Boswell's conspicuous avoidance of them, the
reduction of biography to "mere" eulogy, insofar as "eulogy"
connotes surplus wordage from the bases of monuments, was discredited fairly early in the century. The hero-worshipping impulse was gratified less in rhetoric than in reticence, less in outright praise than in disproportionate stress on a man's virtues and
silence concerning his shortcomings. In biographical practice the
crucial middle term of the hallowed formula, ". . . the *whole* truth
. . .", had little or no place. Biographers seldom lied outright, and
to that extent their professed or implied adherence to the code of
their veracious craft was not disingenuous; but they did not hesi-
tate to adjust facts where desirable, and even more, they felt
bound to suppress whatever, in their judgment, posterity should
not be told. From every side, the spirit of the age pressed the
biographer to select, evade, conceal, and extenuate.

To venerate heroes is, by virtual definition, to subscribe to
existing myths or to create new ones. Either way, the biographer
sacrifices historical realism to the requirements of his ideal portrait. In such portraits, the nineteenth-century commemorative
urge was, as always in hagiography, inseparable from the didactic: the biographer dedicated himself not merely to honoring a
luminous memory, but also to turning his subject's character and
achievements into an *exemplum.* Biography tended constantly
to follow the lines suggested by the current ethical stereotype, the era's conception of the moral man. In the first third of

the century, for example, literary biographers served the cause of moral perfection by finding in their subjects' lives and characters those qualities which the age found most desirable: serenity of mind, lack of affectation, benevolent sensibility, equipoise between seriousness and amiable humor, intellectual cultivation stopping short of pedantry, generosity and probity in money matters, marital affection and fidelity, love of family and home, patience in the face of adversity, and, above all, religious faith.

Not all of these virtues, of course, could be found embodied in a single figure; that was too much to be hoped or striven for, even by the most fervent worshipper. On the other hand, there was always a certain amount of evidence to suggest that the hero was, after all, a son of Adam. But no edification was to be had from revealing that a celebrated poet was indifferent to the cleanliness of his linen, slept with women other than his wife, and rather too often was disabled by drink. Such concessions to historical fact would defeat the whole aim of poet worship. Literary biography, like biography in general, was committed to establishing, or preserving, an image of the man not as he was, but as it was most inspiring for people to think he was, and as they wanted, indeed, to think he was. Readers of the lives of revered writers expected to be given fresh grounds for their reverence; hence the biographer dedicated to maintaining the wishful image was obliged to suppress, or at the very least treat with the utmost circumspection, those elements in a writer's character and those episodes in his life which exposed the common clay.

This in itself need not be wholly deplored. Biography written to praise famous men and inspire a new generation through their example does honor to any age, and to disparage it simply because it often is bad history is to depreciate its motives and its influence for good. But, as the preceding chapter showed, the nineteenth century often managed to vulgarize its nobler impulses with remarkable skill and thoroughness. The high-minded desire to celebrate genuine heroes for the benefit of the race— biography's original *raison d'être,* and its principal one down through the eighteenth century—was now complicated by a cluster of social and cultural necessities which were largely peculiar to the new age.

Hero worship itself, as exhibited in biography, fell off into what Harold Nicolson was to call "the cenotaph urge"—the desire to extol even the patently mediocre talent. From an occasional act of piety, the production of commemorative biographies was converted into a veritable industry, which flourished despite the caustic comments in every year's harvest of reviews. The idealizing motives that lay behind the biography of the truly distinguished man degenerated into simple hypocrisy: any resemblance between the real General Balaclava, Sir Jabez Hinksey, M.P. (the cotton millionaire and philanthropist), or the Reverend Dr. Septimus Chasuble, Bishop of Wessex, and the incarnations of all the Christian virtues portrayed in their respective biographies was entirely imaginary. Few readers, probably, were deceived by such portly sequels to the funeral oration, and even fewer were permanently improved in character as a consequence of reading them. But in their numbers and their all too palpable dishonesty they did the cause of serious biography great disservice, both by bringing the whole art into disrepute and by solidifying to the point of petrifaction the tradition of *de mortuis nil nisi bonum*.

The impulse to wrap even men with third-rate talents in the meretricious dignity of Manchester cloth togas was a manifestation of the widespread confusion and debasement of values which marked the bourgeois domination of Victorian England. A closely related phenomenon was the coarsening of social grace into that towering virtue of a self-conscious middle class, Gentility. The Augustans' aversion to what they called "the vulgar," their insistence on personal decorum, acquired in the new century the solemnity of widespread social sanction. When it reached its full powers after the Regency, Gentility (better known, in certain applications, as Prudery), required that polite literature treat whole areas of human experience with the utmost circumspection, if, indeed, it acknowledged their existence at all. Sex was only one of a number of subjects which, as we shall presently note, embarrassed the biographer as much as it did the novelist. For over biography, as over fiction, ruled the editors, publishers, and circulating-library proprietors, who were, in turn, both the reflectors of, and in most cases unquestioning subscribers to, the spirit of the age. Thackeray's famous complaint in the preface to *Pendennis*—"Since the author of *Tom Jones* was buried, no writer of fiction among us has been permitted to depict to his utmost power a MAN. . . . Society will not tolerate the Natural in our Art"—was just as applicable to the art of biography in his age. Treated forthrightly and objectively, *l'homme naturel* was no more fitting a subject for biography than he was for fiction.[1]

Another aspect of the bourgeois atmosphere of Victorian times was the near-veneration of home and family as social institutions beyond price. A consequence of the same social force that led many popular Victorian novelists to take up domestic themes was the persistent drift of emphasis from the public to the private life of biographical subjects. Writing in 1866, E. S. Dallas defined the phenomenon quite clearly:

> A novel is but a fictitious biography, and in the popularity of the novel we have to deal with precisely the same movement and sign of the times as we find in biography. Our interest in the private life of our fellow-men has been developed into a system, and there is nothing in the way of study which people seem now to desire so much as to peep into the house of a neighbour, to watch his ways, and to calculate the ups and downs of fortune. . . . [There] is a gossipping propensity in human nature which any man of sense can keep within bounds, but which none of us can eradicate. To this gossipping sense the novelist appeals. A novel may be described as gossip etherealized, family talk generalized.

It may or may not have been true that, as some observers insisted, this increased propensity for gossip in literature could be blamed

---

[1] When Southey reprinted "in popular form" (in his life of the poet) Cowper's own account of his religious mania, critics attacked him for giving publicity to a subject that had hitherto been kept decently obscure. It was extremely unwise, they said, "to allow such narratives as that of Cowper to form a common subject of reading for the young and the enthusiastic, especially if their minds are in any degree disposed to religious excitement." (*Edinburgh Review*, LXIII [1836], 349.) Such perils might attach equally to the discussion of any other subject likely to disturb the immature psyche. Thus the possible presence of the impressionable young in the audience of a book designed for adult readers was a circumstance that the biographer, like the novelist, had always to keep in mind.

on the ever-growing number of women readers. But the presence
of women assuredly made itself felt in the pronounced tendency
toward domesticity and antiheroism in literature, as in the other
arts. "Woman," Dallas asserted, "peculiarly represents the private
life of the race. Her ascendancy in literature must mean the
ascendancy of domestic ideas, and the assertion of the individual,
not as a hero, but as a family man—not as a heroine, but as an
angel in the house. The individual as a great public character
withers. The individual as a member of society and in all his
private relations grows in importance." The tendency toward the
writing of "history seen as a domestic chronicle" that Mario Praz
found endemic in nineteenth-century British art characterized
biography as well as the novel. But whereas the burgeoning of
the domestic novel was welcomed rather than deplored, the parallel tendency in biography intensified concern over the deepening threat the vogue of biography offered to individual, or family,
privacy.

It is not hard to understand, therefore, why, if the frequency
and vehemence with which serious periodicals took up the subject in the Victorian era is any indication, the British threshold of
pain was at its lowest point in history. Never had sensibilities
been so easily offended; never had people's right to privacy—
especially the right of the celebrated, whose privacy was most
imperiled—been so insisted upon. The implication of the new
popular journalism was that no family of dignity or substance had
any right to exclusive knowledge of its own affairs. And biography, insofar as it sought to be candid and revealing, was as much
to be feared as the impertinence and disclosures of gossip writers.
Since total opposition was neither practicable nor desirable, the
writing of biography had to be controlled, its candor and revelations replaced by studied discretion.

Whatever small chance there might otherwise have been that
the subject would be treated with frankness shrank with the
diminishing interval between death and biographical entomb-
ment. "The newspapers," commented Edmund Gosse a hundred
years after the debasement of biography into a funerary ritual
began, "now combine the one announcement with the other: 'We

regret to state that the eminent taxidermist, Viscount Beeswax, passed away after a long illness at ten o'clock last night. The funeral will take place on Friday next, and the biography will be undertaken by the Bishop of Bodkin, a life-long friend of the remains.'" The rules which governed the Bishop of Bodkin and all biographers of the recently deceased were devised in response to the sort of difficulties Dr. Johnson had met when he reached Addison in his progress through the roster of seventeenth- and eighteenth-century poets: "As the process of these narratives is now bringing me among my contemporaries, I begin to feel myself *walking upon ashes under which the fire is not extinguished,* and coming to the time of which it will be proper rather to say *nothing that is false, than all that is true.*"

Boswell, in dealing with Johnson, had walked upon the coals as boldly as if he were shod with asbestos—though his *Life* would have been welcomed with fewer reservations had he been more sensitive to the warmth still lingering in the ashes. His successors, on the contrary, picked their way as cautiously as if they were shod with tissue paper. Biographers of men who yesterday were living idols of the nation's readers found it ever more incumbent upon them "rather to say nothing that is false, than all that is true." The necessity of averting offense required them to consider family and public opinion at every stage of their work. Where the truth was unpleasant—where it would shed discredit upon the subject himself, or irritate the reader's sensibilities—it had to be suppressed, or glossed over with elaborate circumlocution, or, if worse came to worst, admitted and then eloquently (and, if necessary, sophistically) extenuated.

Editing the letters of Dante Gabriel Rossetti to William Allingham, Birkbeck Hill found a letter in which Rossetti, describing an interview with Tennyson, "related one or two incidents symptomatic of the more off-hand or unconventional shades of the poet's demeanour"—shades totally unreported in Hallam Tennyson's biography of his father. Hill and Allingham's widow agreed that the letter should be shown to Hallam. Back came an urgent, uncompromising answer: the letter, if printed in its entirety, might be "the death" of Tennyson's widow. So the whole offending section was suppressed. "The incident," remarked William Michael Rossetti, "shows how powerful were the family-feelings in opposition to the publishing of anything which might seem at all to qualify the finer and more dignified traits in the Poet Laureate's character," and it is duplicated a thousand times over in the annals of literary biography in the last century and a half.

Often, it is true, biographers were not given access in the first place to materials that would have made possible a candid portrait of their subject. Owners of letters written by a celebrated man or woman may have refused to let the biographer see them; many portions of George Eliot's correspondence, for example, were withheld from her husband, John Walter Cross, when he was preparing his life of her "as related in her letters." Others to whom biographers applied carefully inked or snipped out sections of letters before handing them over, as did certain of Sir Walter Scott's correspondents when they responded to Lockhart's request for documents. Some of the blame customarily visited upon Victorian biographers should, for the sake of more accurate justice, be redirected toward the people who frustrated them in their quest for information.

Even obscure poets, as Keats was for several decades after his death, were protected. In 1848, after printing a letter in which Keats alluded to Fanny Brawne (but not by name), Richard Monckton Milnes remarked:

> the lady . . . inspired Keats with the passion that only ceased with his existence. Where personal feelings of so profound a character are concerned, it does not become the biographer, in any case, to do more than to indicate their effect on the life of his hero, and where the memoir so nearly approaches the times of its subject that the persons in question, or, at any rate, their near relations, may be still alive, it will at once be felt how indecorous would be any conjectural analysis of such sentiments, or, indeed, any more intrusive record of them than is absolutely necessary for the comprehension of the real man.[2]

This was the attitude, shared by most Victorians, which made the

---

[2] One must remember, of course, that Fanny Brawne was still living.

publication of Keats's letters to Fanny, a generation later, so profoundly shocking an event: "an act of sacrilege to the memory of
Keats," as one reviewer called it, and another, "this hideous
breach of the sanctities of life."

Although there was general agreement that great discretion
was to be observed in writing every life of a contemporary figure,
the exact demarcation between the tellable and untellable was
never fixed. In the case of literary biography the discussion was
complicated by the problem of biography's critical relevance. Did
a writer's personal character and the circumstances of his private
life have any real bearing on what he wrote? In those pre-
Freudian days it could be argued that a great deal of personal
detail was totally irrelevant to a discussion of the man as artist;
the only question was, how much *was* relevant. A powerful section of critical opinion insisted that only a narrowly circumscribed portion of a writer's life, the part that clearly and unequivocally had a bearing on his published work, was open to
biographical scrutiny. At mid-century a writer in *Blackwood's
Magazine,* an organ that traditionally advocated a great degree of
biographical reticence, asserted:

> . . . in compiling the life of a poet, we maintain that a literary
> executor has purely a literary function to perform. Out of the mass
> of materials which he may fortuitously collect, his duty is to select
> such portions as may illustrate the public doings of the man: he
> may, without transgressing the boundaries of propriety, inform us
> of the circumstances which suggested the idea of any particular
> work, the difficulties which were overcome by the author in the
> course of its composition, and even exhibit the correspondence
> relative thereto. These are matters of literary history which we may
> ask for, and obtain, without any breach of the conventional rules of
> society. Whatever refers to public life is public, and may be
> printed; whatever refers solely to domestic existence is private, and
> ought to be held sacred.

Thus the manifold cultural forces that made for reticence in biography at large were supported in literary biography by the critical doctrine that the poet and the man were separable, the one
open to, the other exempt from, public curiosity.

Against this atmosphere of biographical obscurantism Carlyle raged:

> How delicate, decent is English biography, bless its mealy mouth! A Damocles' sword of *Respectability* hangs for ever over the poor English life-writer (as it does over poor English Life in general), and reduces him to the verge of paralysis. Thus it has been said, "there are no English lives worth reading except those of Players, who by the nature of the case have bidden Respectability good-day." The English biographer has long felt that if in writing his Man's Biography, he wrote down anything that could by possibility offend any man, he had written wrong. The plain consequence was that, properly speaking, no biography whatever could be produced.

Carlyle was, in this respect, like his own favorite figure of the Ishmaelite, howling in the wilderness. Few men of his age shared, except as an abstract proposition, his conviction that the principle of biography should be *de mortuis nil nisi* VERUM; it was an ideal more honored by quotation than observance. Ironical as it seems today, when the great burden of complaint against nineteenth-century biography is exactly Carlyle's, that it told too little, in its own time, despite all its suppressions, it was recurrently criticized for telling too much. The term *voyeur* had not yet entered the language, but voyeurism is exactly what, according to a large and influential school of opinion, afflicted many biographers and their readers. In his *Voltaire*, a study of intellectual independence if there ever was one, John Morley, of all Victorian biographers the most liberal in the general bent of his opinions, paused to utter a thoroughly Victorian sigh: "Alas, why after all should men, from Moses downwards, be so cheerfully ready to contemplate the hinder parts of their divinities?"

· 2 ·

In 1838, when Carlyle fulminated against biographical mealy-mouthedness, his cause, forlorn at best under prevailing conditions, was already lost. One event after another had aroused educated public opinion against the prevalence of scandalmongering, and prompted some living authors (partly, one supposes, as an intimation of the course they expected their survivors to follow) to build walls of granite around their own personal affairs. In 1828, as part of the free-for-all squabbling over Byron's grave, Leigh Hunt published a book called *Lord Byron and Some of His Contemporaries,* the first volume of which was devoted largely to a recital of his grievances against the dead idol, with fluent revelations of Byron's personal habits. Hunt, whose own frailties, literary tastes, and political opinions had made him, in certain powerful quarters, one of the most ridiculed and despised men of his time, had every reason to expect the skies to fall on him, and they did. Among other visitations of wrath from Byron's partisans, he was treated to forty blistering pages of invective in *Blackwood's Magazine,* and these lines, by Thomas Moore, in *The Times:*

> Next week will be published (as "Lives" are the rage)
>   The whole Reminiscences, wondrous and strange,
> Of a small puppy-dog that lived once in the cage
>   Of the late noble lion at Exeter 'Change.
>
> Though the dog is a dog of the kind they call "sad,"
>   'Tis a puppy that much to good-breeding pretends;
> And few dogs have such opportunities had
>   Of knowing how lions behave—among friends.
>
> How that animal eats, how he moves, how he drinks,
>   Is all noted down by this Boswell so small;
> And 'tis plain, from each sentence, the puppy-dog thinks
>   That the lion was no such great things after all.
>
> Though he roared pretty well—this the puppy allows—
>   It was all, he says, borrowed—all second-hand roar;
> And he vastly prefers his own little bow-wows
>   To the loftiest war-note the lion could pour.
>
> 'Tis, indeed, as good fun as a Cynic could ask,
>   To see how this Cockney-bred setter of rabbits
> Takes gravely the Lord of the Forest to task,
>   And judges of lions by puppy-dog habits.
>
> Nay, fed as he was (and this makes it a dark case)
>   With sops every day from the lion's own pan,
> He lifts up his leg at the noble beast's carcase,
>   And—does all a dog, so diminutive, can.

> However, the book's a good book, being rich in
>   Examples and warnings to lions high-bred,
> How they suffer small mongrelly curs in their kitchen,
>   Who'll feed on them living, and foul them when dead.

Seven years later, a Yankee puppy dog named N. P. Willis invaded the richly carpeted domains of London society, with the results already noted. Within another year or two Lockhart, who had a main hand in chastising Willis for his journalistic indiscretions, was himself called to task for being insufficiently mealy-mouthed in his life of Scott. If, as seemed horribly certain, the biography of the future was to be a monstrous assemblage of servants' quarters gossip and the contents of one's desk drawers, everything possible should be done to forestall it.

This was one of the topics on which Carlyle and his friend Tennyson, smoking their pipes up the kitchen chimney in Cheyne Row, failed to see eye to eye. Once arrived at an eminence on which he was vulnerable to biographical attention, the poet was gossip's implacable foe. In March, 1849, even before he was made Laureate, he congratulated an unnamed poet on having failed to win fame, thus escaping the posthumous indignity of a "life and letters":

> And you have miss'd the irreverent doom
>   Of those that wear the Poet's crown;
>   Hereafter, neither knave nor clown
> Shall hold their orgies at your tomb.
>
> For now the Poet cannot die,
>   Nor leave his music as of old,
>   But round him ere he scarce be cold
> Begins the scandal and the cry:
>
> "Proclaim the faults he would not show:
>   Break lock and seal: betray the trust:
>   Keep nothing sacred: 'tis but just
> The many-headed beast should know."
>
> Ah shameless! for he did but sing
>   A song that pleased us from its worth;
>   No public life was his on earth,
> No blazon'd statesman he, nor king.

((157

> He gave the people of his best:
>> His worst he kept, his best he gave.
>> My Shakespeare's curse on clown and knave
> Who will not let his ashes rest![3]

"What business has the public to want to know all of Byron's wildnesses?" Tennyson demanded on another occasion. "He has given them fine work, and they ought to be satisfied. It is all for the sake of babble." "He said," wrote his Freshwater friend Julia Cameron, "he believed every crime and every vice in the world were connected with the passion for autographs and anecdotes and records,—that the desiring anecdotes and acquaintance with the lives of great men was treating them like pigs to be ripped open for the public; that he knew he himself should be ripped open like a pig; that he thanked God Almighty with his whole heart and soul that he knew nothing, and that the world knew nothing, of Shakespeare but his writings; and that he thanked God Almighty that he knew nothing of Jane Austen, and that there were no letters preserved either of Shakespeare's or of Jane Austen's, that they had not been ripped open like pigs."

Browning was, if anything, even more fanatically opposed to biographical exposure than Tennyson. His attitude toward personal publicity is embodied in his biting poem "House" (1876):

> I have mixed with a crowd and heard free talk
>> In a foreign land where an earthquake chanced:
> And a house stood gaping, nought to baulk
>> Man's eye wherever he gazed or glanced.

> The whole of the frontage shaven sheer,
>> The inside gaped: exposed to day,
> Right and wrong and common and queer,
>> Bare, as the palm of your hand, it lay.

> The owner? Oh, he had been crushed, no doubt!
>> "Odd tables and chairs for a man of wealth!

---

[3] These lines are thought to have been called forth by the publication of Monckton Milnes's life of Keats in the preceding year. Another, longer poem on the same theme is Tennyson's "The Dead Prophet," published in 1885 and possibly referring to the furor over Froude's biography of Carlyle. Tennyson, however, for whatever it is worth, denied having any particular prophet in mind.

What a parcel of musty old books about!
   He smoked,—no wonder he lost his health!

"I doubt if he bathed before he dressed.
   A brasier?—the pagan, he burned perfumes!
You see it is proved, what the neighbours guessed:
   His wife and himself had separate rooms."

Friends, the goodman of the house at least
   Kept house to himself till an earthquake came:
'Tis the fall of its frontage permits you feast
   On the inside arrangement you praise or blame.

Outside should suffice for evidence:
   And whoso desires to penetrate
Deeper, must dive by the spirit-sense—
   No optics like yours, at any rate!

When, as happened several times in the years after her death, Browning was confronted with the publication, proposed or actually accomplished, of letters from his wife, he had great trouble controlling his wrath. He did his best: "Once," he wrote his friend Isabella Blagden after Thornton Hunt had printed a letter "full of intimate talk about our child's illness," "I should have been angry enough—now, I seem hardly to care after the first feeling of disgust and annoyance—it is as if some clownish person had thrown open the door of a bathing-machine in which I was undressing— the whole company on the beach stare & probably laugh—& a very young lady would be mortified enough." But a year later, writing to Miss Blagden again, he made no such show of indifference: "what I suffer in feeling the hands of these blackguards . . . what I undergo with their paws in my very bowels, you can guess & God knows!"[4]

---

[4] Looking down from the gold bar of heaven, Elizabeth Barrett Browning unquestionably would have applauded his ferocious efforts to guard her posthumous privacy. It was what she wished—*in her own case*. But she had also written him before their marriage: "We should all be ready to say that if the secrets of our daily lives and inner souls may instruct other surviving souls, let them be open to men hereafter, even as they are to God now. . . . Not that I do not intimately understand the shrinking back from the idea of publicity on any terms—not that I would not myself destroy papers of mine which were sacred to *me* for personal reasons—but then I never would call this natural weakness, virtue—nor would I, as a teacher of the public, announce it and attempt to justify it as an example to other minds and acts, I hope." (*Letters of Robert Browning and Elizabeth Barrett Barrett* [New York, 1898], I, 481.)

The most drastic attempt men of letters made to frustrate prospective biographers was the deliberate destruction of their private papers. Tennyson expressed the feelings of many of his fellow writers when he told Gladstone in 1883:

> I heard of an old lady the other day to whom all the great men of her time had written. When Froude's *Carlyle* came out, she rushed up to her room, and to an old chest there wherein she kept their letters, and flung them into the fire. "They were written to me," she said, "not to the public!" and she set her chimney on fire, and her children and grandchildren ran in—"The chimney's on fire!" "Never mind!" she said, and went on burning. I should like to raise an altar to that old lady, and burn incense upon it.

Acting on this principle, Tennyson had his son Hallam burn his love letters to Emily Sellwood, his future wife—"many passages [of] which," remarked Hallam with tantalizing blandness, when he spoke of their destruction in the *Memoir*, "would show the intensity of feeling" his father experienced. The Browning love letters, however, escaped this fate. Although Browning carefully burned his letters to his father and family, he treasured in an inlaid box all those he had exchanged with Elizabeth Barrett, and, surprisingly, in view of his passion for privacy, told his son shortly before he died, "There they are, do with them as you please when I am dead and gone!" Pen Browning published them in 1898, and the ensuing public debate whether or not he should have exposed to the world the intimacies of his parents' courtship was further proof, if any were needed, that the issue of biographical reticence was still as vital as ever.

Fear of inappropriate revelations laid its eradicating hand, sooner or later, on the papers of virtually every man and woman with literary fame or even literary associations. Cassandra Austen destroyed portions of her sister Jane's correspondence. In 1869 Swinburne told William Michael Rossetti he had heard that the step-daughter of Shelley's friend, Mrs. Gisborne, had burned two boxes full of Shelley papers; and the history of Swinburne's own letters, as the editor of the definitive edition observes, "seems like a series of holocausts." His mentor and friend, Benjamin Jowett, directed that all the letters he received, among them many from

Swinburne, be destroyed after his death, and all of the poet's letters to his family were burned after his cousin's death, by her stern order. In 1880, when John Addington Symonds was dismantling his old home at Clifton, he destroyed not only his own correspondence but that of his whole family from the seventeenth century onward, including the papers of an old Independent minister who had known Bunyan and his father's correspondence with John Sterling, Francis Newman, F. D. Maurice, and Jowett. "It was rather pretty," wrote Symonds, "to see Catherine [his wife] and my four children all engaged in tearing up the letters of a lifetime. We sat on the floor, and the dead leaves grew above us mountains high." Still, he confessed, "I feel rather like a criminal to have burned the tares and wheat together of this harvest."

When he moved his possessions to his villa at Gad's Hill in 1860, Dickens, "shocked," as he said, "by the misuse made of the private letters of public men," burned in a field behind the house his accumulated correspondence of twenty years—thousands upon thousands of letters and other documents—and two of his boys roasted onions in the ashes. The smoke was so thick that, according to Dickens, it was the cause of the heavy rain which fell as he finished the task. "Would to God," he cried, "that every letter I had ever written was on that pile!" So, Leon Edel has suggested, might Henry James have exclaimed when, behind his house at Rye, he made a bonfire of the letters he had received for forty years. It was a cry that Hardy would have echoed at Max Gate, as, in the course of selecting papers he wished to use in his (unacknowledged) autobiography, he burned everything he did not wish to survive him.[5]

The frequent publication of personal papers which did escape the flames—acts regarded in many quarters as unforgivable lapses of discretion—had the effect of strengthening owners of other papers in their resolve to guard the secrets of both the dead and the surviving, and so doomed further batches of docu-

---

[5] Another, supposedly less common, means of checkmating biographers was to write letters so dull as to ensure their being burned. This, at least, was the excuse Wordsworth is reported to have offered for the frequent dreariness of his own letters. (R. Ellis Roberts, *Samuel Rogers and His Circle* [London, 1910], p. 49.)

ments to the fire. The appearance of Keats's letters to Fanny
Brawne, Thomas and Jane Carlyle's unrestrained letters to each
other, and the Brownings' love letters—to cite but three out of
many widely censured episodes in the later nineteenth century—
must have resulted in the destruction of countless letters written
by other literary figures.[6]

Occasionally, before setting a match to the originals, Victorian paper-burners more or less obliged posterity by making an
expurgated transcript. When his aged sister prepared to destroy
the diary of Dr. Polidori, Byron's physician and traveling companion and a great-uncle of Dante Gabriel, William, and Chris-
tina Rossetti, she copied it out, but omitted the "improper" passages. One of them, according to William, who saw the original
before it went into the fire, recorded of Byron's arrival at Ostend,
the first stop on his pilgrimage of exile, that "as soon as he
reached his room, Lord Byron fell like a thunderbolt upon the
chambermaid."

But whether anything was salvaged or not, the odor of burning papers permeates the literary history of the nineteenth century: the true-born Englishman's response to the singular new

[6] It was bad enough to contemplate the stripping away of privacy that
publication of a man's papers entailed; it was even worse when the mercenary
element was added. Coventry Patmore, going through his father's effects, found
some unpublished letters from Hazlitt. Recognizing that they belonged to the
series from which Hazlitt had composed his *Liber Amoris,* he sent them to
Hazlitt's son to be destroyed, as "memorials of his father's erotic weakness."
Many years later, to his consternation, Patmore found that the younger Hazlitt
had nonetheless preserved them and left them to his own son, who eventually
sold them for publication. Writing to *The Times* in protest, Patmore remarked,
"I am sorry now that I did not myself burn the whole mass of morbid trash,
instead of intrusting the unpleasant secret of Hazlitt's mental and moral disease
to the tender mercies of his heirs and administrators." (Basil Champneys,
Memoirs and Correspondence of Coventry Patmore [London, 1900], I, 20–21.)
Sometimes it was an unfortunate experience with avarice, rather than any
desire to guard its secrets, that resulted in a family's closing its archives to
would-be biographers. W. J. Evelyn, for instance, a descendant of the seventeenth-
century diarist, had good reason to turn away inquirers from the ancestral house
at Wotton. An autograph collector who had helped William Bray edit the
diary for publication in 1818 also helped himself to scores of John Evelyn's
books and hundreds of his letters, and W. J. Evelyn was forced to spend many
hundreds of pounds to get back his own property when the purloiner's collection
was sold thirty years later. (W. G. Hiscock, "John Evelyn's Library at Christ
Church," *Times Literary Supplement,* April 6, 1951, p. 220.)

democratic axiom that one man's business is, if the public wills it, everybody's business. In this light, the climax of Henry James's *The Aspern Papers* becomes symbolic indeed—symbolic of the end of so many modern biographical quests:

> "What shall you do—where shall you go?" I asked [Miss Tina— niece of the woman James modeled after Jane Clairmont, who once had been Byron's mistress].
>
> "Oh I don't know. I've done the great thing. I've destroyed the papers."
>
> "Destroyed them?" I waited.
>
> "Yes; what was I to keep them for? I burnt them last night, one by one, in the kitchen."
>
> "One by one?" I coldly echoed it.
>
> "It took a long time—there were so many."[7]

· 3 ·

Victorian biographers would not have been Victorians had not most of them sympathized with, and been governed by, the current passion for privacy. Yet there were difficulties. Leslie Stephen opposed the publication of intimate personal documents as a general rule. When the Browning love letters were printed, he suffered from "the feeling that one is looking over the shoulders of the writers at a moment when they would certainly have shown the door to an intruder." But his "instinctive repulsion"

---

[7] At the same time, widespread though the destruction of papers undoubtedly was, not every report of a grand holocaust of a literary man's papers is necessarily accurate. Once in a while a batch of such manuscripts, reputedly burned, proves to be still extant; Fanny Burney's diary, for example, was thought to have perished in the fire that destroyed her cottage in 1919, but it is now in the Berg Collection at the New York Public Library. To assert that so-and-so's letters *had* been burned was the easiest way, if not always the most truthful, to dispose of inconvenient inquiries from prospective biographers: "Dear Lady Northmore, I've hunted high and low and have nothing whatever. My husband evidently, before his death, destroyed everything. I'm *so* sorry— I should have liked so much to help you." James's ironic story "The Abasement of the Northmores" knowledgeably illuminates the behind-the-scenes motives and maneuverings that produced so many life-and-letters volumes. The fiction of the destroyed papers had its uses in the general pattern of ploys and counter-stratagems. But lightly invented fictions have a way of hardening into unchallenged traditions, and this is what modern scholars, hot after the unpublished document, must take into account.

clashed head on with the undeniable attraction the letters possessed; and the best he could do was to conclude that "the case is one of those in which the total result is so impressive and edifying that the ordinary rule may be disregarded"—hoping at the same time that no precedent was being set, with intolerable abuses sure to follow. Shelley's biographer, Edward Dowden, was torn between what he called his "superstitious veneration of written words, as if they were living things," and the attitude of Wordsworth, Browning, and Tennyson; but in the end he could, like St. Francis, "praise God for my brother *Fire*, and think cremation and a few white ashes a noble close and consummation for what has been most living and most dear."

> The accident of ink and paper [he argued] confers no title to perpetuity. Nor need we fear that the fountain of life will run dry and that men will want our little cisterns. . . . One's thoughts and feelings are so very fragile and need so much the interpretation of the living person to do them justice, that they may easily be misused and ruined and do harm instead of good. . . . I applaud the prudence and discretion of choosing what we think best for the world and exercising a strict discretion, leaning towards the side of leaving little rather than much.

Whatever their personal feelings on the matter, in practice biographers were obligated to keep on the safe side of contemporary conventions. For one thing, there was political and religious orthodoxy to contend with. Burns's biographers had to deal in the most circumspect fashion with the democratic opinions of the People's Poet, in order to sweeten his memory in an era when to many people "democratic" connoted all that is implied today by "subversive" and "communistic." When Christopher Wordsworth compiled the memoir of his late uncle, he skimmed over the crucial first twenty-five years in less than a hundred pages, ignoring the crucial drama of Wordsworth's early sympathy with the French Revolution and his temporary acceptance of Godwinian atheism. Did Wordsworth ever, as some averred, "lapse into scepticism"? "No!" thundered the canon of Westminster. "His early education, his love of the glories and beauties of creation protected him from any approach to that." Because all the incriminating passages in his poetry and private letters were suppressed, the Wordsworth interred in those two heavy volumes proved never to have been troubled by a thought inimical to church or state: he was, indeed, a poet in a shovel hat. No wonder that the *Quarterly Review* complained that "in his fear of plucking forbidden fruit," Christopher "has mainly served up the leaves." No wonder too that when the American scholar George McLean Harper came to write what was until lately the most authoritative biography of Wordsworth, he went to the other extreme and overstressed the poet's early radicalism.

Everywhere one looked, there were what the Victorians called "painful topics" or "some aspects of life and character too sacred to be here put down." The skeleton in the closet of Somerset Maugham's Edward Driffield was merely the fictional counterpart of scores of such skeletons in the preceding hundred years. Many of them were common knowledge, but to crystallize literary circle gossip in the hard perpetuity of print was a step no responsible nineteenth-century literary biographer was prepared to take. For easily understandable reasons, family troubles, especially when they involved moral dereliction, were either referred to in terms so oblique as to be inscrutable or suppressed altogether. Such was the case with the extraordinary number of nineteenth-century authors' children who came to bad ends or otherwise proved unworthy of their heritage. The Brownings' adored son Pen left unfulfilled the hopes of his father, who nevertheless was loyal and affectionate to him until the end, finding in his modest success as a painter some compensation for his failure at Oxford, his indolence, and his expensive and somewhat sporty tastes. Lockhart's old age was darkened by the conduct of his son, Walter Scott, who left Cambridge for the army, got involved in "evil company," became the constant prey of moneylenders and the defendant in lawsuits, and eventually died in delirium at a Versailles hotel. Several of Dickens' sons were keen disappointments to their father—who, it must be said in their defense, was not the most conscientious or understanding parent. But little or nothing of these domestic disappointments and worries, which nowadays we consider an integral part of a man's life story, found its way into contemporary print.[8]

Another painful subject that called for all the tact the biographers could muster was insanity. The early biographies of Cowper are curious both for what they say and what they fail to say. In his letters and his autobiographical fragment the poet left a harrowingly detailed narrative of his hallucinations and other mental agonies. But Hayley skirted the subject as widely as he could:

> The misfortune of mental derangement is a topic of such awful delicacy, that I consider it as the duty of a biographer rather to sink, in tender silence, than to proclaim, with circumstantial, and offensive, temerity, the minute particulars of a calamity, to which all human beings are exposed, and perhaps in proportion as they have received from nature those delightful, but dangerous, gifts, a heart of exquisite tenderness, and a mind of creative energy.

Which is a decorative way indeed of saying (again in Hayley's words) that Cowper suffered from a "depressive malady" and "hypochondriacal dejection."

There was much more justification for silence or euphemism, of course, when forthright allusion could cause distress to the living. Those who described Wordsworth in his later years at Rydal Mount ransacked the contemporary vocabulary of hushed expressions to convey the fact that his sister Dorothy had become a helpless lunatic. Even today, the exact nature of the serious neurasthenic illness which repeatedly sent Tennyson to "hydropathic institutions" in the middle 1840's is unknown, because his son—whose own knowledge perhaps was meager—alluded so fleetingly to the occurrence in the official biography. Serjeant Talfourd in his first sketch of Lamb's life (1837) omitted all reference to Mary's recurrent madness and her killing of her mother

---

[8] For a vivid illustration of the difference between Victorian reticence on such matters and modern candor, see Peter Green's *Kenneth Grahame* (1959). The story of Grahame's miserable marriage and the visiting of the parents' sins of omission and commission on their ill-starred son Alastair, as recounted unsparingly but compassionately by Mr. Green, reads like something out of Ibsen —or Euripides.

during one such attack.[9] Only after Mary's death did he print (in his *Final Memorials of Charles Lamb*) passages in Charles's letters that alluded to this overwhelming tragedy of their lives.

But equally troublesome to biographers, in Lamb's case as in numerous others, was the problem of drink. Historically, since at least the age of Dionysius, poetry and wine have been inseparable; but in the increasingly severe moral climate of nineteenth-century England, in which rubicund three-bottle men, holdovers from Fielding's day, were giving way to temperance orators, the association was a poignant embarrassment. The inescapable truth was that Lamb often got drunk, as, given the circumstances of his private life, he had considerable right to do. To concede this, while retaining intact the image of "gentle Elia" that was produced by one of the century's most successful exercises in sentimental mythmaking, challenged both the euphemistic and the sophistical skills of his biographers. Talfourd pussyfooted throughout: "Lamb grew warm as the conviviality of the evening advanced," he said at one point; at another, evenings with his newspaper friends "left poor Lamb with an aching head"; at still another, Lamb was guilty of "occasional deviations from the right line of sobriety," and Mary's face bore a "half humorous expression of resignation to inevitable fate, as he mixe[d] his second tumbler." Lamb's long-lived friend Barry Cornwall used the standard Victorian apology[1] when faced with evidence of frequent drunkenness on the part of one whom it would be unsuitable to call a drunkard: "The truth is," he said, "that a small quantity of

[9] Crabb Robinson's approval typified contemporary feeling on the touchy subject: Talfourd, he wrote in his diary on August 12, 1837, "has showed great judgment in the veil he has thrown over what ought not to be too palpable and intelligible." (*Henry Crabb Robinson on Books and Their Writers*, ed. Edith J. Morley [London, 1938], II, 533.)

[1] How standard it was can be appreciated only by those who have examined all the nineteenth-century biographies of literary devotees of Bacchus. Compare Dr. Beattie on Thomas Campbell: "With a temperament extremely excitable—a hospitality that bordered on profusion, he was too apt to be carried away by his feelings. In his endeavours to promote the hilarity of friends by the 'festive bowl' and brilliant conversation, he may have passed, at some 'witching hours,' the conventional limits; but it is well known to those with whom he lived in familiar intercourse, that a few glasses were too much for his irritable frame; and hence, what would have been only moderation in other men, was little better than excess in him." (*Life and Letters of Thomas Campbell* [London, 1850], II, 407. There are two more pages to the same effect.)

any strong liquid (wine, &c.) disturbed his speech, which at best was but an eloquent stammer. The distresses of his early life made him ready to resort to any remedy which brought forgetfulness; and he himself, frail in body and excitable, was very speedily affected." But Cornwall carried extenuation to the point of silliness when he apologized for Lamb's merely dropping into an inn: "If he now and then stopped for a minute at a rustic public house, tired with the excursive caprices of Dash [his dog] —beguiled perhaps by the simple attractions of a village sign—I hold him excusable for the glass of porter which sometimes invigorated him in his fatigue."

Although Lamb was perhaps more than a "social drinker," he was no sot; Richard Brinsley Sheridan was. Disappointed in his political ambitions and besieged by creditors, the mottle-faced former playwright was known in his later years to every member of the London night watch who stumbled over him in the gutter. But in the two large volumes of his biography of Sheridan, Thomas Moore (himself well known in his youth as a translator of the *Odes of Anacreon*) hinted only once or twice at this notorious weakness—on one occasion praising his "agreeableness and wit . . . (before the Rubicon of the cup was passed)."

By all odds the best publicized, most deprecated, and most ingeniously explained affection for the bottle was Burns's. It was impossible to suppress the fact that Burns drank; he had celebrated the pleasure of tippling not only in his letters but in a whole body of convivial lyrics that had swiftly become part of the Scottish national literature, and even if his bibulousness had not been so abundantly commemorated on paper, it lingered in the memory of his neighbors and companions.

This weakness and Burns's democratic opinions, mentioned earlier, were but two of the difficulties he left to his idolators. A third was his libertinism. To call him a cottage Casanova would probably be both too picturesque and too extravagant; had there been a survey of young males' sexual habits in the rural Scotland of Burns's time, his personal record would doubtless seem unremarkable. But because it had become as much a part of literary history as his drinking, biographers had to deal with it too, and in the very age when, in the official moral code, sexual irregularity had become a more heinous offense than blasphemy or treason. A detailed study of how Burns's numerous biographers dealt with the problem would provide useful instruction in the ethical spirit of the times and the way language could be bent in its service. Much could also be learned from comparing the early biographers' treatment of Burns's loves with their handling of Scott's and Byron's. It may well have been, as Burns insisted, that

> For a' that, an' a' that,
> Our toils obscure, an' a' that,
> The rank is but the guinea's stamp;
> The man's the gowd for a' that.

But when it came to public exposition and interpretation of a man's sexual life, "his ribband, star, an' a' that" made all the difference in the world. No detail of the ploughboy's miscellaneous fornications was left unrecorded, though in the most evasive of language, and with, on the part of his numerous sympathizers, the most elaborate attempts at apology. Confronted with the plain evidence of Burns's "glorying, and only glorying, in his shame" as the father of illegitimate children, Lockhart nevertheless wrote:

> When I consider his tender affection for the surviving members of his own family, and the reverence with which he ever regarded the memory of the father whom he had so recently buried, I cannot believe that Burns has thought fit to record in verse all the feelings which this exposure excited in his bosom. . . . His false pride recoiled from letting his jovial associates guess how little he was able to drown the whispers *of the still small voice;* and the fermenting bitterness of a mind ill at ease within itself, escaped . . . in the shape of angry sarcasms against others, who, whatever their private errors might be, had at least done him no wrong.

But when Lockhart turned to the premarital affections of another Scotsman, of much higher social rank (and his father-in-law to boot), he quickly adopted the orthodox Victorian position that some facets of a man's life are nobody's concern but his own. In speaking of Scott's youth, he allowed himself only the briefest admission that "in this season of hot and impetuous blood he may not have escaped quite blameless" and suppressed almost completely the story of Scott's devotion to Miss Belsches.

Akin in social dignity to Scott and in sexual indulgence to Burns, Byron presented a still different case. However severely the moralists might view them, his numerous liaisons were public knowledge, and they were, in any event, a perquisite of rank. Although in quoting Byron's letters he freely used asterisks to conceal names, inadmissible language, or overexplicit details, Moore gave his readers what was, for the time, a notably candid record of Byron's amours. But the curious relativity of his account throws significant light on contemporary British attitudes and, incidentally, complements Byron's own remarks on the topic in *Don Juan.* Moore suppressed material on Byron's premarital "affairs of gallantry" out of deference, as he said, "to that peculiar sense of decorum in this country, which marks the mention of such frailties as hardly a less crime than the commission of them." But once his narrative moved Byron out of England, "we have . . . shifted the scene to a region where less caution is requisite," and he promised his readers that henceforth he would "give, with but little suppression, the noble poet's letters relative to his Italian adventures." In other words, to the reader of 1830 the propriety of a sin depended on its locale. Illicit sexual adventures on English soil could not be dwelt on, indeed their existence might hardly be admitted, but the same indulgences in Italy might be freely discussed.

Moore may have congratulated himself on recognizing this odd distinction and, as a biographer, making the best of it. But he failed to anticipate (how could he have done so?) the high moral line taken by his reviewer in *Fraser's Magazine,* a periodical that wore the raiment of virtue seldom enough, and most unbecomingly when it did. The writer was outraged by Moore's "salacious" dwelling on Byron's "rejoicing in the low, vulgar, company of the lowest and most vulgar of the women of Venice."

> If no other consideration could have arrested his pen—Mr. Moore should at least have remembered that he had the chastity of his own marriage bed, and the chastity of his own daughters to

preserve, and that little or no benefit could be done to the morality
of his own household by the publication of stories which for copiousness of detail, and minuteness of delineation are not exceeded
by the amplest narratives in *Harriette Wilson.*

Byron would have relished that.

Moore's comparative forthrightness in describing Byron's life
with women contrasts strongly with the way he had earlier dealt,
or rather failed to deal, with Sheridan's philandering. The
dramatist-politician's well-known predilection for alien beds was
euphemized into "those triumphs out of the sphere of domestic
love, to which his vanity, perhaps, oftener than his feelings, im-
pelled him." The very extensiveness of Moore's description of
Mrs. Sheridan's illness and death and the widespread weeping
that ensued seems to have been designed to counteract the current notion, all too solidly grounded, of Sheridan as a confirmed
rake. "The vanity of talent," as Moore put it, may have seduced
him into infidelity, but his "seeking solace . . . in the endearments
of the children" after Elizabeth's death was proof enough of the
sincerity of his love for her. One may take the argument or leave
it, but Moore's earnest attempt at whitewashing the record of a
decidedly dissolute life is characteristic of the biographical practice of his time.

All the personal documents that biographers loaded into their
volumes had, naturally, to be scrutinized for giveaways. No
amount of soft-pedaling or suppression in the biographer's own
text would avail if the subject himself were allowed to blurt out
some unwelcome truth in a private letter quoted on the next page.
In addition to combing out indiscreet or otherwise inconvenient
statements of fact, the biographer had to delete or sharply mitigate phraseology that grated on the sensitive ears of his generation.[2] Biographies, like novels, were often read aloud by the fire-

[2] Some idea of the rise and decline of Victorian verbal prudery may be
had from the fortunes of a quaint episode in Goldsmith's life. Bishop Percy
recounted (1801) that while Goldsmith was writing in his squalid London room,
there appeared to him "a poor ragged little girl of very decent behaviour, . . .
who, dropping a curtsie, said, 'My mamma sends her compliments, and begs the
favour of you to lend her a chamber-pot full of coals.'" The chamber pot survived, in such forthright nomenclature, through Prior's, Forster's, and Irving's
biographies; but just as the latter appeared (1848–49), William Howitt prettied

side, and language that was forbidden to contemporary novelists could not be condoned in a private letter which the celebrity of its author thrust into print. Furthermore, to have permitted an outspoken author to have his say precisely as he said it would have been as culpable as revealing discreditable episodes or traits of character: it would have sent a network of cracks across the ideal image that readers wished to have preserved intact.

It was not a matter simply of reducing to innocuousness expressions involving a big, big D, though this was Thomas Noon Talfourd's principal concern when he printed his early collection of letters by Lamb, a man not averse to using robust expletives in private correspondence. The genteel taste which barred so many effective but "crude" words from polite discourse frowned upon informality in general. The spirit in which nineteenth-century biographers handled their subjects' letters was ordinarily that of William Mason, who, as long ago as 1775, had insisted on presenting his deceased friend Thomas Gray as "Scholar and Poet"—not an ordinary human being in everyday clothes—and therefore polished up the language of his private letters wherever it fell below the best literary standards. He corrected Gray's relaxed "don't" to "do not," his "had wrote" to "had written," his "oaf" to "simpleton" and his "brag" to "boast." "It is probable," as Edmund Gosse wrote, "that in his foolish heart Mason really did consider that he was respecting Gray in thus brushing his clothes and washing his hands for him before allowing the world to see him. He thought that a ruffled wig or a disordered shoe-tie would destroy his hero's credit with the judicious, and accordingly he removed all that was silly and natural from the letters." Although Mason's absurd fussiness was widely condemned in the nineteenth century, the contemporary amending pen kept busy. In 1809 Southey wrote to Scott, "I want to hear that you have conceived of another poem and are parturient." Forty years later, printing the letter, Sou-

---

the utensil into a simple "potful of coals," and Thackeray a few years later—having in mind, it is true, not readers but the family audiences at his lectures—dodged the issue by alluding to the receptacle without naming it: "that queer coal-scuttle we read of." By Austin Dobson's time, however (1888), it was again permissible to call a chamber pot a chamber pot.

they's son erased the whole indelicate metaphor and had his late father write instead, "I want to hear that you have planned another poem and commenced it." When J. W. Cross arranged the letters that constituted the substance of his biography of his late wife, George Eliot, he omitted or altered everything that might conflict with his desired portrait of the novelist as a high-minded woman who would not descend to occasional colloquialism or humor. When she wrote "It is raining horribly here—raining blue devils" he cut out "blue devils." He refused to allow her, posthumously, to speak of German ballet girls as "looking like butchers in chemises." Out went her remark "I am as thin as a medieval Christ," and her facetious report that "My hair is falling off; by next April I shall be quite bald and without money to buy a wig!" And when she said of some misplaced proofs, "I would rather have lost one of my toes," Cross converted the toes into fingers. The result was an image of George Eliot that was too unnaturally "respectable" even for Victorian taste; the novelist William Hale White, for example, protested that he utterly failed to detect in Cross's solemn pages the woman he remembered, "her hair over her shoulders, the easy chair half sideways to the fire, her feet over the arms, and a proof in her hands. . . ."

In striving so hard to develop and preserve an idealized version of their subjects, blue-penciling or adjusting all discordant details, biographers undoubtedly were being faithful to their own concept of their mission as well as to the expectations of most of their readers. One wonders, however, whether their subjects would always have approved. Many years before she even knew of Cross's existence, George Eliot wrote a friend: "I wish you would burn my letters when you have read them once through, and then . . . there would be no risk of a critical third pair of eyes getting a sight of them, which would certainly be a death blow to my reputation for gravity and wisdom—not that I am very careful in this matter—for this bump of cautiousness with which nature has furnished me is of very little use to me." Obviously she was aware of what in our day is called her "public image"; but what her husband-biographer overlooked was the distinctly humorous view she took of it. It is likely that among all the literary men and women who became the subjects of nineteenth-century biography, there were a number who would have been chagrined, to put it mildly, by the figure that after their death went by their name in the public consciousness.

· 4 ·

Thus wherever there was family pride to defend, or respectability to preserve or establish, or current ideals of conduct and philosophy to nourish by biographical example, the forces of suppression, distortion, and special pleading were at work. Probably the most determined campaign to substitute an imaginative reconstruction for the true man was the one waged in behalf of Shelley.

To convert the historical Shelley into a character fit to be idolized by the many Victorians who admired his poetry was a large order, but his doughty daughter-in-law almost succeeded. Jane, wife of Sir Percy Florence Shelley, was the widow of the Honorable Charles Robert St. John, second son of the third Viscount Bolingbroke: such resonant credentials must be recited, the better to understand her anxiety to make Shelley acceptable to her class of Victorian society. From Shelley's widow, her mother-in-law, she acquired the first outlines of an idealized portrait; for in her miscellaneous writings about the poet, Mary Shelley had spoken of him in the golden terms proper to any widow's recollection of her prematurely deceased husband. But Lady Shelley also inherited the painful fact that Shelley deserted his first wife, Harriet Westbrook, and lived adulterously with Mary, the despondent Harriet consequently drowning herself in the Serpentine. This, even more than his radical opinions on politics and religion, was the gravest charge against him. Accordingly, Lady Shelley dedicated herself to suppressing whatever facts had not yet been made public on the Harriet Westbrook affair and to putting the best possible construction on such of Shelley's deeds as were common knowledge.

All this seems to have been much more important to her than to her husband, who, far from being devoted to intellectual beauty, was a throwback to the sporting, country-gentleman type of his grandfather, Sir Timothy Shelley. He was the perfect model of the mid-Victorian dilettante, spending his total leisure pursuing his hobbies, which included photography, tricycling, and yachting. He owned, at one time or another, ten different steam yachts, and the same house which held the "Shelley shrine" also enclosed the private theater in which the poet's son and his friends dabbled in dramatics. All in all, Sir Percy was the sort of character whose modern habitat would be in the fiction of A. P. Herbert, P. G. Wodehouse, or the earlier Evelyn Waugh, and considering the lustrous name he bore, it is not surprising that people like Wilfrid Meynell found "something unsatisfactory about him." Their sense of fitness was disturbed by his genial habit of referring to the poet of *Prometheus Unbound* as "me old father."

While her husband cycled, yachted, and rang the curtain up and down in his snug playhouse, Lady Shelley was busy with the care and nurture of his father's reputation. Since most of the papers vital to a biography were in her hands, she was in a position to oversee and, if necessary, dictate the use to be made of them. Before she came on the scene, there had been a spate of books and articles about Shelley, all of them inaccurate and, in one way or another, injudicious. For one thing, they harped too much on Shelley's eccentricities and outright aberrations. Taken as a whole, they had generated a highly picturesque but unbalanced conception of what Shelley was really like. Her first major move was to entrust the writing of the first "authorized" biography to Shelley's old university friend, Thomas Jefferson Hogg. The result was a scandalous disaster. As soon as Hogg's first two volumes were published, she commanded the instant return of all the papers she had lent him. Apart from devoting more attention to his heavily facetious self than to Shelley, he had manipulated his documents so as to make what were, in fact, references to his own pursuit of Shelley's sister Elizabeth seem to allude to Shelley's coincidental interest in Harriet Grove. Wherever necessary, he drastically altered facts in order to justify his own conduct at Shelley's expense.[3]

Repudiating Hogg as the official biographer, Lady Shelley found a new gadfly to contend with: another old friend of Shelley, Thomas Love Peacock, who in a series of articles in *Fraser's Magazine* (1858-60) made too much, for her taste, of Shelley's peculiar conduct, and, worst of all, was loyal to the memory of Harriet Westbrook. In 1859, therefore, she printed a work called *Shelley Memorials*, designed to counteract Hogg's and Peacock's poisons by setting the record straight. She was especially zealous to show that Shelley's separation from his first wife was the result not of his elopement with Mary Godwin but of unfortunate circumstances in their marriage itself, not least of which was Harriet's own temperament; and, as always, Lady Shelley sought to exonerate her father-in-law from any responsibility for Harriet's death. Rumor, which has never been firmly contradicted, had it that the actual author of the *Memorials* was Richard Garnett, an official of the British Museum and a close friend of Sir Percy and Lady Shelley.

Most of Shelley's surviving friends bitterly resented her attempts to impose a reconstructed Shelley on the world; the old sea dog Trelawny, for example, commented that "all that know [her] abhor her." The book received press notices ranging from hollowly polite to hostile; they agreed, however, that an acceptable biography of Shelley was yet to be written. The Shelleys wished Garnett to undertake it, but he was too busy at the Museum. William Michael Rossetti would have done so, but he had the advantage or handicap (depending on which side one was on) of knowing the truth about the Harriet affair, as told by letters owned by a London bookdealer. In addition, Rossetti had integrity. "Nobody," he wrote Garnett, "is less desirous of paining Shelley's daughter[-in-law] than I am: but I cant be two things at once—I cant be to the public a biographer, and to the family a suppressor of published facts. Besides, I consider that the world,

---

[3] With all its faults (see below, page 217), the book is generally considered to be the most vivid and authentic first-hand portrait of the young Shelley. Hogg finished at least one more volume after the family withdrew its sanction and its papers. No one seems to know whether the manuscript still exists.

now nearly half a century after Shelley's death, has a full right to know whatever throws light upon HIM."[4]

Consequently, the memoir Rossetti prefixed to his edition of Shelley's poems (1870) was written independently of the family, and he was not invited to succeed Hogg as the poet's official biographer. Finally, in 1883, Lady Shelley appointed Edward Dowden, Professor of English Literature at Trinity College, Dublin, to the task: "equivalent in the literary world," he said, "to the offer of a Bishopric." Dowden worked hard for three years. In addition to the family papers placed at his disposal, he examined Shelley materials in many other hands—sometimes having to pay well for the privilege, as in the case of the haul Harry Buxton Forman had made from Jane Clairmont's estate.[5] Garnett was the much-vexed mediator between Dowden—an old friend—and the family; he submitted Dowden's manuscript to them, and they returned their objections through him. He watched Dowden walk a tight rope, attempting to consult Lady Jane's and Sir Percy's "susceptibilities" without being unfaithful to the Shelley of historical record. Once again the treatment of the separation was the crucial issue; diplomatically, Dowden wrote Garnett that "I understand how they must feel a special concern about this portion of the story and it is very desirable that our views should in the main coincide." Eventually they did, more or less; though his striving to maintain a judicious view resulted, inevitably, in the Shelleys' insistence on regarding him as an outright champion of Harriet. In 1886, "oppressed by the duty of considering all Lady Shelley's tender enthusiasms" and balancing them against the claims of Harriet's grandchildren, Dowden saw his two-volume work into print. "I should like nothing worse than that it should be supposed that I had in the slightest degree forfeited my inde-

[4] In 1878, long before numerous other combatants had entered the fray, John Addington Symonds, in his English Men of Letters life of Shelley (p. 186, note), indicated the extent to which the biographical study of Shelley had become a veritable bearpit: "Lady Shelley *v.* Hogg; Trelawny *v.* the Shelley family; Peacock *v.* Lady Shelley; Garnett *v.* Peacock; Garnett *v.* Trelawny; McCarthy [author of *Shelley's Early Life from Original Sources,* 1872] *v.* Hogg, &c, &c." It was one of the least edifying spectacles in the later Victorian literary scene.

[5] Forman's rival in this episode was the ancient mariner from Salem, Massachusetts, Captain Edward Silsbee, who sailed to Italy in quest of the aged Jane Clairmont and her relics of Byron and Shelley—an expedition that gave

pendence," Dowden had written Garnett. But the worst came to pass. Mark Twain, as spirited a defender of Harriet Shelley as her grandchildren, attacked the performance as "a literary cakewalk," Matthew Arnold deplored both Dowden's partisanship and his style, and to many twentieth-century critics of scholarly morality Dowden's has seemed a classic case of a biographer's knuckling under to the demands of his subject's family. Actually it was not that simple. Only by reading the letters Dowden wrote during the period of his travail to Garnett and to his future wife, Miss West, can the full delicacy both of the situation and of his solution be appreciated. Seldom, if ever, did he falsify, though he undoubtedly knew more than he set down. His chief sin was that of compromise. But since his was one of the stickiest positions into which a biographer was ever cast, it cannot be held too much against him.

The year before Dowden's book appeared, a prolific miscellaneous writer named John Cordy Jeaffreson published a 900-page pleading entitled, in anticipation of the modern "debunking" school, *The Real Shelley: New Views of the Poet's Life.* The object of Jeaffreson's corrective wrath was the romantic myth of Shelley which, he said, had been set afloat by the concerted efforts of the family, the numerous Shelley idolators outside it, and the "Shelleyan Socialists"—a term by which he meant neither economic nor political radicals, but advocates of "the pernicious social philosophy, that requires sound-hearted England to abolish marriage and replace it with the Free Contract." The book was unremittingly contentious from beginning to end. Jeaffreson was the prosecuting attorney, quivering with indignation, scorn, sarcasm, sophistry, and rhetoric; the defendant was the pale angel of the Boscombe Place shrine and the modernized *pietà*, who turned out to have been anything but admirable: an ungrateful son, "a

---

Henry James the *donnée* for *The Aspern Papers.* In the ensuing struggle for possession of the Clairmont papers, Silsbee had the initial advantage, since he was in Florence, indeed was living in her very house, when Jane died; Forman arrived two months later. On the other hand, Forman had cash to offer Jane's niece, whereas all Silsbee had was long-term notes. As a result, nearly all the spoils went to Forman, and Silsbee came away with a few relatively unimportant documents, which are now at Harvard. (Kenneth Neill Cameron, *Shelley and His Circle 1773–1822* [Cambridge, Mass., 1961], II, 910–913.)

bad husband to his first wife, and far from a faultless husband to his second," and a perennial liar (or, to use Jeaffreson's triple-negative phraseology, "The poet suffered from a deficiency of that repugnance to untruth which is the prime characteristic of English gentlemen").

The Real Shelley had a hostile reception; its author was branded a calumniator, slanderer, toad, bat, venomous snake, poisonous reptile, Thersites, and Caliban. Even though he performed a useful service in calling attention to the sentimental mythmaking that had obscured some of the hard truths about Shelley, on the whole he deserved what he got. His massive "case" against Shelley was so ill-tempered, niggling, and violently partisan—wherever Shelley's motivation was discussed, it was automatically given the worst construction—that it defeated its own purpose.

Nevertheless, its very appearance, together with the stir it caused, was symptomatic of the time.[6] The vehemence it both contained and evoked suggests the pitch to which biographical controversy could rise by the middle 1880's. At last the official and received versions of celebrated writers' lives and characters were beginning to be called into question. So far, so good: that is what is meant by scientific inquiry. But it was clearly impossible to proceed with the calm detachment that "the scientific spirit" implies. Men's emotions were too firmly committed on one side or another: an impressive measure of the depth to which the admiration of great men had ingrained itself into the Victorian temper and equally of how passionate were the feelings engendered in revulsion from it. The bitterness which biographical disputes aroused in the closing decades of the century—typified, as we shall see in Chapter Seven, by the vituperation that attended the Froude-Carlyle controversy—was no whit less than that stirred up some years earlier by theological furors like those over the heterodox *Essays and Reviews* and Bishop Colenso's critical ex-

---

[6] It was preceded by another two-volume exercise in casemaking from Jeaffreson's pen, *The Real Lord Byron* (1883). Though equally partisan (especially in behalf of Lady Byron), this was, unlike the Shelley book, not iconoclastic; rather, its purpose was, by frankly noticing the cracks in the statue, to divert attention from the feet of clay. Byron was a sinner, but not a monster.

amination of the Pentateuch. Just as, in those disputes, the simple issue of historical truth versus myth was enveloped in a dense, billowing cloud of religious feeling, so the various moral anxieties that had underlain both the creation and the criticism of biography in the past century came once more to the surface. The supreme problem was not so much what the whole truth really was as how much truth it was permissible for a biographer to tell.

CHAPTER VI

The Writing of Nineteenth-Century Literary Biography

✳

Eᴺɢʟɪsʜ biography in the nineteenth century was a rich but unstable compound of history, journalism, eulogy, inspiration, and materials suitable for the study of the mind. How far was it also a form of literary art?

Its examples ranged in size from the seven packed volumes of Lockhart's *Scott* to the pocket-sized monographs of the English Men of Letters series that Macmillan launched, under John Morley's editorship, in 1878.[1] Midway between them was the most

---

[1] The English Men of Letters series probably did more than any other single force to bring literary biography to the attention of a wide public. Among the contributors were Leslie Stephen, John Addington Symonds, Henry James, Anthony Trollope, Edward Dowden, Edmund Gosse, Austin Dobson, and G. K. Chesterton. An interesting sidelight on the fear of innovation in Victorian publishing circles—as well as the stigma attached to cheap books—is the fact that when the series was first planned, John Morley insisted that "for respectability's sake" it should include a volume by "*one* recognized divine": a condition fulfilled by Dean R. W. Church's writing on Spenser. (For a brief history of the series, see Charles Morgan, *The House of Macmillan* [New York, 1944], pp. 115–118.)

After it had been under way for four years, Swinburne described it to Gosse as "a most singularly unequal series—of which I should say that some volumes were about as bad as possible, others—perhaps more—very fairly creditable, and two or three about as good as they could be." (*The Swinburne Letters*, ed. Cecil Y. Lang [New Haven, 1959–62], IV, 281.) This judgment was also that of the reviewers. They welcomed some volumes, usually on the ground that the commission had called forth their respective authors' best powers. But the note of condescension, if not outright disapproval, normally was much stronger. Most of the reasons given were valid: the books were unhappily characteristic of their era, with its passion for predigested, condensed information and its youths' need for quick aids on examination eve; their authors were, as

typical and, critically speaking, the most vulnerable form of literary biography: the two- or three-volume "life and letters." In addition, there was the "life and times," exemplified by David Masson's gigantic study of Milton amid, and too often lost in, the tumult of his age. Then, those other large-scale works, also the fruit of much research but more strictly limited to the man: Prior's *Goldsmith*, Lee's *Defoe*, Courthope's *Pope*, Dowden's *Shelley*, Aitken's *Steele*, Knight's *Wordsworth*. On another shelf were the more slender books that (not forgetting Lockhart) came closest to art: Macaulay's long, brilliant essays, produced for the *Edinburgh Review* and the *Encyclopædia Britannica;* John Morley's studies of Burke, Rousseau, Voltaire, and Diderot, which marked the first firm welding of literary biography and intellectual history; Mrs. Gaskell's moor-haunted account of Charlotte Brontë, and Carlyle's memoir of John Sterling. Last, and in general least, there were the innumerable obituary scrapbooks, called "memoirs" or "lives" only by pretense or courtesy, which were compiled by the widows, sons, daughters, or friends of recently deceased authors.

The variety was ample. But as a genre, biography experienced no such broad-fronted progress as is apparent in, for instance, the history of fiction from Jane Austen to Meredith. In the nineteenth-century English novel, with its dozen or more masters, we can trace profound changes in subject matter, intention, technique; in talking of it we can use, accurately, such terms as "evolution" and "emergence." No such thing is possible with biography. Such novelties as turned up were either modifications of existing types or eccentric productions which had no lasting influence on the art. Within none of the several kinds of biography was there a conspicuous advance toward more sophisticated treatment of materials or greater refinement of artistic form. Apart from the inevitable acquiring and shedding of period characteristics—for example, the disappearance of the elegant style that had been in

---

often as not, unqualified to write on the subjects assigned them; and there was no clearly defined editorial policy, especially in respect to the relative proportions of biographical and critical matter. Nevertheless, the public bought the volumes in large quantities, and some titles went through numerous printings in the course of the years.

fashion at the beginning of the century, the substitution for some decades of Victorian ponderousness, and its eventual replacement in turn by the more spare, direct prose attributable in part to the influence of journalism—there are few formal qualities by which a biography published at the end of Victoria's reign can be distinguished from one written while George III was still on the throne.

The overabundance of purposes that biography was intended to serve helps explain why the history of the form in the nineteenth century is one of artistic potentialities little realized and challenges largely unmet. But a graver difficulty was that throughout the era biography was written in the midst of unresolved critical issues. The fact that it was caught in a backwash of the ancient controversy over the relative virtues of "classicism" and "realism" was perhaps sufficient reason why critics were able to agree on only a few broad principles. One was that biography was indeed, as Wordsworth had written in 1816, a dignified art, with laws of its own. Drifting in the critical air were ideals of perfection. Biographies should provide graphic descriptions of character and episode; they should make intelligent but not excessive use of background; they should manifest a sure sense of relative value, singling out and highlighting the significant facts and minimizing or omitting the trivial and irrelevant; shunning digressions, they should strive for structural unity. Critics agreed also that biography had to obey the canons of "good taste," of decent reticence.

Beyond these easily accepted principles, on every important issue there were vigorously expressed and quite irreconcilable opinions. And in any event, no extensive body of formal criticism existed. No Coleridges philosophized on the theory of biography as one did on the esthetics of poetry. Current thought on the matter must be pieced together from the incidental observations thrown off by reviewers (usually in the early paragraphs of notices that soon turned into long strings of quotations) and, in rare instances, by biographers themselves. What little theorizing was done about biography was superficial, unmethodical, and laden with concepts and terminology borrowed, sometimes inappropriately, from criticism of other branches of literature. It was, furthermore, wholly insular. All issues were referred to the practice of Boswell and Lockhart, who reigned unchallenged as the art's greatest masters. Reviewers betrayed virtually no awareness that France and Germany too had had a history of biographical writing and that biography was still flourishing there in the nineteenth century. The significance of Sainte-Beuve, who for many years assimilated the roles of biographer and critic in his *Causeries du lundi,* was almost wholly overlooked by British critics. The honor he enjoyed in England was due to his eminence as a critic, and it had no effect whatever upon either the criticism or the practice of literary biography.

Superficial and mistaken though it often was, contemporary journalistic criticism of biography still was superior to practice. Although reviewers frequently praised the wrong books, or praised the right books for the wrong reasons, they also could, on occasion, describe the faults of a newly published biography in terms with which a modern reader is bound to concur. On the whole they had more enlightened standards of what constituted good biography than did the biographers themselves, and it is to be regretted that their reiterated complaints and advice went unheeded.

The only considerable study of biography as an art that the century produced was obscurely published (at the Durham seacoast town of Sunderland, in 1816) and completely neglected. Few copies survive today, and few persons have ever looked into it. The 339-page *Essay on the Study and Composition of Biography* was written by James Stanfield, an Irishman who was educated for the priesthood in France, went to sea in a slave ship, and returned to England—one of three survivors of the voyage—as a dedicated abolitionist. Later he became an actor and the manager of a traveling theatrical company in Yorkshire. His son, named for Thomas Clarkson, the antislavery crusader, was a successful Victorian painter and an intimate of Dickens, for some of whose amateur theatrical performances he painted the scenery.

Certainly none of the foregoing explains how James Stanfield happened to set himself up as an authority on biography. None-

theless he did, and he wrote a most sensible book. Once allowance has been made for the special assumption underlying his
argument—the belief, central to the empirical psychology of the
time, that the laws of influence and motivation can be discovered
and formulated, and that therefore the materials of biography can
validly be applied to the "scientific" study of the mind—Stanfield's theory of biography in most repects is quite acceptable
today. His insistence on scholarly impartiality, accuracy, and
skepticism; his emphasis on the importance of environment,
childhood physiological and psychological factors, and physical
traits, which once or twice strikingly anticipates Freud; his
recognition of the significance of personal details and relevant
anecdotes; his conviction that in literary biography the author's
personal life is inseparable from the history of his work; his recommendation that the biographer, far from being a mere chronicler,
use the full resources of art—all these mark him as a critic much
in advance of his time.

Apart from Stanfield, the only nineteenth-century writer before Edmund Gosse who set down fairly full opinions on what
biography should and should not be was Thomas Carlyle.[2] His
essays on Croker's edition of Boswell and on Lockhart's *Scott* are
but the most famous expressions of a consuming interest which
can be traced throughout his critical writings. Time after time he
deplored the low state of what he considered a noble art: "Rich
as we are in biography," he complained, "a well-written life is almost as rare as a well-spent one." To him most existing so-called
biographies were "mere Indexes of a Biography, which each
reader is to write out for himself, as he peruses them; not the
living body, but the dry bones of a body, which should have
been alive." Only Boswell, among Britons, had produced a biography worth counting in the baker's dozen—no more—of "genuinely-good *Biographies* [that] have yet been accumulated in
Literature." The advocate of biography as an art rather than a
process of compilation, Carlyle insisted on "harmonious" compo-

---

[2] Although Leslie Stephen wrote several biographies, edited the *Dictionary of
National Biography* (to which he also contributed 378 articles), and collected
many of his periodical essays under the title *Studies of a Biographer*, he had surprisingly little to say on the actual philosophy and technique of the art.

sition. He deplored the all too familiar method by which "stone is laid on the top of stone, just as it comes to hand; a trowel or two of biographic mortar, if perfectly convenient, being perhaps spread in here and there, by way of cement; and so the strangest pile suddenly arises; amorphous, pointing every way but to the zenith." This was his chief complaint against Lockhart's *Scott*, which, he said, collected all the materials for a fine biography, but was itself formless and far too long.

> The truth is [he concluded in another place], Biographies are in a similar case with Sermons and Songs; they have their scientific rules, their ideal of perfection and imperfection, as all things have; but hitherto their rules are only, as it were, unseen Laws of Nature, not critical Acts of Parliament, and threaten us with no immediate penalty: besides, unlike Tragedies and Epics, such works may be something without being all: their simplicity of form, moreover, is apt to seem easiness of execution; and thus, for one artist in those departments, we have a thousand bunglers.

These rank among the wisest words ever spoken on the condition of nineteenth-century biography. But if Stanfield's wisdom hardly reached beyond Sunderland, Carlyle's was drowned in the roar of his social prophecy.

· 2 ·

A further cause of the prolonged immaturity of biography as an art lay in the social accident described in Chapter Four: the rise of the contemporary man of letters to public prominence. By an inexorable process in which Providence and the new cultural conditions collaborated, every living literary celebrity sooner or later was transformed into a dead subject for biography. The lapse of time between interment and the publication of the first memoir became ever shorter; it was what a newspaper-reading public, living in the present and impatient of delay, required. And the choice of biographer naturally was governed by the chances of association—and by the feeling that a man's posthumous fame should not be entrusted to alien, and therefore possibly unsympathetic, hands.

Thus the first biographers of many nineteenth-century literary figures were men and women who suited the situation's two requirements: they were available to satisfy the public expectation of a quick memorial, and they were dependable, which is to say discreet. One qualification they (with a few noteworthy exceptions, such as John Gibson Lockhart) did not have: genuine competence for the task. Ability to write reasonably grammatical English and to arrange large parcels of personal documents for the printer are the very minimum gifts a biographer should have, and these were all that some biographers in fact possessed.

"The worst of all the diseases of biography," wrote Edmund Gosse, was the widow-biographer. "She is the triumph of the unfittest. Others may have little art, little experience, little sense of proportion; but she exceeds them, for she has none at all. . . . It is to the Widow that we owe the fact that a very large section of recent biography might pass for an annex to Madame Tussaud's gallery." Mrs. Kingsley's memoir of her husband, a saccharine compilation of his letters and the testimonials of many grieving friends, was probably the Victorian era's most oppressive example of the widow-biography; its arduous and all too successful attempt to replace the living, fly-casting Kingsley with a marble effigy gave pause even to contemporary reviewers, whom one might expect, after the long dosage to which they had been subjected, to have built up a degree of tolerance for that kind of performance. Its "very continuity and unbroken strain of goodness, nobleness, and instructiveness," said one critic, "strikes the reader with a certain mixture of weariness and half-distrust." The melancholy that permeated the book, observed another, did scant justice to the essential happiness of a man "who had so keen delight in nature and in home, whose children were healthy and happy, and whose wife was all that this book shows her to be."[3]

[3] The unmistakably malicious intent of the last phrase tempts one to speculate on the motives that led widows to compose, or commission, the kind of biographies they did. In Henry James's short story "The Real Right Thing," the widow of the writer Ashton Doyne, in addition to determining that his biography should be "a full reply to every imputation on herself," views the proposed book as a means of making belated amends for her own insufficiency: "she hadn't taken Doyne seriously enough in life." (One recalls the contrition for his sins as a

Just as unqualified, and no less anxious to conceal indecorous truth under a blanket of filial adulation, were sons and daughters. It was his reading of the fulsome *Memorials of Thomas Hood*, by the poet's daughter and son, which led Thackeray to say to his own elder daughter: "Let there be nothing of this when I am gone!"—a command which long was interpreted as a prohibition of any biography of himself, but which was simply the frank-minded Thackeray's protest against meringue posing as bread. Other blood relatives were hardly better equipped. When the time came to prepare the official biography of Wordsworth, his survivors were frankly dubious of his nephew Christopher's qualifications; Miss Fenwick, the poet's friend and amanuensis, wrote Sir Henry Taylor that he had accepted the task "without much knowledge of his uncle, or indeed of his poetry, and he had had all this to get up," but, she added, "he is a very able man and good," and "on the whole, he might execute the work satisfactorily." Unfortunately, as the Wordsworth circle were the first to admit, he did not.[4]

When the role of biographer fell to someone outside the family, the results often were no happier. In 1828 Thomas Moore, writing his will, named his friend Lord John Russell (later the first Earl Russell) as his biographer. At Moore's death twenty-four years later, Lord John, absorbed in his political career, had neither time nor inclination for the task. But out of affection for Moore, and wishing to assure an income for the poet's widow, he

husband which led the widowed Carlyle to edit his wife's "letters and memorials" and hand them over to Froude for eventual publication.) In Kingsley's case, speculation is stimulated by the fact that the rector of Eversley had an excessively strong libido. As an intended wedding present to his wife, he prepared a manuscript preface to a prose life of St. Elizabeth of Hungary, which he decorated with pen-and-ink drawings of the nude female figure, and before and after their marriage he wrote her letters which a biographer even in 1959 deemed "too intimate for printing." (Robert B. Martin, *The Dust of Combat: A Life of Charles Kingsley* [London, 1959], pp. 71, 132.) Thus at least one Victorian widow had a peculiarly compelling reason to stress her late husband's spiritual qualities before the world.

[4] Although the setting is the early twentieth century, Virginia Woolf's description (*Night and Day*, Chapter III) of a mother and daughter ineffectually trying to write a biography of the latter's grandfather, a great English poet, is an accurate representation of what went on in numerous Victorian households where duty was owed to a deceased author. Too many biographies of the time were produced by the well-meaning but unqualified kind of people, and under the inauspicious conditions, Mrs. Woolf describes.

undertook it, with results that are apparent throughout the eight resulting volumes of almost uninterrupted documents. Politicians are not necessarily good biographers (though John Morley was), nor are doctors, one of whom pasted together Thomas Campbell's life; nor divines, such as A. P. Stanley, who reverently entombed the Thomas Arnold that Lytton Strachey was later gleefully to disinter; nor aristocratic dilettantes like Richard Monckton Milnes, who wrote the first published life of Keats; nor architects like Basil Champneys, who worked under the stern aegis of Coventry Patmore's widow.

In the first two thirds of the century many seasoned men of letters also wrote biographies, but always as a sideline, and often in the inhibiting capacity of a personal acquaintance. Southey, author of lives of Cowper, Nelson, and Wesley, was a poet and writer of controversial prose. Scott, biographer of Dryden and Swift, was primarily a poet and novelist. Byron's first biographers were Leigh Hunt, a poet and journalist; John Galt, a novelist and miscellaneous writer; and Moore, a poet. Lockhart was a critic and editor of the *Quarterly Review*; Mrs. Gaskell was a novelist; John Forster was a barrister, critic, and newspaper editor.

In later decades, biography tended to become a principal occupation of some men of letters, who wrote it with their right hands rather than their left. But even then, their allegiance to the pen was not complete. Masson and Dowden were professors, and Gosse (Congreve, Jeremy Taylor, Donne, Gray, Patmore, Swinburne, Browne, and others) was first an assistant in the British Museum, then a translator in the Board of Trade, and finally librarian to the House of Lords—and in any event, his critical writing far exceeded his biographical output in bulk. Austin Dobson (Goldsmith, Fielding, Walpole, Fanny Burney, Steele, Richardson) worked at the Board of Trade for fifty years; J. W. Mackail (Morris) was in the Education Office, W. M. Rossetti (Shelley, Keats) an official of the Inland Revenue, and J. Dykes Campbell (Coleridge) a veteran of the Mauritius Civil Service.

The conditions under which nineteenth-century biography normally was produced made it unlikely that men and women of boldly original, innovating talent would be attracted to the form. Notwithstanding the frequent asseverations of its dignity as art, when theory gave way to cases it was looked upon as journey-men's work, and only at long intervals do we find biographers themselves revealing their awareness of some of the artistic prob-lems and rewards inherent in their task. "Biography," Thomas Moore remarked to Samuel Rogers, "is like dot engraving, made up of little minute points, which must all be attended to, or the effect is lost." Washington Irving, writing as one biographer to another, congratulated Moore on the "admirable management and indefatigable care" he had exhibited "in gradually developing [Byron's] character, by incident after incident, placed in proper relief, commented upon with a delicate and skillful hand, and illustrated by letters and those scraps of poetry that burst from his heart & his fancy at the time." Edward Dowden, fifty years later, was, as biographers went, unusually self-conscious an artist: "I avoid with horror, argument and purpose and polemics, and delight in getting down a stroke or a bit of colour as the end in itself. The result is that at present I write much of my narrative [the life of Shelley] without comment, with a slight strain of irony throughout—irony being a form of self restraint like the censure of the press, and forcing one to say things in the most dextrous way; and at rare intervals I lift up the story out of the irony by my manner of telling it, by a quickly repressed outbreak of enthu-siasm." The writing of biography was so imaginatively exhilarat-ing to Dowden, in fact, that his own experience contravened the usual assumption that the biographer is tied to his facts, whereas the critic is free to wander where he will: in writing his short life of Southey, he said, "I felt a happy sense of freedom . . . , as if biography were a free work of art, while in criticism I always feel as little free or creative as if I were at work in some scientific investigation." But these glimpses of the nineteenth-century biog-rapher as a conscious artist are rare.

· 3 ·

The artistic problem that most worried both critics and biog-raphers was the value and function of personal detail. Was it desirable that a biography should contain a substantial portion of homely particulars? If so, should the biographer strive for lifelike effect through a process of selection and retouching or through a wholesale accumulation of circumstantial minutiae? The answer depended in part, of course, on the nature of the portrait he wished to paint and his motives in painting it: whether he desired to commemorate a hero in his full moral grandeur, the reader's reverence undistracted by a recital of his small idiosyncrasies, or a man in all, or most of, his common humanity.

For the inclusion of personal details, by whatever manner, there was venerable sanction. Plutarch had shown the way, and Dryden had long ago admired him for it:

> [In biography] you are led into the private lodgings of the hero; you see him in his undress, and are made familiar with his most private actions and conversations. You may behold a Scipio and a Laelius gathering cockle-shells on the shore, Augustus playing at bounding-stones with boys, and Agesilaus riding on a hobby-horse among his children. The pageantry of life is taken away; you see the poor reasonable animal as naked as ever nature made him; are made acquainted with his passions and his follies, and find the demi-god, a man. Plutarch himself has more than once defended this kind of relating little passages; for, in the Life of Alexander, he says thus: ". . . sometimes a word, or a casual jest, betrays a man more to our knowledge of him, than a battle fought wherein ten thousand men were slain, or sacking of cities, or a course of victories."

Early in the eighteenth century, Roger North had not spared the prosaic details, on the ground that "a life should be a picture; which cannot be good, if the peculiar features, whereby the subject is distinguished from all others, are left out. Nay, scars and blemishes, as well as beauties, ought to be expressed; otherwise, it is but an outline filled up with lilies and roses."

But it was Boswell who had established the lavish use of concrete detail as a principle of biographical art. Following his example, the usual large-scale biography in the early nineteenth century was swollen, within the limits of decorum and discretion, with every move the subject made, every story that was told of him, every comment his letters contained on the state of hotel accommodations in Italy or the exasperations he suffered from incompetent household servants. But the misfortune was that, in lack of new Boswells, biography fell into the hands of writers who, in Roger North's phrase, endeavored to "rectify want of art by *copia* of matter." Typical of them was Sir James Prior, author of a superabundant life of Goldsmith, who justified his comprehensiveness thus:

> Biography to be useful must be minute; to be entertaining also it must be minute. Without, in short, it enters into detail, we can never know much of the individual, or of the private history, often not the least interesting portion of the history of his works; we cannot indulge that rational curiosity, which all such persons are calculated to inspire; we cannot trace how his life and his writings bear upon each other; under what particular circumstances the former was passed, and under what incitements or successes, what difficulties or privations, the latter were written. . . . We are not afraid so much of tediousness as uncertainty; not of the accumulation of evidence, but of its scantiness.

The generous inclusion of personal details, again, made it possible for the reader to discover his affinities with the great man—a most valuable moral lesson, as Dr. Johnson had pointed out long ago, and as Thomas Moore reaffirmed for a new age. We "contemplate with pleasure," he said, "a great mind in its undress, and . . . rejoice in the discovery, so consoling to human pride, that even the mightiest, in their moments of ease and weakness, resemble ourselves."

Nevertheless, far from conceding that Boswell had ushered in the biography of the future, some life writers in the decades immediately following him adhered to the neoclassic ideal of dignified generalization. To them the best portraits were those which eschewed such differentiating and humanizing aspects of personality as anecdotes, physical peculiarities, domestic and social habits. But material like this was not wholly rejected, even by biographers most intent upon producing an idealized portrait. Having devoted their main text to the events of a life, they customarily swept together details of physique, mannerisms, daily habits, and the like into a miscellaneous last chapter. These dustbin appendages, often headed "Personal Characteristics" or, in the case of Christopher Wordsworth's memoir of his uncle, "Reminiscences: Miscellaneous Memoranda," were often accompanied by an apology for introducing such "trivialities." The dual implication was that their presence in the main part of the book would have ruined the sought-for noble effect, and that although perhaps they did not deserve to be lost completely, they were included largely as a sop thrown to the curious. The truth was that no amount of neoclassic theory could prevail against the immediacy and individuality afforded by what Boswell called "minute particulars [which] are characteristick" of the man.

The crux of the artistic problem resided, then, not so much in the value of "detailism" per se as in the discrimination the biographer should exercise over the particulars he had assembled and the method by which he should present them. It was generally recognized that the intentions of biography as a literary form could be frustrated as completely by excess as by neglect of detail. Addiction to minutiae could, said Coleridge, "render the real character almost invisible, like clouds of dust on a portrait, or the counterfeit frankincense which smoke-blacks the favourite idol of a Roman Catholic village." What biographers and critics alike ordinarily failed to appreciate was that in the midst of copiousness there could be control. They seldom noticed the distinction between "trivia" that were psychologically meaningful and artistically right and those that merely served the biographer's garrulous urge and the reader's idle curiosity. When reviewers complained, as they often did, of the sagging circumstantiality of a new biography, normally their suggested remedy was drastic reduction: a sweeping application of the shears rather than carefully weighed strokes of the deleting pen.

The fact that the hybrid "life and letters" was the typical form which serious biography assumed is witness enough to biographers' reluctance to perform the artistic act of selecting, reordering, and assimilating their raw material. If their besetting weakness was their tendency, as Ruskin put it, "to confuse epistolary talk with vital fact," the reason was that it was axiomatic that the letters of a man *contained* his life; that, indeed, his life could be narrated most effectively and authentically by reproducing large portions of his correspondence and other personal papers. To this simple circumstance may be laid the formlessness and diffuseness that characterized the century's major biographies, the long delay in acknowledging purposeful selection as a principle of biographical art, and the ambiguity of the biographer's role. He customarily looked upon himself as a mere compiler, and yet he was to some extent, albeit unconsciously, a creative intelligence.

For the verbatim use of documents there was ample and eminent precedent. Izaak Walton included numerous letters in his *Lives,* and so highly valued were those of Donne in particular that 129 of them were also published separately by his son, in 1651. In Walton's time, it is true, there was one uncompromising dissenter. In his brief life of Abraham Cowley (1668) Dr. Thomas Sprat declared:

> The truth is, the Letters that pass between particular Friends, if they are written as they ought to be, can scarce ever be fit to see the light. They should not consist of fulsome Complements, or tedious Polities, or elaborate Elegancies, or general Fancies. But they should have a Native clearness and shortness, a Domestical plainness, and a peculiar kind of Familiarity; which can only affect the humour of those to whom they were intended. The very same passages, which make writings of this Nature delightful amongst Friends, will loose all manner of taste, when they come to be read by those that are indifferent. In such Letters the Souls of Men should appear undress'd: And in that negligent habit, they may be fit to be seen by one or two in a Chamber, but not to go abroad into the Streets.

But Sprat's position found little support. Instead, his dictum became notorious, and men as dissimilar as Dr. Johnson and Coleridge were to attack it. The example to be followed, most people agreed, was William Mason's, in his life of the poet Gray. "I might," he observed with his incurable pomposity, "have written his life in the common form, perhaps with more reputation to myself; but, surely, not with equal information to the reader; for whose sake I have never related a single circumstance of Mr. Gray's life in my own words, when I could employ *his* for the

purpose." Boswell, in turn, frankly emulated Mason, whose practice he deemed ideal, though Dr. Johnson for his part thought the
life of Gray "mighty dull."

The device of telling a story through letters was, of course,
not new in literature. "Epistolary novels" had enjoyed a protracted vogue in Mason's and Boswell's day; at the peak of their
popularity, in the 1780's, scores were published every year. Sequences of letters enabled the novelist to create the illusion of
intimacy, affording the reader a privileged view of the thoughts
and moods of his characters. It was a procedure especially suited
to a literary age when sensibility was in flower. But as new narrative techniques developed, the device's artificiality and restrictions became increasingly apparent; it interfered with the development of the authorial point of view, the omniscience, the free
use of dramatic scene and dialogue that appealed to new generations of novelists. By the early nineteenth century, the epistolary
novel was passé. Ironically, however, its relative, the epistolary
biography, flourished for another hundred years.

There were excellent reasons why letters continued to provide
the main substance of biography. Unlike the correspondences
contrived by fiction writers, these had the supreme virtue of
genuineness. They were precious social and psychological documents, as Hazlitt, in an often-quoted passage, was among the
many to point out: "Letters are certainly the honestest records of
great minds, that we can become acquainted with; and we like
them the more, for letting us into the follies and treacheries of
high life, the secrets of the gay and the learned world, and the
mysteries of authorship. We are ushered, as it were, behind the
scenes of life; and see gay ladies and learned men, the wise,
the witty, and the ambitious, in all the nakedness, or undress at
least, of their spirits." The contents of the library tables of his time
substantiated Hazlitt's claim, for the published letters of Walpole,
Pope, Sterne, Chesterfield, and the bluestockings were sufficient
evidence of the value private correspondence had as mirror of the
human scene and revelation of the human character.

The high estimate the early nineteenth century placed on the
personal letters of the great was one manifestation of the rever-

ence toward documents—the raw, undigested, primary sources of history—that in turn was a symptom of the romantic infatuation with the past. As the credulous excitement over William Henry Ireland's Shakespeare forgeries demonstrated, the passion for newly revealed manuscripts suspended the common sense even of normally reasonable men. As antiquarians went about unlocking muniment rooms of ancient castles and mansions, prying open oak chests in cathedral chapter houses, and blowing the dust of centuries from official records, anything sufficiently ancient seemed worth printing.

The practice of historians and antiquarians, who readied for the press hundreds of volumes containing the texts of old documents, seemed entirely adaptable to the biographer's purposes. The term "compilation" was used as often as "writing" to describe the making of a biography, and no apology was implied. Many a nineteenth-century "life and letters" was produced by the simplest process imaginable: arranging the subject's correspondence and personal memoranda in chronological order, cutting wherever prudent, writing a minimal amount of introductory and connective prose, and sending the resultant manuscript off to the printer.[5] With biography conceived in such terms, Dr. Johnson's remark about Goldsmith was applicable to any practitioner of the craft: "Sir, he has the art of compiling, and of saying everything he has to say in a pleasing manner." That was all that was necessary.

Biographers found a self-conscious virtue in letting their subjects speak for themselves. Apart from providing a man with the means of posthumous self-justification (a principle consonant

[5] This was the fate of uncounted thousands of original letters: the holographs often were not copied, but were simply "edited" by ink or scissors and absorbed into the biographer's manuscript, the whole leaves or snipped-out portions sometimes being pasted on blank sheets of paper, with the consequent loss of whatever was written on the reverse side. Sometimes, as was true of Boswell's *Johnson*, the printer's copy—including, in this case, hundreds of pages torn from Boswell's journal—was returned to the author and so had a chance for preservation. Oftener, however, the printer's copy was destroyed after type was set. Forster often cut from Dickens' letters the passages he wanted to print in his biography, discarding the rest. Although the copy for the first volume survives, that for the latter two was destroyed. For this reason the only texts we have for hundreds of Dickens' most valuable letters are the edited excerpts printed by Forster.

with the Anglo-Saxon ideal of fair play), the method of reproducing personal papers with no overt intervention on the biographer's part suited the age's inductive bias. If the truth of a man's character and career was what the biographer strove to record, where could it be found more faithfully and abundantly recorded than in his private papers? Effacing himself and suppressing his bias—or so he would lead the reader to believe—in a way that often anticipated the strict-objectivity posture of his modern "academic" successors, the biographer said, in effect, Let the record speak, then draw your own conclusions.[6] And if the record was to speak, it should be allowed to speak verbatim. Contemporary opinion opposed any extensive summarizing or digesting, which, it was thought, removed the inimitable flavor that every document possessed in its pristine state and furthermore eliminated many details which, however trivial, had some interest as historical evidence. Burns's early biographer, Dr. Currie, so explained his printing many long documents: "Though the information they convey might have been presented within a shorter compass, it is scarcely to be doubted, that the intelligent reader will be far more gratified by a sight of these original documents themselves."

It followed that art was the enemy of historical truth. If the biographer, instead of reproducing the documents before him, chose to use them as extensive storehouses of facts from which he could draw at will, selecting, rejecting, combining, highlighting as he pleased, he risked being charged with gratuitous interference, with drawing a curtain of artifice between the reader and historical reality. Monckton Milnes spoke for many a biographer when, recalling his dilemma as he set out to write the life of

---

[6] The alacrity with which he let the record speak arouses some suspicion that his motives were not all traceable to the age's reverence for the inductive method. The cat leaps out of the bag in a letter Thomas Moore wrote to Scott in 1826: "I shall not be long in dispatching the book [his life of Byron], as our materials, when united, will be ample, and will enable me, I think, to make Byron *tell his own* story, which is not only the pleasantest sort of biography to the reader but by far the easiest to the writer." (Wilfred Partington, *The Private Letter-Books of Sir Walter Scott* [New York, 1930], p. 235.) Whatever theoretical reasons may be advanced for the wholesale printing of letters in the name of biography, allowance must be made for the familiar fact of human indolence.

((197

Keats, he noted that if he had chosen to be an artist rather than a compiler, "the temptation to render the facts of the story subservient to the excellence of the work of art would never have been absent." Such studied self-denial always earned the critic's praise; as the *Quarterly Review* once noted: "we receive unwillingly those biographies in which the artist is predominant, even when agreeably and skilfully executed; and we are very indulgent with any congeries of materials out of which we can ourselves embody some living personality."

The natural corollary to "Let the subject speak for himself" therefore was "Let the reader form his own image of the man" —without any intervention on the biographer's part. Dr. Beattie, prefacing his life of Thomas Campbell, expressed it this way:

> . . . among the numerous letters quoted in part, or entire, in these volumes, some detached portions may strike the general reader as presenting nothing very characteristic. Taken separately, indeed, they may not; as a whole most likely they will; for if the detached paragraphs be collected like broken pieces of mosaic and *re*set, the character of the piece will be restored, the features identified; and, examined in more intimate connection, they will be found to exhibit a distinct portrait of the original—so at least I have ventured to think. It is not the fragments of a head or a limb, but the nice adjustment of these, that discovers the classic statue—whether a Minerva or an Apollo.

Every man, in other words, his own mosaicmaker.

In practice, the artistic disadvantages outweighed all the values claimed for the kind of biography that was the product of the transcribing rather than the creative pen. Each lengthy letter, each volume of a diary, represented in effect a body of prepackaged data; and its contents, the order in which they were arranged, the way they were presented, and the relative emphasis and proportion their writer had given them—all of these having been determined by an occasion long past—had nothing to do with their present function as components in an artistic pattern.

To fashion a straight, clear narrative out of letters was practically impossible. The composer of a letter-based biography had the same handicaps that Richard Cumberland observed in the

writing of epistolary fiction: ". . . his course becomes more circuitous and subject to embarrassment than when he takes the narrative wholly into his own hands; without great management and
address in keeping his dates progressive, and distinctly method-
ized, his reader is exposed to be called back and puzzled; and . . .
the scene is oftentimes distracted, where we wish it to be entire.
. . ." Other risks were at least as grave. Often a sequence of letters
involved telling the same story to three or four correspondents, or
the repeating of the same opinions over the course of several
years; but it might equally well be confined to letters to a single
correspondent, thus limiting the reader's knowledge to what the
writer wished to tell that person. The writer might simply put
down new developments, leaving numerous tantalizing gaps and
unexplained allusions which the biographer seldom troubled to
fill in or interpret. Thanks to the accidents of both the writing of
letters and their subsequent preservation or loss, the sum of re-
dundancy in a given biography was equaled only by the number
of events omitted. Moreover, a single letter might contain passing
references to many different topics, all—or none—of which might
be pursued, again fragmentarily, in succeeding letters. The reader
had to sort out the tangled, frayed threads for himself. Under the
best of conditions, both the narrative and the personal image
which the reader was expected to construct from the letters were
spasmodic, ill-proportioned, and half hidden from the eye. The
biography-told-in-documents often was, in fact, chaos in three
volumes.

By far the most frequent complaint, however, was that such
books were laden with extraneous and trivial material.[7] In some

---

[7] A reviewer of Cuthbert Southey's six-volume *Life and Correspondence* of his
father (1849–50) put the case as well as anyone: "The biographers of every man
whose name is familiar to the public are sure to imagine that whatever relates
to him has to all men an abiding interest, and if there be nothing to give offence to
men still living, and, indeed, very often whether there be or not, every idle word
becomes fixed in permanent and ineffaceable record. In one volume of biography,
which we have been lately looking over, the bill of the upholsterer who furnished
a poet's cottage is printed; in another a washer-woman's accounts and a tailor's
day-books occupy pages upon pages; a third, mentioning a gentleman's marriage,
gives three letters stating the fact, and nothing but the fact, which had never
been a subject of dispute or doubt, and not content with this, adds an extract
from a local newspaper, and a copy of the entry in the parish register. Why all
this? . . . Books may easily be made too long to be read at all; and it is

instances, scarcity of a man's papers was taken as sufficient excuse for printing whatever survived. In his slapdash *Memoirs of William Hazlitt*, the essayist's grandson introduced one chapter thus: "By some extraordinary *casualty* a few of the letters addressed to Mr. Hazlitt in one particular year, 1821, have escaped the destruction which has been almost the invariable fate of this class of papers in his case. I could desire that those which we still have were more important, but their scarcity must be my apology for inserting them. I regard them as salvage from the waste-basket." At least he was frank.[8]

Ironically, the same age that revered the document had no concern for the literal integrity of its text. No nineteenth-century biographer or editor reproduced with thorough fidelity what he found in his manuscripts. He felt himself wholly at liberty to excise, revise, divide, telescope, and otherwise manipulate his documents before sending them to press. Such editorial license had plenty of warrant among earlier letter writers themselves. At least three celebrated eighteenth-century literary figures had edited their own correspondences. Pope not only arranged for some of his letters to be published in an "unauthorized" edition but elaborately revised them before sending them to the printer.

---

scarcely fair to the fame of Southey, already oppressed by the weight of his own works, to increase the burthen by volume after volume, of whatever in his toil for daily bread he may have set down in his journals, much of which must have been merely as aids to his own memory. . . ." (*North British Review*, XIII [1850], 226–227.)

[8] I do not mean to suggest that modern biographers are universally more sophisticated in their editorial thinking. In 1949 Coventry Patmore's great-grandson Derek printed the following family letter on the sole ground that it was "so brief and noncommittal that I think it worth quoting":

DEAR GEORGE,
This has this moment arrived. I do not know what to do about the check— I think I won't enclose it, as you will get some money of Colbourn.
Baby is quite well.

Your affectionate,
ELIZA PATMORE.

TUESDAY MORNING.
Will you bring Rabbit and Brandy and the things Mrs. Dod is to purchase for me?

(Derek Patmore, *The Life and Times of Coventry Patmore* [London, 1949], p. 31.) Earlier, Patmore's authorized biographer, Basil Champneys, had printed the same letter as "brief and unique."

Sterne, converting his private letters into the published *Letters of Yorick to Eliza,* rewrote them, redistributed their contents, and, like Pope, sometimes changed the name of the addressee. Horace Walpole, who looked upon his correspondence as a continuous historical chronicle destined to be of permanent interest, sometimes got his letters back from a correspondent's heirs and then retouched them before filing them away for posterity. There was no element of crude deceit in the revisionist exertions of Pope and Walpole, at least; to them a private letter was not a mere utilitarian means of communication, but a literary exercise which was entitled to all the improvement, by way of additional wit and polish, that its creator wanted to lavish on it. But they were equally concerned to improve the figure they would present to later generations.

If writers themselves altered their personal papers, it is easy to understand why biographers did not consider original texts to be sacrosanct. They agreed, to be sure, that William Mason had gone too far when he combined extracts from letters of Gray, sometimes as many as five written over a span of several years, and to different correspondents, and presented the result as a single letter, the discrepancies being reconciled by passages from Mason's own pen. Yet they too silently deleted or rephrased passages, moved sections from one letter to another, and even, like Mason, composed brand-new letters from portions of several others. Lockhart, it was discovered when his printed texts came to be compared with the original manuscripts, constantly suppressed, rewrote, combined, and redistributed passages in Scott's letters. Forster's large biography of Landor was replete with misdated, dismembered, and silently altered documents. Thomas Noon Talfourd, having liberally omitted passages from Lamb's letters in his edition of 1837, printed certain of them after Mary's death, in his *Final Memorials of Charles Lamb* (1848). The value of the restoration was, however, somewhat diminished by his failure to indicate to what letters the newly printed portions belonged.

The pervasiveness of these alterations gives a hollow sound to the biographers' customary assertions that they were concerned, above all, to let nothing intervene between their subject and the reader. They did not, in any true sense, let the man speak for himself. He spoke as they wished him to speak, and the reader's response was determined by the form in which they presented the materials for his inspection. Many editorial changes, of course, were dictated by obvious tactical considerations: attentiveness to the wishes of survivors, the manifold pressures of delicacy, decency, and decorum. As for the rest, the conclusion is inescapable: in making the changes they did, biographers were performing a quasi-artistic function. It was the spirit of the letters—and the man—that was to be preserved, not the literal truth. If they were not creative artists in the sense that poets or novelists were, biographers' conception of a reality that transcended the facts in the documents urged them, consciously or not, into the exercise of what we might call editorial artistry.[9] By blue-penciling and reshuffling the contents of a writer's letters and other personal papers, they could, they felt, reveal his essential character more clearly. For documents with their burden of stubborn facts are always awkward materials for art. Their contents tend to wrinkle the smoothly arranged drapery of an idealized portrait, intruding personal details which disturb the consistency that such a portrait should possess and events which might have occurred more fit-

[9] Retroactive authority for such artistry was provided, eighty years later, by Henry James, who conveyed at least this one principle of art wholly unchanged from the mid-Victorian period of his youth into the twentieth century. Writing on November 15–18, 1913, to his nephew, James declared that when he used passages from his late brother William's letters in *Notes of a Son and Brother*, he was concerned to adapt them "into the whole harmony of my text," whose purpose was "to be a reflection of all the amenity and felicity of our young life of that time at the highest pitch that was consistent with perfect truth—to show us all at our best for characteristic expression and colour and variety and everything that would be charming. And when I laid hands upon the letters to use as so many touches and tones in the picture, I frankly confess I seemed to see them in a better, or at all events in another light, here and there, than those rough and rather illiterate copies I had from you showed at their face value. . . . It was as if he had said to me on seeing me lay my hands on the weak little relics of our common youth, 'Oh but you're not going to give me away, to hand me over, in my raggedness and my poor accidents, quite unhelped, unfriendly: you're going to do the very best for me you *can*, aren't you, and since you appear to be making such claims for me you're going to let me seem to justify them as much as I possibly may?' And it was as if I kept spiritually replying to this that he might indeed trust me to handle him with the last tact and devotion—that is do with him everything I seemed to feel him *like*. . . ." (*The Letters of Henry James*, ed. Percy Lubbock [New York, 1920], II, 346–347.)

tingly at some other juncture in a man's life than that certified by the dates.

The spirit in which biographers worked is admirably illustrated in a letter Thomas Moore wrote to the publisher John Murray as he composed his biography of Byron:

> I am getting on very well, having satisfied myself with respect to the Italian Loves, by omitting the whole of the letter about Angelica (making a love the less) and transferring the long account of Margarita from the place of its date (where it jars with our Guiccioli Romance) to an earlier period where it chimes in with his dissolute course of life and thus keeps the character of each epoch more consistently.

Few passages in the history of biographical writing are more calculated to make the modern scholar's flesh crawl than this bland admission of Moore's that he deleted one "Italian Love" from Byron's life and moved Byron's account of another back in time for the sake of artistic fitness. Whether defensible or not, such liberties were inspired by a genuine esthetic purpose, the preservation, or rather the creation, of coherence. If this is not the way things were, Moore implies, this is the way they should have been, and therefore the way they should be transmitted down through the years.[1]

In biographies composed mainly of documents, this subjective tendency was of course fairly well concealed; it could become manifest only if, with the documents themselves at hand, one retraced the process of selection and revision by which a biographer had brought the man of historical record closer to his idealized and simplified conception. But as the demand for shorter, more popular biographies grew, summaries or brief ex-

---

[1] Whatever his trespasses (which also included frequent alteration of the texts of the letters themselves), Moore must be credited with one of the instincts of the true biographical scholar. In his journal for September 19, 1818, he recorded that "Lady Lansdowne said that [Lord Grenville] *has* letters of Sheridan's, but that he will *not* give them. I shall try what effect the knowledge of my having so many letters of his *own* may produce on him. He is said to be very fidgety about his epistolary fame; and, if so, the intelligence may at least give him a sleepless night or two, which he deserves for such sulky uncommunicativeness." (*Memoirs, Journal, and Correspondence,* ed. Lord John Russell [Boston, 1853] II, 166.) The gentle art of blackmail is not mentioned in today's treatises on research, but its employment is not unheard of.

tracts woven into the running text had to be substituted for extensively quoted documents.[2] From ten or a hundred times more material than he could use, the biographer had to choose a limited number of what he regarded as the most significant or representative facts. Biography, as practiced, for example, by Macaulay and, a generation later, by the contributors to the English Men of Letters series was frankly a matter of selection and synthesis. Under these circumstances, a well-defined attitude on the part of the biographer was recognized as not only legitimate but desirable. Biography was allowed to be the product of the writer's intuition, his weighing of the psychological probabilities, rather than an invitation to the reader to perform his own induction from the supposedly unsorted data set before him.

Selectivity came, therefore, to have weightier critical sanction. Every detail, some critics argued, had to justify its place in the total pattern. At the end of the century Charles Whibley asserted that the true biography was "an imagined portrait stripped of all that is unessential, into which no detail is introduced without a deliberate choice and a definite intention." "Rigid selection and lavish rejection of available records," echoed Sidney Lee after long years of blue-penciling *DNB* articles, "are processes which the biographer has often to practise in the sternest temper. . . . Personality is not transmitted on the biographic canvas through overcrowded detail."

Significantly, these were voices in the very age of Henry James. The theory of biographical art was inescapably affected by the new ideal of fiction: selectivity, not uncontrolled abundance; distillation, not elaboration. "How boil down so many facts in the alembic, so that the distilled result, the produced appearance, should have intensity, lucidity, brevity, beauty, all the merits required for my effect?" This was the problem James

[2] Other practical considerations, besides the need to provide lightweight biographies for the growing class of hasty readers, occasionally prodded the biographer to be less of a compiler and more of a craftsman. Southey's effective use in his life of Cowper (1835) of what he called the "mosaic" technique— assimilating many short quotations from Cowper's letters into his narrative rather than reproducing whole series of letters, as was the fashion—was forced upon him by copyright difficulties. Rights to the unrestricted use of the so-called "private correspondence" were owned by the publishers of a rival edition.

posed for the novelist: "to give all the sense, in a word, without all the substance or all the surface, and so to summarise and foreshorten, so as to make values both rich and sharp, that the mere procession of items and profiles is not only, for the occasion, superseded, but is, for essential quality, almost 'compromised.' . . ." It was, as Whibley and Lee suggested, the biographer's problem as well. But his full response to the challenge, though foreshadowed in the compressed biographies of the late Victorian and Edwardian eras, was not to be seen until the canons of fiction were directly applied to the biographical art in the days of Lytton Strachey.

· 4 ·

The ease with which dicta of such late nineteenth-century critics of fiction as Henry James can be adapted to suggest the shortcomings of biography in the preceding hundred years is a reminder that these two major departments of narrative prose were in acknowledged competition throughout the period. Recognition of their obvious affinities and differences kept alive, for one thing, the cliché that a good biography made as interesting reading as a novel—better, really, because it was true. In 1806, Lucy Hutchinson's memoir of her husband, written in the late 1660's but now first printed, was recommended to female readers on the ground that "it carries with it all the interest of a novel, strengthened with the authenticity of real history." "Your work," wrote Washington Irving to Thomas Moore after reading proofs of Moore's life of Byron, "will have a prodigious effect beyond any work of fiction. It has all the variety of scene, passion and incident of the most romantic novel, with the all potent charm of *truth*." Fictitious narratives, in Carlyle's view a few years later, could not hold a candle to biography. "What," he demanded, speaking of all the tales in world literature from the *Iliad* to the latest circulating-library novel, "are all these but so many mimic Biographies? . . . Let anyone bethink him how impressive the smallest historical *fact* may become, as contrasted with the grandest *fictitious event*"—because, in Carlylean metaphysics,

((205

even the tiniest fragment of history was an emblem of the world of spirit, whereas fiction was a representation of nothing.

Meanwhile the weight of the novel's interest was about to be transferred to literary biography's own traditional domain of character portrayal. Each genre, in fact, was invading the other's territory. The proper study of fiction, English criticism was asserting by the middle of the century, was not so much the external events of men's lives (as in Scott) nor social relations (as in Thackeray) as their interior existence, the silent, hidden current of the spirit (as, within a few years, in George Eliot). This shift of emphasis in fiction naturally added significance to literary biography, which had long been offering the raw materials for such exploration, even if the biographers themselves seldom ventured upon the bold interpretation of human experience that was becoming the forte of the Eliot-Hardy-James school of novelists.[3] George Eliot herself praised Mrs. Gaskell's life of Charlotte Brontë for just this reason: it "makes us," she wrote the author, "familiar inmates of an interior so strange, so original in its individual elements and so picturesque in its externals—it paints for us at once the psychological drama and the scenic accessories with so much vividness—that fiction has nothing more wild, touching, and heart-strengthening to place above it."

In an age when the criticism of both biography and the novel was still groping toward formulations, there was much uncertainty over the extent to which the two arts could learn from each other. The post-Boswellian biographical quest for verisimilitude through copiousness had its recognizable counterpart in Dickens' technique of achieving realism through detailed surveys of scene and inventories of a character's appearance and demeanor. Whether or not this was an artistically desirable method was one of the chief issues in the criticism of fiction at mid-century, just as

[3] This development is neatly epitomized in the fact that in 1879 Henry James, writing as a literary biographer, apologized in the traditional fashion for the absence of excitement in his life of Hawthorne, whose career, he said, "was probably as tranquil and uneventful a one as ever fell to the lot of a man of letters; it was almost strikingly deficient in incident, in what may be called the dramatic quality." (*Hawthorne* [New York, 1879], p. 1.) Yet it was James himself, in the role of novelist, who in the next thirty years demonstrated most impressively the intense "dramatic quality" that resides in *inner* experience.

it had been in the criticism of biography for the past fifty years. On another issue, both biographer and novelist subscribed, if only in theory, to the ideal of artistic unity. "The first requirement of a novel," said Fitzjames Stephen in 1855, "is that it should be a biography—an account of the life or part of the life, of a person." The very fact that the increasingly prolific genre of biography had, so to speak, a built-in centrality—a single hero, a single career, therefore a single focus of interest—may well have encouraged the nineteenth-century novel to pull itself together. It became customary to deplore the loose, episodic qualities of much early (that is, eighteenth-century) fiction, and unity of subject and coherence of structure were virtues constantly recommended to the Victorian novelist. Unfortunately, the biographies actually produced were poor models for the novelists to emulate. The superficial unity imposed by the single subject was, in fact, all the unity most of them possessed. Their digressions, superfluities, and disproportions resulted in a formlessness which, as Lytton Strachey was to complain many years later, amounted to a national scandal. Much of this formlessness was due to simple lack of expertness on the part of the biographers. Yet, as some critics justly noted, the biographer worked under a handicap unknown to the novelist: his materials were supplied, and he had somehow to shape his work around them, awkward though the task might be. "In a real biography," wrote a critic in 1858, "the interest lies in seeing the whole issues of a single life; and the reason for threading together periods which, as artistic effects, are complete in themselves, is obvious, namely,—that in real life, and by one greater than any artist, they were so threaded together. But there is no such excuse for a fictitious biography that does not form an artistic whole." The exigencies of the biographical art, in other words, could not be invoked to excuse structural defects in a novel.

If novelists sometimes were warned that biographies were dangerous models, biographers, for their part, were admonished not to imitate novelists. While George Eliot was praising Mrs. Gaskell's *Charlotte Brontë* for its novelistic qualities, the *Edinburgh Review* frowned: "Mrs. Gaskell appears to have learnt the art of the novel-writer so well that she cannot discharge from her palette the colours she has used in the pages of 'Mary Barton' and 'Ruth.' This biography opens precisely like a novel, and the skilful arrangement of lights and shades and colours—the prominence of some objects and the evident suppression of others—leave on the mind the excitement of a highly-wrought drama, rather than the simplicity of daylight and of nature."

It is a further illustration of the way antithetical opinions coexisted through the era, rather than of any pronounced shift of the critical wind, that twenty-two years after the *Edinburgh Review* disapproved of the novelist's venturing into biography, another literary periodical took the opposite view:

> Perhaps the reason why our biographical literature as a rule is so dull and clumsy is that novelists have so seldom taken biography in hand, while the reason of their abstinence from this kind of composition may be that it is so much more troublesome and unsatisfactory than pure fiction. Why should a man spend days in authenticating dates and deciphering obscure records when he can evolve all that he wants so much more easily from his own imagination?
>
> Yet the novelist, whose business it is to occupy himself with the picturesque side of mankind and the inner life which gives human personality its distinction and charm, and who generally succeeds in proportion as he makes his characters appear real, ought to be peculiarly fitted to present men who have crossed the world's stage in flesh and blood as they really were, or as we all desire to see them, in their habit as they lived.

Seldom, however, was there occasion for either censure or rejoicing over the mingling of the forms. Novelists, for whatever reasons, generally held aloof from the writing of biography, and biographers took their responsibilities too seriously to avail themselves of fictional techniques. Least of all did they invent scenes and episodes for which there was little if any authority in their sources. The most notorious among the handful of biographers who gave their imaginations free rein was William Godwin, whose bulky so-called life of Chaucer (1803) was among the worst-received literary biographies of the century. Godwin inherited a body of half-truth and outright myth concerning Chaucer such as had grown up around no other celebrated English author except Shakespeare, and to it he added elaborate embroideries of his own. From the germ of the old story that Chaucer met Petrarch during his travels in Italy, Godwin fancifully reconstructed the interview, during which Petrarch "exchanged with him the glances of mind, and the flashes of a poet's eye," and obliged his English visitor by reading him his just-completed tale of Griselda, a copy of which he allowed Chaucer to take home with him. Godwin's two volumes abounded in such baseless imaginings. Charles Lamb had good reason to reproach him for his "conjecturing spirit, a fondness for filling out the picture by supposing what Chaucer did and how he felt, where the materials are scanty." Apart from Godwin and the sentimental romancers on the life of Shakespeare, however, nineteenth-century biographers ordinarily were satisfied to indulge their creative bent merely by rearrangement of details and the occasional heightening of effect.

The easiest way to lend biography something of the realistic air of fiction is to insert dialogue. As early as William Roper's life of Thomas More, written before 1578, conversational interludes had refreshed the flow of narrative. Often Walton gave what purported to be direct quotations from his subjects' lips, and in the eighteenth century, when the techniques of popular biography and of fiction cast as a biographical narrative were virtually indistinguishable, snatches of talk contributed to the sought-for illusion of reality. The great triumph of dialogue, as opposed to speeches by one figure, came with Boswell, whose remarkable feats of reproducing conversation (supported, one would suppose, by the growing tendency in fiction itself to replace the old-fashioned set pieces of speech with extended dialogue in the manner of the drama) gave new authority for the practice. Hazlitt's *Memoirs of the Late Thomas Holcroft* (1816) had recurrent passages of conversation. More notably, in 1832 Thomas Jefferson Hogg's reminiscences of Shelley at Oxford—magazine articles later absorbed into his ill-fated book—were loaded with lengthy dialogues and Shelleyan monologues. That his is a reasonably verbatim report is, to say the least, dubious. If Hogg's quotations are authentic, he must have been blessed with total recall; if they are not, he had remarkable powers of invention.

But the high valuation which was placed on the very words that issued from the lips of a poet was most extensively demonstrated in the case of Byron. Virtually all the biographies and books of reminiscence appearing in the decades just after his death strove to reproduce as much as the authors could remember, or persuade their readers they remembered, of Byron's talk. More than one hundred and fifty men and women printed, at one time or another, their recollections of his conversation. The dramatic quality of Byron's life made it almost impossible to keep fictional devices out of his biographies. Leigh Hunt, for instance, described, in pages that might easily be thought to be taken from a novel, a Byronic uproar·with his servants at Leghorn, and John Galt turned Byron's deathbed into a scene worthy of a third-rate sentimental novel.

The deathbed was, in fact, the one obligatory scene in nineteenth-century biography, particularly in the earlier decades when biography was most valued as a means of religious and ethical inspiration. For it there was precedent stretching back to the hagiographical beginnings of the art. The prominence and care given it in seventeenth- and eighteenth-century lives reflected the Christian tenet that all of life was but a preparation for the moment of bodily dissolution. Each of Walton's five lives ended with a scene illustrating the manner of holy dying. That his focus on the deathbed as the great climax of the story was deliberately maintained for artistic as well as didactic effect is proved by the manner in which he arranged his material, often at the expense of chronology. When the last illness neared, he anticipated his subject's death by printing his will and announcing the time and place of the passing, and then, having got the factual particulars out of the way, he was free to devote all his art to a representation of his subject's final days and hours.

The vicinity of the grave retained its solemn appeal in the eighteenth century, as was shown by the space given to expiration scenes both in biography and in the new domestic fiction. Just

as Clarissa Harlow's protracted illness and death were the har-
binger of a thousand such passages in later novels, down to Little
Nell, Paul Dombey, and Colonel Newcome, so in biography
Boswell's circumstantial account of Dr. Johnson's last illness
("Sir, you cannot conceive with what acceleration I advance
towards death") was followed by Moore's and other writers'
clinically detailed narrative of the epic struggle in which ignorant
doctors vied to bleed and purge the moribund Byron, and Dr.
Beattie's ample coverage of the death of the poet Campbell in
squalid lodgings in Boulogne. Beattie's long-drawn-out scene,
saturated with religious sensibility, typified the way in which the
great surge of evangelical piety that was one of the early nineteenth century's principal emotional tendencies infused narratives
of an "approaching dissolution" with solemnity. Every change in
the patient's condition, every affecting sentiment that fell from
his lips (his resignation and calmness were uniformly emphasized
and admired),[4] every expression of grief on the part of the devoted
watchers—these provided the spacious climax to the biographer's
story. Probably the most widely praised deathbed scene was
the spasm-by-spasm, prayer-by-prayer account A. P. Stanley gave
of Thomas Arnold's two or three final hours. Only as its subject
lay dying did Stanley's book, until that point one of the most
tedious of biographies, come to life. Lachrymose and sententious
as the deathbed scenes in pre- and early-Victorian biography may
have been, they did afford biographers a chance to exercise
the instincts for dramatization that they otherwise largely suppressed.[5]

[4] One embarrassment Goldsmith bequeathed to his nineteenth-century biographers was the manner of his passing. As his obstinate insistence on saving his
life with Dr. James's powders—the age's best-selling all-purpose nostrum—was
nearing its fatal result, his physician inquired: "Is your mind at ease?" "No, it
is not," Goldsmith replied.

[5] Seldom was it granted Victorian readers to assist at three "final illnesses" of
the same person. Having suffered bad health throughout life, Hannah More, the
celebrated writer on religious subjects, took to her bed in 1820, and, according
to her first biographer, "those friends who had the opportunity of watching her
sick bed, were careful to gather up what fell from her lips while under the
impression of approaching dissolution." Hannah, however, after having dis-
coursed from the brink of the grave for the span of ten pages, made an unexpected
recovery, and her admirers put away their notes for future reference. Two
years later she was stricken again, and the watchers by her bed were given

Understandably, the freest use of the tone and devices associated with fiction was found in the handful of biographies written by novelists. Certainly Lockhart's previous practice as a novelist was responsible for the deftness of his anecdotes in the life of Scott, his constant use of dialogue, his full and closely observed physical descriptions, and above all his re-creation of extended scenes. Two excerpts are evidence enough of Lockhart's artistry:

> The contrast between the two [Ballantyne] brothers was not the least of the amusement; indeed that continued to amuse him to the last. . . . James was a short, stout, well-made man, and would have been considered a handsome one, but for these grotesque frowns, starts, and twistings of his features, set off by a certain mock majesty of walk and gesture, which he had perhaps contracted from his usual companions, the emperors and tyrants of the stage. His voice in talk was grave and sonorous, and he sung well (theatrically well), in a fine rich bass. John's tone in singing was a sharp treble—in conversation something between a croak and a squeak. . . . He was shorter than James, but lean as a scarecrow, and he rather hopped than walked: his features, too, were naturally good, and he twisted them about quite as much, but in a very different fashion. The elder brother was a gourmand—the younger liked his bottle and his bowl, as well as, like Johnny Armstrong, "a hawk, a hound, and a fair woman."

> On rising from table, according to Constable, they sallied out to the green before the door of the cottage, and all in the highest spirits enjoyed the fine May evening. John Ballantyne, hopping up and down in his glee, exclaimed, "Is Rob's gun here, Mr. Scott; would you object to my trying the auld barrel with a *few de joy?*" —"Nay, Mr. Puff," said Scott, "it would burst, and blow you to the devil before your time."—"Johnny, my man," said Constable, "what the mischief puts drawing at sight into *your* head?" Scott laughed heartily at this innuendo; and then observing that the little man felt somewhat sore, called attention to the notes of a bird in the adjoining shrubbery. "And by the by," said he, as they continued listening, " 'tis a long time, Johnny, since we have heard the

---

the fresh benefit of her spiritual wisdom and exemplary patience. Again she recuperated, after having provided ten additional pages for her biographer. The third time, by which point she had become somewhat repetitious, she died. (William Roberts, *Memoirs of the Life and Correspondence of Mrs. Hannah More* [2nd ed., London, 1834], IV, 122–132, 183–194, 337–349.)

Cobbler of Kelso." Mr. Puff forthwith jumped up on a mass of stone, and seating himself in the proper attitude of one working with his awl, began a favourite interlude, mimicking a certain son of Crispin, at whose stall Scott and he had often lingered when they were school-boys, and a blackbird, the only companion of his cell, that used to sing to him, while he talked and whistled to it all day long. With this performance Scott was always delighted: nothing could be richer than the contrast of the bird's wild sweet notes, some of which he imitated with wonderful skill, and the accompaniment of the Cobbler's hoarse cracked voice, uttering all manner of endearing epithets, which Johnny multiplied and varied in a style worthy of the Old Women in Rabelais at the birth of Pantagruel.

One might quote also Lockhart's description of his first visit to Abbotsford, with Scott as his proud guide; and the harrowing narrative of the catastrophe of Scott's fortunes; and, finally, his moving account of the broken man's voyage to the Mediterranean, and his last days at Abbotsford.[6] Of Lockhart's skill as a biographical artist there can be no question; it is only to be regretted, as Carlyle regretted, that he never knew the value of economy.

· 5 ·

Gentleman-conservative that he was, Lockhart would have rejected with fastidious horror the very notion of "popularizing" his life of Scott. It was left for a biographer of Goldsmith, a decade later (1848), to show how literary biography could be written to the taste of the new class of readers who preferred amusement to

---

[6] Lockhart's pages on the great novelist's dying days, though justly admired as art, are now considered unreliable history. Scott's dignity and clear-headedness, as described by Lockhart, cannot easily be reconciled with the independently attested fact that he was then no longer in command of his faculties. His famous admonition to his son-in-law, "My dear, be a good man—be virtuous—be religious—be a good man. Nothing else will give you any comfort when you come to lie here," which in any event has the air of a prepared exit speech, bears a curious resemblance to a physician's report, quoted by Dr. Johnson, of Lord Lyttelton's last words: "Be good, be virtuous, my Lord; you must come to this." It is known, too, that one of Scott's female relatives begged Lockhart to write an appropriate deathbed narrative to prove that Scott was deeply religious. (See Hesketh Pearson, *Sir Walter Scott: His Life and Personality* [New York, 1954], pp. 282–283.)

edification. The very title of John Forster's *Life and Adventures of Oliver Goldsmith* struck a critic as having "somewhat the air of intending fictitious narrative . . . Oliver Twist rather than Oliver Goldsmith." Virtually unique in this respect among the century's biographies, the work boasted a wealth of specially drawn illustrations; just as Dickens' scenes were interpreted by Cruikshank and "Phiz," dramatic incidents in Forster's narrative of Goldsmith's career engaged the talents of such equally popular artists as Maclise, Dicky Doyle, Stanfield, and Leech. Everything in Forster's book recommended it to the clientele of select circulating libraries: his chatty, though, as he admitted, sometimes high-flown prose, full of the historical present tense, *alases*, exclamations, allusions to "our Hero" and "poor Goldsmith," authorial asides and confidences; the huge freight of anecdotes, many from Boswell and other familiar sources but now touched up with every device of the early-Victorian journalist; the leisurely, affectionate pen portraits of scores of "Goldy's" friends; the lavish evocation of the eighteenth-century scene.

Few figures in the period's literary biography were brought more positively alive than Forster's Goldsmith. But it was a very special Goldsmith, adapted, like the gallery of humorists Thackeray was about to unveil in his lectures, to the era's taste: feckless, to be sure, but endearingly innocent, whimsical, courageous, cheerful—in short, a Goldsmith on whom Forster's contemporaries could be depended to splash their affection.

> Through all the distance of time [Forster wrote, in one of a hundred such passages] may not one see even yet, moving through the steps of the minuet, that clumsy little ill-built figure, those short thick legs, those plain features,—all the clumsier and plainer for the satin-grain coat, the garter blue silk breeches, the gold spring buttons, and the rich straw-coloured tamboured waist-coat,—yet with every sense but of honest gladness and frank enjoyment lost in the genial goodnature, the beaming mirth and truth of soul, the childlike glee and cordial fun, which turn into a cheerful little hop the austere majesty of the stateliest of all the dances?

The age of Johnson was seen through Victorian rose-colored glasses; the residents of Grub Street and the habitués of the bluestockings' salons alike were good-humored, well-intentioned, sociable; people in general were solid, normal, hearty, and their worst faults, generally speaking, were nothing more than amiable eccentricities. Forster, indeed, transformed Johnson's Literary Club into a branch of the Pickwick Club, and even when Goldsmith was portrayed starving in his garret, the book exuded an aroma of roast beef and plum pudding.

This *Gemütlichkeit*-laden biography was enthusiastically received in its time. "Here," wrote a *Quarterly* reviewer, "we have depicted the man himself as he moved along his path, and at every turn of the story, which is unfolded with the vivacity and regularity of an actual drama, he stands before us in the vividness of reality, with all the changes which had been wrought in him by each previous stage of his journey. This is real *Biography*." It went through a number of editions, and for twenty or thirty years it was often cited as an example of how lively and engrossing a well-written literary biography could be. But it set no fashion, and in his own later biographies Forster made no attempt to imitate it.[7]

One of the few subsequent writers to try the same kind of easygoing popularization for an adult audience was Forster's admiring friend Percy Fitzgerald, a prolific journalist who composed a two-volume *Life of Laurence Sterne* (1864). Exclamatory, interrogatory, confidential, garrulous, the prose style suggested Forster's watered down for patrons of the cheaper libraries: "The next act of this little piece discovers the pastoral little village, which has become Mr. Sterne's new parish. A pretty spot,

---

[7] Soon after Forster's book appeared, however, an attempt of another kind was made to write Goldsmith's biography for a popular audience. The aged Washington Irving, who earlier had composed two potboiling sketches of the poet-essayist, helped himself to some of the facts in Prior's and Forster's more substantial volumes and served them up anew in, as he said, "as graphic style as I could command." He managed to revive his failing powers sufficiently to produce a jaunty, picturesque book, permeated, as all of his successes had been, with his genial literary personality. The book was not Oliver Goldsmith, but it was authentic Irving. Flavor apart, its most noteworthy feature was the elaborate web of romantic speculation Irving wove around Forster's hint that Goldsmith cherished a hopeless passion for Mary Horneck ("the Jessamy Bride"). "This," exclaimed Forster in a later edition of his own biography (1871, II, 148, note), "is running down a suggestion indeed!—and, with whatever success for romance-loving readers, less pleasantly, it must be admitted, for sober seekers after truth."

with a musically-sounding name . . ." And: "And now that the Rev. Laurence is fairly afloat with his parochial duties, provided, too, with a Mrs. Sterne to play the vicar's lady, let us look into this Yorkshire parish of Sutton, and see how he will adapt himself to a newer and more pastoral shape of life." Reviewers were quick to detect the meretriciousness of the whole performance.

> Some chapters [complained *Blackwood's Magazine*] . . . are scattered through later parts of the work, which advance the story almost as little as certain fantastic chapters in "Tristram" that are half filled with asterisks: they bear inviting titles and are written in an emphatic manner, but leave much the same impression behind them as a page of asterisks might have done. . . . Mr. Fitzgerald's . . . manner of writing . . . is of that class where there is too incessant, too conspicuous effort to be lively and entertaining. . . . He would please more if he trusted to the inherent interest of his subject, and laboured less to keep our attention by the little tricks and artifices of composition.

Biographers' occasional adoption of the familiar style, even if the first-person singular itself was used only sparingly, raised afresh the question, perennial since Boswell, of how far the author should be present in a book which, after all, belonged not to him but to the man he was writing about. The novelist who repeatedly took his readers into his confidence and even suspended the action while he stepped to the footlights to deliver homilies had been a stock character ever since Fielding's day, and with Thackeray and Trollope he returned to front center. Critics of fiction disagreed on whether the intrusive commentator was an asset or a nuisance. Among critics of biography, however, opinion was almost unanimous: he was a nuisance.

It is true that Walton's habit of turning up in odd corners of his *Lives* was not only condoned but approved. But he was one of "our older authors," and his seeming innocent egotism was part of his antique charm. Later biographers enjoyed no such tolerance. Mason's intrusiveness in his life of Gray had never been forgotten. Mason paid himself off for his self-effacement in letting Gray tell the story of his own life by constantly appearing in the footnotes. He insisted on explaining why he included certain letters which might seem trivial to the judicious and why, equally often, he excised certain passages (thus piquing, without satisfying, the reader's curiosity); he added his penny's worth to the opinions Gray expressed in his letters, called frequent and gratuitous attention to the "beauties" of Gray's phrasing, and, not least often, apologized for including references favorable to himself.

Much more censurable, however, was Boswell's alleged over-presence in his *Life of Johnson*. This was one of the gravest defects the nineteenth-century reader found in a generally admirable book. If Boswell was, as Macaulay insisted, a conceited fool, he might at least have had the sense to remove himself from his pages, so that the fact would not have been so obvious. The artistic sin of a dramatist's upstaging his hero was compounded when the dramatist revealed himself as a most undesirable person, the sort of character one would be extremely reluctant to admit to his drawing room.

Some critics nevertheless maintained that Boswell's constant presence was as indispensable as Johnson's. But the charge of "egotism" was one to which biographers coming in Boswell's wake were expected to be peculiarly sensitive. Biographers, it was held, should be neither seen nor heard. Thomas Jefferson Hogg's *Shelley* was attacked, as it should have been, for its excessive attention to the subject of Thomas Jefferson Hogg;[8] and the first volume of Forster's *Life of Dickens* was greeted by the much-quoted, but largely undeserved, sneer that it was really "The Life of John Forster, with Some Account of Charles Dickens"—a complaint to which Forster responded by reducing his personal prominence, and introducing more evidence from other sources, from

---

[8] This was not the only competing topic. Even in an age when strict adherence to the biographical business in hand was not insisted upon, Hogg's waywardness was widely criticized. Into what he termed this "biography of a Divine Poet, to the illustration of whose remarkable character alone every word should tend," he packed many opinionated digressions, including uncomplimentary observations on the legal profession and a disquisition on the philosophy of nakedness, its salutary physical effects, and the views of various people (including ladies) with whom Hogg canvassed the topic. His long narratives of his travels in England, with special attention to the poor roads and dirty inns, may be valuable contributions to the history of transportation, but they are not especially suitable to a life of Shelley—least of all the forty pages devoted to the trip he made to Dublin in 1813 to see the Shelleys, who, it turned out, were not there.

((217

the middle of the second volume to the end. The conspicuously modest biographer therefore could expect a special meed of praise. The *Westminster Review,* for example, lauded Monckton Milnes's tact in his life of Keats:

> When the poet, in verse or prose, sings his own song, Mr. Milnes leaves him to sing it alone, and places himself with his readers, a reverential listener to the melody, which varies from the gayest possible tone of feeling to the most passionate agony; then, when the great soul is silent, he tells us where and how he is, or suffers some one else that he deems will do it better. Thus the book goes on, the poet wandering whither he listeth, his editor following, led on by heart-instinct, and leading us on too, making our pole-star one.

· 6 ·

Biographical theory would have been oddly unresponsive to the intellectual currents of the time had it not stressed the importance of milieu. The vital role of social and cultural environment in forming character had become a commonplace of English thought as early as Boswell's time, and its specific application to literature (environment makes the man, the man makes the poem) had similarly been accepted in current esthetic discussion. Nowhere were the shaping effects of milieu more extensively revealed than in the lives of poets. Hence the biographer was expected to depict his subject's background with special care. As William Godwin put it:

> The full and complete life of a poet would include an extensive survey of the manners, the opinions, the arts and the literature, of the age in which the poet lived. This is the only way in which we can become truly acquainted with the history of his mind, and the causes which made him what he was. We must observe what Chaucer felt and saw, how he was educated, what species of learning he pursued, and what were the objects, the events and the persons, successively presented to his view, before we can strictly and philosophically understand his biography.

Godwin's precepts were unexceptionable, but his practice was deplorable. In the 1,100 pages of his life of Chaucer, the poet appeared only at long intervals; for the most part, he was lost to view behind Godwin's survey of life and manners in fourteenth-century England. Godwin had to describe with some minuteness the architecture of the time, because, after all, Chaucer's eye could not have avoided noticing it; when he mentioned the legend that Chaucer was a lawyer (a possibility so remote that even Godwin, a most accomplished maker of bricks without straw, did not believe in it), he glided into a long discussion of medieval law. Sir Walter Scott, one of the many critics whose wit and indignation were stirred in approximately equal degrees by Godwin's performance, observed:

> . . . the incidents of Chaucer's life, serving as a sort of thread upon which to string his multifarious digressions, bear the same propor-tion to the book that the alphabet does to the Encyclopædia, or the texts of sermons to the sermons themselves. . . . Where the central figure . . . is dimly discoverable in the back-ground, ob-scured and overshadowed by the motley groupe of abbeys, castles, colleges and halls, fantastically pourtrayed around it, we cannot perceive either unity or individuality in so whimsical a perform-ance. The work may be a view of the manners of the 13th [*sic*] century, containing right good information, not much the worse for the wear; but has no more title to be called a life of Chaucer, than a life of Petrarch.[9]

This grand-scale misapplication of environmentalism in biogra-phy, together with the derision it invited, gave the "life and times" study the dubious repute it retained throughout the cen-tury. In literary biography, Godwin's ill-advised exploit remained unsurpassed, at least in scale, until the advent of David Masson, "a sort of Carlyle with a wooden leg, stumping painfully, but with Aberdonian resolution, through the Miltonic period." His *Life of John Milton: Narrated in Connexion with the Political, Ecclesi-*

---

[9] Privately Scott wrote a friend, "a whole edition has vanished—I was at a loss to know how, till I conjectured that, as the heaviest materials to be come at, they have been sent on the secret expedition . . . for blocking up the mouth of our enemy's harbours." (*The Letters of Sir Walter Scott*, ed. H. J. C. Grierson [London, 1932–37], I, 216.)

((219

astical, and Literary History of His Time (seven volumes, 1859–
94) was concerned, as the subtitle suggests, primarily with
events, not, as Godwin's was, with social and intellectual background. But the effect was the same: a "life" was almost wholly
obscured by its "times," and the biographer's overpreoccupation
with a legitimate intellectual interest doomed his book to artistic
failure.

One biographer who succeeded to a modest extent in establishing the influence a man's environment had upon his character
was Lockhart, who in his life of Burns recognized the psychological effect of the country youth's experiences among the Edinburgh literati after the Kilmarnock volume of *Poems* brought him
fame. Burns, he declared, was an artist suddenly thrust into unac-
customed, head-turning, and potentially injurious company. It
was not the last story of the kind that literary biography was
destined to unfold. Even more noteworthy, because conceived on
a larger scale and more skillfully accomplished, was Mrs. Gaskell's description of isolated Haworth and of the schools Charlotte Brontë attended. George Eliot's praise was well merited:
with a novelist's eye and a psychologist's insight, Mrs. Gaskell
re-created both the physical and the social atmosphere that, as she
well argued, had much to do with the formation of Charlotte's
character.[1]

Theoretically the ultimate goal of background exploration in
literary biography is less to trace the development of a writer's
character than to explain the genesis and peculiar qualities of his
art. Sometimes, particularly in the early years of the century,
before formal histories of literature had been written to relieve
them of this self-imposed responsibility, biographers such as
Scott, in his *Dryden,* and Anna Barbauld, in her *Richardson,* in-

---

[1] Mrs. Gaskell's reward for her pains was an immediate outcry in the press
and the threat of legal action. Her description of the Clergy Daughters' School
at Cowan Bridge gave much offense to the master's family and friends. As a
result of this and other breaches of discretion, the second edition of her book
was suppressed and the third contained many alterations to soothe the feelings of
various injured parties; and the author, on advice of counsel, publicly retracted
some of her statements. Our present knowledge of the facts of Brontë biography
makes it plain that Mrs. Gaskell was nevertheless oftener right than wrong.

terlarded their life narratives with generous slices of literary history. But since they merely described the literary events and tendencies that happened to coincide with their subject's lifetime, without attempting to specify the ways in which they affected him, such passages had little bearing on the literary biography itself. A closer connection between the individual career and the literary conditions of the age was occasionally achieved, as when Thomas Moore used the unsettled, questing literary atmosphere of early nineteenth-century England to account for the direction in which young Byron's talents developed. Moore was, for his time, unusually conscious of the relation between the spirit of the age and poetic production. He recognized not only that a writer is affected by the literary and cultural air he breathes in his youth, but also that that same air, breathed by his prospective readers, influences his fortunes as author. Southey too was aware of this factor; in his life of Cowper he made a careful attempt to relate the success of *The Task* to the state of English poetry at the time, and more especially to the condition of public taste. Decades later William Lee invoked the popular taste of Defoe's day to explain why he wrote so many crime stories (*Moll Flanders, Jonathan Wild,* and so forth)—"Books never intended for the drawing-room tables of the nineteenth century."

For the first three quarters of the century no biographer of a man of letters came even close to fulfilling the sweeping requirements Carlyle laid down for a biography that would comprehensively explain the man in terms of his time. Least of all did anyone show the impact of contemporary ideas on his subject's mind. The first English literary biographer to set his figures firmly in their intellectual milieu was John Morley. In his studies of Voltaire, Rousseau, and Burke, Morley was interested less in his subjects' external experience than in the development of their ideas and their place in eighteenth-century intellectual history. His own bent of mind—he was a belated child of the Enlightenment, rationalistic and skeptical—and his laconic style admirably equipped him for his task. But he had no contemporary imitators. The dates of his books (*Voltaire,* 1872; *Rousseau,* 1873;

Burke, 1878) are, however, significant. The decade witnessed a renewed emphasis on environmentalism. In 1875 Dowden published his popular and influential *Shakspere: A Critical Study of His Mind and Art,* the first chapter of which ("Shakspere and the Elizabethan Age") was a noteworthy description of the dramatist's cultural surroundings. Four years later, Henry James's English Men of Letters volume on Hawthorne was less a formal life narrative than an attempt to represent Hawthorne as the product of a particular time and place. By evoking the flavor of the Salem in which Hawthorne's mind and art were formed, and by explaining to an English audience the problem of the writer in the America of the 1840's and '50's, James provided what was for his time "a model of perfection in biography," insofar as perfection was to be achieved by answering Carlyle's question "What and how produced was the effect of society" on the writer? Here and there in literary biography, in the seventies, the effect of Taine's theories of *race, moment,* and *milieu* was beginning to be felt; James, indeed, specifically alluded to Taine in his *Hawthorne.* But this tendency of thought, coming as it did from a foreign quarter, had little immediate influence on the literary biography of the next several decades; for the most part, English biographers, stubbornly insular in their habits, were as little indebted to Taine as their novel-writing contemporaries were to Zola.

· 7 ·

But the central concern of biography, then as now, was the man, not his times—the individual human result of environmental forces, not the forces themselves. The supreme artistic problem, accordingly, was one of portraiture. By the careful selection and arrangement of recorded detail, a man's outward presence could be re-created. A harder task was that of faithfully capturing the most elusive of all personal qualities, his inner constitution: the changing coloration of mental phenomena which eventually became more or less fixed in the form of his mature psyche, and the way he felt and thought at various junctures in his adult life. If sufficient private evidence survived, the biographer might with some confidence describe the climate of his subject's mind, both its habits of impulse and response and the particular quality it assumed in individual circumstances; much more difficult, however, was the problem of *explaining* why he acted and thought as he did.

One must not assume that this interest in making explicit and credible the intangibles of the mind—so pervasive a concern in twentieth-century biography—was universal, or even usual, in biography of the nineteenth century. The fact that many biographies were sponsored by the subject's immediate family, whose desire to protect his privacy naturally extended to his inner self, was hardly conducive to independent speculation and interpretation on the part of the biographer. In any event, the whole Victorian spirit of reticence, drawing a firm distinction between a man's public and personal lives, urged that what went on behind the drawn blinds of his soul was information privileged to him alone. It was a sense of combined impropriety and futility that led many to conclude, as Leslie Stephen did toward the end of the century, that "A little analysis of motive may be necessary here and there: when, for example, your hero has put his hand in somebody's pocket and you have to demonstrate that his conduct was due to sheer absence of mind. But you must always remember that a single concrete fact, or a saying into which a man has put his whole soul, is worth pages of psychological analysis."

Nevertheless, biographers often could not suppress the deep-seated curiosity most men feel in the presence of another personality whose complex, inconsistent traits of character were inscribed, fragmentarily and quite possibly cryptically, on the historical record. This curiosity was reinforced by the whole scientific tendency of the century, which, although it may not have supplied many useful techniques for answering psychological questions, insisted on raising them.

As the century began, biographers frequently rested their portrayal of character on the systematic psychology associated with the Scottish mental philosophers. Sometimes in so many words, sometimes only implicitly, they treated their subjects as typical of a certain predefined class. Thomas Moore accurately expressed his era's confidence in the simplifications made available by the current theories and nomenclature of psychological analysis:

> There are few characters in which a near acquaintance does not enable us to discover some one leading principle or passion consistent enough in its operations to be taken confidently into account in any estimate of the disposition in which they are found.... There is in most minds some one governing influence, from which chiefly,—though, of course, biassed on some occasions by others, —all its various impulses and tendencies will be found to radiate.

Those elements of personality which bound a man most closely to the genus to which he belonged—men of poetic talent, for example—were isolated and stressed, to the neglect of the individual traits which conformed to no textbook classifications. Dr. Currie emphasized Burns's sensibility, a quality which in excess (as supposedly it was among poets) distracts the rational mind, which is the only sure moral gyroscope. In effect, the old generalizing mode of the Theophrastan character, which had hampered the development of genuine biography more than a century earlier, was revived under new, "scientific," auspices. And though the special tenets of empirical, classificatory psychology faded from intellectual favor by the 1830's, its residual effects persisted for some time, most influentially, perhaps, in the thought of Herbert Spencer and Alexander Bain.

With Thomas Carlyle, whose private spiritual odyssey from Edinburgh rationalism to romantic intuitionism marked the path a whole generation followed, biography was again drawn away from more or less realistic psychology, though in a different direction, and, artistically speaking, to greater advantage. A number of his literary essays, notably those on Schiller and Burns, are exercises in biography and criticism, the two interests being so closely entwined as to suggest an anticipation of Sainte-Beuve. Impatient of the moral platitudes, quack-scientific humbug (as he would have said), and perfunctory superficialities that passed for "character interpretation" in his time, he insisted that the biographer's most pressing task was to look deeper, ever deeper, into the very soul of a man. "How," he demanded, "shall that unhappy Biographic brotherhood, instead of writing like Index-makers and Government-clerks, suddenly become enkindled with some sparks of intellect, or even of genial fire; and not only collecting dates and facts, but making use of them, look beyond the surface and economical form of a man's life, into its substance and spirit?" He practiced what he preached. His biographical exercises were spiritual profiles, the imaginative results of his passion to discover men, larger than life, who were governed by superhuman gifts and missions. His conception of human personality was too feverish ever to be confined to the facts as they appeared in the historical records; instead, the Carlylean obsession with a reality that lies behind appearances transfigured his subjects into simulacra at once unhistorical and unreal, visions rather than images.

Whatever its merits as factual biography, Carlyle's *Life of John Sterling*, a memoir of a young clergyman, was a genuine work of art. The urgency of Carlyle's purpose—to counteract Archdeacon Hare's official biography of Sterling, which overstressed his religious heterodoxy at the expense of his character as a human being—gave his prose a spirit and movement that stood in marked contrast to the air of conscientious dutifulness or ill-concealed boredom which distinguished most of the era's biographies. Occasionally, though not as often as such extravaganzas as the "Burns" might lead one to expect, Carlyle turned Sterling into a standard Carlylean hero, "a radiant child of the empyrean, clad in bright auroral hues." To the extent that Carlyle's rhetorical habits made all his figures appear cast from the same mold, Sterling was not individualized. But because he had personal recollections to work from, and because he was intent on presenting Sterling not as a demigod but as a man, Carlyle employed to excellent effect concrete details, anecdotes, scenes, and the devices of dramatic style, including free use of the confidential *I* and *we* and of the historical present tense.[2]

Carlyle's experiments in literary life writing were convenient

[2] One must not forget that in the same book occurs the famous description of Coleridge holding forth on Highgate Hill, a triumph of portraiture which makes Carlyle, surrounded by his fellow biographers, seem like a Titan towering over a company of penny-a-line journalists and bloodless antiquaries.

and picturesque vehicles for the exposition of his philosophy, not authentic reports of personalities and events. He provided no useful model for future biography. Nevertheless, it was wholesome for someone with his eloquence and powers of illustration to insist that the "substance and spirit" of a man's life demanded to be explored, not with the pedantic charts provided by the formulas and categories of "mental philosophy" but with the intuition of a sensitive human being responding to the records of another.

Intuition is a faculty which can pierce to the heart of a psychological mystery or fly absurdly wide of the mark. Though its value to a keen-minded biographer is considerable even in a modern epoch of scientific psychology, it especially recommended itself to biographers in the first half of the nineteenth century, when sentimentalism and free indulgence of fancy had literary warrant. Whenever, as they narrated their subject's inner life, they skated on thin ice or came to open patches of water, biographers of Carlyle's generation could rise on the wings of their intuition. It was a convenient device for supplying the silences of history or amending its undesirable evidence. In a passage in his life of Burns, already quoted in another connection (page 169), Lockhart wrote:

> When I consider his tender affection for the surviving members of his own family, and the reverence with which he ever regarded the memory of the father whom he had so recently buried, I cannot believe that Burns has thought fit to record in verse all the feelings which this exposure excited in his bosom. . . . His false pride recoiled from letting his jovial associates guess how little he was able to drown the whispers *of the still small voice;* and the fermenting bitterness of a mind ill at ease within itself, escaped . . . in the shape of angry sarcasms against others, who, whatever their private errors might be, had at least done him no wrong.

In the very act of sentimental psychologizing, Lockhart made a shrewd observation. The first sentence represents the romantic apologist at work; whatever the facts, the instincts of the sympathetic biographer ("I cannot believe . . .") are a surer guide to truth. But the second sentence, with its recognition of inner conflicts and the deceptive manner in which they are often revealed, has a psychological validity that evokes respect in a post-Freudian age.

Although nineteenth-century literary biographers sometimes arrived at psychological descriptions and explanations which are still valid today, as a rule they were not adept at such insights. There was always a certain amount of random, perfunctory examination of motives, from Scott's attempts (1808) to explain Dryden's religious vacillation to Edmund Gosse's analysis (1899) of the circumstances of Donne's conversion. But what the nineteenth-century biographer most needed, and what the age could not give him, was the aid not only of techniques but of concepts that would enable him to read between the lines of his data. Although the importance of childhood and adolescent experience was recognized—Forster, for example, in describing Dickens' miserable experience in the shoeblacking factory and discussing the autobiographical significance of *David Copperfield*, sought to show "in what way those strange experiences of his boyhood affected him afterwards"—there was little awareness of the continuing process of psychological development in adulthood. The influence of mature personal relationships was seldom perceived, least of all that of marriage. The contribution of a poet's wife to his career was glanced at only to the extent of celebrating her constancy, affection, and patience or deploring the effects of an imprudent and ill-fated marriage.

Of all Victorian biographers, John Morley was the most percipient and level-headed psychologist. His study of Rousseau, nourished, of course, by the *Confessions*, was much more concerned with the philosopher's inner life than with external events. Probably no earlier literary biography in English probed so insistently into its subject's mind. Yet Morley himself lamented the inadequacy of the psychological knowledge his age had at its command. He looked forward to the time "when the great art of life has been more systematically conceived in the long processes of time and endeavour, and when more bold, effective, and far-reaching advance has been made in defining those pathological

((227

manifestations which deserve to be seriously studied, as distinguished from those of a minor sort which are barely worth registering."

· 8 ·

Truth, it might reasonably be concluded from all that has been said in these pages, was not the supreme strength of nineteenth-century literary biography. The diverse forces that made biography what it was in the age combined to suppress, distort, and otherwise render mistaken, inaccurate, or incomplete the record of a life and character as mediated by a biographer from the documentary sources. With exceptions so few as to be negligible—one is the life of John Bunyan (1885) by the Bedfordshire nonconformist minister Dr. John Brown, who managed to discover virtually every fact that survives about the tinker-preacher —no English literary figure was so satisfactorily treated by a nineteenth-century biographer as to make any subsequent life an act of virtual supererogation.

Yet it is also true that a tradition of severe and exhaustive biographical scholarship persisted throughout the century, producing books which, though themselves superseded in time, laid the indispensable foundation for further inquiry. Although it was not until after mid-century that English historical scholarship felt the effect, through Stubbs, Freeman, and other historians, of the von Ranke school of "objective," "scientific" historiography, among English life writers there were, from the very beginning of the century, a heroic few whose ideals of accuracy and thoroughness were no less stringent than those associated with the discipline of the German universities. If the typical nineteenth-century literary biography is notorious, as it deserves to be, for its easy ways with fact, the reason is not that inspiring precepts or instructive models were wholly lacking.

In 1813 James Stanfield, in his remarkable book, set a theoretical standard for scholarly biography that could hardly be improved upon today. He canvassed in detail the sources of "biographical partiality" and credulity, the problem of amassing suitable, dependable, and sufficient materials, and above all the importance of scientific rigor in the handling of data. Already his high standards had been put into practice. Thirteen years earlier, Edmond Malone had published a life of Dryden which embodied the results of a prodigious amount of digging in hitherto undisturbed archives. Often its text was no more than a two-line rivulet running above broad acres of small-type notes. The book has been called "the first genuine scholarly biography of a man of letters," and it well deserves the praise, for Malone, in addition to being tireless in his quest of facts, subjected them to intensive testing on the basis of chronological soundness, veracity of witnesses, and sheer likelihood.[3] The world, it seems, was not yet ready for so assiduous a display of antiquarianism in literary biography; its minuteness, digressiveness, and (to many people) finicky worrying over unimportant discrepancies earned it adverse reviews and even the dubious flattery of elaborate satire. The title of one pamphlet, adequately describing the author's opinion, ran: *"The Essence of Malone, or, the 'Beauties' of that fascinating Writer, extracted from his immortal Work, in five hundred, sixty-nine Pages, and a quarter, just published; and (with his accustomed felicity,) entitled 'Some Account of the Life and Writings of JOHN DRYDEN!!'"*

Between Malone's unencouraging experience and the equally damning reception of Godwin's *Chaucer*—a book superficially resembling it, but poles removed in quality of scholarship—it is little wonder that no further large-scale literary biographies, based on or pretending to exhaustive research, appeared for a full generation. But in 1837 Prior published his life of Goldsmith. Formless though it was, its sheer weight of materials, ranging from Goldsmith's tailor bills (which henceforth became the symbol of biographical irrelevance) to third-hand anecdotes, entitled it to respect; in diligence of investigation and near-neurotic anxiety to test the authenticity and probability of every received

---

[3] A novel feature of the book, which illustrates the comprehensiveness of Malone's notion of research, was the appended list of "Persons in whose Cabinets letters written by Dryden may probably be found." This open invitation to readers to seek further documents in designated places has seldom been repeated by subsequent scholarly biographers.

statement, Prior out-Maloned Malone. Six years later a busy antiquarian, Sir Nicholas Harris Nicolas, inaugurated modern Chaucer study in a small book which, in conspicuous contrast to Godwin's, limited itself to the demonstrable facts of the poet's life. Nicolas expunged from the tradition such myths as those of Chaucer's meeting Petrarch and of his spending his last years in serene retirement at Woodstock; and he refused to make any but the most sparing and cautious use of the supposedly autobiographical clues found in the poems.

In 1859 David Masson published the first volume of his sprawling biography of Milton, which upon completion a generation later incorporated a vast wealth of information drawn from the so-called "life records" of the poet-statesman and from the documents of seventeenth-century English political history. Two years later came the first volume of an equally monumental enterprise of research and critical editing, the seven-volume *Letters and Life of Francis Bacon* by James Spedding, one of the most brilliant men of his age, whose lifelong dedication to the minute study of Bacon was dominated by an attempt to redeem the philosopher's name from Macaulay's aspersions. William Lee, stimulated by his discovery in the State Paper Office of a mass of Defoe's political writings dating from after 1715—the year when previous biographers had assumed he retired from the pamphlet wars—combed all accessible newspapers from the period, with the result that he proposed many new items to add to the canon, rejected from it writings previously ascribed to Defoe, and revised the chronology of his literary career. In the next decade John Forster published (1875) the first volume of a projected life of Swift, which he left incomplete at his death. His wide-ranging research, facilitated by his influential connections in literary and socal circles, led to his gaining access to many previously unused Swift manuscripts. His new material, in addition to fresh data gathered from still other sources, was effectively used in Henry Craik's vigorously written two-volume life of Swift (1882).

As the century neared its close, the early romantic poets, no longer near-contemporary figures, became subjects for disinterested scholarly research rather than of discreet memoirs inhibited by the presence of survivors. Their private papers, located in many hands, were printed for the first time, in long excerpts though not, as a rule, *in toto*. Some years before Lady Shelley appointed him the poet's official biographer, Dowden had begun to accumulate material on Shelley's life, and his correspondence with Richard Garnett, William Michael Rossetti, and others reveals how diligently he sought to establish facts and settle disputed or obscure points. In 1889, three years after Dowden's *Shelley* appeared, William Knight published his three-volume life of Wordsworth, which was noteworthy for the many documents it made public for the first time, among them extracts from Dorothy's Grasmere journal and the entries in Crabb Robinson's diary relating to Wordsworth's circle. And in 1893 J. Dykes Campbell completed the first life of Coleridge based on original documentary sources, including much material left by Coleridge's acquaintances. Thus within a single decade the biographical study of three major poets was set upon a firm basis. Much more remained to be done, but there was great gain in the fact that major portions of the relevant sources had become accessible in print. If nineteenth-century literary biography lacked noteworthy art, it was not for want of raw material.

Nor, one must repeat lest too bleak an impression be left by the necessary emphasis on the deficiencies of nineteenth-century literary biography, was it for total lack of models—the occasional biographies which succeeded in presenting with style and skill a coherent, steady, and lifelike view of their subjects. The artistic merit of some has already been alluded to: Lockhart's *Scott*, Mrs. Gaskell's *Charlotte Brontë*, Morley's studies of eighteenth-century philosophers. In addition, there were Lockhart's *Burns*, with its thoughtful character analysis; Moore's *Byron*, which, despite its suppressions and evasions, remains a masterly portrait of a complex personality; the younger George Crabbe's modest life of his father, which Edward FitzGerald, an intimate friend of the author, no doubt overpraised as "one of the most delightful books in the language" but which charms by its very unpretentiousness; Southey's *Cowper*, distinguished by economy and balance; Alexander Gilchrist's *Blake,* which treated another treacher-ous subject with sanity and understanding; Forster's *Dickens,* which went a long way toward fulfilling Dickens' own desire that, "when my personal dustiness shall be past the control of my love of order," he have "such a biographer and such a critic" as the Forster who had written the life of Goldsmith; and Froude's *Carlyle,* which will appear in the next pages. The great misfortune was that such performances were not more frequent in the long course of the century.

CHAPTER VII

From Froude to Strachey

IN the years between the publication of the first volumes of James Anthony Froude's *Carlyle* in 1882 and that of Lytton Strachey's *Eminent Victorians* in 1918, the general intellectual and literary atmosphere of England became more favorable to realistic biography than it had been since Boswell's day. But the actual writing of biography, ironically, continued to be dominated by conservatism and convention. If anything, the lives of authors written during this generation were more dogged, more dull, more anxious to avoid both giving offense and raising questions, than those which had gone before.

The period was not wholly sterile, of course. In addition to the important documentary biographies of Pope, Swift, Steele, Wordsworth, Shelley, and Coleridge which were mentioned above, there were such substantial works as John William Mackail's *William Morris*, Ethel Colburn Mayne's *Byron*, and Sidney Colvin's *Keats*. Other biographies could boast a certain gracefulness of style, mechanical and faded though the prose of such professional belletrists as Gosse, Dobson, and A. C. Benson now strikes us. But the typical biographical production of the era was on a level not far above that of the numerous volumes put together by the ex-actor Lewis P. Benjamin ("Lewis Melville"), whose competence, not to say ambition, hardly went beyond the ability to arrange many letters in sequence and write bridges of pedestrian commentary.

There no doubt were a number of reasons for this widening

discrepancy between the spirit of the age, which was now discarding, one by one, the obstacles that had stood in the way of candor, and the spirit of its biography, steadfast in its obedience to traditional principles of reticence, its desperate anxiety not to give offense. One reason, however, stands out above all others: the controversy over Froude's *Carlyle*. Protracted, sordid, acidulous, this battle of the books displayed the Victorian character more often at its obscurantist worst than at its courageous best. It is not pleasant to recall, but it is indispensable to our story.[1]

Carlyle, faithful to his old sentiments about mealymouthed biography, instructed his friend and disciple Froude to make whatever use he wished of his personal papers for the sake of a biography which would present him truly as he was. After Carlyle died in 1881, Froude published first the sage's own *Reminiscences*, then (1882–84) his four-volume life of Carlyle, and (1883) the *Letters and Memorials of Jane Welsh Carlyle*, over which her husband had himself worked following her death.

At once Froude was denounced as a traitor to his master's memory. In his pages the man who was the veritable conscience and scourge of Britain, whose eightieth birthday in 1875 had been a national occasion, turned out to have been an extremely difficult man to get along with, selfish, grim, irritable, even violent. From first to last his domestic life had been marked by tensions and fierce outbursts. The spirited Jane Welsh Carlyle, as was revealed by her letters which Froude printed, had been a martyr to the bearded prophet—but far from an uncomplaining one. And Froude, had he chosen to do so, could have presented an even darker picture of unrest in Cheyne Row, for in a passage in her diary which he suppressed she recorded that her arms bore blue marks from her husband's abuse.

This exposé (as it was immediately regarded) of a great writer's bearish personality and his ill-advised marriage to a woman

---

[1] The curious may find the details in Waldo H. Dunn's *Froude and Carlyle* (1930), a book which proved, if nothing else, that fifty years after the battle was joined, neutrality was still beyond reach. Dunn, who had the cooperation of Froude's children while Carlyle's nephew, Alexander, refused him access to his uncle's papers, unequivocally sided with Froude. Subsequent opinion has, for the most part, supported him.

with a will of her own shocked a Victorian world that still cherished its illusions about the moral dignity of author-heroes and the bliss of the married state. To reveal as much as Froude revealed would have meant disaster for any biographer in the era, but it was doubly unfortunate that fate had chosen him to do so. His religious heterodoxy, notorious since he had published his *Nemesis of Faith* over thirty years before, had won him the antagonism of the clergy, who still wielded great influence over public opinion; and his reputation as a historian had already been tarnished by charges of constitutional inaccuracy, partisanship, and general incompetence, laid against him particularly by E. A. Freeman, a scholar of no mean pedantry who appears to have harbored an almost psychotic enmity toward him. Freeman's allegations were generally accepted at the time, though nowadays people are inclined to regard them as an instance of the pot calling the kettle black. However that may be, Froude's soiled status as a historian made him all the more vulnerable to the execration that greeted his successive volumes on the Carlyles. Only metaphors from the autopsy room seemed adequate to convey the critics' outrage. "We have been assisting for the last three years," said the *Saturday Review* when the *Letters and Memorials of Jane Welsh Carlyle* appeared, "at a minute and repulsive double dissection, in which by a hideous process each of the subjects has been made to take a part in demonstrating the morbid anatomy of the other. No such spectacle has hitherto been afforded in the annals of literature"—and much more to the same grisly effect. "No deplorable or shameful detail has been spared," the same organ commented when reviewing the later volumes of Froude's biography; "a minute and exhaustive anatomical demonstration has been made of every morbid structure, the scalpel of the biographer has been ruthlessly employed to lay bare and exhibit all the ravages of disease."

The anti-Froudeians were led by Carlyle's niece and nephew, who, motivated by family pride and also, it has been suggested, by envy of Froude's profits, used every means at their command to denounce his portrait of their uncle. Outside the family Froude's most energetic antagonist was the Harvard professor

Charles Eliot Norton, the close friend of many English men of letters, including Carlyle. Norton now edited (or at least put his name to) a series of volumes of excerpts from Carlyle's correspondence, designed to "correct" the image painted by Froude, who, Norton joined Freeman in asserting, was as unreliable a biographer and editor as he was a historian. The printed texts of the letters in Norton's volumes, it happens, are as untrustworthy as any that Froude put to press. Another of Froude's assailants was Cordy Jeaffreson. One would have thought that the two besieged biographers would have formed a united front against the critics; but Froude was a friend of Lady Shelley, which automatically made him Jeaffreson's enemy. The anomalies involved in this choosing-up of sides—a "realistic" biographer of Carlyle sympathizing with a protectress of Shelley myths, one accused iconoclast ranged against another—are piquant indeed.

But Froude was not without his partisans. It is significant that Carlyle's own brother and sister, hardy old Calvinists who were bred to take human frailties as they came, wrote to Froude approving of his picture. Carlyle's old friend Edward FitzGerald concurred. So did Ruskin, who claimed that he knew "the facts" which supported at least one of Froude's most shocking assertions. "The facts" actually were this one: that a Tunbridge Wells doctor, examining Jane Carlyle, "suspected . . . that the usual marital relations had not occurred"; he told his aunt the story "in confidence" (we shall not pause over the medical ethics involved here); and the aunt happened to be Ruskin's mother. In the light of what is now known of Ruskin's own unconsummated marriage, it is not surprising that Carlyle's putative impotence won his sympathy. By defending Froude, Ruskin sacrificed his close friendship with Norton.

In 1903, twenty years after the publication of Jane's diaries, the controversy over the Carlyles' sexual life was revived by Sir James Crichton-Browne, a physician who, though he had never even seen Jane, averred that her medical history contradicted Froude's view that living with Carlyle had undermined her health. In reply Froude's children—he had died in 1894—published a manuscript found among his papers, "My Relations with Carlyle." In these pages Froude disclosed matters he had omitted from his books on the Carlyles, among them Jane's note about the bruises on her arms and the deathbed statement of Geraldine Jewsbury, her intimate friend, that on the morning after their marriage Carlyle "tore to pieces the flower-garden . . . in a fit of ungovernable fury." To this, Crichton-Browne and Alexander Carlyle replied in a pamphlet called "The Nemesis of Froude," as well as in an article in the *British Medical Journal,* whose offensive tone and content rightly evoked much disapproval.[2]

One need hardly observe that this series of episodes, spread over many years and arousing an incredible amount of acrimony, is not among the most edifying chapters in the history of English literary biography. The debate over what happened, or failed to happen, in the Carlyles' marriage bed is a striking illustration of a supposedly prudish society's capacity for prurience. It is also a classic example of the way irrelevances can distract attention from main issues. For in perspective Froude's real importance lay in the fact that he was, however undeliberately, a rebel against the prevailing biographical policy of concealing warts and smoothing facial furrows. Contemporary critics, in those infrequent moments when they could spare a glance at the artistry of his volumes, conceded that Froude was a portraitist in the style of a Rembrandt. In his presentation of the deep shadows as well as the radiances he found in his materials, Froude sought to realize Carlyle's character not only in its truth but in its wholeness. Like Boswell, he unapologetically admired the subject of his portrait (a circumstance which, though perfectly evident, his critics still found hard to believe); like Boswell, he was nevertheless intent on portraying the man as he was, not as he might have been; like Boswell, finally, he had his own subject's authorization for doing so.

[2] Froudeophobia was virulent in more than one sense. It infected, among others, a member of the Burmese Civil Service named David Alec Wilson, who during his years on the bench in the Orient had earned wide notoriety as "the hanging judge." In his retirement he wrote a six-volume biography (1923–34) dedicated to cleansing Carlyle's fame of all the aspersions with which, Wilson claimed, Froude had bespattered it.

But this not inconsiderable artistic achievement was almost totally obscured by the ethical issue. The Froude affair brought to an angry head—though the final successful lancing was still many years in the future—the old argument over the limits of biographical candor. The sore had already been rubbed raw by the publication in 1878 of Keats's letters to Fanny Brawne. These, as well as other letters of Keats published by Harry Buxton Forman in 1883, shattered one more Victorian dream. Far from being a faithful model for Shelley's Adonais, Keats, it turned out, was a young man with quite human desires and fits of peevishness and despair. The appearance in 1885 of Jeaffreson's *The Real Shelley* further inflamed the sore. Hence the course of late Victorian literary biography was, in effect, determined at long remove by three women, Jane Carlyle, Fanny Brawne, and Harriet Shelley. The disclosure of the roles they had played in the lives of the men who had, each in his fashion, loved them, necessitated a drastic and most unwelcome re-estimate of the character of the men themselves. Neither Carlyle as the often ranting husband of Jane, nor Keats as the feverish lover of Fanny, nor Shelley as the callous deserter of Harriet fitted Victorian moral specifications. What additional bitter surprises were in store if the trend toward biographical realism were not stemmed? And so, at a time when it might otherwise have gradually been drawn aside, the heavy plush curtain of Victorian reticence again was inexorably closed.

Froude's fate proved sufficient warning to virtually all other biographers who aspired toward reasonable frankness. Apart from the familiar argument that candid biography represented an impertinent invasion of privacy, the cry was revived that a man's art is self-sufficient and self-explanatory. E. F. Benson, for example, complained in 1895 that the English Men of Letters series was

> a shelf full of disillusionments. There is scarcely one beautiful life among them; even when the artist is overladen with admirable moral qualities, and free from disgusting habits, he is intensely dull. The life of Wordsworth ought to have for a sub-title, "How to Be Happy though Stupid." . . . Our safest course, unless we are very sure of ourselves, is studiously to avoid anything that deals with the ordinary life of artists. The chances are that, as dished up

for the popular taste, such lives will contain details that will either disgust or weary us, and then, unless we are very sure of ourselves, that knowledge will quite wrongly come between us and the beautiful thing.

Possibly the recent "esthetic" emphasis on the autonomy of art had something to do with Benson's squeamishness. Yet it was his almost exact contemporary, William Butler Yeats, who once said: "I have no sympathy with the mid-Victorian thought to which Tennyson gave his support, that a poet's life concerns nobody but himself. A poet is by the very nature of things a man who lives with entire sincerity, or rather, the better his poetry the more sincere his life. His life is an experiment in living and those that come after have a right to know it."

But it was Benson's view, not Yeats's, that prevailed. The law laid down by *Blackwood's Magazine* in 1849—"Whatever refers to public life is public, and may be printed: whatever refers solely to domestic existence is private, and ought to be held sacred"—was, more than ever, the biographer's working rule. Thomas Wright wrote in the preface to his biography of Walter Pater (1907): "My ambition is that the critics and the public should say of this book—'It tells the truth, though only just as much as the public has a right to know, and tells it in the most delicate manner conceivable.' . . . Pater's home life—his life with his sisters—I have considered absolutely sacred, and there will be found in these pages nothing whatever about it—that is to say, nothing subsequent to his childhood; and, indeed, it is a subject that could not in the least interest the general public."

Other biographers did not flaunt their reticence so defiantly, but they were no less assiduous in their suppressions. Hallam Tennyson's two-volume *Memoir* of his father (1897) is the enduring model of the official, or family-approved, late Victorian biography. It is suffused with decorous domesticity, full of harmless jottings on the comings and goings of titled visitors, the Laureate's trips to London or through the provinces, and the receipt of adoring letters; as a work of biographical art, it is as monstrous and marmoreal as a tomb in Westminster Abbey. Like the florid inscriptions that decorate those sepulchers, it does contain a residue of factual information. But the idiosyncrasies that made him

((239

the engaging and often formidable character he was—his vanity, his atrabiliousness, his shaggy Lincolnshire abruptness which no amount of presence in polite society had modified—were so rubbed down as to turn a wonderfully distinctive personality into an oppressively conventional one. The whole bulky work was executed in a spirit faithful to that attributed to Tennyson's wife in Max Beerbohm's caricature: "Woolner [the sculptor] at Farringford, 1857. Mrs. Tennyson: 'You know, Mr. Woolner, I'm one of the most un-meddlesome of women; but—when (I'm only asking), *when* do you begin modelling his halo?' "[3]

But, as the *Memoir's* cool reception proved, a principle that is generally subscribed to can be practiced too diligently for the taste even of its strongest advocates. It was Hallam's misfortune that among his readers were hundreds of men and women who had beheld Tennyson in all his varied moods, bland or black, or who had heard the numberless picturesque anecdotes told of him; and these readers found the discrepancy between the filial image and the true man too extreme to countenance. It was Graham Balfour's misfortune, likewise, that William Ernest Henley, one of Robert Louis Stevenson's closest friends until an unhappy misunderstanding parted them, chose to review his family-sponsored life of the novelist (1901). Henley had already proved himself a fearless opponent of biographical myth; his essay on Burns, in the Centenary Edition of that poet (1897), had brought Scotland to the verge of a new Border Rising by its refusal to help propagate the vast sentimental legend about "oor Rabbie."[4]

[3] Besides replacing the living Tennyson with, in Edmund Gosse's phrase, a "smooth bust of rosy wax," his son managed to gloss over all the painful, and psychologically the most critical, passages of the poet's life. He scarcely mentioned the rough handling his father's 1832 volume of poems received, and although he conceded that *Maud* was not an unqualified success, he spent far more space on the plaudits lavished on other books. Nor did he say anything at all of the anti-Tennysonian tide that started to run in the mid-1860's.

[4] Henley thus discharged a mission that Stevenson himself had been prevented from completing. In 1875 R.L.S. had been commissioned to write an article on Burns for the *Encyclopædia Britannica*, but what he wrote was, said Sidney Colvin, "too little in accordance with the accepted Scotch tradition" to suit the editors. So Stevenson was paid off, and a more tractable contributor, John Campbell Shairp, engaged instead. (*The Letters of Robert Louis Stevenson*, ed. Sidney Colvin [New York, 1923], I, 231.) Shairp also wrote the English Men of Letters volume on Burns.

Now, in a *Pall Mall Magazine* review that was destined to take its place in the anthologies of "notorious literary attacks," he began with faint praise: "Mr. Graham Balfour has done his best; and his best should rank decently among official biographies." The book, he continued—his disgust mounting—was "a solemn and serious essay in that kind of make-believe in which the biographee . . . did all his life rejoice, and was exceeding glad." The R.L.S. of these sober pages was "an angel clean from heaven, and I for my part flatly refuse to recognise it. . . . This Seraph in Chocolate, this barley-sugar effigy of a real man . . . is not my old, riotous, intrepid, scornful Stevenson at all." Henley's motives in this review were personal, not those of a disinterested critic; by venting his sarcasm on Balfour's book he was working out the bile accumulated during his estrangement from Stevenson, caused, he was sure, by the intervention of Stevenson's wife, who in removing him from his raffish old friends had sought to convert the erstwhile Bohemian into a respectable family man. Behind Balfour stood Fanny Osbourne Stevenson, and it was actually toward her, not the biographer himself, that Henley's bitterness was directed. But at the same time he was asserting the same ideal of biographical art that had underlain his assault on the Burns myth. It was intolerable, Henley felt, that sentimental cant should masquerade as veracious biography. Yet, whether sanctioned by a century-old accretion of national legend or by a family zealous to keep its late hero's laurels green, this was the essential quality of most biography written in Henley's time. Other episodes in the attempt to cultivate the Stevenson legend show how strong and persistent remained the urge toward biographical falsehood that Henley deplored. When Sidney Colvin edited Stevenson's letters for publication (1899 and 1911) he omitted virtually all of the high-spirited phraseology and other evidences of robustness that would have revealed him as a real man instead of a barley-sugar effigy; Colvin's censorship of the manuscripts extended to pasting two strips of paper, one black, the second white, over many of Stevenson's inadmissible remarks. To restore these passages, and correct Colvin's swarming errors of transcription and his constant editorial manipulation, has proved a large task for the editor of the definitive collection of Stevenson's letters. In 1915, again, family pressure succeeded in having the original edition of Clayton Hamilton's *On the Trail of Stevenson* withdrawn from circulation because of various indiscreet statements, some of them true—including the assertion that Fanny and Louis had shared a bed before marriage. One predictable consequence of these and other attempts to control the public idea of Stevenson was a wave of "debunkery" in the 1920's, when adulation was replaced by a leer and the youthful Stevenson was credited, among other improprieties, with possessing a mistress —who eventually proved to be wholly imaginary.

· 2 ·

It is a coincidence worth pondering that the Froude furor erupted at the very time that certain novelists, typified by George Moore and Gissing, were at last defying the code of circulating-library literary morality by imbuing their fiction with something of the naturalism practiced by the Russian and French masters. Refusing to acquiesce, as Thackeray had done, in the ban against Fieldingesque frankness of portraiture, they asserted the artist's freedom to portray men and women as they came. These suffered according to rule: the critics denounced them, their books were banned from the profitable library market, respectable publishers declined further works from their pens. Though the parallel is not complete (Froude was never a crusader, a conscious would-be liberator of biography from the trammels of Victorian mealy-mouthedness) Froude's fate was strikingly like that of the bolder spirits among novelists. In the eighties and nineties Hardy, attempting a moderate realism, was so plagued by editorial complaints and the necessity of toning down offending passages that, eventually tiring of having to make his Angel Clares convey their girls across swollen streams in wheelbarrows instead of in their arms, he quit novel writing entirely. In 1888 the publisher Henry Vizetelly went to prison for issuing a translation of Zola's *La Terre.* "Authors," rumbled the aged Tennyson—

Authors—essayist, atheist, novelist, realist, rhymester, play your part,
Paint the mortal shame of nature with the living hues of art.
Rip your brothers' vices open, strip your own foul passions bare;
Down with Reticence, down with Reverence—forward—naked—let
  them stare.
Feed the budding rose of boyhood with the drainage of your sewer;
Send the drain into the fountain, lest the stream should issue pure.
Set the maiden fancies wallowing in the troughs of Zolaism,—
Forward, forward, ay, and backward, downward too into the abysm!

Notwithstanding the Laureate's outrage, literary Zolaism was a sign of the future, and implicit in it were numerous forces in the late Victorian and Edwardian social and intellectual climate. These ranged from so incidental yet significant a phenomenon as the spread of photography, which habituated a new generation to graphic realism,[5] to the influence of scientific thought, which required men to see things not as they ought to be but as they are. Scientific psychology—a quite different study from the "mental science" under whose auspices biography had been written a century earlier—demanded a large supply of sound biographical data; and, as Havelock Ellis complained in "An Open Letter to Biographers," written when he was completing his research for his *Study of British Genius* (but not published until many years later), the hungry mouths were not being fed. "You . . . tell me a great many things that I have no desire to know," he proposed to tell contemporary life writers. Concentrate instead, he urged them, on the personal, including the physical, life of a man, "the influences, physical and moral, which surrounded the period of his conception, the welfare of his pre-natal life, whether he was born naturally and in due season," the facts of his adolescence ("you cannot tell us too much real biography—the description of life—concerning these youthful years"). The biographer should pay due attention to his subject's frailties—"you must know a man's weakness before you truly know his strength"—and be himself an expert psychologist. "The writing of a biography is

---

[5] As early as 1864, Charles Allston Collins, Wilkie's brother, had pointed out that with the coming of photography, the eulogistic biography, which he found analogous to a painted portrait, seemed more and more unrealistic. "The written portrait and the painted are alike in unlikeness." ("Biography at a Discount," *Macmillan's Magazine*, X [1864], 159.)

no facile task; it is the strenuous achievement of a lifetime, only to be accomplished in the face of endless obstacles and unspeakable prejudice." It was, in fact, a task demanding the patience, candor, and fortitude of a Zola.

The critics did little to break down the "endless obstacles and unspeakable prejudice" that frustrated the writing of honest biography. Such debate as there was centered timidly on the possibility that discretion might, under certain conditions, be tempered with candor. Some critics revived the old proposition that biographers should be governed by a statute of limitations: so long as a man's memory was still fresh, and his family and friends survived to be solicitous for his good name as well as their own, a biographer should tread lightly over the still-warm ashes; but after a lapse of two or three generations, a great man belonged to the ages, and all that was to be learned about him might, without offense, be made public. The general opinion was still that summarized at the end of a typical assault on "The Rakers" in 1911: "When a beautiful soul has created a masterpiece, and paid his debt to the world, we might well allow his light to shine throughout time undimmed and undisturbed by the miasma of malignant and malicious gossip."[6]

Yet here and there protesting voices could be heard. In a talk given in that same year, H. G. Wells weighed the relative claims of biography and the novel:

> The case for biography, and more particularly autobiography, as against the novel, is, I admit, at the first blush stronger. You may say: Why give us these creatures of a novelist's imagination, these phantom and fantastic thinkings and doings, when we may have the stories of real lives, really lived—the intimate record of actual men and women? To which one answers: "Ah, if one could! But it is just because biography does deal with actual lives, actual facts, because it radiates out to touch continuing interests and sensitive survivors, that it is so unsatisfactory, so untruthful. Its inseparable falsehood is the worst of all kinds of falsehood—the falsehood of

[6] The "malignant and malicious gossip" against which so many advocates of biographical reticence protested during these decades was found (though in the modern view both epithets are too strong) in the popular periodicals, seldom in formal literary biographies.

omission. Think what an abounding, astonishing, perplexing person Gladstone must have been in life, and consider Lord Morley's "Life of Gladstone," cold, dignified—not a life at all, indeed, so much as embalmed remains; the fire gone, the passions gone, the bowels carefully removed. All biography has something of that post-mortem coldness and respect. . . .

The most insistent voice raised against biographical taciturnity, in these turn-of-the-century decades, was Edmund Gosse's. The biographer's anxiety, he said,

> should be, not how to avoid all indiscretion, but how to be as indiscreet as possible within the boundaries of good taste and kind feeling. He should start determined to reveal as much as possible, to drag his coy and retreating subject as far as can be done into the open light of day. . . . Let the biographer be tactful, but do not let him be cowardly; let him cultivate delicacy, but avoid its ridiculous parody, false delicacy. . . . He is bound to preserve the decencies, he is required to consider the feelings of survivors. But his first consideration, his first duty, is to truth.

This advocacy of truth, however circumscribed, is the most admirable of Gosse's several roles in the history of literary biography and one for which he has received too little credit. Sheer justice requires it, because he also has much to answer for. It was he, more than any other writer after 1880, who was responsible for the widespread corruption of criticism by anecdote. In innumerable essays and reviews, and finally as the belles-lettres expert of the *Sunday Times*, he habitually diverted the talk from the artistic merits of a book to familiar chitchat about its author. This rejection of esthetics (a dull subject) for biography (a lively one) was responsible for his success as a literary commentator-by-appointment to the middlebrow public. He had many imitators, and among them they fixed the level of much so-called criticism in the lean decades after Arnold and Pater. To those who entertained a more exalted notion of the critic's function, "appreciation" offered in place of serious judgment was bad enough, but appreciation flavored with genial but irrelevant scraps of biography and personal reminiscence was intolerable. When, in the 1920's, I. A. Richards and his followers spread a revulsion against the biographical element in criticism, their protest was not against biography per se but against the indulgence of biographical causerie in the name, or place, of criticism.

As a critic of the art of biography, however, Gosse was distinctly ahead of his time. A conformist, a social climber, a snob, and in most literary matters conservative and unimaginative, he nevertheless had the independence and courage to initiate the post-Victorian revolt against biographical evasiveness and eulogy. If it was Lytton Strachey who finally toppled the false front of traditional biography, Gosse must be credited with having undermined its foundations for the preceding thirty years.

As a practitioner too Gosse has his honorable place in the story. His obituary article on Queen Victoria in the *Quarterly Review* for April, 1901, however innocuous it now seems, aroused sharp criticism by its treatment of the late sovereign as, first of all, a woman with human weaknesses. *Father and Son* (1907), an avowed but unsigned autobiography centering about one of Victorian England's most painful situations—the emotional and intellectual gulf separating the generations, typified in Gosse's case by the tragic lack of sympathy between a father of fanatically rigorous religion and a son of liberal beliefs—was a milestone in the slow progress toward biographical realism.

Ironically, in writing his life of Swinburne (1917), Gosse succumbed to the very pressures he had so long and vigorously decried. Whatever his ambitions to present Swinburne as he lived —especially the roaring boy of the sixties and seventies—they were frustrated by the family, particularly by Swinburne's cousin, Mrs. Disney Leith, a lady of such formidable constitution that at the age of seventy, while holidaying in Iceland, she took daily swims (not mere dips) in the chill ocean. Gosse, as the recent editor of Swinburne's correspondence observes, "was not merely hampered by personal loyalty and paralyzed by a Damoclean sword, he was pursued by the Eumenides." In a letter to Maurice Baring, he enumerated the "disadvantages" (a heroic understatement) under which he labored:

1. The extraordinary hostility of the family. 2. The embargo laid on any mention of drunkenness. 3. A still heavier sexual embargo. 4.

The weight of the Watts-Dunton legend [i.e., the version of Swinburne cultivated by the pompous lawyer-*littérateur* who supervised his life from 1879 onward], which I had to break down without seeming to do so. 5. The fact that I was obliged to keep the Correspondence for another publication.

"I think," Gosse added, "no biographer ever had more to contend against. If I could, I would withdraw the whole book, and re-write it from the beginning to end."

But the heavily bowdlerized book was published in the version that Mrs. Leith read in manuscript, accompanying her numerous demands for excision with no single word of approval. Gosse was allowed to say nothing of Swinburne's early propensities either for the bottle or for the flagellant rod; the closest he could get to intimating that Swinburne was not a sober, unexceptional citizen was in recurrent vague allusions to his "eccentricity," his "excitability," his "nervous malady," which seems always to have attacked him in the city, never in bucolic surroundings, where he was the most charming and innocent of company: "it is not necessary to dwell on much that was distressing, and even alarming, in his town habits." He never could specify that the "bilious attacks" of which Swinburne so frequently complained were, in fact, monumental hangovers, and when he alluded to the circumstances which, "widely related at the time," led to his enforced resignation from the Arts Club in 1870, he had to leave a new generation in the dark as to what the circumstances were.

Unhappy as he was with the book, Gosse quickly discovered that it satisfied few readers. To some, the unreconstructed inheritors of the Victorian tradition, it revealed too much—much that should have been decently left unmentioned; to others, aware of the large and flamboyant mass of Swinburne scandal that still passed from mouth to mouth, it revealed too little. "The attempt of a silly and pompous old man to present a man of genius," said Ezra Pound, who proceeded to regale the readers of *Poetry* magazine with fragments of deliciously crude Swinburniana that Gosse, even if his taste had allowed their inclusion, could not possibly have got past Mrs. Leith's censorship. Gosse, in his most ambitious and delicate biographical undertaking, had (depending on one's point of view) either been too faithful to his principles or not faithful enough.[7]

And then, in the spring of 1918, a much younger and wittier man, a scion of the Victorian intellectual aristocracy—a man to whom very little was sacred, least of all the grave eminences of the age to which his own family had added dignity and brilliance —published a best seller. In the book's preface, which immediately assumed the force of a manifesto, Lytton Strachey summed up all Gosse had been saying since before the twentieth century began. But because his strictures were applicable to the history and current condition of literary biography in the United States as well as in England, and because they, along with the book itself, would touch off a revolution in the art on both sides of the Atlantic, it will be suitable at this point to review what had been happening, meanwhile, in America.

[7] Barred from printing all he knew, Gosse left to the British Museum a long "Essay (with Two Notes) on Swinburne," which was eventually printed in *The Swinburne Letters*, ed. Lang, VI, 233–248. Its descriptions of the poet in his cups, his patronage of a high-class house of flagellation in St. John's Wood, and his friends' unsuccessful project to acquaint him with normal sexuality through the cooperation of Adah Menken offer a tantalizing sample of the biography Gosse could have written had circumstances permitted.

CHAPTER VIII

Literary Biography in America

✳

I

N 1800, while cultivated Britons were reading Dr. Currie's biography of Burns, a poet who even in his lifetime had been acclaimed a national hero, in the new federal republic across the Atlantic Mason Weems was riding his book-peddling circuit as usual. This time he had a new, fast-selling item in his saddle bag: a life, largely derived from the "parson's" own imagination, of General George Washington. That, in a hickory nut shell, was the difference between the state of literary biography in Britain and America as the new century began. There were no full-length biographies of American men of letters, nor would there be any, with but one or two exceptions, until after the Civil War.

But meanwhile, biography that dealt with distinguished non-literary Americans flourished. A country that was young, vigorous, and cocky never tired of reading about its national heroes. For every Englishman's Wellington, the American had his Washington; for every Nelson, a John Paul Jones. Books narrating the exploits of the British sea dogs and explorers had their American counterparts in the glibly written and eagerly devoured sagas of Davy Crockett and Daniel Boone. With the passing of the decades, new heroes appeared, and the requirements of democratic politics brought into being a kind of life writing as yet undreamed of in England, the campaign biography, to which even such able writers as Hawthorne and Howells put their hands.

((249

As literacy spread, and improved transportation carried cheap books into the mountain villages and the settlements on the prairies, virtually all the types of popular biography that had taken root in England found ready sale. The religious literature that reached the people through Sunday schools, denominational magazines, and booksellers contained at least as heavy an incidence of didactic biography as it did in "our old home." Under the aegis of the Society for the Diffusion of Useful Knowledge—the American offshoot and namesake of a bustling British organization dedicated to accelerating "the march of mind"—inspirational and prudential life stories flowed from the presses.

In the flourishing lyceums too (Yankee adaptations of England's mechanics' institutes of the thirties and forties), biographical lectures were constantly delivered, along with recommendations to borrow biographical volumes from the little libraries attached to the meeting halls. Though some of the anxieties that prompted many Englishmen to read biography were not present in the sanguine American psychology, other motives were identical on both sides of the Atlantic. Emerson, beginning his long career as a public lecturer in 1835 with a series of discourses on Michelangelo, Luther, Milton, George Fox, and Burke, was, in this respect as in others, the New England Carlyle. His *Representative Men* (1850) was the American version of his friend's *Heroes and Hero-Worship* (1841). "There is no history. There is only Biography," wrote Emerson in his journal in 1839. Carlyle could go no further.

> The great value of Biography [Emerson had written in 1835] consists in the perfect sympathy that exists between like minds. . . . We are imprisoned in life in the company of persons painfully unlike us, or so little congenial to our highest tendencies, and so congenial to our lowest, that their influence is noxious, and only now and then comes by us some commissioned spirit that speaks as with the word of a prophet to the languishing, nigh dead faith in the bottom of the heart, and passes by, and we forget what manner of men we are. It may be that there are very few persons at any one time in the world who can address with any effect the higher wants of men. This defect is compensated by the recorded teaching and acting of this class of men. Socrates, St. Paul, Antoninus,

Luther, Milton have lived for us as much as for their contemporaries, if by books or by tradition their life and words come to my ear. We recognize with delight a strict likeness between their noblest impulses and our own. We are tried in their trial. By our cordial approval we conquer in their victory. We participate in their act by our thorough understanding of it.

This was the gospel—or one aspect of it—that he spread throughout ante-bellum America, from the platform and through his printed essays. The instructional value of biography was emphasized, furthermore, by current writings in periodicals and by the American encyclopedias (many of them simply reprints of English works) that had an entry on the subject. Study of the lives of great men was as much a part of the program for self-improvement in young Abraham Lincoln's America as it was in Lord Brougham's England. As in England, it was often a frank substitute for the reading of history. "I have read books on magic and astrology," the twenty-six-year-old James Russell Lowell told a friend in 1845, "and yet never looked into a history of England. All that I know of it I have acquired by reading the biographies of men whose lives *are* the history of England."

Biography, considered as a branch of literary art, from time to time engaged the thoughts of American writers. One of the most intelligent of all nineteenth-century discussions of the topic, by an unidentified author, appeared in the *Southern Literary Messenger* in 1856. Faithful to its origin in a democratic society, it opposed the "statuesque" school of Victorian biographical opinion by arguing that by showing all sides of a figure, candid biography helps "diminish that blind admiration for men which is appropriately named hero-worship. . . . The popular hero appears as he is, divested of his stateliness, his assumed dignity, and his other artificial trappings of greatness." It stressed that the ideal biographer should exercise both "reason" (to be historically accurate) and "imagination" ("to so combine existing and actual materials in proportions that have already existed, that, while absolutely true, they shall possess all the novelty of original conceptions"). And the writer recognized the critical value of biographies of literary men: "Our pleasure in reading [literary] works

((251

is greatly enhanced by a knowledge of the circumstances under which they were written. The incidents and passions of private life giving rise to the book, tinging the author's conception and being incorporated in his mind as a part of the conception—a consideration of these incidents and passions is absolutely essential to a full appreciation of the book itself. The dim outline only of an author's figure looms before the reader as he peruses the attractive pages [of his works]. But furnished with the facts of a writer's life public and private, he enjoys the rare satisfaction of beholding the hitherto dim and receding figure rounded into natural proportions and starting from the page with life-like verisimilitude."

The singling out of literary biography is particularly noteworthy. In the America of 1856 literary biography was represented almost exclusively by imported books. Virtually all English biographies of importance or current interest participated in the brisk commerce from Paternoster Row into the bookshops of Boston, New York, and Philadelphia—and also into the hands of printers who speedily used them as copy for cheaper, made-in-America editions. Boswell, Southey, Scott, Moore, Lockhart, and the other well-known biographers of the period 1791–1850 were part of every American's liberal education, if not his personal library.[1]

This very fact illustrates America's cultural dependency on Britain. Though hundreds and thousands of men, and even a sizable number of women, were writing for print, there was as yet no national literature in the sense that the nation itself was conscious and proud of an indigenous literary tradition. The most influential and respected literature continued to come from abroad. Emerson and others, in the thirties and forties, called for the country to stand on its own two feet intellectually, but it was too busy with other affairs to do much honor to its native-born authors—except, as we shall see, the author of "Diedrich Knickerbocker's" *History of New York* and *The Sketch Book of Geoffrey Crayon*. Writers in America between the close of the Revolution

---

[1] The New York man of affairs Philip Hone copied into his diary thirty pages of extracts from Lockhart's life of Scott.

and the outbreak of the Civil War had a hard row to hoe. The journalist Joseph Dennie remarked, about the turn of the century, that "becoming an author in America was as hopeless as founding an academy of science in Lapland," and a generation later Stephen Longfellow wrote his son: "A literary life, to one who has the means of support, must be very pleasant. But there is not wealth enough in this country to afford encouragement and patronage to merely literary men." No early American author, apart from Irving and Cooper, could live by books alone. He could not hope to compete with the popular British writers whose work, unprotected by international copyright, was pirated by American publishers at will. Whatever the solid benefits to the nation at large of this wholesale importation of English culture, the authors' profession in these early decades could have stood a degree of protection. As it was, the only real livelihood to be gained from the literary pen was to be found in the magazines, and the uncertainty of such an occupation is sufficiently illustrated by the difference between N. P. Willis' fame and prosperity and the vicissitudes of Edgar Allan Poe as contributor and editor.

The man of letters who lacked advantages such as dignity of family or membership in one of the recognized professions had little social standing in early nineteenth-century America: at least as little as his English colleagues in the same period. In the South especially he was looked down upon; his lot was contempt and neglect. Henry Timrod wrote that "it would scarcely be too extravagant to entitle the Southern author the Pariah of modern literature." But conditions were not much more favorable elsewhere. The anti-intellectual and above all the anti-belletristic forces of a pushing materialistic culture were not counterbalanced, as they were in England, by the existence of a silver-fork society eager to lionize a poet risen from the lower bourgeoisie. Nor had America any baronetcies or peerages to bestow on authors who had enriched the nation's literature; the closest approach to such an honor, by its very nature tainted with partisanship and of uncertain duration, was the political sinecure awarded to writers like Irving and Hawthorne.

Hence there was simply no occasion or demand for native

((253

literary biography. If literary giants walked the earth of Jefferson's or Buchanan's America, they were for the most part unrecognized; celebrity, such as it was, went to the ephemeral "magazinists"—"Fanny Fern," Lydia Sigourney, Willis, Fitz-Greene Halleck (whose statue was erected in New York's Central Park in 1877). The first book-length memoir of an American man of letters was Pierre Irving's *Life and Letters of Washington Irving* (four volumes, 1863–64).[2] The story it told represents the only exception to the general truth that until after the Civil War, the United States did not overexert itself in cherishing its own men of letters.

Washington Irving was the nation's first literary gentleman. During his long years abroad, his fellow Americans read with growing pride of his becoming the toast of European society: a native New Yorker, a popular writer at that, sought after by the most exalted literati and hostesses in England and on the continent, rumored even to be engaged to marry the Empress Maria Louisa! News of every fresh triumph, quickly copied from paper to paper when it arrived on the latest ship, was wonderfully soothing to the young country's gnawing sense of cultural inferiority. The English popularity of Irving's volumes was sufficient answer to Sydney Smith's scornful "Who reads an American book?" And the well-publicized fact that Irving made considerable money by his pen increased still more the respect in which he was held.

Returning to the United States in 1832, Irving received a hero's welcome. He was given a typical testimonial dinner of the era, held in the New York City Hall and attended by three hundred carefully selected guests, who participated in a six-hour-long orgy of speechmaking and cheering. Thereafter to his death twenty-seven years later, he was as much a part of the American consciousness as the president for whom he had been named or

[2] It was preceded by William Dunlap's (and Paul Allen's) *Life of Charles Brockden Brown* (1815), but this strange two-volume production is actually a gallimaufry of selections from Brown's writings, published and unpublished. Only three or four percent of the work, at the most generous estimate, can be called "biography."

the millionaire fur trader, Astor, whose biography he wrote. Magazines and newspapers never ceased printing his portrait and accounts of his travels and new honors abroad; he was prevailed upon to join, and then to become an officer or trustee of, numerous societies; books were dedicated to him, medals were awarded him, literary societies were named after him, replicas of Ball Hughes' bust of him sold by the hundreds at fifteen dollars each; and at Sunnyside, on the Hudson, the old man was an oracle to whom young and old alike repaired for advice and encouragement. Like his English contemporaries, he was betrayed by popular journalism—and he reacted precisely as they did. In 1857 a private letter one Charles Lanman had written to a friend was printed in a Washington newspaper under the headline "A Day with Washington Irving." "I can only say," wrote Irving to Lanman with unconcealed irritation, "that I wish you had had a worthier subject for your biographic pen, or that I had known our conversation was likely to be recorded; I should then have tasked myself to say some wise or witty things, to be given as specimens of my *off-hand table talk*. One should always know when they are sitting for a portrait, that they may endeavor to look handsomer than themselves, and attitudinize."

On the whole, Irving was venerated more for his character and the way his brilliant international career nourished American pride than for his literary gifts. Popular though his books were—he was a walking classic, studied in the schools while yet alive—it was rather as a man of affairs, a diplomat, an antiquary, a confidante of titled personages that he received homage. The quality of his fame, in fact, like that of much of his writing, was somewhat old-fashioned; it had the flavor of the eighteenth century. In Bryant's New York, Irving resembled a belated, Federalist, Franklin.

But meanwhile, in America as in England, adulation of literary heroes was springing from new sources, taking new and more picturesque, sentimental, and democratic forms. Just as romantic idealization of the poet had been in the English air long before Carlyle and (posthumously) Shelley gave it eloquent expression in 1840, so in America, Emerson merely put into famous words a spirit that had been exciting a certain number of his compatriots for decades. In "The Poet" (1844) he wrote:

> The poet is the person in whom these [visionary, prophetic] powers are in balance, the man without impediment, who sees and handles that which others dream of, traverses the whole scale of experience, and is representative of man, in virtue of being the largest power to receive and to impart. . . . The poet is the sayer, the namer, and represents beauty. He is a sovereign, and stands on the centre. For the world is not painted or adorned, but is from the beginning beautiful; and God has not made some beautiful things, but Beauty is the creator of the universe. Therefore the poet is not any permissive potentate, but is emperor in his own right. . . . The poet has a new thought; he has a whole new experience to unfold; he will tell us how it was with him, and all men will be the richer in his fortune. . . . O poet! a new nobility is conferred in groves and pastures, and not in castles or by the sword-blade any longer. The conditions are hard, but equal. Thou shalt leave the world, and know the muse only. Thou shalt not know any longer the times, customs, graces, politics, or opinions of men, but shalt take all from the muse.

Fittingly enough, and by no means accidentally, it was to Wordsworth, the gray-headed English *fons et origo* of this view of the poet, that romantically inclined Americans, including Emerson himself, gravitated when they went abroad. "From the letters we have read from Americans in England," commented *Holden's Dollar Magazine* in 1850, "we are led to believe that the majority of them, the moment they get their trunks out of the Custom House, start off in a cab for the railroad station and procure tickets for the North, in pursuit of the author of Peter Bell." But behind "Peter Bell" lay the preface to *Lyrical Ballads*, with its ringing assertion of the poet's sublime mission, and it was this spirit that moved Americans in quantity to visit Rydal Mount and Abbotsford, and elsewhere to beg for a withered rose that Byron had touched.

The devotional impulse was not, of course, unmixed with less lofty considerations, preeminent among which was simple curiosity. While some Americans, their heads still in the clouds, wrote home of their first sight of poets (genuine poets: not Americans), others, like N. P. Willis, put into democratic print what would, a century later, be called the low-down on fashionable English literary life. In either case it is noteworthy that the growing American interest in literary personalities could at this period be satisfied only by sentimental three-thousand-mile pilgrimages to the native soil of *English* literature.[3]

Except, that is, when the hero traveled to his adorers, as happened in 1842, when Dickens' first visit excited the populace to the hysterical display that forms one of the most colorful chapters of American social history. In the frequent association of Dickens with Washington Irving during the former's stay, there was a significant symbolism of contrast. Both were rousingly cheered whenever they appeared in public; but whereas Irving owed his fame to his being a public man, patrician, and cosmopolitan as well as an author, Dickens was simply "Boz," man of the people, ex-newspaper reporter, and creator of *The Pickwick Papers, Oliver Twist, Nicholas Nickleby,* and *The Old Curiosity Shop.* He was the first man to become a hero in America solely on the strength of his writing, and not until the advent of Mark Twain would any other literary figure claim so many thousand column-inches of American newspaper space.

No sooner was he settled in the Tremont House in Boston than he had to deal with thousands of requests for his autograph and hundreds of formal greetings and invitations from every variety of cultural, educational, and legislative body from Maine to the Mississippi. At the theater, as the band played the "Boz Waltzes," he was cheered three times three, and at a sculptor's studio, while he sat for his bust, a mob of female Bostonians snipped bits of fur from his coat. En route to New York, at every station Yankee faces were poked into the train, bawling "Is Mr. Dickens here?" In New York, the Boz Ball at the extravagantly decorated Park Theater attracted eight thousand men and

[3] See Washington Irving's "Stratford-on-Avon" (*The Sketch Book*) and Hawthorne's "Some of the Haunts of Burns" (*Our Old Home*), in which Americans of two separate generations comment, with a mixture of amusement and fully shared awe, on British literary shrines and hero worship. A delightfully ironic pendant to these is Henry James's story "The Birthplace."

((257

women, of whom five thousand, failing to gain admittance, milled around in the street outside. The grand march, quadrilles, and tableaux were followed, a few nights later, by an equally elaborate Boz Dinner, over which Irving presided. It was not surprising that after he left the seaboard, the exhausted Dickens made it a rule not to accept any public entertainment. But whenever he appeared in interior cities and villages he attracted large and frantically enthusiastic crowds, blissfully ignorant of the figure they were destined soon to cut in *Martin Chuzzlewit*. Had he returned to America in the mid-forties, after the publication of *American Notes* and *Chuzzlewit*, his reception would have had a quite different temper. When Dickens eventually did come back, in 1867, all was more than forgiven, and the night before tickets went on sale for his readings, lines of people formed outside Steinway Hall, shivering in New York's bitter cold, fighting, dancing, and singing. By morning there were five thousand in the crowd, waiters hustled breakfast from nearby restaurants, and scalpers began operations. Though Dickens fever ran as high during this second visit as during the first, there was a noticeable decrease in the vulgarity that had marked the behavior of the street mobs; America was learning to take its heroes in stride, and the quid-distended cheek of aggressive egalitarianism was no longer so painfully in evidence.

One further connection Dickens had with the developing American interest in authors as people was odd and oblique. A certain Thomas Powell, a friend and fellow clerk of Dickens' brother Augustus, by a series of forgeries stole £10,000 from his London employer. Avoiding prosecution by producing a certificate of insanity, Powell fled to America in 1849 and made the rounds of the New York papers as a self-described London *littérateur* and hobnobber with contemporary literary celebrities. An article of his on Dickens, published in the *Evening Post*, resulted in Dickens' sending a strong letter of denunciation to be printed in the *Tribune*, upon which Powell sued Dickens for libel and Dickens retaliated by exposing Powell's criminal record in the American press. While this dustup was in progress, Powell published a volume called *The Living Authors of England*, a collection of essays on a variety of writers, from Tennyson and Browning downward. Though its emphasis was purportedly critical, the book obviously aimed to profit by Americans' curiosity about authors' private lives and personalities. Was So-and-so happily married? What did Brown, Jones, and Robinson look like? Was the poetic Miss Doe a sprightly conversationalist? Powell, like an émigré N. P. Willis, set out to tell—tell, in fact, considerably more than he knew. With an easy assurance that must have taken in numerous American readers, he confided what (he alleged) Browning once said to him at dinner and which authors were notorious for their habit of forgetting large favors that people did them.

Even if Dickens' attacks in the American newspapers had not warned them of Powell's undependability, readers only moderately conversant with the English literary scene would have discovered that his book abounded with errors and fabrications. But then, as always, accuracy counted for little when weighed against the privilege of gazing on famous writers when—they thought— they were not on display. Powell, whatever his moral shortcomings, was an alert student of American taste. Already the welcome given the anthologies of Rufus Griswold, whom we shall meet in a little while, had proved that readers were avid for the biographical sketches that constituted one of their distinguishing features. Howitt's *Homes and Haunts of the Most Eminent British Poets* had been published in America in 1847, immediately after its appearance in England, and almost at once it had its American counterparts. In 1853, for example, appeared a typical gift book of the period, *Homes of American Authors; Comprising Anecdotical, Personal, and Descriptive Sketches, by Various Writers,* with steel and wood engravings, facsimiles of manuscript pages, and essays by such luminaries as William Cullen Bryant, George William Curtis, Henry Tuckerman, and Edward Everett Hale. Henceforth books like these became a familiar product of American presses, culminating—if that is the right word—in what was undoubtedly the most famous series, Elbert Hubbard's "Little Visits" to the homes of English and American authors.

The omens were unmistakable. Americans were becoming

insatiably curious about the personalities, dwelling places, and domestic habits of their own authors. When "homes and haunts" books began to appear, pilgrimages and letters beginning "I beg you will pardon this intrusion on the part of an unknown ad-mirer" were bound soon to follow—and after that, biographies in abundance.

· 2 ·

From mid-century on, therefore, Americans interested in au-thors as people had two broad and picturesque landscapes to scan. With telescopes supplied by Powell and somewhat more reputable guides such as William Howitt, they could pursue at their own firesides the pastime of looking in upon the great Eng-lish authors who still figured prominently in American magazines and bookshops; and now, close by and opened to their gaze by a host of busy journalists and engravers, were the homes, haunts, and habits of numerous native celebrities. In this development the activities of the Bostonian James T. Fields were particularly noteworthy. Fields was a valued friend of many British authors, whose work he published both in book form, under the imprint of Ticknor and Fields, and in the *Atlantic Monthly,* which he owned and for nine years edited. Probably no other American of the day had so many and so diverse personal contacts with the Eng-lish literary scene. Fields looked back on them in *Yesterdays with Authors* (1871), a series of affectionate reminiscences of Thack-eray, Dickens, Wordsworth, Miss Mitford, and the Barry Corn-wall group. Fields's tone is sufficiently exemplified by his open-ing sentence: "Dear old Thackeray!—as everybody who knew him intimately calls him, now he is gone." Chatty but discreet, confidential but not intimate, Fields gave an air of total respecta-bility to the purveying of literary gossip. Not only did he achieve this through his own writings; just as important, he encouraged relatives and friends of recently deceased American writers to publish their reminiscences in the *Atlantic*—Elizabeth Peabody on her brother-in-law Hawthorne, for example, and Emerson on Thoreau.

As Fields well knew, publishing these various kinds of memoirs, a practice that amounted in effect to laying the foundation stones for the formal literary biography of the future, helped stimulate sales of the works of the authors with whom they dealt. An enterprising businessman as well as a gentleman of culture, he recognized, probably before any of his British colleagues did, the value of encouraging public interest in the personality behind the book. For frankly promotional purposes, his firm issued from time to time illustrated brochures of "Boston Authors" (that is, those on the Ticknor and Fields list), with pictures not only of their bearded selves but of their homes—Longfellow's Craigie House, Lowell's Elmwood, Webster's home at Marshfield. In addition to planting favorable reviews of their books in strategic newspapers, he sometimes contributed gossipy articles on "What the Literary Men Are Doing in Boston," "which," admitted Longfellow, one of the literary men, "I do not much affect."

Nor, presumably, did he much affect some of the other consequences of Fields's priming the pump of literary journalism. In a Sunday paper appeared "The Study at Craigie House," an article typical of the inventories of authors' studies that popular taste demanded—a relentless ticketing of every article of furniture, the contents of the poet's desk top, his bibelots, mementos, pictures, down literally to the very wastebasket. In America, as in England, the inquisitive journalist was abroad, and hardly a weekly newspaper or magazine, at some time or another in its career, was without its long series of "Authors at Home" sketches, as the New York *Critic* entitled the one it ran in the middle 1880's.

As one of Boston's leading citizens, Fields was prominent in arranging for the testimonial dinners and celebrations of the seventieth and eightieth birthdays of eminent writers. Extended bouts of feeding, toasting, and oratory had, of course, been institutions in American politics—Eatanswill in the New World—since the century's earliest decades. The same recreations had acquired a literary rationale in the annual dinners of the Shakespeare and Burns societies that sprang up in every American community which boasted both cultural pretensions and a fair supply of expatriate Englishmen or Scotsmen who seized this means of renewing their sentimental bond with the old country. On the hundredth anniversary of Burns's birth, in 1859, there were over sixty celebrations in America: not only in the obvious centers of culture such as Boston and Philadelphia, but in fairly unexpected places—Keokuk, Savannah, Schenectady, Pottsville— all of which were entitled to fancy that Burns, had he emigrated to America in 1786 as he planned, might have become one of their founding fathers or even their mayor. But Shakespeare and Burns were present at these commemorations only, as it were, in the spirits, and the full purpose of dinners and other celebrations is achieved only when the recipient is there to hear the cheers. Irving and Dickens, we have seen, attended monstrous dinners in their honor, and as, one by one, the New England worthies aged, they too were wined, dined, and presented with elegantly engrossed testimonials. When Whittier turned seventy in 1877, the *Atlantic Monthly*'s publishers proffered him a dinner attended by, among others, Emerson, Holmes, Longfellow, Howells, and Mark Twain, whose frostily received speech, in which he attempted to enliven a Brahmin-sponsored birthday party with frontier humor and parody, was the most resounding *gaffe* of his career. Ten years later, a banquet of the Essex Club in Boston initiated a five-week-long national celebration of Whittier's eightieth birthday, climaxed by the arrival at his home of a trainload of celebrities headed by the governor of Massachusetts. No such function was complete without felicitous verses from Oliver Wendell Holmes's ever-ready pen ("Bryant's Seventieth Birthday," "For the Burns Centennial Celebration," "For the Moore Centennial Celebration," "For Whittier's Seventieth Birthday").

This custom was not confined to New England. Walt Whitman was treated to a series of birthday dinners, at the last of which (1891) a stenographic report was made of the conversation over the champagne bottles. Although the practice declined in the twentieth century, large testimonial dinners to William Dean Howells, the "dean" of American letters, were repeatedly arranged by Colonel George Harvey, president of Harpers, who published his lucrative books and whose magazine Howells edited. In 1912 Howells' seventy-fifth birthday banquet was attended by the retiring president of the United States, the Colo-nel's close friend, William Howard Taft.

Such celebrations received copious publicity all over the country; every newspaper printed accounts of the proceedings, and the higher-toned weeklies sometimes put out special supplements dealing with the life, character, and writings of the honored guest. But such contact between personage and public was still vicarious. Much more effective in encouraging the sense of personal relationship was the popularity in America, from the 1830's onward, of lectures. In opera houses, town halls, schools, and churches from the Atlantic coast westward—for the lecturer was only a few miles behind the frontiersman—the American people came face to face with writers. They listened to them, shook their hands, and memorized their appearance and accents. Emerson in his own time was far better known (and paid) as an itinerant lecturer than as a writer for the printed page: during his forty-eight-year platform career (1833–81) he gave some 1,469 lectures in 283 towns in the United States and Canada. His Transcendentalist colleague Bronson Alcott took to the road with his series of quasi-Coleridgean "Conversations," and, though the going was rough for a while, eventually he became so welcome a figure that he was on the circuit from Kansas to Florida for seven months in every year and continued his career until he was past eighty. Dr. Holmes was in constant demand, and so were the poet-traveler Bayard Taylor in his Arab robes and, for a season, Mark Twain and George Washington Cable in a rather ill-advised dual act. Decade after decade, American writers supplemented the income from their books (or tried to compensate for its nonexistence) by reciting for bread.

Great though the demand was for American author-lecturers, it was even greater for British ones, who possessed, in addition to a strange way of speaking, the glamor of a far-off country for which many American hearts were still nostalgic. Native lecturers had their undoubted homespun virtues, but those from abroad were redolent of London clubland and their conversation full of Tennyson at Farringford and the Brownings in Florence. Thackeray came in 1852 and 1855 to read his lectures on "The English

Humourists" and "The Four Georges." Wilkie Collins, following in his friend Dickens' footsteps, gave readings across the country in 1873–74; Charles Kingsley made an American tour at the same time; and in 1882 Oscar Wilde spread the gospel of estheticism from the Atlantic seaboard to Colorado miners' camps. In the severest possible contrast to this exponent of *préciosité* came, a year or two later, Matthew Arnold, who made a generally unfavorable impression on his audiences, his platform demeanor suggesting nothing so much, said a Detroit paper, as "an elderly bird pecking at grapes on a trellis."

If one could not see one's literary heroes in person, either on the platform or in their everyday habitat—by the sixties pilgrims were walking to Cambridge to touch the latch on Longfellow's gate and even out to Concord for a glimpse of Emerson's woodpile—the next best thing was to hear of them from a returned traveler. Howells, returning to Ohio for a visit about 1870, stopped over at Congressman Garfield's house at Hiram, and as they sat on the veranda in the evening he began telling familiar anecdotes of the Boston literary circle. "Just a minute!" interrupted the congressman, who ran across the lawn to his neighbors' fences. "Come over here," he shouted to the families sitting on their own back porches. "He's telling about Holmes, and Longfellow, and Lowell, and Whittier!" Out of the dusk came figure after figure, men, women, and children, eager to take their places on the Garfield steps. "Now go on!" said Howells' host, and Howells did, to everyone's immense satisfaction, while the whippoorwills, as he recalled many years later, "whirred and whistled round, and the hours drew toward midnight."

It would be hard to find such a scene duplicated today, in or out of Ohio, and on or off congressmen's porches. But the wide circulation of the periodicals in which the leading writers' work appeared and was discussed, and the generous space most newspapers gave to their public activities, made such names as Holmes, Longfellow, Lowell, and Whittier household words in the quite literal sense. Nor may we underestimate the part that American women especially played in spreading this popular interest in writers as people. It was they, in the decades just before and most conspicuously after the Civil War, who held high the torch of literary culture; as both foreign and domestic observers of the American scene often remarked, the men were too busy making money to care very much about authors, let alone read their books. Not only did women form a principal segment of the reading public, thus influencing the course current literature was to take during those years. As in England, it was their character-istically feminine interest in domestic life—in an author's fore-bears, for example, and the appointments of his home, and his joys and sorrows in the midst of his family—that encouraged journalists to seek out and publish what would become in time some of the fringe materials of literary biography.

Appropriately, it was a woman who left the most intimate glimpse of the effect all this had upon the author himself—or herself. The successful American writer of the post-Civil War era paid the same price for his fame as did his English contemporary; no form of author-bothering known in Britain was foreign to western shores, as Louisa May Alcott, writing from personal ex-perience, revealed in an amusing passage in *Jo's Boys* (1886):

> Strangers demanded to look at her [the successful writer, Mrs. Bhaer], question, advise, warn, congratulate, and drive her out of her wits by well-meant but very wearisome attentions. If she de-clined to open her heart to them, they reproached her; if she refused to endow pet charities, relieve private wants, or sympa-thize with every ill and trial known to humanity, she was called hard-hearted, selfish, and haughty; if she found it impossible to answer the piles of letters sent her, she was neglectful of her duty to the admiring public; and if she preferred the privacy of home to the pedestal upon which she was requested to pose, "the airs of literary people" were freely criticised.

The world beat a path to the Bhaers'—or Alcotts'—door as if superior mousetraps, instead of popular novels and books for children, were manufactured inside. On one presumably typical day, a reporter for the *Saturday Tattler* called, and was ejected only with difficulty; Mr. and Mrs. Erastus Kingsbury Parmalee of Oshkosh and their three interesting daughters called on the way to view "Holmes and Longfeller, and the rest of the celebrities," offering to leave their albums so that the authoress could write in them at her leisure and then post them back to Oshkosh; the whole student body of a young ladies' seminary picnicked on the lawn, "freely expressing their opinion of the place and its possessors" before they left; seventy-five youths from the Young Men's Christian Union, arriving in a rainstorm, dripped and slopped all over the house; and the day ended with the arrival of a lady who collected grasshoppers from the grounds of "famous folks" as well as famous folks' castoff clothing for a rug she was making—a vest of Emerson, a pair of Holmes' trousers, a dress of Mrs. Stowe.

Mark Twain's experience of the fruits of fame was even more varied. For forty years he was a celebrity precisely to the American taste, always available, and drawling out wisdom—or what his admirers accepted as wisdom—wreathed in cigar smoke and laughter. Gladstone's England had its Tennyson, remote, austere, legendary; McKinley's America had its Mark Twain, timing his Sunday morning walk down Fifth Avenue to the moment when the crowds were coming out of church, gratifying doorbell-pulling reporters with some opinion that would automatically make the next day's headlines. For, unlike the inaccessible Tennyson, Twain, a former newspaperman himself, was the interviewer's delight; "no comment" was not in his vocabulary, and so he was called upon, as Albert Bigelow Paine said, for his views on politics, polygamy, and women's suffrage, of heaven, hell, and happiness, of the latest novel or the trouble in China. His name, and observations credited to him, penetrated where no other man of letters was ever spoken of: to Mr. Dooley's saloon, and the barbershops of a thousand country towns.[4]

Acknowledging that his life story, no less than his personality, was public property, on a sudden impulse in 1906 Twain took on a Boswell: Albert Bigelow Paine, a former itinerant photographer and dealer in photographic supplies at Fort Scott, Kansas, who

---

[4] But at least the visages of a few other eminent men of letters were at home in the milieu of beer and shaving mugs. Those of Ruskin, Burns, and Howells appeared on cigar boxes. In the same locale, the name of Wilkie Collins was well known, having been given to a trotting stallion of some celebrity. The novelist was delighted to learn, in a pamphlet extolling the powers of his namesake, that "Wilkie Collins covers mares at $75 each." (Kenneth Robinson, *Wilkie Collins* [New York, 1952], pp. 306–307.)

had come to New York and enjoyed some success as a journalist. For the four remaining years of his life, he and Paine held innumerable autobiographical sessions, as Mark, sitting up in bed and prompted by Paine, reminisced furiously, with copious free association and imaginative embellishments, and a stenographer took it all down. Gradually Paine became Mark's boon companion, going everywhere with him and observing and hearing a great deal that was not designed for the formal biographical record. But Paine, unluckily, had none of Boswell's literary gifts; his 1,700-page biography is an artistic failure, an immense monolith from which later biographers, despite Paine's testy assurance to Bernard De Voto that "nothing more need ever be written about Mark Twain," have carved better books.

Fourteen years before the Twain-Paine collaboration began, another giant of American letters had finished assisting at the creation of his own legend. As early as 1868, the precise period when London shopwindows displayed photographs of Swinburne and Adah Menken, Washingtonians had been buying pictures of Walt Whitman—*sans équestrienne*—and getting the poet, a familiar figure on the city's pavements and horsecars, to autograph them. In his crippled but articulate old age, Walt Whitman held court in his little house on sooty, odorous Mickle Street in Camden, New Jersey. As Bliss Perry was to write, he was "visited by hundreds of persons eager to look upon his very noble face and to touch the hand which he used to extend with a royal graciousness. . . ." Artists painted his portrait; sculptors made busts; photographers, knowing that Heaven might never send them another such subject, photographed him until, as Whitman himself remarked, the very cameras were weary.

Whitman, singer of himself, knew that posterity was bound to be at least as much interested in him as it was in the Brahmins who were passing, one by one, into the shades. Despite his protestations that "he did not want his life written, that he did not care in any way to be differentiated from the common people, of whom he was one," he was determined to shape his own myth. He had already written a portion of the book published under John Burroughs' name as *Notes on Walt Whitman as Poet and Person*, and in the early eighties he contributed numerous unsigned pages on his ancestry and youth to a volume by his Canadian disciple, Dr. Richard M. Bucke. To admirers who came to Mickle Street, he was unstinting in his communication of autobiographical data, some of which, to the confusion of the record, later turned out to be nothing more than exuberant invention. Chief among the visitors for whom Whitman poked his stick through the great pile of personal documents on the floor, occasionally extracting a pertinent paper, was his own Boswell, a self-educated Camden printer named Horace Traubel. Traubel, later to become a small-time socialist propagandist, supporter of Eugene Debs, and himself the center of an adoring coterie, took down in "condensed longhand" the old man's memories and fancies as they fell from his lips. Within an hour of each visit, the occasion still fresh in memory, Traubel expanded his notes into a bulky manuscript, sections of which have been printed at intervals since 1906.

· 3 ·

So, in the fullness of time, the occasion and the demand for literary biography arose in America. Its beginnings lay in three heavy double-columned anthologies edited by the journalist and critic Rufus W. Griswold: *The Poets and Poetry of America*, which, appearing in 1842, sold out eight editions in five years, *The Prose Writers of America* (1846), and *The Female Poets of America* (1848). Devoted chiefly to excerpts from the works of native writers, most of whom have not been heard of since, Griswold's volumes also contained prefatory biographical and critical sketches, ranging in length from a paragraph to two or three pages. In 1856 the same sort of personal material, but much more of it, occupied the two volumes of Evert A. and George L. Duyckinck's *Cyclopædia of American Literature*, which, as the title suggests, was less anthology than dictionary. As a group, the compilations of Griswold and the Duyckincks marked the stage in American literary biography through which the English had passed more than a century earlier, with the series of biographical dictionaries stretching from Fuller's *Worthies* to Cibber's *Lives.*

This same Griswold touched off the first extensive biographical controversy over an American writer. He and Poe, as fellow critics and editors, had had a touchy, off-again-on-again relationship, exacerbated by an attack in 1843 on *The Poets and Poetry of America* which he suspected, probably with good reason, that Poe had written. Two days after Poe died in a Baltimore hospital, Griswold published in the New York *Tribune,* over the signature "Ludwig," a venomous attack on the poet's character. He amplified his charges in the memoir he wrote, by request of Poe's mother-in-law, for the collected edition of Poe's works that began to appear in 1850. Despite the vigorous counterattacks of Poe's friends, Griswold's picture of Poe as a drunken, quarrelsome, vindictive genius *manqué* falsely colored the whole Poe biographical tradition on both sides of the Atlantic. Not until the 1940's was the full extent of Griswold's malign slipperiness as a life writer revealed. It is now known that he inserted in his transcripts of Poe's letters remarks that Poe did not make but that would have been characteristic of him had he been the sort of man Griswold made him out to be. In addition, Griswold invented letters of his own to which Poe's (perfectly genuine) letters were falsely represented to be replies—the context thus contrived serving to change the whole tenor of Poe's letters, "revealing" him as both conceited and sycophantic, and Griswold, not incidentally, as a fine critic. But Griswold's most reprehensible device was this. In the "Ludwig" letter he quoted a passage from Bulwer's *The Caxtons* with the aim of showing, in his words, that Poe "was in many respects like Francis Vivian" in that novel. When he reprinted the same passage in the *Memoir,* however, he omitted the quotation marks, so making it appear that the description was a literal one of Poe, not of Bulwer's fictional character. Thenceforward the description was reproduced by Poe's biographers as Griswold's own well-grounded opinion; and the damage it did was compounded by the fact that the *Memoir* in which it was preserved accompanied virtually every new edition of Poe's works.

Irving's death, ten years after Poe's, was an occasion for national mourning; and so was the subsequent passing of each of the great generation of Massachusetts writers. Thoreau died in 1862, Hawthorne in 1864, both of them celebrated, either shortly before or after death, by reminiscent articles written by relatives, neighbors, friends, and business associates and published, almost inevitably, in the *Atlantic Monthly*. Thereafter, one by one, the elaborate seventieth- and eightieth-birthday celebrations proved to be among the farther milestones on the path that led to the grave. Bryant—the only expatriate New Englander of literary stature, who had spent most of his years of fame in New York— died in 1878, Longfellow and Emerson in 1882, Lowell in 1891, Whittier in the following year, and Dr. Holmes, the last leaf on his generation's tree, in 1894.

Book-length biographies followed in due course. In the United States as in Britain, the "age of biography" had been preceded by an era of brilliant historiography. The decades before Boswell's *Johnson* had had their Hume, their Gibbon, their Robertson; in America during the middle of the nineteenth century there was the equally brilliant constellation of Parkman, Prescott, Motley, and Bancroft. The only difference—and a considerable one it was—was that no American Boswell came after them, to supply inspiration and challenge for the ensuing generation of biographers. In the history of American literary biography there is no towering landmark like the *Life of Johnson*. Instead, the quality of the genre during its first half-century of existence was determined by that prevailing in England at the same time. The earlier biographies of American authors were neither better nor worse than the contemporary English biographies after which they were modeled. But at least the drought that had prevailed down to the 1870's was ended. Macmillan's English Men of Letters series, besides adding a few American writers, among them Hawthorne and Whitman, to the honor roll of English literature, undertook an "American extension," which produced half a dozen titles before it died of malnutrition. A more ambitious series was the indigenous American Men of Letters (Houghton Mifflin), in

which some of the best as well as the most mediocre performances appeared.

The art of biography in nineteenth-century America was oppressed and inhibited by the same forces that were aligned
against it in Britain. Some biographers wrote under the shadow of
their subjects' explicit or inferential disapproval. Whittier, echoing Tennyson and (by anticipation) Browning, had pleaded:

> Let Love's and Friendship's tender debt
>   Be paid by those I love in life.
> Why should the unborn critic whet
>   For me his scalping-knife?
>
> Why should the stranger peer and pry
>   One's vacant house of life about;
> And drag, for curious ear and eye,
>   His faults and follies out?
>
> Why stuff, for fools to gaze upon,
>   With chaff of words the garb he wore;
> As corn-husks when the ear is gone
>   Are rustled all the more?
>
> Let kindly Silence close again;
>   The picture vanish from the eye:
> And on the dim and misty main
>   Let the small ripple die.

Lowell, in his essay on George Chapman, had set forth at length
his severe views on the exposure of poets' private affairs; and the
other members of their New England literary generation, if only
as children of their time, could be assumed to expect the utmost
discretion on the part of their biographers. Their wishes were
thoroughly respected, the more so because their survivors and
biographers alike not only were witnessing the unedifying and
apparently termless war of words between Poe's detractors and
defenders but in addition remembered Pierre Irving's experience.
In his biography of his uncle, Irving had suppressed all reference
to the elder man's love for Emily Foster. To the third volume of
the English edition, however, the publisher Richard Bentley had
appended, presumably as a device to secure copyright, two new

chapters containing extracts from the diary of Emily's sister and from Irving's letters to the Foster family—documents which drew the veil from the story of his fruitless second romance. The furious Pierre, denouncing the London publisher's unauthorized addition as "without precedent in the annals of literature," had no choice but to add the new chapters to the final volume of the American edition, and so to shatter the cherished national legend that Washington Irving had remained faithful throughout life to the memory of his earlier sweetheart, Matilda Hoffman.

It was to forestall such blows as this that the families of other eminent American authors took special precautions to eradicate whatever evidence of a man's character and experience they deemed unfit for the world's knowledge. Sophia Hawthorne inked out hundreds of "intimate" passages in her late husband's notebooks—only to have her exertions nullified many years later, by the application of infra-red light to the manuscripts. Samuel Longfellow mutilated, garbled, telescoped, and invented his brother's letters and journals with an abandon that was excessive even in those days of virtually unlimited editorial license. The documentary records of nineteenth-century American authors' lives fared, in fact, not a whit better than those of their English contemporaries. The comprehensive surveys of extant and vanished manuscripts which preface Jay Leyda's *Melville Log* and his *Years and Hours of Emily Dickinson* are acrid with the smoke of scores of bonfires that put forever beyond reach an incalculable amount of first-hand information about the novelist and the poet, and the same melancholy story can be told of the papers of many other American authors.

In the United States, as in England, zeal for decorum was manifested not only by a desire to make an author, even in his private jottings, conform to the current proprieties of language, as Sophia Hawthorne played William Mason to her late husband's Thomas Gray. Equally powerful was the insistence upon idealization or, on a less defensible level, foisting on the world a predetermined image of the man, whether idealized or not. It is as refreshing as it is rare to find someone in the nineteenth century protesting against this pervasive impulse to harness biography to the wagon of moral inspiration. When Emerson was preparing a selection of Thoreau's letters for publication in 1865, he explained to Thoreau's sister Sophia that his intention was to present the essayist as "a most perfect piece of stoicism"; he debated, therefore, whether to include some homely passages which "marred his classic statue." Miss Thoreau ventured the opinion that "it did not seem quite honest to Henry" to omit such passages. Emerson's publisher, Fields, backed her up, and a few were retained, despite the danger to the classic statue.

Whatever the diligence of its historical scholars, from Jared Sparks on down, in literary studies America had as yet produced no researching Malones, Priors, or Forsters. If a biographer had ample materials at hand, as in his subject's family archives, well and good; but seldom did he exert himself to garner fresh information from scattered and obscure sources. George Edward Woodberry's two lives of Poe were probably the most scholarly biographies of an American literary figure produced before the First World War. The earlier volume (1885) was introduced, justifiably, as "a documentary biography" whose author "has verified all facts positively stated at first hand, and has felt obliged to assign the authority followed, in any questionable assertions, in footnotes." The two-volume expansion of this monograph (1909), containing virtually all the information on its subject hitherto printed, was weighted with apparatus, including numerous "Notes Mainly on Obscure and Controverted Points" and a whole series of appendices. It was, in fact, a monument, virtually unique in earlier American literary biography, of thorough and (except for Woodberry's misplaced faith in Griswold) critical fact-gathering. Yet Woodberry admitted that since the publication of his earlier book he had "never engaged in personal investigation." The large second biography merely assembled whatever windfalls had been contributed by others, as well as the extensive Poe-Chivers and Griswold papers, which Woodberry earlier had edited for magazine publication. The shocking (to the modern eye) degree of his lethargy as a scholar is exemplified by his allusion to the crucial letters from Poe to the Allan family, in the Valentine Museum at Richmond. "I remember with great pleasure," he wrote, "an evening spent with their custodian in 1884; but as he did not offer to show the letters, I did not ask for them. . . . He confined his information to saying that my knowledge of Poe's military career was correct. I have no further knowledge of the contents of the letters, which I have never sought to see and which have been very carefully guarded, except of the slightest derived from a Richmond correspondent at my request in respect to a small detail." It is impossible to resist the conclusion that Woodberry, like nearly all the American literary biographers of his age, preferred the role of gentleman to that of the library-ransacking scholar.

As a work of art, the 1909 *Poe* was negligible. So were the other life-and-letters compilations that had followed Pierre Irving's: Samuel Longfellow's and Julian Hawthorne's accounts of their brother and father, respectively, James Elliot Cabot's *Emerson*, Samuel T. Pickard's *Whittier*, Parke Godwin's *Bryant*. About all that can be said of them, as of their English prototypes, is that they were the source books from which later biographers have had to draw, especially for the texts, however corrupt, of documents which are available in no other form. They were the products of the transcribing rather than the freshly narrative and descriptive pen, and the only qualitative distinction that can be made among them is the degree of deftness with which each biographer-compiler arranged his quotations into an easily followed story. Probably the most successful of these large-scale treatments was Horace Scudder's *Lowell*. Scudder took his artistic responsibilities seriously, preferring to absorb short quotations from Lowell's letters and other writings into his running text rather than to follow the prevailing custom of piecing long extracts together, end to end. He took pains to achieve narrative clarity, and he tried to present a unified interpretation of Lowell's personality, even to the extent of standing back and commenting on his attitudes, motives, and moods at a given juncture.

It was normally in the shorter, monograph-length biography, exemplified by the volumes in the American Men of Letters series, that literary craftsmanship and interpretation were found if they were to be found at all. The proportion of narrative to personal and literary comment varied from book to book, as did the success with which each was accomplished. One of the best was George Rice Carpenter's *Whittier,* a workmanlike interweaving of biography and criticism which placed the Quaker poet as a dramatic figure against the background of his abolitionist age. Carpenter's artistic aims were modest enough, but few other biographers of his era attempted even as much as he did. Faced with what seems to us the stimulating challenge of capturing the significant events of a life and the spirit of a complex personality within 200 or 250 pages, they were ordinarily content to play it safe, by confining their narrative to well-known facts and their commentary to one or two qualities that they found predominant in the men of whom they wrote.

Carpenter's *Whitman,* for instance, written in the stiff-collared academic prose of the Theodore Roosevelt period, failed to convey the flannel-shirted flavor inherent in its subject; by concentrating on Whitman's alleged "mysticism" to the neglect of almost all his other characteristics, Carpenter seemed anxious to overlook both his intellectual and his literary radicalism. But the problem of Whitman was practically insoluble in an age when literary biographers, most of them Bostonians or professors or both, were bound to the "genteel tradition" of American letters. Whitman fared no better at the hands of the Harvard professor Bliss Perry, who tempered his personality to proper Bostonian taste. The poet, he asserted, was really a gentleman: "Instead of the 'terrible eyes and buffalo strength' which might have been expected, [his visitors] found a quiet, slow man, pleasant-voiced, reticent, studiously chaste in speech and modest of manner; a man, in short, as little like the 'New York rowdy' of *Leaves of Grass* as could be imagined." Deprived of all his burly robustness for introduction into Beacon Street parlors, Perry's Whitman is a pallid effigy, and the book itself a classic example of the mismatching of biographer and subject.

Their English counterparts had to deal with five centuries' harvest not only of saints but of philanderers, drunkards, and all other varieties of sinner as well; but American literary biographers were fortunate. Their subjects, at the end of the nineteenth

((275

century, were still few, and with few exceptions these had led lives of unimpeachable rectitude. There was little to hide or extenuate, nor was there much to moralize over, as Thackeray had moralized over Steele and Sterne. The chief exception was Poe.[5] It was in describing his career alone that the accents of the temperance tract, so conspicuous in early lives of Burns, were introduced into American literary biography. Hear Woodberry in his early life of Poe: "He ate opium and drank liquor; whatever was the cause, these were instruments of his ruin, and before half his years were run they had done their work with terrible thoroughness—he was a broken man. He died under circumstances of exceptional ugliness, misery, and pity, but not accidentally, for the end and the manner of it were clearly near and inevitable." But narcotic and alcoholic indulgence was not the whole of the story. Apart from his wife and Mrs. Clemm,

> no one touched his heart in the years of his manhood, and at no time was love so strong in him as to rule his life; as he was self-indulgent, he was self-absorbed, and outside of his family no kind act, no noble affection, no generous sacrifice is recorded of him. . . . Solitary as he was, proud and selfish, how could he kindle his works with the vital interest of humanity? Other interests they have, but not this crowning one which is the supreme excellence of the works of men. Thus ever more remote from mankind ran the currents of his life and genius, interminably commingling, until their twin streams, glassing at last the desolation they had so often prophetically imaged, choked and stagnant in midway of their course, sank into the waste. The pitiful justice of Poe's fate, the dark immortality of his fame, were accomplished.

This grand finale passage illustrates not only the quality of biographical moralizing when it did occur, but also the level of the literary criticism which the typical early biography of an American author contained. Neither, obviously, was high. Nowhere in the literary biographies of the period was profound or acute criticism to be met. Nor did the writing achieve distinction. Poe, once more, proved an evil influence; as the quotation from

[5] Another might have been Melville, whose adventures in the South Seas had elements of scandal that were attested to by some of his surviving shipmates. But Melville did not attract the interest of any biographer until 1921.

Woodberry suggests, and as a glance at the rich, beautiful, and absurd prose of Harrison's biography would corroborate, he tempted his biographers into the worst excesses the style of their time afforded. When they were engaged upon less spectacular figures, however, biographers seldom gave rein to their prose, either for better or for worse. They were content to write literate English, and if they did not often succumb to affectation, just as infrequently did they aspire to art.

In fact, the only American of his era who steadfastly regarded biography as a high art and dedicated his life to its practice was the invalid of Wellesley Hills, Gamaliel Bradford. A fervent devotee of Sainte-Beuve, Bradford sought to capture the inner essence of men as diverse as Robert E. Lee and Dwight L. Moody, Samuel Pepys and Darwin. In all, this self-styled "naturalist of souls"—a term he borrowed from Sainte-Beuve—examined well over a hundred specimens. But only five were treated in full-length books; all the rest were glimpsed in the brief sketches— Bradford called them "psychographs"—which had been Sainte-Beuve's forte. Moreover, in Bradford's work the narrative was always subordinated to the portrait, and though the reading of diaries and letters that lay behind each of his psychological profiles was extensive, it was intuition, rather than methodical induction from all the facts, which guided Bradford's judgment. Only in the loosest sense, therefore, can he be called a biographer.

Hence the history of literary biography in the United States before the twentieth century's third decade affords little scope to the would-be chronicler of lively episodes, and even less satisfaction to the critic. Among the biographers there were no Froudes to become the centers of acrimonious squabbles, and among their subjects there were, apart from Poe, none whose personal characters were held in bitter dispute. Differences in interpretation there may have been: compare Woodberry's inadequately concealed distaste for Poe with Harrison's admiration for him as a southern gentleman, despite his inability to cope with the demands of southern conviviality. Legends there were: after Henry James's suave little English Men of Letters volume on Hawthorne, it was generally agreed that the author of *The Scarlet*

Letter had been a morbid, misanthropic recluse, a veritable hermit of Salem, and despite the modifications introduced in biographies like Moncure Conway's, with their stress on his domestic happiness, the myth went undispelled until the 1930's. But for the most part, the biographies of 1870–1920 were conservative, cautious, and colorless. Their deficiencies were well described by William Roscoe Thayer, writing in 1905:

> Biographers have not kept pace with novelists in skill to reproduce the actual man; they still work too much from the outside; they should live in the heart and brain of their hero and let us see the very springs of action; for the demand for veracity, stimulated by science and by fiction, has grown so keen that readers will no longer tolerate the old school of biographers. . . .

Thayer looked forward to the day when "biography, taking a fresh start, will go on improving until its masterpieces shall be as many and as excellent as those of the other great arts." But like Edmund Gosse, writing to the same effect at the same time, Thayer preached to no avail. Only after the First World War, when scholars and a new generation of critics alike discovered the true breadth, originality, and excitement of American literature, would the writing of American authors' biographies become a major literary adventure. Then, at last, the decorous surfaces painted by the older biographers would no longer suffice; character had to be probed to its depths. Sketchy narratives would be fleshed out with the thousands of details accumulated through pioneering research. Legends and received interpretations would be subjected to ruthless scrutiny. And, by no means least, the writing would often become lively, even brilliant. All of these happy developments, however, had to await the appearance of Lytton Strachey's *Eminent Victorians* in 1918. With that event, the two streams of English and American literary biography would merge into what Edgar Johnson, borrowing a phrase from Shelley, was to call "one mighty torrent."

III

The Modern Age

III

The Modern Age

CHAPTER IX

The Stracheyan Revolution

✳

T HE new age of biography was heralded by this vigorous blast of Lytton Strachey's horn, in the preface to *Eminent Victorians*:

> The art of literary biography seems to have fallen on evil times in England. We have had, it is true, a few masterpieces, but we have never had, like the French, a great biographical tradition; we have had no Fontenelles and Condorcets, with their incomparable *éloges*, compressing into a few shining pages the manifold existences of men. With us, the most delicate and humane of all the branches of the art of writing has been relegated to the journeymen of letters; we do not reflect that it is perhaps as difficult to write a good life as to live one. Those two fat volumes, with which it is our custom to commemorate the dead—who does not know them, with their ill-digested masses of material, their slipshod style, their tone of tedious panegyric, their lamentable lack of selection, of detachment, of design? They are as familiar as the *cortège* of the undertaker, and wear the same air of slow, funereal barbarism. One is tempted to suppose, of some of them, that they were composed by that functionary, as the final item of his job.

Although the wall did not topple down in one piece, Strachey's manifesto proved its eventual doom. After *Eminent Victorians*, biography could never be the same.

The book's critical reception was mixed—Gosse, for instance, though generally disposed to welcome it, regretted Strachey's lack of sympathy with his subjects—but of its popularity, and what in a later decade would be called its newsworthiness, there was no question. In London drawing rooms it was discussed as excitedly as the first cantos of *Childe Harold* had been in 1812; and if its impact at the universities was somewhat less, the reason was only that most of Britain's impressionable youth were at war. But they read the book in the trenches or, as "Hugh Kingsmill" (H. K. Lunn), one of Strachey's future imitators, did, in German prison camps. Another prolific biographer of the next several decades, Hesketh Pearson, serving in Mesopotamia, happened to pick up in the Baghdad Officers' Club a copy of an Allabahad newspaper reporting the stir the book was creating in London. He ordered it from home, and when it arrived several months later, he "realised at once that it was something new in English letters and that it marked an epoch in biographical literature." Pearson's and Kingsmill's delight was shared by a somewhat older participant in the war, Bertrand Russell, whose laughter as he read the book in his conscientious objector's cell brought the warder running to remind him that a jail was intended as a place of punishment.

Strachey's ironic iconoclasm was exquisitely attuned to the nation's mood. His book's very title, indeed, was part of its fortune: "Eminent," with a wry curl of the lip which bore witness to all that four years of war had exposed of eminent men's capacity for stupidity and selfishness; "Victorians"—a single word which stood for all that (it was now thought) had been wrong with British society for the past fifty years. The pejorative significance of the latter term had been deepening for two decades. Among the bright young literary men of D. H. Lawrence's generation, "Victorian" was synonymous with "Tennysonian," which was bad enough; but in addition, it was the Victorians, or the Victorian mentality, that bore the blame for the agony England had undergone since August, 1914. *Eminent Victorians*, making game of the personal absurdities, pretensions, artificial pieties—the moral littleness—of four selected specimens of high Victorianism, epitomized the cynical spirit of the surviving young and middle-aged as they looked back upon catastrophe and forward into a land of meager promise. It was, in a way, a funerary volume such as its author denounced in his much-quoted preface; but the grave it gayly marked was that of a nation's idealism. The book was not quite what Gosse and others had had in mind when they urged the reformation of English biography, but it signalized the long-delayed event nonetheless. In this twilight of the Victorian gods, both the spirit and the technical brilliance of Strachey's perform-ance aroused almost hysterical enthusiasm among the emanci-pated. There had been nothing even faintly prophesying Boswell's *Johnson* before 1791. *Eminent Victorians* was just as unheralded and, given the mood of 1918, even more welcome.

Neither Cardinal Manning's printed sermons nor Miss Night-ingale's *Notes on Nursing* nor General Gordon's *Reflections in Palestine* fall within the ordinary definition of literature; of the four celebrities Strachey anatomized, only one, Dr. Arnold, has even a modest place on the periphery of literary history. *Eminent Victorians* is not, therefore, literary biography. And yet (to bor-row one of Strachey's characteristic mannerisms) the book cannot possibly be neglected here, because it not only acclimatized biog-raphy to the twentieth century but—equally important—finally vindicated biography's claim to be considered as an art. Every biographer since 1918, from the producer of weighty "definitive" lives to the confector of romantic trifles, has necessarily written in the shadow of Strachey.

The four narrative portraits that comprised Strachey's volume were as graphic and intimate as one could wish: Florence Night-ingale in her imperious ruthlessness, Arnold with a perpetual "slightly puzzled" look on his face, Manning contemplating the vigil lamp of insatiable ecclesiastical ambition, Gordon alternat-ing between Bible and brandy bottle. Once more it could be as-serted that biography had all the interest of fiction, with the addi-tional advantage of being true. For the will to believe in Victorian biography according to Strachey was strong, and was not Strachey's *bona fides* sufficiently proved by the bibliography of sources appended to each account?

No longer would readers be satisfied with the pedestrian style that had always been tolerated in biography—a duller prose, perhaps, than was admissible in any other branch of literature. Strachey had a style, and one of such pronounced and individual qualities that no one could overlook it, however irritating it might be to some tastes. E. M. Forster, long after the initial excitement died down, continued to find it "admirable." It was witty; it had epigrammatic terseness; it had a seemingly inexhaustible liveliness. It was also, on occasion, vulgar, as when Strachey portrayed young Manning tempted by the glamor of the Oxford Movement: "Really to mean every word you said, when you repeated the Athanasian Creed! How wonderful! And what enticing and mysterious vistas burst upon the view! But then, those vistas, where were they leading to? Supposing—oh heavens!—supposing after all they were to lead to—!" And it betrayed an amazing fondness for clichés, hundreds of which jar with singular infelicity against the normal urbanity of Strachey's prose.[1] But whether or not his taste was always sure, he set an example of conscious artistry which in the long run notably raised the stylistic standards of biography. He worked at his sentences like a Pater; he managed his effects with the care of a Proust.

Strachey was less a narrator than a portraitist. It was the inner, not the outer, life of his subjects that engrossed him, and his creative resources were concentrated on depicting it, along with the scenes and events that helped illustrate it. Having adopted a key to a seemingly enigmatic and even paradoxical character—a kind of psychological leitmotif, such as Arnold's pompous, pathetic earnestness—he traced the development, dominance, and consequences of that trait from youth to the grave. To support and enhance his psychological portrait he marshaled all the devices of the novelist and dramatist: interior monologues, speculation on subconscious motives (expressed with a wholly deceptive air of innocence), revealing details of appearance and manner, dramatization. One measure of his craftsmanship is found in his expert use of subordinate characters as foils to his (non-)heroes or in other illustrative capacities. The gentle, unworldly, even bewildered Newman played the dove to the energetic, ambitious Manning's eagle; Florence Nightingale was surrounded by a whole cast of minor figures who, in one way or

---

[1] One may argue, of course, that Strachey deliberately indulged in false flights and clichés for rhetorical effect—as the stylistic equivalent of his subjects' own commonplaceness, their moral platitudinousness. If so, it is one Stracheyan ironic device that fails to come off.

another—one thinks of Arthur Hugh Clough in her service, obediently wrapping brown paper parcels—pointed up her "demoniac frenzy," her grim efficiency which, if one were to believe Strachey, made strong men shiver in their blucher boots.

Thus Strachey demolished the old notion that a biographer should be no more than an assembler of facts which, when laid out in a long row, would automatically tell the true story of a life and faithfully reflect a character. The organizing, speculating, interpreting intelligence a biographer brought to his task was at least as important as the data with which he worked. It is true that Strachey allowed himself to be too prominent an intermediary between reader and subject, just as he carried other innovations too far. But it is also true that he turned the biographer back into an artist.

Unfortunately, however, these momentous contributions to the progress of biographical art were made under the auspices of a steadfastly iconoclastic spirit. Strachey's work would have been sounder, and its immediate effect on biographical practice healthier, had he not viewed both his characters and their age with the combination of fastidious disdain and supercilious amusement that was a hallmark of the Bloomsbury group. His ambition seemed to be to break into the Tussaud Gallery of Victorian Dignity and commit all kinds of mischief—painting clown faces on the waxworks' solemn countenances, rearranging the figures in absurd poses and questionable juxtapositions, stripping off their outer garb and revealing them in their somewhat patched underclothes. To this impish purpose all his craftsman's devices were directed: a vocabulary weighted to maintain a consistent attitude (*horrid, alarming, distressing, regrettable, odd,* and so on), the habit of rendering high and solemn matters ludicrous by association with, or absorption in, the humble and trivial (a trick that served him well as he deflated the pomposities of Victorian religion and morality), bland but devastating innuendo, rhetorical questions, ironic anticlimaxes—and above all, the clever and wicked selection of detail.

In modern times, at least, almost every eminent person leaves behind him an abundance of personal data which, skillfully

((285

manipulated, can prove him to have been a fool or a knave. In-nocuous personal details and casual episodes, if sufficiently em-phasized, described with archness, and placed in a misleading context, can be as damaging in their effect as plain evidence of dim intellect or villainy. Strachey's recurrent allusions to Man-ning's "piercing eye" and his custom of "drawing up elaborate tables" as he sought to make a decision underscored the cardi-nal's supposedly shrewd and calculating nature; Dr. Arnold's habit of alluding to "general principles" in his arguments enabled Strachey to ticket him as a stupid man who, despite his pose as a profound thinker, could not cope with any principles that were other than "general" and therefore, by Stracheyan extension, vague and meaningless.

Once he had determined the attitude he would take toward his subject, Strachey had no scruples against the conversion of facts to his own purpose. He valued every fragment of data he possessed according to its usefulness to his design: would it con-tribute to the dramatic effect for which he was striving, and would it harmonize with his dominant interpretation? He admit-ted having invented but one detail—Dr. Arnold's legs, which "perhaps, were shorter than they should have been." Everything else, presumably, could be found in the sources; but a number of scholars have shown how recklessly he wrenched facts from con-text, touched up quotations, read more into a statement than it contained, overlooked or conveniently forgot evidence that failed to suit his interpretation, and, in short, violated most of the other injunctions in the scientific historian's decalogue.[2] Though a con-

---

[2] In his profile of Cardinal Manning, Strachey clothed in sinister mystery the interview Manning had with the Pope three years before he went over to Rome: "Precisely what passed on that occasion never transpired"; "In the light of after-events, one would be glad to know what precisely passed at that mysterious inter-view. . . ." As a matter of fact, "what precisely passed" is on record, in the very sources Strachey used; but to have mentioned it would have spoiled the effect of Machiavellian intrigue with which he sought to infuse this study of nineteenth-century churchmanship. Time after time, in the "Florence Nightingale," Strachey seized upon perfectly unremarkable scraps of evidence and distorted them for the sake of demonstrating the woman's alleged obsessiveness. His account of General Gordon's adventures in China was founded on a diary which was well known to be a fabrication, and there is no basis for his assertion that Gordon was a dipso-maniac.

noisseur of irony, Strachey apparently never realized that he committed on a large scale the very sin of which Victorian biographers were guilty—pressing evidence into the service of a preconception. The methods were the same; only the purpose was different. Strachey's suppressions and distortions were motivated not by devotion to the dead or obedience to the canons of contemporary decorum, but by the very reverse. He focused his attention not on what could be said for his subjects but rather on what could be held against them. Because he was a gay artist, his quick sketches of celebrated Victorians are infinitely more engaging than the heavy gilt-framed biographical portraits commissioned by their contemporaries, but they are no more faithful to history. Strachey's people are as "flat" (in the terminology of novel criticism) as any of Ben Jonson's or Smollett's or Dickens's humor characters. Their truth is the truth of caricature, which, admittedly, may be considerable—but still far from complete.

Having disported itself among the ruins of four Victorian reputations, the reading audience happily anticipated Strachey's next book, *Queen Victoria*. The Queen was, *ex officio*, the most eminent Victorian of them all, and Strachey was depended upon to outdo himself. In some respects he satisfied the highest hopes. In the book, which appeared in 1921, appeared the Queen's nasty old uncles, the Prince Consort's *éminence grise* Baron Stockmar, and the succession of prime ministers, climaxed by the "romantic charlatan" Disraeli, who twisted the Queen round his dandiacal finger. All were done to a turn. And yet it was obvious that, although it would be too much to assert that Strachey had come to scoff and remained to pray, he did succumb to a certain reluctant affection for the short, stout monarch. G. M. Trevelyan observed that "the most important event in the history of English biography in the twentieth century is not the portrait of Queen Victoria by Lytton Strachey, it is the conquest of Strachey by Queen Victoria." In the midst of much incidental entertainment —though there was less outright farce than in the earlier book— ran a serious theme: the incongruity between Victoria's exalted position, which became all the more exalted when Disraeli

((287

crowned her Queen Empress, and her thoroughly bourgeois character, sentimental, strong-willed, unintellectual, yet somehow
admirable.

Replete though it was with the familiar Stracheyan rhetorical
devices, along with an audacious novelty, the deathbed-reverie
montage at the very end, *Queen Victoria* was less a *tour de force*
than an advance toward more thoughtful and methodical biography. In contrast to *Eminent Victorians, Queen Victoria* comprised a full-length biographical narrative. Strachey traced the
transformation of the Queen herself, the person behind the Royal
Presence, from a timid, awkward girl to a mature woman with a
mind of her own, quietly assuming the burdens of state with
which the death of the Consort left her to deal singlehanded, and
thence into a regal old age marked by two jubilees. This careful
treatment of change, along with Strachey's tempering of iconoclasm with a measure of sympathy, made the book a better example of narrative biography than the earlier one. It was less
scintillating than *Eminent Victorians,* but it was also less irre-
sponsible.[3]

No sooner did *Eminent Victorians* and *Queen Victoria* capti-
vate the popular fancy than a whole shoal of imitations appeared,
bad and indifferent. Never before in literary history, perhaps, had
an innovation been so swiftly seized upon and vulgarized. Strachey's books were honest literary coinage, much as some people
disliked the design; those that followed them in the next decade
were, for the most part, tinny counterfeits. This no doubt was
inevitable. Like Boswell, Strachey seemed so very easy to imitate.
His technique appeared, after all, to consist only of a few tricks
that any reasonably agile literary talent could soon learn: the
artfully contrived innuendo, the innocent question with the built-

---

[3] Those who saw evidence of Strachey's maturing and mellowing in *Queen
Victoria* had hopes that, once he outgrew his superciliousness and his passion for
effect at the expense of truth, he would become a thoroughly serious biographer.
But he was already forty-one when the book came out; and his only subsequent
biography, *Elizabeth and Essex: A Tragic History* (1928), proved to be an inferior work obviously written for the market Strachey had created. Its fictionaliza-
tion was too pronounced, and its dubious thesis—that Elizabeth suffered from a
physical abnormality—contributed to its general cheap air.

in answer, the clever paradox, the glib antithesis, the exposure of the unheroic detail, the conversion of a solemn incident into farce. And his condescending posture could be adopted by anyone who was capable of malice. Beginning with (for instance) the assumption, so fashionable in those years, that the Victorian age was one of intellectual stagnation, tastelessness, pharisaism, and unctuous religiosity, one could select almost any Victorian celebrity and have two or three hundred pages' worth of fun at his, and the age's, expense. It was a cheap and easy way of making a salable book, and many writers, to Strachey's embarrassment and the damage of his own reputation, took it.[4]

· 2 ·

Although it was widely assumed that "the new biography" necessarily involved iconoclasm—a mistake that bred endless confusion, and not a little injustice, in contemporary criticism— the association was fortuitous rather than fundamental. The statue-toppling aspect of Strachey's art was, understandably, the most discussed, and in the wider context of biography, it was symbolically appropriate. Biography was, as Strachey suggested, the literary emblem par excellence of Victorianism, a product faithful to the old era's habit of misapplied and exaggerated hero worship, with all its attendant hypocrisy and evasiveness. In their pronouncements on the subject, it was often hard to tell which the members of Strachey's generation were angrier about—

---

[4] In contemporary discussions of "the new biography," the names of Strachey and André Maurois were linked, along with that of Emil Ludwig, who first gained widespread attention in England and America in the middle and late twenties with translations of his psychologically oriented lives of Bismarck, Wilhelm II, Napoleon, Goethe, and Christ. If they formed a "school" at all, it was a totally fortuitous one. Neither Maurois nor Ludwig was influenced by Strachey, nor he by them. It was simply a case of three men, with widely different backgrounds, simultaneously and independently turning the spotlight of biography from a man's outward career to the recesses of his soul. Still another popular "Stracheyan" biographer was Philip Guedalla, whose colorfully written books, among them biographies of Palmerston, Gladstone, and Wellington—as well as a collection of essays on Victorian women called *Bonnet and Shawl*—contributed to the general realization that the English nineteenth century was populated by people, not statues. Guedalla, however, did not deal with literary figures.

Victorianism itself, or the literary vehicle that epitomized it. "The Victorian biographer," asserted André Maurois, "always describes a mask, and refuses to look behind it." And Virginia Woolf—was this perhaps one manifestation of her subconscious rebellion against the memory of her father, Leslie Stephen?—lamented that "where the Mrs. Hutchinsons and the Izaak Waltons had wished to prove that their heroes were prodigies of courage and learning the Victorian biographer was dominated by the idea of goodness. Noble, upright, chaste, severe; it is thus that the Victorian worthies are presented to us."[5] The general feeling was that Victorian biographers had formed a gigantic conspiracy of silence. It was therefore fitting that a radically altered type of biography should provide the stage upon which gleeful iconoclasts destroyed the myths—at first, specifically Victorian—that had had so long a run. For the occasion, the heavy plush draperies of traditional biography were replaced by brightly colored settings, and the stage directions called for sprightly instead of measured movements. The air was festive indeed, and it was filled with prophecies. At the height of the excitement, in 1930, Hesketh Pearson declared that "there can be little doubt now that biography is to be the leading literary art of the future and will attract the best writers and some of the best brains among our successors. . . . It is the day of the biographer; he is the dramatist, the essayist, the romancist of the future."

Such euphoria was due only in part to the substitution of candor for concealment; the revolution in biography went far deeper, and had many ramifications that were just as important. At last, biography, like the postwar generation itself, had been liberated from the shackles of dead conventions and allowed to catch up with the times.

Unlike other genres of literature, it had given, as we have seen, no signs of significant advance in the past two decades. Among the more adventurous poets there had already been a reaction against Tennyson-derived pastoralism; with Wells and

---

[5] Mrs. Woolf perhaps forgot that it was her father's own *Dictionary of National Biography* which had steadfastly refused to admit eulogy to its pages. "No flowers, by request" was said to be its unofficial motto.

Bennett fiction had been taking long further strides toward realism; on the stage Shaw's impudent heterodoxy and Galsworthy's bold—for the time—discussion of social problems had brought vitality to a drama that had languished during most of the preceding century. Only biography had been untouched by the winds of Edwardian and early Georgian change. Now, under the hands of Lytton Strachey and his most gifted successors, it too became an art responsible to its immediate literary and intellectual milieu. Much more than at any time in the past, it mirrored, and was affected by, ideas that helped color and define the spirit of the moment. Writing of "the new biography" in 1929, Gamaliel Bradford observed:

> I feel that it is really more than anything else one of the varied aspects of the application of the scientific spirit, which has so widely moulded our whole intellectual and spiritual attitude in the closing nineteenth and beginning twentieth centuries. The influence of Darwin has wholly changed not only our science, but our religion, our economics, our sociology, our fiction, and our poetry. Why should it not revolutionize our biography also? I believe it has. In other words, instead of trying to write a man's eulogy, or commemorate his achievements, or hold him up as a profitable example, we are simply trying to understand what manner of man he was, to analyze his character and motives, and to classify him and put him in his place with other groups of human beings.

The spirit of realism, which in its modern manifestation had originated in the Victorian scientific revolution and then spread through literature—most notably in the novel—had at last reached biography. It encouraged biographers to present, and readers to accept, a historic figure as he lived, no matter how unattractive or downright wicked he may have been. For the twentieth-century mind had room for all kinds of people; frankly accepting the fallen state of man, it could look with complete aplomb at human spectacles which would (or should) have shocked and grieved readers in the eighteenth and nineteenth centuries. Biographers found an audience prepared to take men and women as they came, neither lamenting what they were nor pretending what they were not.

((291

But the most powerful of all the intellectual influences that animated biography in the postwar years was the appearance of new theories and schools of psychology, which drastically revised man's view of himself and opened vast new fields of speculation. Freud's theories had begun to affect advanced thought in the English-speaking world before the outbreak of the First World War. In simplified and usually distorted form, they had also made their way into the popular consciousness—in America more than in Britain—through magazine articles and easy-to-read books, which catered to the contemporary appetite for the daring by stressing the specifically sexual implications of Freudianism. But it was not until the early 1920's—"this super-sexualized beginning of the twentieth century," as Amy Lowell called it, "when every school-boy babbles Freud"—that psychoanalysis made its full impact on either the smart set or the man in the street. Only then did English and American biographers begin to babble Freud, with consequences we shall observe in the next chapter.

Iconoclasm, realism, psychoanalysis: these topics and attitudes of the day, made palatable by borrowed fictional techniques, comprised a sparkling and heady brew. The modish biography of the 1920's and '30's was as characteristic a product of its age as *Chrome Yellow, The Green Hat*, and *Babbitt*.

The "biography boom," as it soon was called, became one of the chief literary phenomena in the English-speaking world from 1920 to the middle of the thirties. Brightly written, studiously irreverent biographies by the hundreds competed with novels on the best-seller lists. Bliss was it in that dawn to be alive, but to be biting grandfather's leg was very heaven. In both Britain and America the book-length debunking of heroic reputations became a literary fad. "For some years," wrote Bernard De Voto in 1933, when the sport was beginning to lose its zest, "biography in America seemed to be no more than a high-spirited game of yanking out shirt-tails and setting fire to them." The muckraking spirit of a former decade, which had exposed the corruption of such majestic institutions as Philadelphia and Standard Oil, was transferred to national heroes—the Washingtons, now revealed to have used profanity, invested in the liquor traffic, and otherwise comported themselves like subjects of Warren G. Harding, and the Lincolns, whose newly exposed crudities as backwoods Neanderthals came as no surprise to those whom H. L. Mencken had educated in the grotesque realities of the American subculture.

From the worst excesses of (so-called) Stracheyism or debunking, literary figures were relatively exempt, perhaps because so many more tempting Aunt Sallies were available. The principal literary targets, naturally, were authors who either had acquired a special reputation for stuffiness or whose intelligence and gifts had presumably been overrated. The ill fortune Dr. Arnold had suffered at Strachey's hands was visited upon his son in Hugh Kingsmill's incredibly tasteless biography, in which the poet was habitually referred to as "Matt"—an act of *lèse-majesté* comparable only to calling Henry James "Hank." The revelation that Wordsworth in his youth—itself, according to the received idea of the poet, an improbable concept—had fathered an illegitimate child provided Hugh I'Anson Fausset with an opportunity to portray the solemn admirer of nature's simple plan as having been, in reality, a guilt-ridden neurotic. But even worse was Fausset's book on Tennyson, an elaborate compound of petulance, misrepresentation, and pretentiously bad writing which, anticipating by two decades W. H. Auden's announcement that Tennyson was "the stupidest English poet," depicted the Laureate as an intellectual nullity, living his whole life drinking, or bathed in, the emotional syrup of his smug and adoring age. Donald Carswell adopted a crushingly condescending attitude toward the hero who had made so noble a figure in Lockhart's biography: Scott, he declared,

> never really understood anything, for though he had solid reasoning powers, he had little insight. He lived in terms of feeling and believing and willing, and spent his days pursuing incompatibles with unremitting diligence and spectacular, if sometimes sad, results. He was a professional man who aspired to be a feudal lord and could not keep his fingers out of trade; a Jacobite whose devotion to the House of Hanover became a byword; an enthusiastic admirer of the material progress of his age who would not accept its social and political consequences; an Anglophobe in principle who in practice found England altogether admirable;

an historian who knew everything about history except its meaning. To a moderately clever man these absurdities would have been obvious, but Scott was not even moderately clever. Of the metaphysical diathesis that is said to distinguish his countrymen he had not a trace. He loved to talk, but was never at ease in a discussion and never said anything worth remembering. His writings are as bare of ideas as his conversation was.

In America at the same time, and in the same spirit, Herbert Gorman portrayed Longfellow as "a sort of American Queen Victoria . . . the emblem of Victorian America, kindly, benign, urbane, moral, and safe," endowed with "mental feebleness" and no poetic talent whatsoever. Written almost entirely in the historical present tense, calling its luckless hero "Henry" throughout, and dismissing the whole Victorian era as a "sugary epic," Gorman's book represented flapper-age literary biography at its most flamboyant and futile.

To writers of popular biography, the chief attraction residing in the annals of literary men was not so much the ease with which such persons could be revealed as muddle-headed, pretentious, ambiguous, and hypocritical, as the rich psychological and dramatic qualities—the "romance"—with which their histories abounded. For overinflated reputations to prick, one turned to statesmen, military heroes, and millionaires; but for genuine human interest and ready-made drama, the Poes, Byrons, Shelleys, Wildes, and Brontës were the thing. Moreover, as the success of many new literary biographies proved (and as Boswell, Lockhart, and Mrs. Gaskell among others had demonstrated long ago), one could make a good story out of the life of an author without saying much about his works: it was what he was, not what he wrote, that counted. By regarding authors solely as colorful human beings who led eventful lives (André Maurois, for example, treating the life of Shelley as a light comedy, barely managed to hint that "Ariel" was a poet), popularized literary biographies appealed to countless readers who had little interest in literature as such and were not especially eager to acquire any knowledge of it. For every reader of a vividly written biography of Byron who went on to sample *Don Juan*, there were thousands who were content to have enjoyed a guided tour through his love life.

In literary history could also be found numerous men and women whose lives could be interpreted as "illustrations" of history, again without necessary reference to their artistic achievement. The saga of Washington Irving, as exhaustively related by Stanley Williams, was a panoramic reflection of the state of contemporary taste in America and Europe; its subject was not so much who Irving was and what he wrote as the reasons why he was, apart from Cooper, the first American writer to become an international celebrity.

Among the biographies of American writers produced after 1920, a number were noteworthy for their interpretations of the fate of the individual in the successive epochs of American culture and of the unique qualities of that culture as manifested in the fortunes of some of its most sensitive products. Newton Arvin, a leading advocate of the conception of Hawthorne as "solitary," asserted that the novelist's experience was a paradigm of the dominant tendency in the America of his day: "Dispersion, not convergence, has been the American process. . . . He was at odds with the society about him; but the elements of that society were, in a special sense, at odds with one another. . . . His very estrangement from his fellows was but emblematic of their own estrangement from one another or their collective estrangement from the main body of human experience." Lawrance Thompson saw in Longfellow's career "the spirit and character of a national and cultural adolescence. . . . The essential traits in his character were moulded by the repeated inner struggle between his inherent Yankee opportunism and his dominantly romantic attitude toward life"—a struggle that took place in the breasts of countless other young Americans of his generation. And if young Longfellow was a Yankee Everyman of the 1820's and '30's, men like Dreiser and Sherwood Anderson were no less typical of another kind of American in the early twentieth century: self-educated for the most part, profoundly influenced by contemporary rationalism-materialism-determinism, pulled one way by their lower-middle-class antecedents and another by their intellectual ambitions, and ending up as pathetically confused radicals. Their biographies were epitomes of the groping bourgeois quest for some kind of philosophical position and the artistic means of defining it. They—and, later, Scott Fitzgerald, Sinclair Lewis, and other ill-fated children of the American twentieth century—became, in the hands of their biographers, Representative Men.

Sometimes these books were not merely descriptive but argumentative as well: they were, in fact, vehicles for the conveyance of theses. From the beginnings, of course, literary biography had contained moralizing and other incidental propaganda. Dr. Currie's life of Burns had warned against the pernicious effects of drink, and in several passages in his life of Goldsmith, John Forster had argued the case for more liberal payment and more stringent legal protection to authors—a cause much agitated in the middle of the nineteenth century and admirably supported by Goldsmith's continual poverty despite the amount of literary work he turned out. But seldom had a book-length biography of a literary figure been used primarily to disseminate its author's pet doctrine. Now, in the 1920's, appeared biographies that were frankly tracts for their time. Van Wyck Brooks's studies of Henry James and Mark Twain were propaganda pieces, addressed to the intellectuals and artists who, in protest against the coming of a new Gilded Age, were sailing for Europe by the boatload. Granting the sorry history of America's cultural life and its shabby treatment of its sensitive spirits, Brooks argued through his parables of James and Twain, escape was not the answer; it was time for the American artist to take a stand on his native ground. "Read, writers of America, the driven, disenchanted, anxious faces of your sensitive countrymen," exhorted the peroration of *The Ordeal of Mark Twain;* resist the fate of Twain, "the saddest, most ironical figure in all the history of this Western continent . . . the supreme victim of an epoch in American history." Later Bernard De Voto, wielding a frontiersman's sledge hammer on Brooks's book in his *Mark Twain's America,* proposed a devil theory that was as specifically characteristic of its time (1932) as Brooks's detestation of the frontier and the anti-artistic mood of the Grant epoch had been of 1920, namely, the proposition that if anything stifled Twain's native woodnotes wild, it was the encrusted gentility of the Holmes-Howells world centering in Cambridge, Massachusetts.

One hesitates to decide where honest, responsible thesis advocacy ends and polemical ax grinding begins; all that need be said is that the annals of literary biography between the two World Wars record numerous instances of both. Hugh Fausset's portraits of Wordsworth and Tennyson were largely excoriations based on the odd insistence that, as poet-prophets, they should somehow have prevented the catastrophic course of nineteenth-century England which led eventually to the Marne. Katharine Anthony portrayed Margaret Fuller and Mary Lamb as feminists who lived before their proper time, and adopted a Freudian argument to rebuke twentieth-century women who declined to join the march:

> The feminism of women, like the corresponding form of sex-solidarity among men, is based on a social impulse which is in turn, rooted in an erotic impulse towards others of one's own sex. The destruction of this impulse is neither possible nor desirable. Women who are unfriendly and unsympathetic toward the mass problems of their own sex are defective on this side of their emotional development. Somewhere along the road of their evolving characters, they have lost the capacity for a social emotion of a very high value.

Even Marxists, not content with the number of living authors they recruited in the 1930's, proselyted the dead. T. A. Jackson, followed by several other less doctrinaire biographers, viewed Dickens' life as "the progress of a radical" who was a Marxist in all but name, and Jack Lindsay found the life and writings of George Meredith permeated with similar leanings.[6]

---

[6] Everything is possible to the zealot. In another book, Lindsay found that possession of a mistress enabled Dickens "to embody in his novels the change in relations between the sexes which the advance of industrialism in the post-1848 situation was bringing about." (*Charles Dickens: A Biographical and Critical Study* [New York, 1950], p. 348.) This neat cementing of a nexus between Dickens' sexual life, his view of society, and his art compels wonder, if not precisely belief.

((297

Overt and comprehensive theses were but the most conspi-cuous manifestations of a trait that marked literary biography in general after it was stirred from its long intellectual lethargy: the effort to interpret as well as to assemble. The biographer sought not only to present data but to search for pattern and dominant meaning. No longer was the writing of a man's life a matter of mere compilation, or even of careful chronological narrative; the ideal biographer had to analyze his material, see it from many different angles and in many different lights. He had to be simul-taneously an expert psychologist, a student of intellectual and social history, something of a philosopher—and an artist with a sure sense of artistic values. Few practitioners, of course, quali-fied on all counts (to which had to be added, in the case of literary biography, the possession of a sound critical faculty). Many post-Stracheyan biographers, ill-prepared to be psycholo-gists, historians, critics, or literary artists, produced books that were as bad as any the nineteenth century had spawned. But others were triumphs of scholarship and controlled imaginative-ness.

Whether the presence of a substantial body of pertinent criti-cal theory helps bring out the best in an art at any given period is a readily debatable proposition. It is beyond question, however, that the successes biography had in the decades after 1920 were due to no such assistance. Although many believed, with Frank Harris, that "of all the literary arts, biography is the most diffi-cult," the lack of shrewd and stimulating criticism persisted in the new age. The very circumstances that had unexpectedly made biography a vehicle of expression peculiarly suited to the period had multiplied the demands made upon it; yet the biographers had to solve their problems empirically. Despite the critical and popular prestige the newly vivified art had acquired, the level of discussion was not high, and the same grain was sifted over and over. For a number of years the single most debated point was the legitimacy of Strachey's attitude and method. Few denied that some advantage was to be found in his replacement of the mor-tuary attendant's wax and rouge with the candid pencil of the freehand sketcher, but was there not something indecent in his refusal to be reverent, or even respectful, in the presence of men and women of substance and dignity? And was any biographer entitled to the license Strachey took in dealing with factual materials? On the more basic artistic issues confronting the biographer, however, critics seldom touched. In the preceding century, criticism, uninspired though it usually was, had been several steps ahead of practice; now the reverse was true. Neither the intellectual restlessness nor the zeal for experimentation which attended the emergence of the "new" biography generated a criticism worthy of the occasion.

It is hard to tell how self-conscious was the biographers' coming to grips with the demands of their art. Among them was no counterpart of a Keats, confiding to his correspondents the insights into the nature of poetry that his struggles with the art produced, nor a Henry James, reflecting in his notebooks, and more publicly in his prefaces, on the goals and effects to be sought by the novelist. The chronicles of the modern biographical art contain no such extended and intimate records of a writer's day-by-day contemplation and toil as one finds in, say, Flaubert's *Correspondance* and André Gide's diary of the creation of *Les Faux-Monnayeurs*. The closest approach to such records, perhaps, is to be found in the journals and letters, and several formal essays, of Gamaliel Bradford. But Bradford was for various reasons a lonely figure, residing some distance from the main stream of the biographical art; and it is doubtful whether many biographers read either his numerous collections of "psychographs" or the volumes of private papers (*Journal,* 1933; *Letters,* 1934) in which his most astute observations appear.

Most of the commentary written from the practitioners' point of view after 1920 came from the so-called popularizers, André Maurois, Harold Nicolson, Hesketh Pearson, and one or two American ladies. On the whole, apart from Maurois' Clark Lectures at Cambridge (published in 1930 as *Aspects of Biography*) and some of the same writer's scattered essays, it was superficial and platitudinous; and readers could not help noticing, time after time, the discrepancy between the various writers' lofty and unexceptionable doctrine and their actual practice. One of the few extended discussions that deserved the name of serious criticism was written by Henry James's scholarly biographer, Leon Edel, whose Alexander Lectures on *Literary Biography* (1957) demonstrated how stimulating a topic the aims, techniques, and problems of the biographical art could be when treated with a combination of common sense and literary sophistication.

CHAPTER X

The Oath

❈

"A BIOGRAPHER," wrote Sir Desmond MacCarthy in his essay on Lytton Strachey, "is an artist who is on oath." The conception of biography embodied in those nine terse words was not new in the twentieth century; it, or something very much like it, underlay the theory of the genre from its beginning. But the most significant fact about biography after 1920—the respect in which it most conspicuously differed from that of preceding eras—is that the two requirements of veracity and art were taken more seriously than ever before. Each made greater claims upon the biographer, who had to work harder to satisfy them. And because they pulled him in different directions, intensified emphasis on each increased the tension between them.

The higher the standards, the sharper was the biographer's awareness that he could no more be a wholly faithful historian than he could be a free artist. As an artist he was limited to the facts he had to work with; as a historian he was limited by the quantity and nature of his materials. For any ambition to present a rigorously accurate account of a man and his life is, when examined closely, impossible of achievement. All a biographer can hope for, under the best of conditions, is to present an image—incomplete, distorted, flawed, shadowy though it has to be—which is not unlike the original, however short it may fall of complete fidelity.

In the course of a single day, a person performs thousands of overt acts, thinks thousands of thoughts, responds to as many thousands of impulses, makes subconscious gestures beyond counting. Multiplied by the number of days in a year, and then by the years of a man's life, they constitute the staggering sum of data the biographer would need were he to have the absolute command of his subject that in practice is reserved for God. But total knowledge of another man's continuous existence from birth to death, embracing everything from the most public act to the most secret motive, is obviously beyond the reach of mortal being. Even the most systematic of self-watching diarists—a Pepys, a Boswell—succeeds in recording but a small sampling of his conscious acts and thoughts during a specified period, and nothing whatsoever, naturally, of his subconscious life; how much less, then, can one man know of another's!

Thus only an infinitesimal fraction of the events in a life ever has been or can be recorded. What comes down to the biographer, under the best of conditions, is a small selection, and one that is almost wholly accidental. It has no necessary bearing on the genuinely crucial episodes and concerns of a man's life; it is merely the aggregate of the data which happened to be set down, for reasons that seldom had anything to do with their ultimate biographical importance, less all which, though once recorded, has subsequently perished. Many centrally significant events, furthermore, were never recorded in the first place; they were locked in the unwritten memories of those who participated. The habit of recording personal events has always been more exceptional than customary, even among men and women who have been most given to self-observation. And even if there is a rough correlation between the amount of data preserved on a certain series of events and the intrinsic importance of those events, their meaning can be only crudely assessed; "there is," as Walter Bagehot once put it, "no idea of the countless accumulation, the collision of action, the web of human feeling, with which, in the day of their life, they were encompassed."[1]

---

[1] The variations on this melancholy truth are many, and they might well be inscribed above every biographer's desk to enforce a humble spirit:
    When I read the book, the biography famous,
    And is this then (said I) what the author calls a man's life?
    And so will some one when I am dead and gone write my life?

The biographer is sentenced to labor under the brutal certainty that he can at best construct only a rough approximation of the life that was actually lived, of the personality that actually existed, and changed, from this year to that; and that most of the important knowledge he needs is never to be had. His situation is like that of the archaeologist who must infer the full appearance and habits of a prehistoric man from the few fragments of bone and artifacts he finds in a barrow.

But biography seems to thrive in an atmosphere of hopelessness, and the sheer gigantic dimensions of his handicaps give the biographer a kind of desperate strength. If a minuscule representation of a life is all that can be attained (with a large, irreducible amount of distortion assured), at least he can try to learn and report the truth insofar as it is humanly possible to do so. By shrewd inferences from the extant data, and by an equally careful process of selection and arrangement, it may be possible to recreate a man and his life, if not in their full literal truth, then in their essence. Such is the hope that has always sustained biographers as they have gone about their impossible task.[2]

(As if any man really knew aught of my life,
Why even I myself I often think how little or nothing of my real life,
Only a few hints, a few diffused faint clews and indirections
I seek for my own use to trace out here.)
　　　　　　　　　　　　　　　　(*Leaves of Grass*)
"When Plutarch placed in noble array for the contemplation of ages to come his images of heroes and sages, or when Dr. Johnson drew that gallery of poets, so many of whom only survive in his portraiture, the writers must have been conscious how little of the real men lay behind those strong or graceful representations, how much that was even faithfully recorded may convey a false impression, how much was inevitably omitted which might contradict every deduction and alter every estimate." (*Quarterly Review*, CXIX [1866], 154-155.)
"The biographer may reconstruct an episode, present a picture, or reflect a mood by which the reader is enabled to feel something of the glow of personality and know, perhaps, a little of the substance of the past. In so far as the historian can accomplish this his work is a success. At best his labor will be pathetically incomplete, for whatever its detail and its resemblance to life, these will record mainly but an outward expression, behind which was the mighty sweep and tumult of unwritten thought, the overwhelming proportion of any life, which no other human soul can ever really know." (Albert Bigelow Paine, *Mark Twain: A Biography* [New York, 1912], III, 1586.)
　[2] A more relaxed view was Robert Louis Stevenson's: "I like biography far better than fiction myself," he once wrote Gosse; "fiction is too free. In biography you have your little handful of facts, little bits of a puzzle, and you sit and think, and fit 'em together this way and that, and get up and throw 'em down and say damn, and go out for a walk. And it's real soothing; and when done, gives an

A major reason for the flowering of biography after the First World War was that hope was fed anew from several sources. Strict canons of historical criticism, developed over many decades, came to exert a stronger control over the handling of biographical facts; a combination of circumstances was opening to the biographers of many figures quantities of material that had hitherto been inaccessible; and new techniques of interpretation, such as that provided by psychoanalysis, became available. In this stimulating atmosphere it was possible to believe that, if the complete truth about a life remained beyond reach, biographers could approach it more closely than ever before.

In the nineteenth century, as we have seen, there was no lack of theoretical belief in the historian's—and, by extension, the biographer's—obligation to scrutinize every piece of data before admitting it to his pages as established fact. A small handful of British literary biographers had applied the acid of critical intelligence to the error-encrusted mass of received information. But most biographers were content to print their data without worrying too much about its absolute accuracy. If they offered their readers information previously unknown, the novelty of these supposed facts tended to still any doubt of their truth; and if they drew their data from preceding biographies, they implicitly assumed that prior existence in print was warrant enough of reliability.

In the post-Stracheyan era, biographers who derived the substance of their books from preceding ones, without attempting either to test the received facts or supplement them, remained in the majority, as they always will. They placidly passed on the errors they found in their sources, along with fresh ones bred by their carelessness or their desire to supply silences or tidy up discrepancies. But in the upper reaches of the craft there was a notably intensified spirit of skepticism, which resulted in a ceaseless campaign to purge from the body of biographical knowledge

---

idea of finish to the writer that is very peaceful. Of course, it's not really so finished as quite a rotten novel; it always has and always must have the incurable illogicalities of life about it. . . . Still, that's where the fun comes in." (*Letters*, ed. Colvin [1923], IV, 211–212.)

all the myths, biases, unsupported assumptions, misinterpretations, and sheer mistakes that had crept past the unvigilant eyes of earlier biographers.

Just as indispensable, in this high conception of the biographer's responsibility, was thoroughness—the determination not to let a single recoverable fragment of information escape view. Research was governed by the premise that nothing is potentially without some meaning. "The tiniest scrap of biographical fact," wrote Jay Leyda, "might be the very detail needed to help grasp a cluster of associations, the missing piece in the puzzle that makes plain a series of relationships in the life that in turn reveals a major theme or continuity in the poems."

This scholarly attitude was cultivated most assiduously and effectively in the American universities, where, before the First World War, a new generation of biographers were trained in the seminars of men who had themselves been baptized Ph.D. at the primal fonts of modern "scientific" scholarship, in Berlin, Göttingen, Munich, Heidelberg, Leipzig. During the first decades of academic literary scholarship, at the turn of the century, the emphasis had been heavily on pre-seventeenth-century literature. The great figures to be studied were Chaucer and Shakespeare, and whatever research did not directly bear upon them was addressed to the works of their contemporaries and to the philological problems associated with medieval and Elizabethan writings. The later epochs, for the study of whose authors biographical material was much more abundant, received comparatively little attention. But as the first years of the twentieth century passed, scholars' horizons gradually broadened, and despite the commanding presence of George Lyman Kittredge, whose specialties were Chaucer and Shakespeare and who wielded immense but not always salutary influence over the academic study of literature in the period, the lives of post-Elizabethan writers began to be re-examined. American professors, quick to detect the inadequacies of the existing biographies, prepared to rewrite them with the aid of newly examined, and in many instances newly discovered, documents.

The first great American biographer of English literary figures was Wilbur Lucius Cross, known to his Yale students as "Uncle Toby" on account of his devotion to *Tristram Shandy*. His two biographies, of Sterne (1909) and Fielding (1918), were the first extensive and critical lives of their respective much-maligned subjects, and in many ways they are still the best. At Princeton, meanwhile, was George McLean Harper, whose life of Wordsworth (1916) finally put the study of the poet on a firm foundation. Taking the documents which William Knight had printed in inaccurate and expurgated form in his discreet biography, Harper studied them for the sake of the thoughtful, well-informed interpretation of his subject's life and character which he rightly conceived to be the biographer's business. The book's thoroughness and its steady attempt to define the sources and nature of Wordsworth's ideas and relate them to the events of his earlier years made it a landmark in the development of modern scholarly biography.

Harper and Cross were the two pre-1918 American literary biographers whose works were entitled to be called "magisterial." But among their contemporaries were two Columbia teachers, Carl Van Doren, whose life of Thomas Love Peacock appeared in 1911, and William Haller, author of *The Early Life of Robert Southey* (1917). And at the University of North Carolina, Archibald Henderson, a mathematician, was devoting his avocational life to writing successive large biographies of his idol, George Bernard Shaw.[3]

These were pioneers in what, beginning in the 1920's, became a major American academic industry: the production of exhaustive, meticulously documented biographies of English and American literary figures. Ransacking libraries, private collections, and official archives in America and abroad, conducting extensive cor-

---

[3] The most fateful personal encounter in the history of literary biography—Boswell's first meeting with Johnson, in Tom Davies' bookshop in 1763—occurred totally without benefit of press coverage. In contrast, Henderson's first meeting with Shaw in 1907 was, thanks to Shaw, adequately publicized. All Fleet Street was invited, and the subsequent headlines read:
SHAW MEETS BIOGRAPHER ST. PANCRAS STATION
DECLARES BIOGRAPHY A TERRIFIC TASK
SAYS ONLY A DESPERATE CHARACTER COULD WRITE HIS LIFE
(Henderson, *George Bernard Shaw: Man of the Century* [New York, 1956], p. xii.)

respondences with fellow scholars, librarians, collectors, descendants, and everyone else who was possibly able to help, accumulating piles of photostats and, later on, reels of microfilm, professors from coast to coast were busy amplifying and correcting the world's knowledge of virtually all important literary figures. They soon had their counterparts in the English universities and, sometimes, outside. The result of this international scholarly effort was a succession of portly books upon which, because they contained all the data then known on their respective subjects, all subsequent narratives necessarily were based.

The amount of primary material available for use had multiplied many times since the beginning of the century. Earlier, it is true, there had been no lack of data on some authors; as the lengthy acknowledgments prefixed to scholarly biographies like Courthope's *Pope* and Aitken's *Steele* testified, energetic biographers could find manuscripts and obscure printed works relating to their subject in scores of private hands, in various depositories of public records, and in such libraries as the British Museum and the Bodleian at Oxford. But many more collections of papers had vanished, or remained inaccessible. Virtually every biographer had been deprived of certain classes of documents which he had reason to believe were in existence—somewhere. The new generation of biographers set out to find them. Besieging every library and private house where their quarry might lie, indefatigable in their search once they were admitted to the premises, they succeeded in bringing to light large quantities of withheld or forgotten documents.

They were not, of course, uniformly successful. Loyal to their Victorian heritage, some families—both the immediate survivors of a distinguished man and those who were removed from their celebrated ancestor by several generations—sought either to discourage all biographers or to keep close control over what a biographer wrote. Everyone in the literary world knew that Somerset Maugham drew from life when he depicted the second Mrs. Driffield, anxious proprietress of the posthumous fame of her late husband, the last of the great Victorians, and Alroy Kear, the pussyfooting biographer who announced that "I don't want to say anything that's untrue, but I do think there's a certain amount that's better left unsaid."[4] This was the attitude which governed many a widow, a son, a daughter as public interest, whetted by Strachey and his followers, demanded frank and ample biographies of recently deceased men of letters. With varying degrees of adamance—one thinks of Coventry Patmore's survivors, suppressing the details of his passion for Alice Meynell and his taste for pornography; and of Carrie Kipling's indomitable guardianship over her late husband's reputation—they sought, Lady Shelley-like, to fix their late husband's or father's public image. To ensure privacy beyond the grave, celebrated authors themselves took precautions reminiscent of the nineteenth century: Willa Cather and Ernest Hemingway both left injunctions against the publication of their letters, and in his eighties Maugham publicly requested his friends to destroy all the letters from him which they possessed.

In the printed commentary on biography, even in an age priding itself on its liberal spirit, belated Victorians could still be found urging the moral necessity of telling less than one knew and of refusing to speculate on private matters. In 1925, lecturing before the Royal Society of Literature, A. C. Benson, once the

---

[4] Readers of *Cakes and Ale* will recall that Edward Driffield, the great novelist, provided a difficult subject for an honest biographer. His first wife was a robust and extravagantly unfaithful daughter of the earth; instead of the "sea chanteys or old English country airs . . . the sort of thing they used to sing at fairings," which his novels would lead readers to expect he himself sang, he was partial to music-hall favorites like "Come Where the Booze is Cheaper"; "he was just a wee bit unscrupulous in money matters and he had a kink in him that made him take a strange pleasure in the society of his inferiors and some of his personal habits were rather disagreeable." His prospective biographer admitted that "It would be rather amusing to show the man with his passion for beauty and his careless treatment of his obligations, his fine style and his personal hatred for soap and water, his idealism and his tippling in disreputable pubs; but honestly, would it pay? They'd only say I was imitating Lytton Strachey." Malicious though Maugham's portrait of Alroy Kear is, the situation in which Maugham placed him evokes sympathy. It is a useful reminder that as late as 1930 literary biography was occasionally the product of an understanding between an exigent widow and an acquiescent biographer. As it related to Thomas Hardy, however (the presumptive model for Edward Driffield), Maugham's satire was somewhat wide of the mark. The chief guardian of Hardy's public image was not his second wife but Hardy himself. It was he who wrote all but four chapters of the two volumes of his "official" biography—*The Early Life of Thomas Hardy* (1928) and *The Later Years of Thomas Hardy* (1930)—the presence of Florence Hardy's name on the title page notwithstanding.

writer of discreet lives of FitzGerald, Rossetti, and Pater, attributed to the ideal biographer the hope that "the memory of
something fine and beautiful and beloved should be . . . recorded,
that it may stand as a living witness to life and beauty," and
urged that "he need not violate privacy or sacredness, any more
than a portrait painter need insist on always painting from the
nude." As late as 1940, the American Albert Jay Nock asserted in
the *Atlantic Monthly* that "the [only] legitimate function of
modern biography . . . is to help the historian." There was, he
said, no place for any personal details which did not obviously
bear on the public character of the subject; the biographer had no
reason to acquaint the public "with a variety of matters which not
only are devoid of historical significance, but also are preemi-
nently none of the public's business."

But these were the voices of anachronisms, raised in behalf of
an already lost cause; and although they unquestionably represented the view of many families unreconciled to the modern demand to know all, their sentiments were implicitly repudiated by
the many other families who, sharing the general approbation of
candor, divulged information that had previously been kept from
public knowledge. At Wentworth House, London, and Crabbet
Park, Sussex, Byron's great-granddaughter, who like her forebears
had forbidden any but incidental examination of the largest and
most intimate existing hoard of the poet's private papers, finally
capitulated and threw it open to the fortunate Mrs. Doris Langley Moore. A just estimate of Thackeray's life, shadowed as it was
by the tragedy of his young wife's insanity and complicated by
his Platonic attachment to Mrs. Brookfield, became possible when
his grandchildren consented to the publication of his letters and
other personal papers. The descendants of Wordsworth, Coleridge, Scott, and De Quincey similarly opened their family archives to students. In America the rediscovery of Herman Melville was aided by his granddaughter, Mrs. Eleanor Metcalf, who
made available to a succession of biographical interpreters Melville's surviving papers and her personal memories. Some bastions
remained impregnable for many years, but even they eventually
fell: the Longfellow papers, withheld from most students and

opened to others only under galling restrictions (the footnotes in Lawrance Thompson's *Young Longfellow* record many instances in which he was allowed to see, but forbidden to quote, important material), found their way to Harvard; Mark Twain's manuscripts, over which Albert Bigelow Paine had long been a watchdog, became available after their transfer to the University of California; and Emily Dickinson's, the subject of protracted family feuding which had resulted in her poems and letters being printed only in part and in mangled form, were acquired by Harvard and Amherst College and adequately edited at last.

Meanwhile, the "great age of collecting"—the period, roughly from the later Victorian era to the First World War, during which millionaires such as J. P. Morgan and Henry E. Huntington competed for the possession of literary and artistic treasures—brought still more biographical documents to light. The combination of economic pressure and the prospect of imposing sums of American dollars induced owners to sell private papers that had descended to them. Occasionally even gentlemen's clubs and cathedral chapters succumbed to temptation or necessity. Some of these documents were purchased by university libraries and, in most cases, were soon made available to biographers. A larger portion, however, was snapped up by private collectors, some of whom, unsympathetic with the aims of scholarship or convinced that publication even of excerpts would reduce their resale value, barred access to their newly gained riches. But as the years passed, these great private collections were given to, or were themselves transformed into, research libraries, and the manuscripts became accessible for study. At Yale and Harvard, in New York, Washington, and San Marino; in the British Museum, the Bodleian, and dozens of other libraries in England—everywhere, year by year, still more boxes of private papers, untouched for decades or centuries, were opened and examined. The effect was circular: as scholarly libraries acquired manuscripts and the money with which to buy additional ones, still more families were persuaded to seek out and, if found, part with the papers of their eminent ancestors. The most famous coup of this kind was the discovery and subsequent acquisition by Yale of the incredible

caches of Boswell papers at Malahide Castle in Ireland and Fet-
tercairn House in Scotland.

An especially noteworthy illustration of the steady increase of
biographical source material could be found in the numerous new
collected editions of authors' letters. Comparison of the manuscripts of newly available private letters with the versions given
in older biographies or editions revealed how undependable were
the existing printed texts. This awareness of the faulty props on
which so much biographical information rested stimulated the
publishing of letters edited according to the standards of modern
scholarship. Texts were reproduced with a fidelity that reached
down to the most insignificant punctuation mark; dates and addresses were supplied where lacking; allusions were explained in
thick layers of footnotes. In these collections were gathered the
personal documents which constituted the basis of many an author's biography: in the English eighteenth century, Addison,
Steele, Defoe, Swift, Pope, Chesterfield, Goldsmith, Gray, Burke,
Gibbon, Walpole, Sterne, Johnson, Burns; in the nineteenth,
Wordsworth, Coleridge, Keats, Shelley, Scott, Thackeray,
Clough, Eliot, Trollope, Wilde; in America, Emerson, Cooper,
Poe, Melville, Whitman, Emily Dickinson, Dreiser.[5]

The net of research took in long-neglected files of newspapers
and magazines; public documents in places ranging from the
great English national depository in Chancery Lane, London, to
courthouses on the American prairies; the records of old business
concerns and land surveys. In lawyers' offices were discovered
new letters of Dickens (by the accident of a clerk's having been
sent for the "Forster deed-box" and returning with the wrong

[5] A few statistics will serve to suggest the quantity of personal documents with
which present-day biographers sometimes must cope. Over 11,000 letters of Dickens are to be in the new Pilgrim edition; over 8,000 of Jane and Thomas Carlyle,
more than half of which have not been published, have been located and tran-
scribed for a forthcoming edition; Leon Edel examined in excess of 12,000 letters
of Henry James; Joyce Hemlow had some 15,000 manuscript items to study for
her biography of Fanny Burney; Cardinal Newman left at least 20,000 letters.
The spirit falters as it considers that Lewis Carroll's "Register of Correspondence"
records his having written or received 98,721 letters between 1861 and 1898 and
that Bernard Shaw once estimated, perhaps with some exaggeration, that he had
sent out a million postcards and letters. Such figures are reason enough why some
biographers, echoing St. Francis and Edward Dowden, are inclined in spite of
themselves to praise God for fire.

one) and legal documents which proved that the persecutors from whom De Quincey fled were no figment of a paranoid imagination, as had been supposed, but all too substantial creditors. The variety of sources the modern biographer uses is illustrated in the reference notes to such books as Dixon Wecter's *Sam Clemens of Hannibal*, Stanley Williams' *Washington Irving*, Arthur Quinn's *Poe*, and Jay Leyda's exhaustive compilations of primary material, *A Melville Log* and *The Years and Hours of Emily Dickinson*. In his book on Robert Louis Stevenson, J. C. Furnas acknowledged the aid of the United States Department of State, Weather Bureau, Coast Guard, and Military Academy; the Cunard-White Star Line, the New Zealand *Herald*, the Office of H.M. High Commissioner for the Western Pacific, the Consulate-General of the Netherlands (New York), the National Tuberculosis Association, the American Telephone and Telegraph Company, the California State Department of Public Health, the Pennsylvania Railroad, and the Museum of Modern Art. Boswell, who ran over half of London in order to ascertain a single date, had worthy successors in the biographers who traversed two continents to consult old maps, steamboat timetables, family scrapbooks, army muster rolls, and records of colleges and jails.

As a result of all this activity, well-known passages in authors' lives could be studied in greater detail, and their implications perhaps reinterpreted; fresh light was thrown on obscure episodes; previously unknown episodes were finally made public. A Tennyson grandson, drawing upon oral tradition and many hundreds of family letters which had never before been examined, revealed that the poet's melancholy, shyness, and various neuroses stemmed from the wretched circumstances of his childhood and youth—circumstances not even dimly suggested in Hallam Tennyson's bland account. The atmosphere of the remote country rectory, dominated by a disinherited father who was subject to black moods and increasingly sought oblivion in drink, was that of a Wuthering Heights transplanted to the Lincolnshire wolds, and it explained, more satisfactorily than had been possible until that time (1949), the brooding, sometimes despairing, quality of some of Tennyson's best poetry. Leon Edel, enjoying full access to Henry James's papers, was able to show that the novelist's mysterious injury, popularly supposed to have been some kind of sexual disability, was in all likelihood a back injury sustained while helping fight a lumberyard fire at Newport, Rhode Island; and in a subsequent volume of his biography Edel revealed for the first time James's close but in some respects ambiguous friendship with the American writer Constance Fenimore Woolson. In 1949 the Marchesa Iris Origo told, from some 150 previously unpublished documents in private and public archives in Italy and elsewhere, the full story of Byron's final liaison, with Teresa Guiccioli, and his concurrent involvement in the Italian patriotic movement. In the course of an unedifying squabble between partisans of Ruskin and descendants of his wife, who, after their marriage was annulled, married the painter John Millais, intimate and confidential documents relating to the annulment were published for the first time: among them Ruskin's formal statement rationalizing his failure to consummate his marriage and his former wife's letter to the mother of Rose La Touche, object of Ruskin's presenile obsession, warning her against him. A series of controversy-stirring discoveries, beginning in 1934, gradually peeled away the seals that had kept his contemporaries' knowledge of Dickens' liaison with the actress Ellen Ternan from being shared by later generations. The curious story of Wilkie Collins' illicit domesticity—his possession of two mistresses, the first of whom, Caroline Graves, he temporarily married off to a distiller's son, and the second of whom bore him three children, one of them after Caroline's return to Collins's protection—came to light only in 1939.

This great accretion of new facts unincorporated in the existing "standard" biographies made imperative the writing of works that would absorb them into a single large-scale narrative. The necessity of Newman Ivey White's two-volume life of Shelley (1940) was pointed up by the fact that whereas Dowden, the first relatively thorough biographer, had had access to 150 Shelley letters, White had over 600. Mary Moorman's *Wordsworth* (1957) incorporated a mass of biographical details brought to light by researchers in the wake of Émile Legouis and George

((3 I 3

McLean Harper, most notably Ernest De Selincourt and Helen Darbishire, whose editions of the Wordsworth letters and journals typified the comprehensive, accurate, and heavily annotated source books which now formed the principal foundation of much literary biography.

The appearance of so much fresh material was not an unmixed blessing to biographers. On more than a few occasions it resulted in false emphasis and disturbance of artistic balance. In the early 1930's Herbert Read and Hugh I'Anson Fausset overstressed Wordsworth's affair with Annette Vallon, partly because it had been so long suppressed and partly because no story was better suited to exploitation in the era of Stracheyan idol-toppling and Freudian preoccupation with the bitter fruit of remorse. Derrick Leon and Peter Quennell, in their almost simultaneous lives of Ruskin, laid what future generations may possibly consider disproportionate emphasis on the Rose La Touche story, the full complexity and consequences of which were largely unrealized before the release of the many letters relating to it. In 1949 John Connell's life of William Ernest Henley was based almost wholly on the six bound volumes of Henley's letters and three chapters of an unfinished biography which Henley's close friend and journalistic colleague, Charles Whibley, left behind. Its failure to discriminate between the significant and the trivial in Whibley's collection was a typical consequence of the not infrequent tendency to equate importance with novelty.

· 2 ·

Fidelity to their vow to report nothing but the truth led biographers to reconsider the trustworthiness not only of the texts but of the substance of their documents. Those which presumably came closest to reporting truth, the avowedly autobiographical writings and oral statements of the authors themselves, were by no means always to be trusted as expressions of literal fact. Autobiographies, though more polished and continuous than such other forms of personal record as diaries and letters, are the products of sober second thought, hindsight, and filtered memory; they very often represent episodes as they should have been rather than as they happened, and present youthful character as the mature man chooses to regard it as having been. They are influenced, in addition, by the writer's conscious or unconscious desire to control the impression his own and later generations would have of him. Often they throw more dependable light on their authors as they were at the time of composition than as they were at the time written about.

More than celebrated figures in other professions, the writers of imaginative literature have proved almost incapable of separating autobiographical fancy from fact. Mark Twain, both in his printed recollections and in conversation—above all, in the sessions he spent reminiscing to Albert Bigelow Paine—had a genius for embroidering, to say nothing of inventing, the events of his life. So, as we have noticed, did Walt Whitman. Of the autobiographical writings of another American, Sherwood Anderson, Irving Howe declared that "it is possible to extract [from them] almost everything but reliable information. . . . He felt some deep need to construct an elaborate public legend about his family and his boyhood self." Barrie, in such reminiscent books as *Auld Licht Idylls* at the beginning of his career and *The Greenwood Hat* at the end, could never resist the temptation to imagine what had never happened: "Once he had given himself an inch," wrote Denis Mackail, "he would go on until he had taken several almost absolutely unfounded ells." So too with others of that generation who blandly called their books autobiographical, even so titling them. George Moore lavishly altered details, adjusted chronology, and performed other operations that becloud the biographical record. Yeats was much given to manufacturing myths about himself. Of Conrad's version of the obscure phase of his life which he spent in Marseilles, his biographer Jocelyn Baines remarks that "there are aspects . . . which are hard to reconcile with the known facts or are directly contradicted by them." And Bernard Shaw, whose life, once he achieved fame, was in a sense a running autobiography, found an impish delight in concocting stories about himself, some plausible, some unbelievable. Archibald Henderson took a humorless view of such antics: "His voluminous autobiographical outgivings are often unreliable and unconvincing, because of internal contradictions and irreconcilable antinomies. Such self-contradictions are to be expected, since it is impossible to play simultaneously and subjectively the role of psychiatrist and patient." But Hesketh Pearson, who as a former actor (he played Metellus in the first production of *Androcles and the Lion*) and as a biographer with an insatiable relish for such foibles was better equipped to appreciate them, found Shaw's inveterate humorous posing and yarn spinning a delight. "He believed in what, for want of a proper word, I shall call 'tries': that is, a combination of truth and lies. He declared that a literal account of anything is neither true nor false; and so, in order to achieve essential truth, he would embroider an episode and sometimes even invent one, as in his account of dancing round Fitzroy Square with a policeman in the early hours of the morning."

The recurrent demonstrations that contemporary authors' autobiographies contained a large element of fiction gave added point and necessity to a similar examination of earlier autobiographies, which had always figured prominently in the opening chapters of their respective authors' lives. Cowper, Burns, Scott, Southey, Carlyle, and Dickens, among others, had left such fragments, few of which, however, managed to progress beyond adolescence. In the absence of the various means by which more recent authors' accounts could be tested (including the living presence of the man himself, open to challenge by his Boswell), it was harder to separate fact from fancy; but the most scrupulous biographers did their best. If, sometimes, statements made by Scott and Dickens concerning their earliest years are still given more credence than may be warranted, it is only because there now is no way of proving their errors.[6]

[6] The precise motives and methods involved in writers' retrospective revision of their early lives would repay study. One rather unusual, but plausible, source of autobiographical misrepresentation was suggested by J. C. Reid: literary emulation. The well-known story of Francis Thompson's being given refuge by a faded flower of the street, although perhaps essentially true, may well have gained romantic coloring from his recollection of the more famous episode of De Quincey and his Ann. "The golden-hearted prostitute, from la Dame aux Camélias onwards, is a prettified stereotype much more frequently found in literature than in

The general reassessment of autobiographical materials extended, of course, to the substance of letters. In belated reaction against nineteenth-century biographers' assumption, implicit in their ordinary lack of discrimination, that all letters have equal usefulness and equal authority, modern biographers worked on the principle that letters as instruments of unwitting self-revelation have widely differing grades of value. Some men have the gift and will to smooth out their crumpled souls in correspondence, whereas others shrink from the very thought of such exposure. Keats, in letters to close friends and relatives, spread on paper in passionate urgency his latest discoveries about himself and his art; Samuel Richardson, on the other hand, wrote stolidly on for many pages and said nothing that any reader since his letters were first published in six volumes in 1804 has managed to find of much interest.

Nor is it a matter only of individual temperament: the age in which they were written has at least as much to do with the biographical significance of letters. Most surviving letters from before the eighteenth century have little value as clues to character; they are formal and studied rather than spontaneous. Of Pepys's capacity for ruthless self-examination, as reflected in his diary, his letters give no hint. In his and earlier ages, personal feelings might be revealed in poetry, but seldom in private correspondence. If a hundred of Shakespeare's letters were to be miraculously discovered today, they would in all likelihood tell us little about his essential personality. In the eighteenth century, with the strong flowing tide of sensibility and introspection, the personal content of letters deepened—a development which immediately inspired the epistolary device in popular fiction. But as Lord David Cecil has remarked, to the more elegant minds of the century

> objective topics—politics, books, works of art—seemed . . . far
> better worth talking about than the fluctuations of the individual

---

life." Reid wondered whether Thompson "may not have unconsciously heightened, on the deep-sunk model of De Quincey's experience, a chance association of less consequence than he made it appear." (*Francis Thompson: Man and Poet* [London, 1959], p. 44.)

mood, the condition of the individual soul. It was not that they were ashamed of expressing emotion, like a modern public-school boy. If they felt unhappy or affectionate or out of temper, they said so and as eloquently as they could. But they were not interested to analyse these feelings; and they expressed them with a formality of phrase that somehow makes them unintimate.

Only in the late eighteenth and early nineteenth centuries did all the bars fall, as romanticism, the most powerful stimulus to confession the modern world has known, encouraged the outpourings of the Cowpers, Keatses, Shelleys, Byrons, Lambs, and Carlyles. Even then by no means everyone, but only those who were innately most responsive to the romantic impulse, committed their souls to paper. Later in the century, the reaction against "Byronic" confessionalism ushered in a new reserve; most of Browning's letters after his marriage, in strong contrast to those addressed to Miss Barrett, are studies in nonrevelation. The letters of authors down to the present day have continued to range over the whole gamut, from the impassive countenance at one extreme to the bleeding heart at the other.

On other aspects of the evaluation of letters modern biographers inherited considerable practical wisdom from their forerunners. It had long been recognized, though not uniformly remembered, that immediacy of report is not necessarily a guarantee of accuracy. The "facts" set forth in a letter written soon after the event described may have been misstated because of the writer's excitement or the imperfection of his knowledge; or they may have been distorted to suit his purpose (self-justification, for example) or to accord with what his correspondent expected or wanted to hear. Accurate interpretation of tone, also—the private wave length upon which the writer communicated with each correspondent—was indispensable to the correct evaluation of a letter's contents; and this depended upon knowledge of the unwritten assumptions, the private jokes, the implicit intellectual and emotional sympathies that lay between the two, as well as the particular circumstances in which the letter was written.

Lockhart's remarks on the reporting of conversations were readily applicable to exchanges of letters:

To report conversations fairly, it is a necessary prerequisite that we should be completely familiar with all the interlocutors, and understand thoroughly all their minutest relations, and points of common knowledge, and common feeling, with each other. He who does not, must be perpetually in danger of misinterpreting sportive allusion into serious statement; and the man who was only recalling, by some jocular phrase or half-phrase, to an old companion, some trivial reminiscence of their boyhood or youth, may be represented as expressing, upon some person or incident casually tabled, an opinion which he had never framed, or if he had, would never have given words to in any mixed assemblage—not even among what the world calls *friends* at his own board. In proportion as a man is witty and humorous, there will always be about him and his a widening maze and wilderness of cues and catchwords, which the uninitiated will, if they are bold enough to try interpretation, construe, ever and anon, egregiously amiss—not seldom into arrant falsity.[7]

Elsewhere (in his life of Burns) Lockhart observed that "it is . . . very necessary, in judging of the letters, and drawing inferences from their language as to the real sentiments and opinions of the writer, to take into consideration the rank and character of the persons to whom they are severally addressed, and the measure of intimacy which really subsisted between them and the poet." He applied this principle when he attributed the "grossness of thought or rant, extravagance, and fustian in expression" in some of Burns's letters to the buckish character of his Edinburgh correspondents: Burns was not displaying his true nature, but merely adapting his language to that of the absent company. Lockhart's axiom is handy for special pleading, as in this instance, but it is nevertheless rooted in common sense.

Underlying these various portions of advice is the truth that a letter or a report of talk represents an occasion which cannot be

---

[7] The special difficulty of preserving humor beyond the occasion is underscored by a protest Mark Twain once wrote to the editor Edward Bok: "Now, in your interview, you have certainly . . . set down the sentences I uttered as I said them. But . . . what my manner was at certain points is not indicated. Therefore, no reader can possibly know where I was in earnest and where I was joking; or whether I was joking altogether or was in earnest altogether. Such a report . . . can convey many meanings to the reader, but never the right one." (Quoted by Gladys C. Bellamy, *Mark Twain as a Literary Artist* [Norman, Okla., 1950], p. 37.)

reproduced in all of its details and nuances. The most the biographer can hope to do is to come as close as he is able to the meaning the document was intended to convey at the moment of its origin, and to use his knowledge of the two or more persons involved, and of the attendant circumstances, to avert misreading. Such awareness can, for example, lead to the discounting of exaggerations which earlier biographers accepted at their face value. One reason for the long-held belief that Hawthorne was a brooding recluse was a letter he wrote to his fiancée in 1840 stressing his solitariness. As Randall Stewart put it:

> The phrases "lonely youth" and "lonely chamber" recur with affecting iteration; his life was one of "solitude" and "seclusion"; he was "chilled and benumbed." It is not necessary to question the writer's sincerity or the core of truth in the description. For a young man of Hawthorne's sensibilities and literary aspirations, the Muse was an exacting mistress. . . . But the pathos which pervades the letter . . . must be discounted somewhat in the light of the circumstances of composition. When writing a love letter, a man may be tempted to darken his former years so as to brighten by contrast his present felicity. In a more sober and responsible mood, Hawthorne later described these same years as "tranquil and not unhappy."

In the Carlyles' letters too, pitched as they customarily were on a shrill note of complaint and sheer anguish, it had to be recognized that gross overstatement was an ingrained habit on the part of both husband and wife. If either Thomas or Jane had suffered a mere tithe of the physical and mental trials they described in graphic superlatives, they would, one feels, have thrown themselves into the nearby Thames soon after they arrived in Chelsea.

With letters the question of authenticity is simple: either a letter is genuine (or a faithful copy of a genuine one), or it is not. With conversations, however, the question is more difficult. Seldom, if ever, are the oral statements or colloquies reproduced within quotation marks in biographies derived from stenographic notes made on the spot. Hence it must be assumed that the extended printed versions of the discourses in which Coleridge and Byron indulged are at best only approximations of what they said and the way they said it. Even so, there remains the high probability that the auditors who first wrote down and published these reports were less concerned with literal accuracy than with fidelity to the *spirit* of the man and the occasion. They had no qualms about rewriting conversations as freely as nineteenth-century biographers improved the "tonal consistency" of letters, and for precisely the same reasons.

Often as abundant as direct evidence, but even more treacherous when analyzed for its possible content of fact, was the veiled autobiography presumed to be present in a writer's poems, novels, or essays. To the old practice of searching works of imaginative literature for the "soul" of their author—as well as for modified accounts of events in his life—modern psychology gave a fresh sanction: the premise that most if not all art is a projection of the artist, and therefore a kind of involuntary, however fragmentary, self-portrait and autobiography. A writer's works, it was believed, could make possible any or all of three principal kinds of biographical inferences, which might substantiate or amplify existing information, or else disclose information not contained in the historical documents. By describing analogous events under the guise of fiction, they might throw light on the external experiences of his life; they might reflect facets of his character and personality, his moods and attitudes; and, with the assistance of depth psychology, they might reveal whole tracts of his subliminal life. A writer's formal literary output could therefore be as valuable to the biographer in search of the complete man as any private material; in the case of some authors, far more so.

The extent to which biographers felt justified in extracting supposedly factual evidence from art varied as widely as it had since the search began early in the nineteenth century, and so did the plausibility of their conclusions.[8] The poetry of the great romantics was scrutinized as a set of shorthand spiritual autobi-

[8] In the post-Stracheyan era, however, no writer of serious repute—the eccentrics are always with us—carried the custom of interpreting works of art as extensive cryptobiography to the lengths displayed in Frank Harris' *The Man Shakespeare and His Tragic Life-Story* (1909). This incredible performance brought the subgenre of impressionistic biography to its peak (or nadir, depending on one's viewpoint). Shakespeare, of course, had been the sentimental biographers' initial victim, and he remained their favorite subject for well over a century. The most influential such treatment, affecting the way a whole generation and more conceived of Shakespeare the man and his "spiritual travail," was Edward Dowden's *Shakspere: A Critical Study of His Mind and Art* (1875). Compared with Harris' fantasy, Dowden's was the essence of sweet reasonableness.

ographies—a particularly suitable exercise, since not only had they and their generation been responsible in the first place for this approach to other men's poetry but in addition their own poetry was avowedly autobiographical. The survival of many concurrent personal documents, moreover, made it possible to fit the testimony of the poetry more precisely into the whole biographical narrative. In tracing the development of his sensibility and intellect, every biographer of Wordsworth relied as heavily upon his earlier poems and the autobiographical *Prelude* as upon the more direct records embodied in his and Dorothy's letters and journals. Shelley's biographers turned, with equal assurance, to "Julian and Maddalo" and "Epipsychidion," which had long been assumed to be fraught with autobiographical significance; but they managed to prove only that the same poems could be made to yield several quite different accounts of events.

Now that the novel as an art form was looked upon with the seriousness once reserved for poetry, it too was valued as a repository of biographical clues. One could discern in Thackeray's novels many reflections of his experiences—his love affair with Mrs. Brookfield, for instance, and his detestation of his mother-in-law, Mrs. Shawe—as well as ruefully ironic self-portraits (as in the character of Pendennis). Jocelyn Baines pointed out that the "revelatory value" of Conrad's *A Personal Record,* which was written as autobiography, and *The Arrow of Gold,* which was written as fiction, "varies in inverse proportion to their proclaimed autobiographical content; *A Personal Record* tells scarcely anything of interest [specifically in regard to the Marseilles period], whereas *The Arrow of Gold* tells a lot." From the refracted evidence in Melville's novels, Lewis Mumford, Newton Arvin, and others constructed elaborate narratives of their author's odyssey in the strange seas of Polynesia and metaphysics; his friend Hawthorne also had his biography rewritten time after time along the lines suggested by new interpretations of supposedly personal evidence discovered in his fiction.

Among the great novelists, Dickens probably was the most hapless victim of biographers seeking to find the creator written large in his creation. He had himself, all unwittingly, licensed the hunt when he admitted that *David Copperfield* was to some extent autobiographical and that he occasionally had drawn figures from life, Mrs. Nickleby, for example, deriving from his own mother. Dickens, however, could not have foreseen the sometimes frantic enthusiasm with which some of his biographers, from the 1930's onward, ransacked his works for clues to his tortured psyche. Some saw in the names he gave to his later heroines anagrams of "Ellen Ternan"; others found themselves able to trace, in his treatment of frustrated love and the early death of maidens, the reverberations of the sudden death of Mary Hogarth, with whom he was in love even as he was married to her sister Kate. But the most uninhibited search for hidden Dickensian autobiography was that conducted by Jack Lindsay, some of whose hypotheses concerning Dickens' personal conflicts were in fact quite sensible but who did not know when to stop. In a protracted analysis of the minor story "The Haunted Man" Lindsay not only took the opportunity to observe that Dickens himself was the *psychically* haunted man but found in the fact that the central figure's grizzled hair hung about his face "like tangled seaweed" an evidence of "Dickens's regret for his youthful good looks." The emphasis on the word "respectable" in connection with Mr. Vholes, in *Bleak House,* was proof of "Dickens's discomfort about his own respectability," and the choice of scene for the opening of *Edwin Drood,* an opium den, might be traced to Dickens' having taken laudanum during his American tour.

It is true that evidence found in a writer's work can often be used, legitimately and effectively, to supplement and clarify knowledge gained elsewhere, as well as to supply tentative answers to otherwise unsolvable problems. But it is also true that every attempt to infer biographical fact from an imaginative composition carries its inherent hazards. The element of sheer invention or literary borrowing can easily be underestimated, an error against which contemporary writers themselves protested. Thomas Wolfe "told how some residents of Asheville not only swear that certain occurrences [in his novels] are true but that they witnessed them themselves—when the incidents were really invented out of whole cloth." And T. S. Eliot remarked: "I am used . . . to having my personal biography reconstructed from passages which I got out of books, or which I invented out of nothing because they sounded well; and to having my biography invariably ignored in what I *did* write from personal experience."

Furthermore, in many literary works in which the writer's personal experience, as well as his personality, is indisputably present, there is the difficulty of disengaging the true person from the mask he has adopted. A classic case is that of Sterne: how much of *Tristram Shandy* and *A Sentimental Journey* can the biographer assume to be literal truth? Percy Fitzgerald, writing the first full-length biography of Sterne a hundred years ago, assumed that most of the incidents, whether comic or pathetic, were taken from Sterne's own experience, but his successors were not so sure. Wilbur Cross's comment was the most sensible. "This question," he wrote, "can never be quite answered; for all that a biographer can expect is corroborative evidence here and there from external sources. . . . He knows that incidents in Sterne's life, all the way from boyhood down to near death, are in Sterne's books; but he knows also that they are entangled with much that belongs only to the realm of his art."

Nor did biographers always allow for the fact (long ago embodied, as we saw, in Browning's distinction between the "subjective" and the "objective" poet) that some writers are temperamentally inclined to infuse a great deal of themselves into their work, whereas others create, as it were, from a distance. Biographers dealing with the former kind are, generally speaking, on more solid ground when they repair to literary works for evidence than are those who deal with the latter. But even the most introspective and self-revealing of artists are not strict autobiographers; the lyric "I" is not necessarily the "I" of a private journal. Seldom does a poem or a work of fiction contain a transcript of experience so literal, or a reflection of the writer's character so faithful, that it can be laid into the smooth surface of a biographical narrative with merely the substitution of a real name for a fictitious one or the elimination of some patently invented details. Refraction and distortion are always present, even where the substance is clearly drawn from life. The very essence of the imaginative process is change, and to use supposedly autobiographical material with accurate effect, whether or not the writer labeled it autobiographical, the prudent biographer has to take into account the idiosyncrasies of his subject's personal vision—the special manner in which it exaggerated, selected, modified, enriched, and idealized the raw data of fact. By such means he can provide himself with a corrective touchstone with which to separate biographical fact from its accretions of imaginative fancy.

The *caveats* which the spirit of careful scholarship enforced upon biographers when interpreting evidence deriving from their subject himself were equally applicable when the data came from sources outside the author. Prominent among the various kinds of information inherited from earlier biographers were anecdotes, often valuable for their capsule revelations of a trait of character and indispensable where a touch of personal color or of humor was desired.[9] Once embedded in a biographical tradition, these stories, whether calumnious, flattering, or merely picturesque, and irrespective of their origin, had proved to possess a staying power that increased rather than weakened from generation to generation. To discredit—hopefully, for good—the demonstrably false ones and to revise others in the light of the ascertainable facts required some of the strongest efforts on the part of scholarly biographers. Dryden's bleak prophecy "Cousin Swift, you will never be a poet" had been found in virtually every life of Dryden and Swift, and many other places, for over two centuries; but the odds are that Dryden never said it. R. W. Ketton-Cremer, Gray's best modern biographer, found no substantiation for the old story that the reason for Gray's transfer of residence from Peterhouse to Pembroke Hall, Cambridge, was that a false alarm of fire, raised by prankish undergraduates, had forced him to use the rope ladder he kept in his room. This was one of the innumerable stories which Edmund Gosse, in his love for anecdotal

---

[9] "To this intent I have purposely interlaced (not as meat, but as condiment) many delightful stories, that so the reader, if he do not arise, which I hope and desire, *religiosior* or *doctior*, with more piety or learning, at least he may depart *jocundior*, with more pleasure and lawful delight." (Thomas Fuller, "The Design of the Ensuing Work," *The Worthies of England.*)

literary chitchat, either embellished or invented outright. (Leonard Whibley's copy of Gosse's *Gray*, which Ketton-Cremer used, is "black with his [Whibley's] remorseless corrections.") It was Gosse also who told the pleasant story that the aged Wordsworth, symbolic spokesman for a passing age of poetry, once drank a gracious health to Browning, representative of the coming age: according to the diarist Crabb Robinson, Wordsworth had left the dinner when the toasts began, and long before Browning's name was reached. And it was Gosse who reported that Landor, his face purple with rage, forced a diffident Swinburne to accept the gift of a dubious Correggio from his wall in Florence ("By God, sir, you shall!"); but Swinburne never mentioned the episode, there is no other evidence linking the picture with him, and Landor, eighty-nine years old at the time, was unable to speak above a whisper. Sometimes the expunging of an anecdote from the record was accompanied by a certain regret, for to many biographers, as to many readers, fiction often is more attractive than fact; but other biographers accomplished the operation with a severity typified by Bernard De Voto's curt remark in the introduction to his *Mark Twain's America:* "Many people have told me anecdotes about Mark Twain. I have used none of them."

As with anecdotes, so with all other circumstantial accounts received from the past. Two stories associated with Laurence Sterne's demise survived unchallenged until Wilbur Cross, less credulous than his predecessor, Percy Fitzgerald, examined them. According to the transmitted narrative, Sterne, his fame largely vanished, died in mean lodgings, attended only by a servant or two who robbed him of his remaining trinkets, while a group of his friends were having a convivial dinner around the corner. The truth is that Sterne's fame was still high at his death; his lodgings, far from wretched, were in a fashionable street; and although none of his friends happened to be present at the moment of death, he was by no means neglected or forgotten, as the story implies. In the shape the story assumed when first told may be discerned elements of Aristotle (the tragic fall from high estate), Hogarth (the final scene in *The Rake's Progress*), and the standard legend of the great writer dying neglected in a garret. It is probable that the other unsupportable legend about Sterne's end had a similar literary inspiration. Although there is no credible evidence that his body was in fact stolen from its London grave and carried to a Cambridge dissecting table, or that his skull was subsequently preserved in the university's anatomical museum, who could resist the temptation to devise such a story about a writer whose transparent persona, in his most famous book, was named Yorick?

In the history of many literary lives persist tantalizing gaps which all but the most self-denying biographers feel a powerful urge to paper over with the tissue of reasonable speculation. Whether discouraged by caution or by mere intellectual lethargy, most nineteenth-century biographers had hesitated to suggest any but the most casually contrived solutions to mysteries. William Godwin's example, and that of the rough reception his *Chaucer* had received, doubtless had been sufficient warning. But a further sign of the intellectual liveliness that marked the revival of biography in the modern era was growing confidence in the ability of shrewd reasoning to repair tears in the narrative fabric. Beginning with the known facts on either side of the gap, the most responsible biographers sought to connect them with the strongest available probabilities.

Inevitably, many attempts to fill in the blank space went far beyond the evidence and the limits of sober conjecture. In the 1930's and '40's, for instance, biographers competed with one another to fix the identity of the person or persons with whom they were convinced Emily Dickinson must, on the evidence of her poems, have been in love at one time or another. The list eventually included a naval officer (Helen Hunt Jackson's first husband), who blew himself up while testing a submarine rocket at the Brooklyn Navy Yard; two clergymen, George Gould and Charles Wadsworth; the young principal of the Amherst Academy, Leonard Humphrey; her father's law student, Benjamin F. Newton; a Salem lawyer and judge, Otis Lord; and, on the lesbian side, Kate Scott (Anthon), a former schoolmate of her sister-in-law. The evidence put forth for some of these identifications was not always impressive; it included such dubiously useful items as

((327

the sworn statements of a certain "X," "Y," and "Z," otherwise unidentified, that they had had information on a given love affair from surviving members of the Dickinson family and household help; a valentine printed in Amherst's little magazine in 1850; and, in the case of the harbor-and-lighthouses man, the fact that Emily's poetic images often dwelt on the sea, the harbor, mathematics, military affairs, and science. The argument for her homosexual attachment rested principally on a wholesale reinterpretation of her love poems: wherever the manuscript read "he," one had to assume she really meant "she," for, wrote the discoverer of this "secret," "there is no man—no real man—anywhere in the poems . . . pronouns do not make a man in the poetry of any woman."

It was no doubt inevitable, given the public's perennial interest in the topic, that so much attention was lavished on the mysteries, actual or fancied, of writers' loves. Encouraged by the sensational publication in 1913 of Charlotte's letters to the Brussels schoolmaster Constantine Heger, which documented a feverish episode of which there had earlier been only faint indications, a long procession of Brontë biographers toiled, usually with more ingenuity than cogency, to attribute further romantic attachments to the sisters. Some biographers, less committed to proving an *amour*, canvassed the clues only to admit defeat. Because the sentimental hypothesis of Washington Irving's alleged proposal to, and rejection by, Emily Foster was so deeply embedded in the received story of his life that it could not be ignored, the meticulous scholar Stanley T. Williams felt obliged to devote sixteen closely printed pages to the subject. He could reach no verdict, but nonetheless, admitting that "It is dangerous, perhaps, to hazard a word on her reasons for a rejection which may never have occurred," went on to a disquisition on the presumable emotional significance to Irving of the unproved event. Often, however, there was even less factual basis for such conjecture: the biographer's assumption seemed to be either that the character of his subject clearly required a romance, or that no biography was complete without one. L. A. G. Strong, for example, spent considerable wordage wondering whether there was a premarital "episode" in Thomas Moore's life; since no evidence whatsoever pointed to any, apart from vague and wholly conventional references in his songs, the speculation was bound to end nowhere.

· 3 ·

In the summer of 1909, Henry James and John Buchan spent a weekend going through transcripts of Byron's letters to Caroline Lamb (Lady Melbourne) written during the years before his marriage. They were owned by Buchan's wife's aunt, the widow of the poet's grandson, Lord Lovelace, who wanted a summary of their contents deposited in the British Museum in case someone later destroyed the papers themselves. "So," wrote Buchan long afterward, "Henry James and I waded through masses of ancient indecency, and duly wrote an opinion. The thing nearly made me sick, but my colleague never turned a hair. His only words for some special vileness were 'singular'—'most curious'—'nauseating, perhaps, but how quite inexpressibly significant.'"

James's unabashed absorption in the "quite inexpressibly significant" psychological implications of the papers accurately foreshadowed the modern—post-Jamesian—biographer's concern to discover the truth about his subject's inner life; and the very fact that James examined the documents without turning a hair pointed forward to the virtual disappearance of the old restraints upon the biographer's interest.[1] As he gathered the materials which, in many ways hitherto undreamed of, cast light into the farther reaches of personality, nothing was to be beyond his purview. As research revealed previously unmentioned and sometimes disturbing aspects of a writer's character and deeds, the use biographers made of them might be condemned as mere scandalmongering (which, in the first years of emancipation, it often

---

[1] Published in 1922, the papers contain an important body of evidence tending to prove Byron's incest with his half-sister. Controversy on the subject, ignited by Harriet Beecher Stowe's disclosures in 1869–70 of Lady Byron's allegations, had flamed again in 1905, when Lord Lovelace issued his *Astarte.*

was); but under more responsible auspices it also represented a search for psychological truth far more penetrating than that in which any previous biographers had engaged.

Biographers began, naturally, with the outside, striving to portray with fidelity and minuteness the externalities which had been the sign of the man within. Their goal was Boswell's: to make the man come alive, so that the reader could not only see and hear him, but feel as well the whole effect, by whatever mixed and subtle means it was communicated, of the man's personality. Although only occasionally was there acute disagreement among the witnesses on details of physical fact (which of Byron's feet was the lame one?), on the wider questions of temperament there was bound to be discrepancy—a great deal of it in the case of figures whose positive, manysided, and mercurial personalities struck their contemporaries in sharply conflicting ways. Attempts had to be made to adjudicate among these different viewpoints; which, for example, was the "truer" Wordsworth, the benign poet-philosopher of Rydal Mount or the complacent fuddy-duddy whom a younger generation of poets and critics viewed with a mixture of detestation and ridicule? Whether a biographer reached a decision or frankly confessed his bafflement, his weighing of divergent accounts helped assure his readers that they were beholding not a bloodless statue, whose qualities were simple, harmonious, and self-evident, but a member of the human race who, like all his less distinguished fellows, aroused quite different feelings in different people.

Deserting the photographic studio with its careful arrangement of furniture and lights, the modern biographer trailed his subject through the records, his candid camera and hidden microphone ever alert for the incidental detail that was worth a thousand words of description. The odd turn of phrase in a quoted letter; a friend's report of his burly laugh, or of the sudden sadness that clouded his face when he thought he was off display; a glimpse of his frayed shirt cuffs or a meticulously ordered writing desk or a dog-eared book whose underscorings recalled the emotional gropings of a troubled adolescent; a vivid scar on the cheek that flushed in anger, a passion for prawns, a habit of forgetting to cash checks—these were treasured by biographers bent upon producing an effect of lifelikeness as persuasive as any illusion the novelist could create.

Whatever their eventual place in the biographer's design, external facts, including all that served as indexes to his personality, could be established with reasonable confidence, if the pertinent documents survived; the biographer's task was largely one of reconstructing the whole portrait from the tiny pieces into which the accidents of time and memory had shattered it. But when he sought to represent the inner life, of which the physical portrait was at best an incomplete and approximate indication, the insistent curiosity of a new age pressed him further. Like most preceding biographers, he had available the psychological image presented by the man himself through his letters, conversation, and conduct, as well as the admittedly or inferentially "autobiographical" passages of his formal works. But did this image represent the man as he really was—or was it another work of his art?

The problem was especially pertinent in literary biography, for in most artist-natures there is a certain amount of *poseurisme*. In some it finds its expression in the dramatic projection of art, thus affording the biographer an indeterminate amount of quasi-autobiographical material. But in others the urge to lay a disguise over one's genuine character takes the form of role playing in actual life. This fact, of course, was no discovery of the twentieth century. Probably the most famous example in English literary history, Byron's dedication of his later life to the creation of a personal legend, had been recognized for what it was in his own time, though it remained for biographers in the last few decades to probe the psychological implications of the phenomenon. The Victorians, who prized "frankness," lack of pretense, as a high ethical virtue, had been quick to detect and deplore the affectations of some writers. "Pope," complained *Fraser's Magazine* in 1850, "wrote for effect. So did Cowper sometimes: compare his correspondence with Newton and Hill. The writer can scarcely be identified. Horace Walpole made himself up for the Post, as for a theatre. You see at once that he is padded. The shape of his thoughts is always artificial. Gray's crow-quill was an emblem of his manner. Byron imitated the worst style of Walpole and Gray. He is not himself for a hundred pages together."

With the sharpened modern awareness that in human psychology appearances are both deceptive and (when the deception is recognized and explained) revelatory, the element of pose found in the letters, conversation, and conduct of men of letters gained greater importance. Numerous famous writers seemed to have been acting, intermittently or consistently, either before an audience of their contemporaries or before posterity; or before both. Poe's life, as an enthusiastic student devoted a whole volume to explaining, could be interpreted as that of an actor *manqué*, his histrionic instincts having been acquired from the genes of his player-parents. Walt Whitman, as Henry Seidel Canby and others saw him, adopted a whole series of roles, some of which were captured in posed photographs: a carpenter-poet, a male Florence Nightingale, a Broadway Bohemian, a crippled old man in Camden. Bernard Shaw, whose finest comic creation was his public self, acted so indefatigably before the world that it forgot the possibility that there was another G.B.S. who lived in solitude, with thoughts and feelings he never communicated.

Authors who had dual, or even multiple, personalities therefore offered special problems to biographers. One was that of discerning, isolating, and then piercing beneath the pose—removing the mask, whether assumed for an occasion or a permanent disguise cultivated over many years—in order to discover the "real," or irreducible, personality. Another, even more difficult, was to discover the reasons for the assumption of, so to speak, a working persona: a sense of inferiority? a desire to escape from an uncomfortable psyche into a more satisfying, though fictitious, one? a penchant for arousing admiration or even—masochistically—dislike on the part of others? or the more prosaic ambition to sell more books through exploitation of their writer's personality?

Such questions were typical of the new climate in which biographers worked to find the truth of a man's self. The goal of thoughtful biographers in the nineteenth century had been to discover, in the midst of apparent contradictions, an internally consistent cluster of traits which formed the key to character. In striving to bring out their subjects' "moral harmony," biographers like Lockhart had chosen, arranged, and emphasized their data, the result being an idealized conception—a partial portrait—which, although not necessarily false to nature, was more consistent than nature usually allowed. In fashioning their smooth figures, they had largely ignored the anomalies, the obscurities, the loose ends which interspersed their data. Instead of expanding the reader's field of vision, they had contracted it by blacking out those portions of the available knowledge that failed to suit their intention. If the word "dishonest" is too severe to apply to this procedure, "unrealistic" is accurate enough. The whole truth was sacrificed in the interests of what the biographer conceived to be the main body of truth, or a "higher" truth.

This loftily motivated method, however, no longer recommended itself. The secularization that marked every phase of intellectual life as the nineteenth century gave way to the twentieth resulted, for one thing, in the drastic devaluing of the "moral image": whatever its other uses, biography was not the didactic art it had once been conceived to be. And inseparable from the secular impulse was the awareness, fed from many sources both scientific and literary, of the complexity of the human personality, which biography, in its zeal for harmonious portraiture, had tended not to recognize.

Mere description of surface phenomena no longer sufficed. The interest of twentieth-century readers lay less in what a man's own writings recorded having occurred in his conscious inner self than in the more complicated and intriguing mystery of what happened in the realm beyond awareness and articulation, and above all, why. For it was becoming axiomatic—with much assistance from novelists, who, Freud said in his seventieth birthday address, had made the discovery before he did—that in human behavior, the overt thought or act is less significant than the subconscious, unacknowledged motive. The hidden springs of action, the silent dialogue of the mind with itself, the unacknowledged emotional climate behind events, were becoming the prime subject of psychological conjecture.

((333

Analysis and explanation, therefore, not description alone, were the biographer's task. Realizing that in every soul are dim recesses, in every life aberrant actions, which no formula yet devised could explain, he nevertheless had to find a touchstone that could somehow bring the discrete forces and phenomena of its subject's psyche into a comprehensible relationship. To be a realistic portrait, in other words, biography had to make allowance for the chaos within a man, yet to be esthetically and intellectually satisfying, it had to be organized around a single conception or closely knit set of conceptions.

By a stroke of fortune at least equal in its impact to the advent of Lytton Strachey, Freudian psychology appeared at the very moment that biography was most in need of what it had to give.[2] In it seemed to lie the means of reconciling the seeming contradictions and anomalies of personality and of rationally accounting for "irrational" conduct; it gave the biographer a torch by which to move from the comparatively well-lighted territory of the manifest into the shadowy one of subliminal drama. The hitherto inexplicable was capable, after all, of systematic explanation, and for the now useless "moral image" could be substituted a diagnosis. The spirit of the shrine gave way to that of the clinic.

The promise that psychoanalytic concepts held for biography had already been suggested by Freud himself, in his study of Leonardo da Vinci (1910). In his journal *Imago*, founded in 1912, there appeared from time to time psychoanalytic interpretations of works of literary and graphic art and, less frequently, of the artists' own characters. By the 1920's it was evident that the mutually contributory bond between psychoanalysis and the biography of artists, in particular, was extraordinarily strong. In common with the other arts, and in contrast, most of the time, to

[2] Though their coincidence has led some to believe otherwise, as influences on biography Strachey and Freud were wholly independent. Strachey's brother James, a well-known psychoanalyst and translator of Freud's works, wrote in 1956 that "none of the E[minent] V[ictorians] character sketches were influenced in the slightest by Freud; and the same may also be assumed of Q[ueen] V[ictoria]. ... The great psychological influence on him at the E.V. & Q.V. period was undoubtedly Dostoevsky—who, after all, reveals a lot of the same material as Freud, and whom Freud himself regarded as the greatest of novelists." (Quoted by Martin Kallich, "Psychoanalysis, Sexuality, and Lytton Strachey's Theory of Biography," *American Imago*, XV [1958], 359.)

such occupations for the "normal" as soldiering and statecraft, literature seemed to have attacted the psychologically ill-balanced; some argued, indeed, that such imbalance was a prerequisite for artistic creation. Literary annals contained a long list of men and women whose neurotic or downright psychotic nature was obvious: Cowper, Dr. Johnson, Poe, Ruskin, Swinburne, Coleridge, Blake, Swift, Chatterton, De Quincey, Mary Lamb, Lewis Carroll, Emily Dickinson, Shelley, Wilde, and so on and on. Richard Aldington's later observation, apropos of D. H. Lawrence, was applicable to any number of men and women who were the subjects of literary biography: "If he had not been a great writer, these strange and painful traits of character, his sufferings and misunderstandings and adventures, his instabilities and tantrums, would be a theme for the psychologist, not for the biographer. If he had not written a word he would still have been an interesting personality, and, if known, an almost classic case for the psychoanalyst."

Furthermore, the casebook potentialities of literary biography were enhanced by the very nature and abundance of the material provided by the subjects themselves. A widespread assumption among professional psychoanalysts, who had no difficulty convincing some biographers and critics, was that art was but a great mass of clinical data:

> Psychoanalysis has made it increasingly apparent . . . that the production of an artist is almost entirely subjective. The painter's canvas is no more than that large area upon which he sets out his own inner problems. The poet's lyrical woe is but an echo of his own personal woe. The average novel is but a vast autobiography. . . . An artistic creation may be analyzed entirely in the manner of a neurosis, its various elements being viewed as symbolic expressions of certain emotional constellations, just as neurotic symptoms are. . . . The characters in a work of fiction are but disguised representations of the novelist's own personality.

Members of no other class, except possibly graphic artists, left behind as rich and revealing records of their psychic histories as did men of letters. It was inevitable, then, that the materials of literary biography, including works of literature itself, should be prized as contributions to the knowledge of psychodynamics. Especially in the earlier years, when living patients were scarce, these biographical and artistic records served as clinical data, with famous names and personalities replacing the faceless Fräulein X's, and were duly analyzed in the professional journals under such titles as "Psychological Symbolism of Guilt and Isolation in Hawthorne," "The Confessions of William Shakespeare," "The Defenses against Creative Anxiety in the Life and Work of James Barrie," "Samuel Johnson's Character, a Psychoanalytical Interpretation," "The Case of John Ruskin: A Study in Cyclothymia," "The Respiratory Neurosis of Charles Kingsley," "Flight from Home: Some Episodes in the Life of Herman Melville," and "Psychopathological Glimpses of Lord Byron."

The scientific use which psychoanalysts made of data from the lives and works of authors had its counterpart in the literary use which biographers made of psychoanalytic techniques. So far as the lives of English-language authors were concerned, the exchange of information began in 1920. In that year the *American Journal of Psychology* printed Lucile Dooley's "Psychoanalysis of Charlotte Brontë, as a Type of the Woman of Genius" and Lorine Pruette's "Psycho-Analytical Study of Edgar Allan Poe." In the same year came also the first of the psychoanalytical literary biographies, called "Freudian" for convenience but oriented for the most part toward Adler, with their emphasis upon inferiority complexes, compensations, sublimations, defense mechanisms, and the like. One such book was Katharine Anthony's sketch of Margaret Fuller, the New England bluestocking, who suffered, it appeared, from a father fixation, adolescent dreams with erotic content, hysteria, and latent lesbianism. Another was Van Wyck Brooks's *The Ordeal of Mark Twain*, a biography only to the extent that it had a generally chronological movement, in which Twain was portrayed as a desperately unhappy man, whether he knew it or not. He was haunted by the memory of his mother's forcing him to promise, over his dead father's body, to turn respectable, and by his guilt over having sold out to the Gilded Age, to a materialistic culture that was willing to pay well for a good belly laugh, but nothing at all for Shelleyan poetry or Swiftian satire—either of which, Brooks asserted, was easily within Twain's powers.

For the next thirty years, the great creators of English and American literature, one by one, were beckoned to the couch. Suddenly gifted with "the God's-eye view," biographers ransacked their subjects' private documents and literary works, the testimony of witnesses, and evidence of family conditions and social environment for the kind of telltale data that could be worked up into a case history with a literary aura. The result was a biographical literature which today is of interest only as a bizarre memorial to the spell psychoanalysis in its infant years cast over a whole generation.

Poe's psychotic personality was explored in half a dozen books, no two of which agreed on what was the matter with him except that the disease was deep-seated and complex. (Was it, as Joseph Wood Krutch maintained in 1926, a case of traumatic childhood humiliations aggravated by psychic impotence or, as N. Bryllion Fagin asserted in 1949, one of frustrated histrionicism? If neither of these hypotheses seemed adequate, several others, exhaustively argued, were available.) Swift, whose numerous, well-documented psychopathological symptoms made him an exceptionally tempting subject, was "explained" time after time. A study of *Gulliver's Travels* revealed in 1942 to a member of the staff of St. Elizabeth's mental hospital, Washington, that "Swift was a neurotic who exhibited psychosexual infantilism, with a particular showing of coprophilia, associated with misogyny, misanthropy, mysophilia, and mysophobia." Seventeen years later another professional analyst, in a volume comparing Swift with Lewis Carroll somewhat in the manner of a psychiatric Plutarch, diagnosed Swift as being the victim of (among many other ailments) "severe anxiety and diffuse hypochondriasis of the type which so often accompanies an unusually severe castration complex, in which pregenital determinants are strong." Carlyle with his digestive troubles and (putative) impotence (a classic case, said one writer, of anal sadism); the alleged recluse Nathaniel Hawthorne; the brooding Melville; Dr. Johnson, with his manifold anxieties and compulsions; Charles and Mary Lamb,

((337

bound together for life by memory of the matricide that they had both subconsciously willed and Mary had, in fact, accomplished; Stephen Crane, burdened with an Oedipus complex—the list of the patients attended by Freudian literary biographers could be indefinitely extended. Even writers who were conspicuously normal and well-adjusted came under scrutiny; for was not the very appearance of normality an ominous sign? Thus, for instance, Betty Miller discovered the hearty Browning to be a bundle of neuroses centering in his lifelong desire for dependence upon women older than himself, beginning, obviously, with his mother.

The heyday of the blatantly "Freudian" biography, replete with a terminology as alarming as the malaises it attributed to figures of history, was the period 1920–35. The popularity of the biographies written in the first flush of discovery reflected the exhilarating impact of the new science: its bold novelty, its naughtiness (as it was happily interpreted by a public seeking titillation through means short of pornography), and its seemingly boundless power to explain human behavior. In the late 1930's the fever subsided. No longer—perhaps because Marx had become more modish?—was psychoanalysis, especially if it had a dash of sex, a sure-fire fuel over which to boil a literary pot. Furthermore, the early crudities of the science were giving way to a more refined method, and its enthusiasts' overconfidence was declining in response to a candid recognition of its limitations and pitfalls. Psychoanalysis was, after all, neither the final word nor an infallible guide; there were more things in heaven and earth than were dreamed of in the Viennese philosophy.

Although Freudianism was unquestionably one of the two best publicized and most heatedly debated innovations in biography at the time (the other being Stracheyan iconoclasm), it was scarcely as pervasive as the amount of attention given it in the press would suggest. Like the lavishly misapplied adjective "Stracheyan," "Freudian" was, to adapt an epigram of the biographer Philip Guedalla, a handy stigma with which to beat a dogma. Numerous literary *biographies à thèse* of the time which deserved a better fate were reviewed as "Freudian," the suggestion being that they were laden from beginning to end with psychoanalytic interpretations. Actually, they may have contained no more than an occasional flavoring of such hypotheses, without presuming to use Freudian, Adlerian, or any other doctrine as a means of comprehensive psychic explanation.[3]

The best corrective to an exaggerated view of the place of Freudianism in modern biography is to remember how many intelligent biographers declined to explore the psychoanalytic implications of their material. De Quincey left behind him the kind of evidence which some analysts prize beyond almost any other—that of his dreams. But Edward Sackville-West withstood whatever temptation he may have felt:

> It forms no part of my present intention to attempt a Freudian assault on De Quincey's opium dreams. Their general provenance will, however, be fairly obvious to anyone with a little knowledge of psychology: the prevalence throughout of anxiety, the suspicion of persecution, the feeling of dread, of irrevocability, above all of guilt—in short all the preoccupations, expressed in easily recognizable symbols, which harassed his waking mind in moments of unhappiness, or when the outside world exerted pressure upon his consciousness to the extent of demanding from him action. . . . The whole contents of his dream emporium are from first to last exceptionally transparent, though not, for that reason, in any sense superficial. . . . And that is as far as his biographer need go, even if he has the ability (which I lack) to go further.

Southey also bequeathed his biographers what Jack Simmons, writing in the 1940's, called "a fascinating record" of "his weird, astonishing dreams . . . that a modern psychiatrist might with advantage explore." But the curious reader had to refer to the obscure place where it had been printed in 1881—Southey's correspondence with Caroline Bowles—for Simmons did nothing whatsoever with it.

---

[3] A good example of a well-executed book which was destined to be unfairly classified as a museum piece of Freudian biography was Lewis Mumford's *Melville* (1929), which contains, according to my count, no more than seven passages directly based on psychoanalytic postulates. It is significant that the copy I read had previously been gone through by a student who had marked all the places at which Mumford had fine opportunities for psychoanalytic comment and *did not use them.* They were far more numerous than the places where he did.

Reluctance to conduct psychoanalytic autopsies ordinarily could be attributed not merely to the biographer's distrust of his own competence but, more important, to his misgivings about the validity of the whole procedure. The grounds for his—and many readers'—skepticism were, and are, several. Foremost among them is the biographer's inability to subject the "patient" to dynamic, directed interrogation and self-revealment. As Howard Mumford Jones put it, "Since psychoanalysis depends upon the uncovering of submerged memories through free association under skillful guidance, it seems fair to remark that a dead author has neither memories nor associations nor the capacity to be cross-examined." Suggestive though the biographical documents may appear to be, their true meaning cannot be established and its ramifications pursued by application to the author. They are inert testimony to a psychic state that was once alive, constantly changing, and possessed of a long and obscure history—testimony which, in addition, has no absolutely stable meaning. Though an author's literary remains, as Jones went on to say, "may contain overt or hidden symbolism of considerable psychic significance, the interpretation of these symbols varies so greatly from practitioner to practitioner as to reduce control of the material to zero" —an inconvenient truth which is illustrated by the frequent inability of biographers and critics to agree on the hidden biographical implications of a poem or novel.

Nor is it possible to tell which literary evidence is fraught with true biographical significance and which is not. The premise, quoted above, that all art is but a projection of psychic states collapsed under its weight of absurd comprehensiveness, for it neglected the equally important other aspects of artistic creativity: the pressures of tradition, convention, and current taste, and, if it came to that, such other subliminal influences as those emanating from the Jungian collective unconscious. It requires a one-sided view indeed of literary genetics to find a poem or novel to be the product of an inner being utterly unaffected by external, or historical, circumstance.

Ironically, the system of psychoanalysis, which was hailed as an instrument for discovering coherence in the complexities of human behavior, had the effect of overlooking the complexities of life which lay outside the individual mind but nonetheless affected its deeds, including those of creation. Especially in the hands of amateurs, its concepts and patterns, relieved of their complications, qualifications, and subtleties, became handy over-simplifications, glib formulas by which everything could be explained. At their crudest, they were as mechanical and arbitrary as any formulations devised, in its own pride, by the "mental science" of the late eighteenth and early nineteenth centuries. In this respect psychoanalysis merely substituted one fashionable vocabulary, one set of *idées fixes,* for another, and so sacrificed realism and human truth. "Nothing," as Bernard Shaw said in another connection, "can be more unnatural and biographically worthless than a rigid single estimate with everything else forced into harmony with it: it is like an instantaneous photograph of a horse transfixed by the camera in the act of galloping."

Psychoanalysis proved also to be an inadequate way of accounting for some of the crucial facts of a literary artist's life. It might be possible to trace to psychic sources the specific content of his work and even relate the quantity of his output, year by year, to the rise or fall of his psychic energy and the events of his life; but no amount of analytic reconstruction could explain a sudden, dramatic outburst of genius, such as occurred in the miraculous year of Keats. And even if a biographer succeeded in identifying the particular neurotic pattern that governed a writer's inner life, the only effect of the revelation might be to place him in the company of many other men. As Julian Symons remarked, referring to the hypothesis that Carlyle's fundamental trouble was anal sadism: "To characterize a man by a compulsion apparently so common is hardly to characterize him at all. There are—if we can believe Carlyle's psychiatric interpreter—hundreds of thousands of anal sadists in the world today; but they do not write or think like Carlyle."

It is easy to write disrespectfully of psychoanalytic biography, and, when one contemplates the typical product turned out by authors who knew too little about the facts of their subjects' lives and thought they knew enough about psychoanalysis, it is not excessively unfair. The neglect or twisting of historical facts and the reckless adoption of a psychological theory proved time after time to be a lethal combination. But one cannot dismiss out of hand all psychoanalytic biographies as abortive offspring of a literary art in the process of rehabilitation and a revolutionary science trying to gain general acceptance. To do so would mean overlooking both the individual biographies which have made genuinely profitable use of psychoanalytic techniques and the permanent benefits which the development of depth psychology conferred upon the art as a whole.

For the truth is that, despite all the excesses and foolishness that marked the flirtation years, the advent of depth psychology momentously expanded the scope and art of biography as a whole; and the union may now be taken as permanent, and healthily fruitful. Though the identifying jargon is now mercifully suppressed and we are, in any event, so habituated to the modes of thought underlying psychological interpretation in present-day biographies that we tend to overlook their origin, Freudian assumptions continue to permeate much biography, simply because they have become an ineffaceable part of modern man's thought.

The gain is beyond debate. As a result of Freudianism, biographers were equipped with a whole battery of interwoven assumptions and techniques by which they could approach the problem of personality. All the data relating to a life had to be examined afresh, because the new lighting under which it could be seen revealed a multitude of significances that had never before been recognized. No longer, considering the devious ways in which the subconscious worked, could any useful distinction be made between the trivial and the important, the irrelevant and the pertinent. It became axiomatic, in fact, that no scrap of information, whether a seemingly pointless entry in a documentary record or a suggestion hovering in a line of poetry, was without its potential value for psychological inference. The relative importance of various classes of information radically shifted. Some facts which had always been deemed insignificant suddenly became crucially revelatory of motive and character. Others which had customarily been the center of the biographical story acquired new meaning through their freshly exposed connection with still other events. Data dealing with such forces as early family environment, traumatic events, and mature personal relationships were restudied for the influence they presumably had on the development of personality and attitudes. In one great sweep, also, Freudianism (assisted, of course, by other liberating influences of the time) destroyed the prohibitions and inhibitions that had prevented biographers from using certain classes of information. Although the most publicized, as it was the most immediately noticeable, effect of this new freedom was in the realm of sex, in the long run what counted most was the establishment of candor in respect to every facet of a man's life, whether it be shady financial transactions or a gift for crude language.

But in literary biography the greatest advance which psychoanalytic concepts made possible was that toward a tighter and more comprehensive bond between the artist and his art. The romantic critics' assumption that the soul of a man is written large in the lines of his poem was dramatically validated by science. And not only was the poet present *in* the lines: more important, he could, with the aid of the new analytic instruments, be discerned *between* them, in the complex and subtle implications audible only to the "third ear." Though there was much advantage in being thus enabled to see the writer more intimately, through the fantasies that comprised the substance of his imaginative art, the supreme gain lay in the finer understanding of the poem itself. Insofar as the poem could reasonably be read as the projection of its creator's inner self—the fulfilment of a psychic need—modern psychological insights enabled the critic to apply biographical knowledge for the enrichment of comprehension. To the extent to which a psychological reading of a given literary work could be accepted as justifiable, Freud and his followers could therefore be said to have given literary biography the means by which, at long last, it could accomplish its critical mission.

· 4 ·

As realization grew of the intricacy of the reaction between the internal and external, or constitutional and accidental, circumstances in a man's psychic history, biography not only probed into the hitherto concealed recesses of the personality itself; it sought to establish, more firmly than had before been possible, the relation of a man's character and deeds to the whole social and cultural environment in which he lived. The aim itself was far from new. The effect of environment upon character and genius had figured prominently in eighteenth-century speculation, and Carlyle had rephrased the cluster of questions for his own generation:

> ... if an individual is really of consequence enough to have his life and character recorded for public remembrance, we have always been of opinion, that the public ought to be made acquainted with all the inward springs and relations of his character. How did the world and man's life, from his particular position, represent themselves to his mind? How did coexisting circumstances modify him from without; how did he modify these from within? With what endeavours and what efficacy rule over them; with what resistance and what suffering sink under them? In one word, what and how produced was the effect of society on him; what and how produced was his effect on society? He who should answer these questions, in regard to any individual, would, as we believe, furnish a model of perfection in biography.

Little attempt was made to meet Carlyle's demands at the time. But toward the end of his century and at the beginning of the next, a new and emphatic strain of sociological determinism entered the English mind. In fiction Zola's theory and practice were having their effect: one of the novelist's ultimate goals, he said, was "portrayal of the human being in the environment which he himself has made and alters daily, and in the midst of which he in turn undergoes continual transformation." And, though as usual at a lag of some decades, biography began to make more sophisticated use of environmental detail, for the sake of explaining not only a man's character but his ideas and attitudes as they were eventually to appear in his writings. Weaving together and interpreting a mass of antiquarian detail, James L. Clifford evoked the cultural ambience of Lichfield as it had been in Dr. Johnson's youth, and, among other clues, found in the strong lingering local memories of the Cromwell era the source of his Toryism: "Such stories of the Civil War [as circulated in Lichfield] were enough to color Sam's feeling about the Commonwealth for the rest of his life. With vivid recollections of what had happened to his own town, he could never be completely objective in his attitude toward Cromwell, Milton, or any of the Puritans. He could never overcome his fear of revolution, or his doubt of the value of any sudden change."

In like fashion, Herschel Baker, in his life of Hazlitt, provided a panoramic survey of the ideas and personalities that dominated English intellectual life at the time of the French Revolution, thus accounting for the essayist's political and religious orientation. Dixon Wecter and Bernard De Voto, remedying Albert Bigelow Paine's omission, put Mark Twain's successive locales under the sociological microscope; Irving Howe dissected the late nineteenth-century, small-town Ohio milieu which determined Sherwood Anderson's outlook on life; Gay Wilson Allen minutely analyzed the atmosphere on Long Island and in Manhattan in the midst of which Walt Whitman came to maturity.

It was not alone for intellectual clarification—exploration of cause and effect—that some biographers sought to relate their subjects to their shaping backgrounds. For environmentalism also implies historical relativity, a recognition that both moral standards and literary taste change from generation to generation. This too was no new discovery. "Giving appelations to the conduct and notions of men, according to our own estimation, or the opinions of the present day," Stanfield had written in 1813, "is not the fair light in which to set a biographic picture." The biographer should discriminate between the attitudes and values proper to his own day and those that prevailed in his subject's time, thus forestalling anachronistic and unfair judgments. Some Victorian critics and biographers, consciously opposed to their age's moral parochialism, strove to estimate their subjects' characters and literary

((345

works in terms appropriate to the age in which they lived and worked. Most notably, perhaps, they used the argument of shifting moral climates to account for (though not necessarily to extenuate) the lasciviousness to which the Restoration dramatists were notoriously addicted, both on stage and off. But historical perspective in evaluating actions and attitudes came into much commoner use in the twentieth century. George Sherburn, for example, drew upon his great knowledge of Pope's immediate environment, including the nature of his friends and enemies and the complicated quarrels in which they were engaged, to neutralize the moral indignation with which previous commentators had discussed these murky matters and clarify the rights and wrongs as they would have appeared to contemporary observers *au courant* with the details. And Edward Sackville-West, discussing Wordsworth's dropping De Quincey after the latter had married the girl who had borne him a child, sensibly pointed out that, whatever opinion a modern reader might entertain, Wordsworth's attitude "was in fact unavoidable by anyone who pretended to a life based on the principles current in provincial society at the time."

Close scholarly knowledge of a past time and place sometimes enabled biographers to create the convincing illusion that more is known about a figure than is actually the case. Little direct and authentic information survives on the personality and character of Daniel Defoe; but James Sutherland inferred the sort of person he was by postulating what a youth and man of Defoe's specific background and position—late seventeenth-century dissenting, trading-class Londoner—was most probably like. From a wide range of the faceless data that general history provides, as well as the many quasi-autobiographical hints in Defoe's writing, Sutherland constructed a portrait of the journalist (*Defoe*, 1937) which, although it inescapably contained much speculation, seemed to make good sense because it was based on good scholarship.

His procedure, in a word, typified the union of scholarship with imagination which produces the best biography. For although biographers are required by their oath to found their work upon established facts, neither strict history nor strict science (depth psychology, for example) suffices to give the coherently meaningful account of a character and career that is their eventual goal. There must be something more: the intangible contribution of the biographer's intelligent intuition and sympathy.[4]

One consequence of the "scientific" emphasis of twentieth-century biography, especially that practiced in the university, was an insistence upon what was called objectivity: a term combining, in its widest sense, the absolute effacement of the biographer as a person, the avoidance of imaginative indulgence where facts were not adequate, and the refusal to offer any opinions. The principle was laconically expressed in the foreword to the "definitive" life of Edward FitzGerald: "In writing my narrative, I have striven to be objective and impersonal, for I believe that, unless it is unavoidable, a biographer must not intrude between his subject and the reader." The biographer's function, according to this austere view, was confined to the gathering and exposition of tested facts and to rigorously controlled conjecture on the basis of those facts. He could not permit himself what was taken to be the luxury of evaluating the human meaning of those data, in respect, for example, to the moral character of men and women, their probable motives, the ethical or philosophical implications of their deeds. Like his nineteenth-century predecessor, he was obligated to let facts speak for themselves: the intrusion of his personal views was an impertinence. Nor, in this interpretation of the biographer's proper role, was there room for literary criticism, even in the life of a literary figure, because criticism involved going beyond the provable into the perilous realm of subjective judgment.

The usual results of this insistence on impersonality were books that were juiceless, unventuresome, loaded with reliable

---

[4] Reliance upon intuition without even cursory regard for facts was a characteristic of not a few popular biographies written in the 1920's and early 1930's. Their versions of their subject seemed to have been conceived not in a library but in a trance. Female biographers of the Brontë sisters in particular were given to evolving their intensely personal—and aberrant—conceptions. Such books, which throw more light on the biographers than on their respective subjects, are of clinical interest only, and may be relegated to the crowded shelf of curiosities which the practice of biography has engendered during its prolific history.

information and devoid of intellectual stimulation and humane relevance. With much reason they could be—and were—defended as the storehouses from which later biographers could draw; but they contained no more art, and no more sense of personality, than an encyclopedia. It was disturbing to read impressively documented biographies that showed no evidence the data had made any impact upon, or been assimilated into a comprehensible pattern by, an independent intelligence. Newman Ivey White acted upon sound instinct when, at the conclusion of his monumental life of Shelley, he appended a thirty-five-page "Review and Interpretation" in which he offered his personal view of all he had narrated.

White, along with most other responsible biographers, recognized that fidelity to the biographer's oath is far from requiring a total renunciation of the imaginative and intuitive faculty. The true content of a biography is not a fortuitous assemblage of facts but the historical personality to the reconstruction of which they tend to converge. The extant records of a life are, at best, desultory and fragmentary; they are, in addition, often ambiguous. To achieve the leap from the known to the possibly knowable makes imperative some degree of imaginative intervention, and to bring out the ultimate significance of the life thus re-created requires the exercise of personal judgment. Informed speculation, therefore—the attempt to fill in the gaps of the record by postulating what probably happened, and why—is not only permissible but indispensable if a coherent and meaningful story is to be fashioned from the shreds of fact.

If a biographer is anything more than a research machine, moreover, he is bound to react to the fellow human beings with whose story he has become deeply involved—those enigmatic, inconsistent men and women with their mixed motives, their virtues and occasional lapses into sin. The problem in the post-Stracheyan era remained: What attitude should a biographer possess toward his human material? The one Strachey himself assumed, that of ironic amusement which his imitators corrupted into "debunkery", had its hectic day, but its limitations and palpable injustices were immediately apparent, and the law of diminishing returns set in. Condescension, ridicule, the smirk—these were attitudes which served their moment but did not advance understanding. And so most critics of biography revived, in spirit if not in phrase, the recommendation uttered long ago by Othello, speaking, it would seem, on behalf of all the subjects of biography: "Speak of me as I am, nothing extenuate, Nor set down aught in malice."

Less terse than Othello's plea, but more adequately recognizing the delicacy of the modern biographer's position, was John Galsworthy's statement in his Romanes Lecture (1931):

> A biographer's temperament must in every case colour to some degree the recreated figure of his hero. But the less his temperament deviates the natural colours of the re-creation, the greater the achievement. In a sense the biographer's art is as much the art of criticism as of creation, and true criticism has a certain divine detachment, a devotion to truth, at the expense of, rather than to the gratification of, the critic's self. This is why the good critic and the good biographer are almost as rare as the unicorn. The good biographer, like the good portraitist in oils, must be made of sponge and of steel. All must he absorb, and all sieve, and then must have at once constructive sympathy, and resistant power of the finest temper. Himself he must resist, curb both his sense of the ludicrous, and his sentimental impulses, yet withal keep warm and colourful.

Explanation but not apology, understanding but not partisanship, insight and yet detachment: these were the biographer's debt to the man whose life he wrote, and no less to himself as an artist dedicated to the revelation of truth. To it he had to devote his best powers—as a wise psychologist, as a historian cognizant of the special pressures that influenced conduct in the time of which he wrote, and above all as a candid observer of his own human self.

In his necessary search for the ultimate meaning of his story, therefore, the biographer had to go beyond facts—never to disregard or contravene them, but to read their deeper significance. In his quest the historical data were related to the moral essentials, the "higher truth," as rind is to juice. To penetrate to the juice called for the exercise of imagination and intuitive sympathy, qualities more readily identifiable with the wise artist than with the "objective" historian. And if the artist's human response was necessary before the biographer could perceive the truth toward which his data pointed, those other attributes of the artist, the powers of selection and shaping, were required to enable him to portray his vision of that truth. From a jagged, tangled mass of events both related and unrelated, trivial and crucial, plain and obscure, he had to evolve a well-knit, esthetically pleasing structure that would show where they all belonged and represent, in itself, the sum of their meaning. To make his book a work of art while remaining faithful both to the facts themselves and to the truth they implied was the biographer's supreme challenge.

The Artist

✳

Vɪʀɢɪɴɪᴀ ᴡᴏᴏʟғ maintained that biography is, properly speaking, a craft rather than an art, because it does not permit unrestricted invention: "the invented character lives in a free world where the facts are verified by one person only—the artist himself. Their authenticity lies in the truth of his own vision. The world created by that vision is rarer, intenser, and more wholly of a piece than the world that is largely made of authentic information supplied by other people. . . . The artist's imagination at its most intense fires out what is perishable in fact; he builds with what is durable; but the biographer must accept the perishable, build with it, imbed it in the very fabric of his work." But the terminology really does not matter. Artist or craftsman, the biographer has the task of giving order, shape, and coherent meaning to the data he possesses. By the selection and arrangement of his material, by his apportionment of emphasis, he strives to communicate his personal view of the essential texture and tendency of a man's life.

This conception of the biographer's role as shaper and interpreter was not a product of the twentieth century; something like it was implied in the most thoughtful nineteenth-century commentary on biography. But it was brought into the open, and widely adopted as a working principle, only after a considerable amount of formalistic criticism had been written to guide the study and practice of the sister narrative art, fiction. If much of the increased concern for technique that marked the biographies of the modern era could be traced directly to Strachey, equally much could also be traced to the post-Jamesian interest in the novel as a high form of art. Literary biography reached its maturity in the age—or wake—of James's own critical prefaces (later collected as *The Art of the Novel*), Percy Lubbock's *The Craft of Fiction* (1921), E. M. Forster's *Aspects of the Novel* (1927), and the mass of critical writings devoted to specific works of fiction. This body of criticism had such great influence on literary thought from the 1920's onward that the sheer excitement of its neighboring presence stirred biography into an unprecedented awareness of its own opportunities and technical problems. The now-dignified art of the novel supplied it with ambitions it had not developed on its own.

The intensified study of the great French and Russian novelists as well as a more penetrating examination of the masters in English had shown that fiction was a powerful instrument for exploring the depths of the soul. An inner plot, it became clear, could sustain a novel as surely as the traditional plot of external events. This expanded conception of the scope of narrative and portrait art, applied primarily to the novel, widened the potential of biography as well. So far as his material permitted, the biographer might legitimately strive to achieve the goals of novelists like Balzac, Dostoevsky, Eliot, Hardy, and James. He too could write of men's spiritual adventures, their battles and victories and defeats: but his subjects would be men who had actually lived and in some fashion recorded their experience.

With his artist's eye, he appraised afresh the personnel of literary history.[1] Although the demand for subjects made virtually

[1] It is not art alone that affects the biographer's choice of subject. Leon Edel and others have remarked that the attraction is sometimes determined by his psychological necessities, such as the need for a father figure—an explanation which might apply to any number of nineteenth-century venerative biographies. Amy Lowell, it has often been said, adopted Keats as a surrogate son—an assertion supported by the generally protective attitude she adopted toward him throughout her biography, to say nothing of the tendency of such exclamations as "Poor little shaver, so pitiably unable to cope with his first great sorrow!" and "How he tortured himself, poor boy!" Keats, in more than a facetious sense, was her baby. André Maurois confided that he chose Shelley as the subject of his first biography because "I felt that to tell the story of his life would be in some measure a deliverance for myself. . . . I wanted to kill the romantic in me; and, in order to do it, I scoffed at it in Shelley." (*Aspects of Biography* [New York,

every writer eligible for biographical treatment, it was plain as ever that there are some literary figures about whom a vivid or even moderately interesting narrative cannot be written and others about whom it is almost impossible to write a dull one. The biographical artist is, indeed, at the mercy of both the nature and the quantity of his materials. On some figures, there are abundant data; on others, little. Some who left copious personal archives behind may, however, have belonged to the large class of people who reveal little of themselves even in private letters or diaries; others may have left relatively little, but what remains has an extremely high autobiographical content.

Most authors before the age of Swift defy full-scale biographical treatment simply because not enough revelatory personal documents survive. Many biographies have been written of them—Shakespeare is an obvious case in point—but whatever illusion of intimacy the authors achieve is due more to their imaginative skill than to hard facts found in their sources. In some instances considerable material is available, but it is of a kind that seldom affords a view of the spirit behind external appearances and public deeds. Augustine Birrell's observation concerning Andrew Marvell, "We know all about him, but very little of him," applies as well to many of Marvell's forerunners and contemporaries. It is possible to trace Joseph Addison's political career in detail, but because, as his first large-scale biographer, Peter Smithers, remarked, "Addison abhorred irrelevant self-revelation by authors, and was meticulous in his own avoidance thereof," one cannot see, close up, that portion of the man which figures in literary history. Hazlitt left few personal papers. Wilkie Collins, Charles Reade, and Bret Harte—three writers whose books enjoyed great popularity in their own time and who therefore were themselves in the public eye—can now be seen, as persons, only through a

---

1930], pp. 121–122.) Henry James's *Hawthorne* reflects James's deep personal preoccupations: he saw in Hawthorne's frustrated career as an artist in the unsympathetic American environment an anticipation, a generation earlier, of his own predicament. On another level, one might point out the temperamental affinity which led Hesketh Pearson, a former actor, to write biographies of men who were themselves theatrical by nature or profession: Shaw, Dickens, Disraeli, Wilde, Sydney Smith, Gilbert and Sullivan.

clouded glass. Even more resistant to close biographical treatment are two dons, Walter Pater and A. E. Housman, and the
American poet Edwin Arlington Robinson, all of whom built such
high walls around themselves that few persons truly knew them
when they lived, and no biographer has since been able substan-
tially to reduce the world's inherited ignorance.

Other figures, some of whom left extensive personal records,
offer literary biographers challenges of other sorts. Some were, as
persons, simply uninteresting. Samuel Richardson was complacent, respectable, sententious, and dull; possibly the best one
could do with him would be to portray him as the model of
Hogarth's industrious apprentice, which is not a very exciting
enterprise. Externally, Henry Thoreau was hardly distinguishable
from thousands of other mildly peculiar New Englanders who
spent their lives walking around in work clothes and doing odd
jobs; apart from his lead pencils and surveys, Thoreau in the
world's eye was a typical nonproducer. Melville's personality was
so reticent as to have left little impression on those who knew
him; it was scarcely conceivable that he had had exotic adventures in the South Seas. Trollope and Arnold were irreproachably
proper Victorian civil servants; people mistook Browning for a
successful financier; there was no hint of glamor, only an equine
cast of countenance, about George Eliot. Whatever biographies
were written of them had to derive their attraction either from
dramatic single episodes (as in Browning's case) or from the
records their subjects left of their inner lives.

If some great writers lacked personal color or adventurous
histories, others were—or so most of the records suggest—
basically and irremediably disagreeable. To write at length about
such people is a thankless task; to turn them, without doing violence to history, into persons one would wish to have known is a
hopeless one. The eccentric E. H. W. Meyerstein nevertheless
devoted a 600-page volume to Thomas Chatterton, the "acrimonious prodigy" who managed to make himself thoroughly un-
loved before committing suicide at the age of seventeen. Because
Hazlitt has undeniable importance as a critic and essayist, he was
the subject of several biographies, none of which, however, fully

succeeded in counteracting the impression, current in his lifetime, that this enemy-prone man was indeed "pimpled"—if not in a literal sense, certainly in the word's moral connotations. There were also new biographies—sometimes several on a single figure —of James Fenimore Cooper and Walter Savage Landor, litigants, polemicists, and general curmudgeons; George Gissing, glum, despairing, and the foredoomed victim of two disastrous marriages; Coventry Patmore, a stony dogmatist who imperfectly sublimated and rationalized his sexuality in eroto-religious poetry; the heavy-jowled, pugnacious Hilaire Belloc, monopolizer of conversation and strident anti-Semite. There is a point, however, at which personal unattractiveness becomes so extravagant as positively to recommend a man to adventurous biographers: Frank Harris, for instance. Professionally, as a magazine editor and man of letters, much was to be said for him: he was original, enterprising, and often helpful to good young writers. As a man "he was," wrote Bernard Shaw *to* Harris, *of* Harris, "simply the most impossible ruffian on the face of the earth." Boor, lecher, liar, blackmailer, traducer, braggart, fraud, Harris was one of the worst men of his time; the sheer versatility of his wickedness, the variety of reasons why people itched to horsewhip him, commands admiration.

But in this modern age, the chief delights of biographers as well as of their readers remained men who had in effect done much of their biographers' work for them, by being the kind of vivid and generally agreeable persons they were, by bottling the essence of their personalities in the readily usable form of conversation, letters, and diaries, and (to fill the cup to the brim, in some instances) by living lives whose stories seemingly were predestined for the purposes of art.

The annals of authorship, in fact, provided such ready-made plots in gratifying abundance. So artistically molded were some writers' lives that suspicion was occasionally voiced that they were conducted with the deliberate intention of serving biographers. "Why was Wilde so good a subject for a biography?" demanded Shaw. "Just because his stupendous laziness simplified his life almost as if he knew instinctively that there must be no episodes to spoil the great situation at the end of the last act but one. It was a well made life in the Scribe sense." J. C. Furnas recalled that Henry James, among others, saw the story of Robert Louis Stevenson's life as one that Stevenson himself might have written:

> The story is both kinetic and ironic. Much of its detail has style. And, like most who knew him, the hero found the character of Robert Louis Stevenson fascinating. But the implication that he himself helped to construct the story is rather pretty than pertinent. This life was as active as a water bug, romantic as an elopement, wide-ranging as a tramp ship, dramatic as a duel to the death, even, as he would have liked it, moral as a tract, after his own morality, that is. But it is not in his own literary manner. *The Adventures of a Changeling* was not among the novels aborted by his unexpected death.

Nevertheless, Furnas went on, the narrative "has the asymmetric consistency of great composition." It is a "novel of actuality," a "case history with the values of fiction."

Aided by their own temperaments and the encouragement they received from the spirit of their romantic age, Byron, Keats, and Shelley lived—and in their letters and diaries wrote the substance of—true novels. Byron's life, in a sense, was an amalgam of the best and worst features of several popular kinds of contemporary fiction: the crippled heir to a peerage, the unloving mother, the frustrated idyllic love (with Mary Chaworth), the search for adventure in the Near East, the forbidden passion for a half-sister, dazzling literary and social success, a marriage attended by melodramatic scenes and insane rages, permanent exile by national demand, despair, a new attachment (the Countess Guiccioli), and then the great climax, death in the service of an oppressed nation struggling for independence from the pagan Turk. Keats, like Byron, imparted his engaging personality—his enthusiasms, fancies, anxieties, indignations, and profound insights into self—to his letters, and thence into biographies; and though modern writers saw him through quite different lenses than did the Victorians, neither the passage of time nor familiarity could detract from the miraculous tale of the quick flowering of his genius, the tragedy of his death less than two years later, and the mystery of his destiny as man and poet had his life been spared. Shelley's life, viewed artistically, was a swift series of rising and falling actions, climaxes, reversals, and grand symbolic conclusion. The final scene is a splendid and fitting climax unexcelled in the world's drama: the young man, who from earliest youth had had a strange urge toward boats and water, drowns in a sudden squall and his mutilated body is ceremoniously burned on a pyre, half Greek, half (by anticipation) Wagnerian.

Thus the biographer, eager in this new age to match talents with the novelist, had no lack of strong plots from which to draw. A few, he found, recurred time after time in literary history. One, exemplified by the lives of the great romantic trio—the years of youth lived with a hard, gemlike flame, poetic gifts flaring up and then extinguished by fate's hand, promise scarcely fulfilled—presented itself again in the truncated lives of the tuberculous and suicidal young men of the decadent nineties, Ernest Dowson, Lionel Johnson, Aubrey Beardsley, Francis Thompson, and John Davidson, who died at an average age of less than forty; in that of Rupert Brooke, who became the subject of a twentieth-century sentimental myth, and, still later, in Dylan Thomas' reckless progress toward death in a New York hospital.

Another recurrent plot in literary biography is Greek-classic in suggestion rather than English-romantic. Scott's life followed the Aristotelian tragic movement: a man of noble moral qualities rises to immense wealth and fame, but is toppled by pride (his ambition to be a great landed laird) and misplaced faith in his associates. His paper principality collapses and, refusing to take refuge in bankruptcy, he devotes his failing strength to writing books that will pay off his enormous debts. He kills himself in the effort, but he almost attains his goal. In the even more harrowing final movement of Dickens' life the pace of tragic events is measured, not by discounted notes and the other paraphernalia of commerce, but by the clinical data of pulse, temperature, blurred vision, fainting fits, and muscles unable to respond to the nerves' command—the cost of a frantic obsession to keep busy at all costs, for the sake of anesthetizing the tortured mind. As initially related by John Forster and with added detail by Edgar Johnson eighty years later, the narrative of Dickens' last reading tours, which amounted to a kind of serialized suicide, is one of the most horrifying yet engrossing passages in literary biography.

At the very time the "new biography" was emerging, the lives of several British and American men of letters were working themselves out in the same pattern, thus providing biographers with contemporary instances of fatality. Arnold Bennett, like Dickens a novelist of commonplace social origins who worked his way to fortune and celebrity, paid a comparable price for his rewards: "the high-voltage friendships he was enjoying and forming, the glittering circle of new acquaintance of which he was often a centre of admiration, the brilliant night life, the dancing, the unending dinner parties, the gay talk, the persisting party mood and spirit of the early 1920's in London's West End"—and all the while the insomnia and neuralgia grew more unendurable, the sense of creative failure more oppressive.

Against the brassy background of America, other lives— shorter, the pace of moral disintegration more hectic—were generating the flamboyant and tragic stuff of future literary biography. F. Scott Fitzgerald lived the plot of one of his own novels, supplying Arthur Mizener with the narrative of a best-selling biography: the delusive dawn of sophomoric power and glory at Princeton; year after year of wild parties, drunken misdemeanors, membership in the smart international literary set; a wife's insanity, beginning, with an improbable appropriateness that fiction would reject, in a mania for dancing; failing health, assisted by alcoholism and intolerable periods of abstinence; a pen divided between turning out despised commercial fiction for the sake of quick money and writing affectionate letters to his daughter.

The life of Hart Crane, meanwhile, a Greek tragedy played out in a Dos Passos setting, offered the plot for a brilliant biography by Philip Horton. If the portents of Fitzgerald's doom could be read the moment he received his first praise as a novelist and took his first Prohibition drink, Crane's were to be seen in his emotional impalement between his divorced but still warring parents. His suffering embraced pennilessness, continual drunkenness, physical violence, many arrests, and a homosexual urge that led the poet of *The Bridge* time after time to the Brooklyn waterfront, there to be beaten and robbed by his sailor pickups. The end came when, after a totally fruitless Guggenheim year in Mexico, with Katherine Anne Porter as his frightened neighbor, he leaped from a liner off Florida, in bright sunlight and calm sea.

This was the kind of powerful plot-stuff that the annals of the postwar era furnished literary biographers. If the biographies of Fitzgerald, Crane, Dylan Thomas, Sinclair Lewis, Vachel Lindsay, Eugene O'Neill, and Thomas Wolfe were more explicit in their narration of a man's descent into the depths than those of earlier figures who suffered a like fate, it was not only because the terrible details were so much more accessible, most often from the lips of witnesses. More important, under the conditions that affected all literature in and after the 1920's, the biographer, like the novelist, was not merely free but often compelled to tell the story of an agonized life with naturalistic frankness. It was in the books dealing with contemporary figures, above all, that the liberation of literary biography from mealymouthedness was most evident. No longer could it be maintained that biographers and undertakers belonged to the same guild. These books may not have been delightful to read, but they possessed a terrible immediacy, a dramatic tension and at the same time an inexorable movement toward doom, that Gosse and Strachey had never found in the discreet chronicles they denounced.

Most literary lives, however, are not so expertly preshaped for transference into biography; like the common run of men, celebrated authors usually prove to have blundered through the years in a style that was uneventful, monotonous, almost wholly devoid of sharp climax and drama of any sort. Jane Austen's story amounts to hardly more than an excerpt from the simple annals of the well-to-do, and so placid was the tenor of Edward FitzGerald's unambitious life that it refused to be disturbed by the only event having the potentialities of drama, his hardly explicable marriage to a lady who promptly left him. Yet even in such artistically unpromising narratives, according to his friend Carlyle, the perceptive eye could find shape and dramatic intensity: "The life of every man," Carlyle quoted his alter ego, Herr Sauerteig, as saying, "the life even of the meanest man, it were good to remember, is a Poem; perfect in all manner of Aristotelean requisites; with beginning, middle, and end; with perplexities, and solutions. . . ."

Many lives, too, seem from the biographer's standpoint to be discouragingly miscellaneous: they are characterized by a lack of center, continuity, and focus, or what Matthew Arnold called, in another connection, "confused multitudinousness." But this apparent lack of artistic promise, observed Wilbur Cross, could serve as a challenge to the biographer's powers of insight and discernment:

> A biographer who keeps his mind upon human nature as it is and upon facts as he finds them, will surely discover that the outcome, far from being a mere collection of events, more or less discordant, will be groups of events which on reflection fall into a connected series having a beginning and an end and never quite breaking asunder. In other words, the incidents of real life as well as of fiction have their import and their logic. At length a sort of natural plot, lacking the precision of perfect art, emerges, and at last the man's character and achievements become reasonably clear.

· 2 ·

If the nature of the story prevents him from achieving "the precision of perfect art," the biographer can at least work toward that goal. Sometimes, however, he is permanently frustrated by the accidents that deprive him of evidence relating to some of the most important years in a life. Hazlitt disappears almost wholly from view between 1826 and 1830; there are wide hiatuses in our knowledge of De Quincey's whereabouts and occupations; and the long later portion of Thomas Love Peacock's life, after his relation with the Shelley circle ended and he entered the India House, is obscure. In numerous other instances, there is no correlation between the amount of information available on a given period of a man's life and the importance of that period. Seldom is history so obliging as to match the quantity of the surviving records to their biographical significance.

One of the biographer's hardest jobs, therefore, is to preserve his sense of relative value in the face of masses of evidence that adequately document the uninteresting stretches and leave the rest of a life in shade. As George McLean Harper pointed out, except for its bearing on his art there is nothing that distinguishes the last four decades of Wordsworth's life, "in any singular degree, from the lives of many other Englishmen of his time. Letters, anecdotes, records of his conversation, and other biographical material, are far more abundant for this later period than for the years when he was comparatively obscure. Owing to this fact, it is the aged Wordsworth that the world knows most about"— Christopher Wordsworth's *Memoirs* devotes two thirds of its space to this span—"and this is extremely unfortunate." To Harper, the critical years of the poet's life were his twenties, the relatively undocumented period of his political radicalism and Godwin-induced rationalism. He therefore felt obliged to reverse Christopher Wordsworth's emphasis, devoting the whole of his first volume (441 pages) to the years down to 1802, when Wordsworth was thirty-two, and skimming through the final thirty years, 1810–50, in a mere hundred pages.

Apart from the hazard of letting the availability of data control his book's proportions, the biographer faces the fact that most lives, seen in long perspective, are themselves ill-shaped. The natural climax of an author's career, the period during which he produces his best work or enjoys his greatest fame, may come decades before the end of his life. The man continues to live, enduring monotony and the darkening reminders of mortality, long after the artist has reached his fulfillment. English and American literary history abounds in such anticlimaxes. In addition to Wordsworth's there was Coleridge's, who, afflicted with the burden of unrealized projects as well as with personal miseries, spent his last eighteen years at the home of a Highgate physician, doing little of note except delivering high-flying metaphysical monologues to admiring visitors. Swinburne at forty-two, having cut a swath through London literary and Bohemian circles, fluttering the dovecotes of Victorian propriety with his strange new music and hints of exotic vices, was transported in that most prosaic of vehicles, a hansom cab, to that most prosaic of suburbs, Putney, where he was to live out the rest of a long life in the enjoyment of sobriety, regular hours, and the company of a tamed muse. Walt Whitman, having published *Leaves of Grass*, settled in Camden and spent the next twenty years in a drab monochrome of partial paralysis, constant revision of his poems, reception of pilgrims, and ferryboat rides to Philadelphia. Every such instance represents a biographer's quandary. Shall he pursue the story to the long-drawn-out end with as much detail, now that his subject has entered the twilight in which millions of undistinguished lives merge, as he gave to the period of the man's conspicuous individuality? Or shall he abridge his recital of those comparatively meaningless and certainly undramatic last years?

The decision ordinarily depended on the biographer's dominating purpose. If he wished to concentrate on his subject as artist, he felt justified in spending most space on his literary career—or the most enduringly resultful part of it—and hastily summarizing the remaining years. If, on the other hand, he meant his book to be a complete chronicle of a life, he felt bound to retain throughout the scale of treatment adopted for the period in which the writer's claim to literary remembrance was being established. When Austin Dobson wrote his English Men of Letters volume on Fanny Burney, he compressed the last forty-eight years of her life, during which she wrote nothing of importance, into a single chapter called "Half a Lifetime." A half-century later, however, Joyce Hemlow (who admittedly had the advantage of quantities of unpublished manuscripts that were unknown to Dobson) treated the latter half of Fanny's life, which was full of adventure, on the same generous scale she allotted to the first half, which saw Fanny not only achieving fame as a novelist but recording in her vivacious diaries the comedy of London literary and court circles.

Although the second half was not necessarily anticlimactic, lives that broke somewhere near the middle into two unlike parts offered similar problems in proportioning and treatment. Southey's arrival at Greta Hall, Keswick, in 1803 marked the great watershed in his life. The earlier part had been characterized by restlessness, constant change of residence, sporadic flares of ambition soon quelled by lack of application—a kind of existence best described in episodic terms. Henceforth his life was to be, as Jack Simmons said, "quiet, simple, remote; static, though not stagnant; punctuated by births and deaths, the visits of friends and occasional trips to other parts of England or to the Continent; above all, given over to books, by choice as well as from necessity; one of the most even, admirable careers English literature can show." But since a quiet life cannot be narrated dramatically, the technique had to be altered to one of description, with relatively little concern for chronological sequence.[2]

Leigh Hunt's life witnessed a shift of another kind. Until he was about forty-six, his interest to the biographer centers in his intimate but often troubled relations with Keats, Byron, and Shelley, and his story necessarily is told largely in terms of those associations, with somewhat less attention given to his own busy career as journalist, critic, and poet. "After 1830," as Edmund Blunden wrote when he reached that point in his biography of Hunt, "he produced a quantity of good literature, principally reflective and commendatory; he conversed with most of the eminent Victorians in the world of books; he saluted and helped many young poets of distinct endowments. But we are now faced with the long postscript, or at least the afternoon, to his truly active period." In short, Blunden believed that once Hunt's great companions have left the scene, he is incapable of sustaining the drama by himself. For the remaining twenty-nine years, Blunden contented himself with patching together a variety of interesting scraps on the later Hunt, and the chronological thread, seemingly no longer important, was largely lost.

The course of Melville's life and the nature of the materials

---

[2] Edward Dowden had recognized the problem many decades earlier. In one of the private letters which reveal him to have been the most deliberate artist among nineteenth-century biographers, he wrote: "The rock in my 'Southey' was how to shape a unity out of a life eventful, in some degree, up to about mid-way, and then absolutely stationary and without incident. I think I mastered that difficulty skilfully." (*Fragments from Old Letters, E[dward] D[owden] to E. D. W[est] 1869–1892* [2nd. ser., London, 1914], p. 153.)

concerning it presented his biographers with a several-sided problem, which each solved in his own way. For one thing, Melville's
life was anticlimactic (or so our knowledge of it suggests): after
four or five years of youthful adventure in the South Seas and six
or eight more in the intellectual and emotional fever of expanding
his experience of the world into a densely woven fictional commentary, he vanished for his remaining forty years into the shadows of a New York customs shed. The burning center of the
Melville story (the sequence of physical deeds and inner turmoil
that generated the great books) occurs before the man is out of
his twenties. Moreover, the character of the data changes. Since
prime documents of self-revelation—letters, diaries, and the rest
—are notably scarce in Melville's case, the chief evidence upon
which biographers must rely at any point in his career is that of
his books. But the earlier ones, from *Typee* to *Pierre,* are of much
greater autobiographical value than the later; from the 1850's
onward, Melville the man becomes more and more of an enigma.
Thus among the many tasks his biographers face are those of
making the transition in mode from the drama of his inner self
(the years of contemplation and creative fulfillment) to the later
narrative, which necessarily is fragmentary, external, and at all
events superficial; and of finding a just balance between the crucial years, in which the interest of Melville the genius is concentrated, and those numerically preponderant decades of his later
life.

There were, of course, many writers besides Melville whose
fame was due chiefly to the literary uses to which they put the
scenes and experiences of youth, but who, unlike Melville, continued to draw upon this fund for many years. Wordsworth again
is a case in point; as is Mark Twain, the first twenty-five or thirty
years of whose life, the years of Hannibal, the river, and the
western mines, provided the stuff of his most characteristic books.
For this additional reason the chronological structuring of biography was affected by the special character and emphasis of its
subject's works. Only by fully exploring the "things past" of
which a writer's most notable productions were an imaginative
remembrance could biographers achieve maximum critical rele-

vance in their narratives, though at the risk of seeming to linger too long over his youth.

Persons whose careers were only partly literary posed another question of scale and emphasis. If a substantial portion of a man's life was spent in occupations without bearing on literature and yet the chief, if not the only, reason for writing a biography of him resided in the fact that he did contribute something to literature, where was one to draw the line between the relevant and the irrelevant? Conrad was a sailor until he was past thirty-five; Oliver Wendell Holmes, like Smollett and Goldsmith, was a medical man; Rossetti was a painter; numerous others were diplomats, politicians, divines, academic men, and only secondarily or latterly writers. Peter Smithers, allowing the abundant documents on Addison's political and administrative career to control his book's scope, argued:

> The study of Addison has suffered in the past from preoccupation with his literary work. The circle of wits in the coffee-house, their writings, their friendships and their quarrels, which made up so large part of the lives of many of them, are of secondary significance in Addison's career. He was and envisaged himself as an important figure in the administrative and political life of England, and he held posts for which the aristocratic and wealthy competed fiercely. So fully rounded was his view of life that literary output became a by-product, though a very important one, of a life well lived. . . . His literary achievement, by which he will always be remembered, cannot be understood except in the light of his own purposes.

Hence Smithers' book, although adequately treating Addison's *Tatler* and *Spectator* contributions and his popular tragedy, *Cato*, is less a literary biography than a work primarily of interest to specialists in the era's political history. In Sheridan's case, biographers have had to deal not with two careers but with three: dramatist, politician, and theater proprietor. The first career, which alone entitles books about Sheridan to be called literary biographies, ended before he was thirty; it was the second, even though a series of disappointments, by which, as Lewis Gibbs says, Sheridan would have wished to be remembered. To concentrate on the brief period of *The Rivals* and *The School for Scandal* to the relative neglect of his other, lengthier, careers is to distort the actual tendency and burden of his life; yet what else is a literary biographer to do?

And what, furthermore, is he to do in a case like Defoe's, whose printed output, though enormous, was in great part ephemeral journalism and propaganda, of concern only to modern historians of his age? A biography that presents him mainly as the author of *Robinson Crusoe, Moll Flanders, The Apparition of Mrs. Veal, A Journal of the Plague Year,* and the handful of other works that are mentioned in the histories of English literature recounts only a few small, incidental pieces of Defoe's story, hardly more than by-products of his incredible industry. Yet a biography that puts them into perspective among the 400-odd other works he is known or thought to have written, from pamphlets to whole runs of periodicals, ceases to be a "literary" biography and becomes, instead, a case history of one man among many who were caught up in the swirling political life of their time.

Shifting intellectual theories and attitudes continued to affect the proportions of both the beginning and the end of biographies. In an older England, or a New England, where much importance was attached to a celebrated person's pedigree, the opening pages reached back through parish registers, tombstones, land records, and family Bibles to the first discoverable Foes, Quinceys, and Hathornes. Such extensive canvassing of a man's social antecedents could also be justified by the assumption that his character, and even the germs of his literary genius, could be traced to his chromosomes. But as both reverence for quality of blood and belief in the genetic transmission of character traits declined, the amount of space devoted to genealogical facts similarly shrank. In a few modern instances, however, this general tendency was reversed. Gordon Ray's minute study (in his life of Thackeray and, more extensively, in a separate volume, *The Buried Life*) of Thackeray's older relatives was justified by two facts: first, the family's Anglo-Indian background and the peculiar position that Englishmen returned from India occupied in early nineteenth-century society had much to do with Thackeray's own social attitudes; and second, many of his relatives demonstrably served as models for characters in his fiction.

At the same time, the next following phase of biography, devoted to the subject's home environment and the incidents of his childhood, was restored to the prominence it had occupied a century earlier, when even the most trivial data on a child's early experiences, his sayings and studies, were prized as raw material for the study of developmental psychology. (In the interval, despite eroded confidence in the scientific value of such information and the reiterated complaints of bored reviewers, some biographers had persisted in setting forth at intolerable length the record of their subjects' formative years, partly because custom was still strong and partly because such material had widespread sentimental appeal in an epoch that cherished the cult of the child.) In the post-Freudian era, the same data were extensively presented for quite a different reason: their contribution to an understanding of the subconscious forces that, originating in childhood, determined the nature of the mature personality and, it might be, of his art as well.

At the other extreme of life, the lengthy, often loquacious expiration scenes which so often had formed the last pious glory of biography were generally dispensed with: a secular age no longer placed store in the deathbed as an awe-filled religious symbol. Although no biographer could hope to outdo the laconism of the final sentence in Lawrence and Elisabeth Hanson's *The Four Brontës* ("She [Charlotte] grew weaker, and on the last day of March 1855 she died"), the tendency was toward unsentimental economy. One seldom met such lavishness of detail as that at the end of Leslie Marchand's *Byron*, where, as in Moore's first biography, an international consortium of doctors was beheld speeding the poet toward death. For the edifying or clinical details with which nineteenth-century biographers had laden their concluding pages, Lytton Strachey, by a much-imitated stroke of irony, substituted a passage devoted to a a wholly fanciful phantasmagoria of remembered scenes that coursed through the dying Queen Victoria's half-conscious mind.

In such a fashion, biographies written in an era of intensified concern for form reflected the pressures of contemporary thought. Whatever the ideal proportions recommended by art, in practice the space allotted to a man's heredity, his early environment, and finally to his demise was determined not only by the availability of information but by revised social values, sentiment, genetic and psychological theory, and attitudes toward life and death. The shape a modern biography assumed was, among other things, a function of the thought prevailing in an increasingly scientific, unsentimental, and secular age.

· 3 ·

Many of the influences that affected the structure of a biography affected also its pace and rhythm—additional artistic features about which older biographers had seldom been concerned, but which the twentieth-century critics of fiction had made it impossible for any narrative artist to ignore. The extreme alternatives available to such an artist, possessing a mass of events that he must somehow distribute and group, had been accurately described, two centuries earlier, in *Tom Jones* (Book II, Chapter i):

> Though we have properly enough entitled this our work, a history, and not a life, nor an apology for a life, as is more in fashion; yet we intend in it rather to pursue the method of those writers who profess to disclose the revolutions of countries, than to imitate the painful and voluminous historian, who, to preserve the regularity of his series, thinks himself obliged to fill up as much paper with the detail of months and years in which nothing remarkable happened, as he employs upon those notable eras when the greatest scenes have been transacted on the human stage.

> Such histories as these do, in reality, very much resemble a newspaper, which consists of just the same number of words, whether there be any news in it or not. They may likewise be compared to a stage-coach, which performs constantly the same course, empty as well as full. The writer, indeed, seems to think himself obliged to keep even pace with time, whose amanuensis he is; and, like his master, travels . . . slowly through centuries of monkish dullness, when the world seems to have been asleep. . . .

Now it is our purpose . . . to pursue a contrary method. When any extraordinary scene presents itself (as we trust will often be the case), we shall spare no pains nor paper to open it at large to our readers; but if whole years should pass without producing anything worthy his notice, we shall not be afraid of a chasm in our history, but shall hasten on to matters of consequence, and leave such periods of time totally unobserved. . . .

My reader then is not to be surprised, if, in the course of this work, he shall find some chapters very short, and others altogether as long; some that contain only the time of a single day, and others that comprise years; in a word, if my history sometimes seems to stand still, and sometimes to fly.

The alternative Fielding chose was to be the one employed by those modern biographers most bent upon producing the effect of a novel. They gave maximum prominence to pivotal events and subordinated, even telescoped, the incidental ones; and sometimes, where the extant data or their powers of judicious invention allowed, they alternated detailed and dramatized scenes with rapid summary, giving their books that same variety of movement by which novelists had long since learned to avoid monotony, while at the same time implying the relative importance of events. To accomplish this without doing violence to the logic of the received facts required no little skill. Biographers had not only to train themselves to recognize those events which were both significant and dramatically useful; in addition each event, once selected, had to be magnified or minimized, singled out or merged, highlighted or cast into shadow, according to the effect to which it was expected to contribute. To retell a series of occurrences in authentic historical sequence, but to regulate the very passage of time, so that it might stand still while the crisis of a few days occupied a dozen pages and then fly while the comparatively unimportant incidents of a year were condensed in a single page—and to accomplish all this while the reader remained unaware of the illusion—called for a skill no less fine than that of the expert novelist.

Rhythmic structuring was as desirable as well-regulated pace, and although the formless body of material a literary biographer inherited seldom gave outward sign of possessing inherent divisions, a closer examination sometimes revealed that a life did indeed possess an implicit series of separate movements. Dr. Johnson had observed in 1760 that the lives of writers were divided into epochs by the completion or publication of their books and the tides of their reputations. The growth of a writer's *oeuvre*, together with the counter-rhythm of his inner existence— what Christopher Hassall, in his life of Sir Edward Marsh, called "crises of the sensibility"—contained at least the elements of pattern. As the biographer sifted material and gained perspective, he often perceived an inherent design that he needed only to bring into more prominence to produce the pleasing sense of recurrence, and so of unity, that his artistic ambition sought.

In addition, a few biographers went so far as to introduce thematic devices which served the purposes of both form and argument. Strachey showed the way with his numerous repeated symbols, one of the most memorable of which was the cardinal's hat as the symbol of Manning's temporal striving, a motif culminating in the final sentence: "And he who descends into the crypt of that Cathedral which Manning never lived to see, will observe, in the quiet niche with the sepulchral monument, that the dust lies thick on the strange, the incongruous, the almost impossible object which, with its elaborations of dependent tassels, hangs down from the dim vault like some forlorn and forgotten trophy —the Hat."

More elaborate and even more closely integrated with argument was the rhythmic device Elizabeth Stevenson employed. At successive stages in her life of Henry Adams she introduced, like fragments of subplots, the concurrent phases of the careers of Adams's close friends, John Hay, John La Farge, Clarence King, Henry James, Augustus St. Gaudens, Henry H. Richardson, and Alexander Agassiz. Though all these lives are interesting in themselves, they were adopted for two purposes directly connected with Adams himself: to illustrate the intellectual "cross-fertilization" occurring in this closely knit group which deeply affected his own mind, and also to use the successive achievements of these gifted men as a benchmark by which to measure Adams's progress.

At the opposite pole from biographies distinguished by a conscious management of rhythm and symmetry were those which owed their formal coherence, such as it was, to their very monotony. Produced now by indefatigable academics (as well as by some nonacademic writers whose industry exceeded their artistry), these imposing stores of unassorted information were the modern descendants of the laborious chronicles which, as we saw, the Victorians often dignified with the name of biography. In vain had critics, for better than a century, ridiculed Goldsmith's biographers for printing his tailor's and washerwoman's bills; the distinction between the meaningful and the trivial still eluded some biographers. Week by week, month by month, like the newspapers of which Fielding spoke, they doggedly recounted whatever the records contained, totally regardless of its importance. Triviality was piled upon irrelevance. In Landor's childhood "At least two childhood diseases swept the family: the four eldest children had the whooping cough—we do not know exactly when—and in June 1780 the same four suffered from the measles." Every time Landor's luggage went astray, the fact was entered in the book. Day by day his movements were traced: "Elizabeth kept him at Warwick until about August 12, but he begged Forster to join him at Bath and to stay until the seventeenth or eighteenth, when he had promised Mrs. Sawle to visit her in Cornwall. Forster accepted the invitation, and was at Bath for four days from August 14." So the recital went, the presiding effect suggesting a painstakingly kept engagement book or household diary rather than the life narrative of a passionate man.

These annalistic biographies, heavy with facts that were meticulously arranged but wholly unassimilated, were commoner than they should have been in an age which had raised its standards of biographical excellence. From eight packing cases crammed with correspondence and elaborately indexed scrapbooks filled with the gleanings of the clipping services, S. Foster Damon compiled an obese chronology of Amy Lowell, of which the following paragraph is sufficient sample:

> The summer in Dublin [New Hampshire] was occupied chiefly with correcting the proofs of *Men, Women and Ghosts* and writing

her lectures on the American poets. On July 22, she sent her car over to the MacDowell Colony to fetch the young composer and conductor, Chalmers Clifton, and a poet friend, to dinner. James Whitcomb Riley had just died; when a reporter telephoned her the news and asked for a comment, she said she was very sorry. On July 29, Carl Engel was married; she went down to Brookline for the wedding. He was another of her young men to get married (Fletcher had taken the same step not two months before); it meant the end of those informal long talks that filled evenings absolutely without regard for time. She never was wholly reconciled to the fact. In early August, she had Robinson over from the Colony, to discuss her forthcoming lecture on him. On the nineteenth she read from her poems at the Dublin Lake Club, and though depressed by their reception, was cheered by having Dorothy Foster Gilman, a new admirer, to dinner on the twentieth. On the twenty-sixth she addressed "The Out-Door Players" (Marie Ware Laughton's pupils) at Peterborough on "Poetry as a Spoken Art." Braithwaite, who came up to hear it, reported it in the *Transcript* (September 2, 1916); and Martyn Johnson, who had just bought the *Dial*, and had come to Dublin to talk things over, asked her to boil the speech down for his paper. On Labor Day her house was full in consequence of a Bazaar for the Allies.[3]

Reviewing Mark Schorer's *Sinclair Lewis*, another swollen *omnium gatherum* (though of higher literary quality than Damon's prosaic calendar), Marius Bewley complained with justice that "The biographer-critic or artist, who should be in control, gives way to the chronicler of the quotidian; an extended analysis of the subject's artistic production is likely to give way to

[3] Other modern biographies suffering from the same fault included Denis Mackail's *Barrie*, which in 1941—a year when paper was scarce in England— devoted 719 pages to a relentless recital of Barrie's routine activities; *The Later Years of Thomas Hardy;* Christopher Hassall's *Sir Edward Marsh;* and Rupert Hart-Davis' *Hugh Walpole.* Leon Edel, writing of this last volume, points out that the annalistic method sometimes suits the material; Hart-Davis, "by giving us the recurrent pattern, year by year, of Walpole's life, has made vivid for us how that skillful storyteller lived out a success story—as if life were an engagement book." (*Literary Biography* [New York, 1959], p. 145.) It might also be argued that the same seemingly indiscriminate recital of teas, dinners, country weekends, cruises, and the rest provides a valuable sense of the changed social orientation of the professional author. Late Victorian and Edwardian writers were remarkably gregarious, belonging to numerous interlocking circles—and the more successful the author, the more exalted the company. But one fears that in some biographies the effect, however suitable, was produced by accident rather than design.

the address of his tailor or the school of his analyst. In short, we learn everything except what it is important for us to know. . . . Mr. Schorer decided to throw vast—*really vast!*—quantities of literary refuse . . . down that hole [of Lewis' personality] in the hopes of filling it up." This severe judgment could have been delivered of an uncomfortably large number of modern biographies whose authors were subject, if not necessarily to the calendar, then to the tyranny of their bulging note files. The more they found out, it seemed, the more they felt bound to print.

It could be argued, of course, that no tiniest scrap of information is without its potential significance, whether it be on the day-to-day state of Wordsworth's bowels, De Quincey's tangled financial affairs, the 201 stage roles Poe's mother played, or the schedule of the Boston-Portsmouth stage upon which Hawthorne rode. The increased sophistication with which the interplay of events was studied in the twentieth century, and above all the realization, after Freud, that it is perilous to dismiss any fact of experience, however small, as "irrelevant," provided something of an intellectual justification—though a specious one—for the wholesale inclusion of unsorted detail. But the result inevitably was a type of biography that could be referred to but could not be read with any pleasure, a triumph of miscellaneity that stirred the reader to invert Queen Gertrude's plea and cry out for less matter and more art.

Despite these occasional bulky reminders that the ideal of biography as an art of the shaper had not wholly prevailed, intelligent selectivity, a principle which lay at the heart of the international movement represented by Maupassant, Pater, James, and their followers, was generally accepted as an admirable rationale and guide for biographers no less than novelists. Only by purposeful economy could order and meaning and dominant effect be extracted from the amorphous sequence of events called a life and the chaos of data it had left behind. "Life being all inclusion and confusion," observed Henry James, "and art being all discrimination and selection, the latter, in search of the hard latent *value* with which alone it is concerned, sniffs round the mass as instinctively and unerringly as a dog suspicious of some buried bone." It was this buried bone of value that the artist-biographer, equally with the artist in fiction, sought to unearth. His ultimate aim (to shift the Jamesian metaphor) was the discovery of a significant figure in the carpet of a life; and the figure, once determined, could be represented by a constellation of shrewdly chosen details, those which most accurately differentiated the subject from other human beings and, it might be, also had a symbolic importance as the key to an aspect of character or motive. The artistic success of a biography was determined, in large measure, not by the quantity of details it contained but by the expertness with which its author had selected and used the most pregnant.

Inseparable from the principle of selectivity, in the influential Jamesian critical theory, was the concept of "point of view." The choice of detail for the sake of delineating essential meaning implied the presence of an intelligence that would govern the angle or perspective according to which details would be interpreted, evaluated, and selected or rejected. From the nineteenth century, the twentieth had inherited the almost sacrosanct principle that the most authentic biography was that which let the man speak for himself: that is, present everything from a single point of view, the subject's own. The closer biography approached the mode of autobiography, the better—more faithful, more just—it was. But it became apparent that this was a hollow assumption. Every editorial or interpretive gesture on the part of the biographer—selection, excision, arrangement, commentary—implied interference with the consistent point of view that was supposedly accomplished by limiting the narrative to materials from the subject's own pen. At the same time, it was recognized that, however intimate and authentic a biography limited to such materials might be, it was bound to be one-sided. A biography compiled in the spirit of an *apologia* was scarcely a biography at all.

The life-as-told-by-himself, therefore, gradually disappeared as a distinct type of biography. Either a book was a genuine autobiography or it was not, in which latter case it embraced points of view beyond that of the subject himself. The most prominent of these other angles of vision remained that of the biographer.

In the modern age, as earlier, he could sometimes claim personal acquaintance, perhaps even kinship, with the person whose life he told. Such a man enjoyed the advantages Boswell, Lockhart, and Forster had had as they recounted the lives of Johnson, Scott, and Dickens: he could report from first hand a man's appearance, manner, conversation—all external expressions of character, in fact; and he might often be able to narrate scenes he had witnessed and quote his subject's oral reminiscences of other events. His testimony possessed the unquestionable virtue of immediacy and, presumably, authority. But the handicaps and risks of a biographer in his position were considerable. His first-hand knowledge was confined to a certain span of years and a limited number of occasions; friendship or family relationship was bound to lead to emotional involvement and thus to bias; and the accidents of social relationship might lead him to emphasize his own role in his subject's life and underrate that of others, as Forster unfairly minimized Wilkie Collins' place in Dickens' life.

A major criticism of Forster's *Dickens,* as it had earlier been of Boswell's *Johnson* (and, on a lower level, of Hogg's *Shelley*), was that the biographer himself was too much in evidence. The degree to which a biographer should limit his presence in his own pages remained a matter of dispute in the twentieth century. If he were writing simply a memoir (in the restricted sense of a biography confined to the writer's personal experience of his subject) the issue was not so urgent: the very definition of memoir allowed for his constant participation in the events described. It could scarcely be argued that John Malcolm Brinnin, for instance, in his *Dylan Thomas in America,* was too prominent; the value of eyewitness immediacy in such books considerably outweighed the risk that the narrator would attract attention which rightfully belonged to his subject. But the same tact which would permit a biographer to be on stage, yet not claiming the spotlight, was more pressing in the case of a full-dress biography. The natural temptation was for him to allot disproportionate space to those passages of his subject's life with which he had some connection. With much justification, remembering the way in which most contributors to the swelling biographical literature on D. H. Lawrence had kept themselves in view, Richard Aldington, in his own Lawrence biography, "held personal recollections severely in check." Aldington obviously could have said much more about Lawrence as he knew him, and said it with considerable pungency; but he restrained himself. And Elizabeth Nowell, writing the biography of Thomas Wolfe, referred to herself in the third person in those episodes in which she, as Wolfe's literary agent, inevitably figured.

The proper role of the biographer as an actor in his own drama is one thing; the extent to which he may be allowed to comment on the action from the edge of the stage is another. Carlyle, the irrepressible, editorialized his dogmatic way through his life of Cromwell, pausing with almost every quoted letter to enforce his interpretation of character and events upon the reader. But he was an exception to the general nineteenth-century rule that the ideal biographer should let no ideas or responses of his own disturb the theoretically uninterrupted communion between subject and reader. In more recent times, however, especially with the recognition that a wholly objective biography cannot be written, the right of the biographer to comment and interpret at appropriate junctures, indeed the desirability of his doing so, has been widely acknowledged. But two provisos remain: one, that the biographer should not draw attention to his presence by use of the first-person singular, as some unpracticed hands, bent upon the closest possible rapport with their audience, have done; and the other, that the expression of opinion be immediately related to biographical issues and not extended, as in St. John Ervine's life of Shaw, to an airing of the biographer's own views concerning everything about which his subject also expressed strong notions.

As the techniques by which dramatists and novelists created "rounded" characters were better appreciated, and as scientific ideals stressed the desirability of gathering as much evidence as possible on a given event or aspect of character, biographers made greater use of the testimony of all who had known their subject. A truly comprehensive idea of a man, doing ample justice to his complexity, his human variability and inconsistency, could be had only by seeing him through many eyes. Personal recollections, supplemented sometimes by such disparate other evidence as newspaper reports and even—though the peril is obvious—fictionized portraits for which the real person was known to have supplied the model, provided modern biographers with the small variations of impression, the nuances of light and shadow, the telling incidental details that threw revealing sidelights on men who otherwise might be seen only full face. The great variety of such data in some instances—each source constituting, in its way, an additional point of view—was perhaps most impressively demonstrated in Edward Nehls's "composite biography" of D. H. Lawrence, a three-volume collection of letters, reminiscences, and other statements, written and oral, left by witnesses of Lawrence's life.

But the very diversification of distances, directions, and slants from which the man and his life could be seen had the effect of placing the biographer in a more commanding position than ever. From the various viewpoints a single predominant one had finally to be synthesized, if a coherent version of truth was to be salvaged from fragmentary and discordant witnesses whose reports often conflicted with the account derived from the man himself; and this eventually governing view, only the biographer, the controlling intelligence, could supply. It was his interpretation of character and events that had to prevail.

Even were there not many different accounts to synthesize and so far as possible reconcile, biographers of some figures faced a sufficient challenge in their subjects' own inherent manysidedness. Perhaps the classic example in English literary biography of a man with multiple and mercurial personalities is Byron:

> Now [wrote Peter Quennell] he is Childe Harold, the gloomy wanderer who grandiloquently accepts his fate: now Don Juan, the man of the world who spars against it with defensive irony: now, having abandoned verse-writing, he confronts us as the wayworn traveller, still a man of many different moods, flippant and fatalistic, resolute and disillusioned, yet prepared to sacrifice his existence to a cause in which, he admitted himself, he did not always quite believe. From these images the biographer's task is to produce a comprehensive literary pattern.

((377

There were numerous "real" Byrons; there were also numerous disguises. Somewhere in their midst was the essential, unchanging man himself. And the man was also a poet.

In that last fact lay the supreme problem facing every biographer whose subject is an artist: how to mediate between the two very different yet vitally related aspects of his figure. On the one hand, *l'homme moyen sensuel,* more or less the duplicate of a million others, a thoroughly commonplace mortal with digestion, small impulses, a modest bank account: a Mr. Polly, a J. Alfred Prufrock, interesting only as an atom in a panorama of human mediocrity. On the other hand, the artist, clearly distinguishable from a million other men for the penetration of his vision and his gift of language. Two lives in one, each inseparable from the other, but at opposite poles of significance and adaptability as biographical material. How could two such different characters coexist in the same garment of flesh? This, Bernard Shaw told Archibald Henderson, was the riddle biographers were expected to solve:

> Point out as a matter of common sense . . . that the real George Bernard Shaw was born into the world not by parthenogenesis but in the vulgar way, and inherited all the weaknesses, follies, and limitations of his kind—that he goes about on two legs, blowing his nose and flailing and fudging along as best he can in an extremely prosaic way, perceptibly short of many accomplishments which are fairly common, and in some ways an obviously ignorant, stupid and unready man. Then state your task, which should be, the explanation of how this prosaic reality produces this romantic effect, and does actually get a certain quality into his work, creative and critical, which distinguishes it from the work of men with much more remarkable natural qualifications.

The riddle was, of course, unsolvable: it always has been, and for the present—pending further developments in psychology—will remain so. But it defined the artistic problems, peculiar to their choice of artists as subjects, which literary biographers met in various ways.

First, there was the overriding question of how to apportion attention and establish the relation between the man's outer

and inner lives and, in the case of the latter, between his general
emotional and intellectual tendencies and those which bore most
directly upon his literary productions—the problem, as Henry
James put it, of "the seam between the talent and the soul." Here
a biographer's decision was affected to some extent by the nature
of the available data. Some writers, dreading spiritual exposure,
went to great lengths to conceal their inner lives from the public
gaze. "I have written," said Robert Frost to his friend Sidney Cox,
"to keep the overcurious out of the secret places of my mind both
in my verse and in my letters to such as you." Browning too
sought to camouflage his true self by donning the mask of the
dramatic monologue, and in his outward behavior and utterances
kept Robert Browning, the eminent public figure, and "R.B., a
poem" in two distinct compartments. Frost and Browning,
like Housman and Edwin Arlington Robinson, were reacting
against the free confessionalism of such figures as Byron and
Keats, who provided their future biographers with abundant intimate data from which to construct histories of their minds.

Apart from the adventitious element of material, however, the
choice remained the biographer's. Was his book to be primarily a
narrative of outward events, or was it instead to concentrate upon
the currents of the mind or, for a third possibility, upon the personal sources of the man's art? Roughly, this was the difference of
emphasis one might expect among a historian, a clinical psychologist, and a literary critic. Some biographers, typified by the prolific and readable Hesketh Pearson, unequivocally chose the first
course. But more numerous, and more closely adhering to the
spirit in which the modern age regarded the artist and his art,
were biographies that attempted to explore the inner life of a
writer and to explain, with various degrees of thoroughness, the
origins and development of his talent and its successive products.
The purpose of most literary biography, as distinct from biography in general, was accurately described by Carl Weber, an
American authority on Hardy:

> In dealing with an author emphasis must be placed upon those
> facts which determine his emotional personality, for from them
> emerge his writings. Above all, the biographer must remain keenly

((379

alert to detect those radical discords which result in literary activity. His task is to unravel the psychological complexity and unrest that find release in a work of art. In every author's heart there is, as in Hamlet's, a kind of fighting that will not let him sleep. It is the duty of his biographer to discover the causes and effects of the author's adjustment or maladjustment to his world. . . . One must penetrate into the inner life of the man, learn what he read and what he thought, inspect his secret desires and ambitions, and study his rebuffs and disappointments. The literary biographer's task is not so much to appraise the pearl as to explain why the oyster grew it.

And so the basic emphasis of literary biography, putting into practice what during the nineteenth century had for the most part been confined to theory, was psychological and genetic. Occasionally it resulted in books which touched only incidentally upon external events and paid little heed to strict chronology: Fausset's *Coleridge,* for example, Krutch's *Poe,* Ellmann's *Yeats,* and Arvin's *Melville, Whitman, Hawthorne,* and *Longfellow.* But, more usually, biographers tried to harmonize the course of external events with that of the brain and the sensibility, to relate the exercise of a writer's genius to his experience as a man, and thus to bring into a single focus the separate purposes of strict biography and literary interpretation.

Where the relevant material allowed, biographers could trace the genesis and growth of a poem or novel as one thread among the many concurrent events of the narrative. Under the most favorable circumstances, indeed, it was possible to exhibit so close an interplay between external circumstance, private emotion, and literary creation that the three biographical themes naturally merged into one. Mary Moorman, blessed with the full texts of the letters and journals in which Dorothy and William Wordsworth recorded not only walks and talks and reading but William's day-by-day writing, described each individual poem— itself a fragment of autobiography—as it issued from his pen. By providing a running narrative of his whole creative life integrated with his personal affairs, Mrs. Moorman made clear that the writing of poems *was* Wordsworth's life.

Unlike Wordsworth, who wrote one poem after another and

then periodically collected them in volumes, and Dickens, who wrote novel after novel, James Joyce devoted much of his literary career to gestating one book. He began storing up memories for *Ulysses* in his childhood, but began writing it only in 1914. Richard Ellmann's narrative technique was ingeniously adapted to this sequence of events. He described the origins of *Ulysses'* characters, places, and events in the order in which Joyce encountered them as a child and young man. Then, having reached the year 1914, Ellmann stopped the film and in a retrospective chapter reran the reels with a different filter, this time drawing out from the chaos of events a leading theme previously undiscussed: Joyce's artistic development, the emergence of peculiarities of technique which were destined to make *Ulysses* so revolutionary a work of fiction, and the slow formation of an over-all plan for the book. Once Joyce was seen to be prepared for the great work of his life, Ellmann resumed the narrative and watched the author putting his long-meditated plans into execution.

One more technical problem peculiar to literary biography, and by no means the least, stemmed from another question of purpose. Was it true or not that, as Weber maintained, the biographer's task was "not so much to appraise the pearl as to explain why the oyster grew it"? Some took the position that appraisal was as much their duty as explanation. They had, therefore, to adjudicate in their writing between the conflicting claims of narrative, which moves in time, and interpretation and criticism, which do not. The usual solution was to suspend the chronological recitation of events for a page or two, or even, occasionally, for whole chapters, while the biographer turned critic. The interruption, no matter how suavely managed, could not help irritating some readers, but the major alternative, delaying all critical commentary to the book's latter pages, had equal disadvantages. One indisputable argument for interspersing the motion picture of narrative with the still photographs of criticism was that it gave an expert biographer the opportunity to relate each literary work with the life events which had immediately preceded or accompanied its composition. In his biography of Dickens, Edgar Johnson paused periodically for interchapters in which he not only evaluated each successive novel but integrated it with the larger movement of Dickens' life and art. By skipping these chapters, readers intent only on learning of Dickens' personal life could follow an unbroken narrative. Thus Johnson afforded his readers the clear-cut choice of seeing the drama through without interruption, or having the actors frozen in place while the commentator took the center of the stage.

· 4 ·

As biography grew more comprehensive in scope and had ever larger amounts of data at its disposal, certain other technical problems of long standing grew more pressing. One concerned the way to handle the various strands of concurrent events: a poet's external experiences, both public and private (categories that could be indefinitely subdivided); the development of his intellect; his emotional life; and his literary career. The modern concept of a complete biography required adequate treatment of all of these. Yet the fact that they not only were concurrent but constantly impinged on one another posed a large task. The records might show that on a certain day a great novelist paid overdue bills, worked on a fresh chapter, argued with a brother-in-law, suffered a recurrence of his neuralgia, had a chance meeting in the park with a former mistress, attended a meeting of a committee of authors, and read some pages of Schopenhauer. How was it possible to represent intelligibly this tangled skein of experience?

Ideally, the simultaneity of events and currents of interest should be shown by a kind of narrative superimposition, as if a dozen films were thrown on a screen at once. But the restrictions of language do not permit this effect. One way to achieve a rough approximation of it is to employ a strictly chronological method, the diversified events of each day or week being recited in a tight juxtaposition which suggests the manner in which they overlapped with and colored one another. As was observed above, in connection with swollen catchall biographies, this is not, even under the best of auspices, a very satisfactory technique. The annalistic method is, in fact, the biographer's straitjacket, as James Stanfield pointed out in 1813:

> [It] presents nothing but a chequered display of occasional interest and habitual occurrence; resembling life in the mere glance at appearances, but utterly unlike it in a close view of that seemingly-interrupted, yet *persevering pursuit of objects,* which constitutes the very essence of rational being. . . . Where an interesting process occurs, it should be pursued through the links of purpose, progress, and attainment, shutting out, for a time, the synchronous incidents, which would divert the attention to confused objects, and break the clue of rational investigation; . . . it is [the biographer's] province not only to describe, but connect; not only to narrate, but philosophize.

The biographical artist's aim, Stanfield suggested, was less to produce an effect of verisimilitude—an impression of the illogicality and disorderliness of daily life—than it was to extract the significant themes from the welter of surrounding circumstance. A biographer striving to do so, therefore, was required to do a great deal of sorting and reassembling and, in the end, to quietly violate chronology—as Boswell had done, and as, to select one notable recent example, Leon Edel did in his life of Henry James. At each point where he introduced a hitherto unmet writer or a fresh social circle into his narrative, Edel proceeded to follow out the whole course of James's subsequent experience with this particular influence in his life. This isolation of topic was artificial at best; it bred almost as many difficulties as it solved. The deliberate pursuit of one thread of narrative while others were left in abeyance risked losing the reader in a confusion of dates. But it was a chance that had to be taken in the attempt to reduce the chaos of life to the order of art.

One old coherence-producing device, however, virtually disappeared, and with reason: the conventional final chapter which belatedly described the man's personality and character. One possible reason for its rejection was that a novel could not conceivably contain so isolated a portrait, least of all after the narrative was concluded; why, then, should biography? The biographer's problem, insofar as the myriad details of character were concerned, was one of distribution and assimilation: how best to integrate portrait with narrative. Various solutions were found. Possessed, say, of a dozen short sketches of various aspects of his subject's personal appearance and habits, received from people who knew him, the biographer might choose to reproduce them more or less *in toto,* at appropriate junctures in the story; or he might knock them all down into their hundred component elements (the stammer, the bitter wit, the smoldering dark eyes, the impetuous acts of generosity, the dislike of cats, the reading of the Bible every night before retiring) and insert each separate element where it best fitted into the wide mosaic of the book. Gradually, as the narrative proceeded, the man came alive: page after page, the timbre of his voice, his stride along the pavement, his posture against the mantelpiece, his fits of melancholy, became part of the total definition, and the reader's recurrent glimpses coalesced into a vivid picture.

In developing this personal portrait, the biographer had to convey a sense of maturation and aging, while at the same time preserving the essential consistency that belongs to an individual from childhood to death. It was a matter of keeping a sort of contrapuntal balance between the man's unchangeable, lifelong characteristics and the natural alterations brought about by experience and the sheer logic of the life process. In his biography of Carlyle, Julian Symons traced the steps by which the young Scotsman's attractive, if unpolished and excessively dogmatic, personality hardened with the years into stony intolerance and an unpleasant habit of talking down everyone else—the captive of his ferocious prejudices. And as Forrest Wilson unfolded Harriet Beecher Stowe's busy life in *Crusader in Crinoline,* he showed her as having been, at first, inoffensive and even attractive; but after the explosive success of *Uncle Tom's Cabin* she turned stubborn, self-confident, vain, plausible, even capable of deceit.

Of the many problems of craft inherited from older biography, none was more satisfactorily solved in the new age than that presented by letters. The appearance of definitive, textually sound, and copiously annotated editions of many literary men's correspondences made possible the virtual extinction of the old dual-purpose "life and letters." The full texts of letters were put in their place—in another book; and the life became a sustained narrative, constantly under the control of the writer. The mosaic method, in refined form, became standard: the letters' substance was absorbed, most often in the form of brief extracts, a sentence or a paragraph at a time, into the running text. Although the practice had certain disadvantages, such as the irritant effect of too many quotation marks and, sometimes, the incongruity between the biographer's style and that of the quoted matter, the advantages were greater. By selecting from letters exactly as much as he needed for each occasion, the biographer could borrow his subject's voice and point of view to enhance the effect of authenticity and immediacy; but he remained in control of the artistic process.

In working toward the tightest possible coherence, biographers had to consider afresh how far it was desirable or permissible to allow others to share the spotlight with the central figure. Roger North's was, after the passage of two hundred years, still good doctrine:

> And because it is impossible to account for the lives of busy men, without touching upon some certain dealings of those persons with whom they transacted; whose behaviour and tempers will be interwoven, and make good the fulness of the relation, as things of different complexions distinguish each other; and the most retired converse is material to characters, because a man is known by the company he keeps: it will be proper to insert in this work, the portraits of some persons, consorts and coadjutors, as well as adversaries in business.

Boswell had handled his large supporting cast with skill, but nineteenth-century biographers learned little from him. They either failed to pay sufficient attention to the nature and meaning of their subjects' relations with others, or they embedded, in what was intended to be the history of a single person, a distracting series of miniature biographies, as Southey did when he abandoned Cowper for long chapters while he reviewed the lives of Charles Churchill, Bonnell Thornton, and others who had some connection, often only tenuous, with the poet.

((385

In the new age of psychological probing, it was recognized that many hitherto unexplained aspects of personality could be traced to the influence of a writer's close relatives and friends. It was necessary, therefore, to inquire what, precisely, their roles in his life had been. Secondary portraiture was often essential to the accurate delineation of the central figure. Parents, for instance: in the imperious possessiveness of Ruskin's mother, acquiesced in if not abetted by his father, lay the germ of the psychic agonies their gifted son endured. Hence biographers like Derrick Leon and Peter Quennell had to give the parents the same intensive scrutiny they directed toward John himself. Much of Yeats's early intellectual development centered in his revolt against his father, who had himself revolted against mid-nineteenth-century orthodoxy. And what—could it be known—was the precise nature of Emily Dickinson's relationship with her cold, austere father, a kind of Amherst counterpart of Edward Moulton-Barrett?

Brothers and sisters sometimes handily served biographers' artistic purposes besides casting light on psychological questions. Once her letters and journals were fully published, Dorothy Wordsworth provided her brother's and Coleridge's biographers with a steady point of view, as witness of and participant in the two poets' lives during the years when their gifts first bloomed. The ill-starred Branwell Brontë played an opposite role in at least one biography of his sisters, that by the Hansons: instead of providing a point of view, he was the object seen. His sisters' respective reactions to the successive steps in his moral degeneration supplied an out-of-ordinary means of characterizing them. Their responses on each occasion revealed how far their individual temperaments and capacity for sympathy differed.

Wives too claimed attention. Lavinia Clemens, Emma Hardy, Kate Dickens, Frieda Lawrence, Mary Shelley, Sarah Coleridge— these were among the women whose effect on their husbands' characters and careers was studied. More tantalizing, because more dimly seen, were such figures as Jane Burden Morris, who, Oswald Doughty argued in 1949, had, even when married, a secret love affair with Dante Gabriel Rossetti; and Fanny Wightman, the utterly respectable successor in Matthew Arnold's affections to the mysterious French girl "Marguerite" to whom he had lost his heart one summer in the Swiss Alps, and who inspired some of his finest lyrics. Closer knowledge of these obscure ladies awaited the discovery or release of still unused private papers. There were lifelong happy matches to be celebrated, the Wordsworths', for instance, and the idyll of the novelist-turned-prime minister, Benjamin Disraeli, with his doting Mary Anne. There were others—Milton's, Meredith's, Barrie's, Bennett's, Gissing's —the particular causes of their ruin to be described or speculated upon; and a few, such as John Middleton Murry's tragic third, to be passed over with near silence because the time had not yet come for the lurid facts to be made public.

Although the old-fashioned "life and friends" kind of biography, a characteristic product of the Victorian admiration of amiable gregariousness, faded from favor, an occasional book still devoted excessive space to a more or less irrelevant canvassing of its subject's social circle. This was particularly true of books dealing with early nineteenth-century authors—E. V. Lucas' still unsuperseded life of Lamb, for example, and P. P. Howe's *William Hazlitt*. Less defensible was St. John Ervine's devoting whole chapters in his life of Shaw to the careers of the Webbs, Annie Besant, Granville-Barker, and other celebrities—the subjects of books in their own right—whom Shaw knew. And Robert Cantwell had even less reason for the lavish attention he paid to everyone whose path had at any time crossed Hawthorne's or even merely run parallel to it. It was hardly enough to allege, as Cantwell did, that they had "so much to say of themselves, Hawthorne, Salem, New England, literature, politics, commerce, journalism, life, that it would have been uncivil not to have written of them in all the detail possible." In the new scale of biographical values, significance came far ahead of civility: how had each friendship affected a writer's character or evoked otherwise latent qualities? how had it, perhaps, diverted the whole course of his life? what effect, above all, had it had on what he wrote?

The joint Italian pilgrimage of Byron and Shelley mingled two spirited and articulate retinues—Jane Clairmont, Leigh Hunt, Captain Medwin, Edward John Trelawny, Edward and Jane Williams, the Hoppners. The presence of so diversified a company, self-seeking and altruistic, devoted and jealous, honest and guile-ful, clustering about two magnetic figures during the climactic years of their lives gave biographers a double task: first, to dis-entangle an extraordinarily complicated and unstable set of rela-tionships, for the sake of determining who acted upon whom, why, and to what effect; and second, to evaluate the many ac-counts these men and women left of the poets around whom they circled in a fantastic dance of personalities. Considerably simpler in its pattern, but of even greater importance to biographers, was the coterie of men around Keats—Charles Brown, Richard Woodhouse, John Hamilton Reynolds, Benjamin Bailey, Charles Dilke, and others—whose personal loyalty to that most likable young man won them a place in literary history to which their private talents never entitled them. The several volumes Hyder Rollins dedicated to an exhaustive collection of data on "the Keats circle" struck some as academic busywork, but the new light they shed on the poet's friends also, it turned out, illumi-nated Keats himself.[4]

Yet another concern which modern biographers inherited was

[4] In the lives of more than a few writers occur persons whose influence on the central figure was negligible, yet whom the biographer could not overlook without loss: persons interesting for their own sake, whose presence adds a further reminder of the comédie humaine in which all biographies, regardless of their in-dividual temper, are played. In the Lamb circle was found Thomas Griffith Waine-wright, an artist and journalist of some stature whose propensities for forgery and murder by poison were, in Lamb's time, still unrevealed. Among Blake's friends was another artist, John Varley—a pre-Dickensian eccentric with an overdevel-oped urge to give away his money and a love for wholesome exercise which led him and his pupils, when they tired of boxing, to toss an obliging Mrs. Varley from one to another across a table. In Edward FitzGerald's biography one meets his brother John, a religious fanatic to whom the only joy in life greater than listening to sermons was the delivering of them, which he did, at incredible length, whenever an empty pulpit presented itself. The variety of more or less walk-on characters who add color to literary biographies is, indeed, endless: it ranges from Fanny Burney's beloved Daddy Crisp, the embodiment of eighteenth-century benevolence, past Mark Twain's ingratiatingly hapless brother Orion, whose life, Mark once said, should be called "The Autobiography of a Damned Fool," to the tragic Fred Hankey, a sex-obsessed young man who was Paris pur-chasing agent for Richard Monckton Milnes's extensive museum and library of erotica. Sometimes, also, a literary life may have attached to it an episode that has nothing to do with the central character (except as a leading topic of con-versation in which he surely engaged), yet which cannot easily be omitted. One thinks, for example, of the arrest, eight months' imprisonment, and trial of Jane Austen's aunt, Mrs. Leigh Perrot, for the alleged shoplifting of a card of lace.

the integration of the individual life with its temporal and local milieus. They were part of the *mise en scène,* the representation of which could invest biography with the colorful verisimilitude of a novel. With a few notable exceptions, such as Godwin's regrettable *Chaucer,* Lockhart's *Scott,* Forster's *Goldsmith,* and Mrs. Gaskell's *Charlotte Brontë* (the last a book criticized for its very success in this respect), nineteenth-century biographies had made only fitful attempts to depict the physical and social background of authors' lives. Late in the century Austin Dobson managed to envelop his biographical cameos of Horace Walpole, Fanny Burney, Fielding, Steele, Goldsmith, and Richardson in a circumstantial charm distilled from his appreciative knowledge of the eighteenth-century social scene. But full recognition of the artistic importance of background, not only to re-create the ambience of a life but to forge a link between it and the writing that emerged from it, came only in the modern era. To emphasize the profound impact of place and era upon Virginia Woolf's sensibility, Aileen Pippett evoked the sights, sounds, and everyday habits of Edwardian and Georgian England—the architectural appearance of Bloomsbury, the city's noises, the atmosphere of Covent Garden and Richmond and Sussex—that permeated not only Mrs. Woolf's consciousness but, through it, her prose. In his life of Arnold Bennett, similarly, Reginald Pound devoted two chapters to a detailed topographical and atmospheric survey of "Burslem," down to the very arrangement of rooms in the houses and the rent paid for them, for the sake of illustrating the materials that would form the main substance of Bennett's Five Town novels. In this documentary film technique Pound also exemplified the naturalistic method which Bennett himself employed.

Biographies that succeeded in exploring with tact and truth the nexus between person and scene, between art and environment, were not common. Oftener encountered, regrettably, were those which, following the pedestrian pattern of the old "life and times" volumes, were padded with lengthy and largely irrelevant excursions into political history, topography, current events, and other topics. In F. Homes Dudden's ponderous life of Fielding, every event had to be prepared for by a general reconnaisance of the ground upon which it would eventually take place; twenty-three pages on the London theater of 1729 were the preliminary to the story of the appearance of Fielding's first play, and twelve on the London crime situation had to precede the publication of his *Enquiry on the Late Increase of Robbers in the Metropolis.* Sometimes, also, slices of background description were inserted seemingly only from a sense of duty. When Ralph Rusk moved Emerson to Paris and then to London, he inserted from contemporary newspapers blocks of information on what was going on in those cities at the moment of Emerson's visits; but he failed to show what bearing, if any, these events had on Emerson. Another, earlier, biographer of Emerson went even further. Self-consciously experimenting with the method that was later to dominate the five volumes of his "Makers and Finders" series on the history of American literature, Van Wyck Brooks saturated his pages with atmospheric details intended to evoke the nineteenth-century New England scene in its full picturesqueness. Despite its erudite authenticity and the skill of its inlay, the technique resulted in an illusion of reality no more compelling than that in a Maxfield Parrish painting. It gave the effect of Yankeedom under glass.

At least the seriousness of Brooks's artistic purpose could not be questioned. But other biographers, using the same general method, were too patently seeking the way to the best-seller lists. Just as Forster had loaded his life of Goldsmith with quaintness, giving it a Wardour Street quality not unlike the fake antiquity of a third-rate historical romance, "popular" biographers turned their narratives into costume dramas, the plot and central characters barely keeping themselves visible against the lavish settings. In these hands physical details became mere upholstery; such biographers neglected the great principle that, like the best stage designs, background in biography must be carefully fitted to the purposes and mood of the play that is enacted before it, and extraneous and distracting detail excluded.

At the same time they were addressing themselves with fresh ambition to questions that had confronted their craft from its beginning, biographers after Strachey, compelled by the affinities between fiction and biography, experimented with devices newly suggested by the novel and, in some instances, by the motion picture as well.

Relieved of their heavy apparatus of genealogy, his opening pages gave the biographer a chance to engage his reader and define his theme with the dispatch that had always been available to the novelist. Sometimes he presented an imagined scene. Harold Nicolson's *Byron: The Last Journey* began with the Countess of Blessington, newly arrived in Genoa, anticipating in her diary her first meeting with Byron, which occurs the next day and is immediately described in her words. Thus at the outset Nicolson introduced his hero as he affected one particular sensibility. Sometimes the whole introductory chapter was deliberately limited in scope. In her biography of Henry Adams, Elizabeth Stevenson concentrated, to the exclusion of such customary topics as domestic affairs and juvenile episodes, on a single element in Adams's first years: the way his childhood environment was pervaded by his family's talk of, and participation in, national politics. She thereby announced the theme of her whole book: that "the national self was a second skin for Adams; what wounded the nation wounded him," and that his eventual disillusionment, as a mature man, with the social and political affairs of his country was a prelude to his disenchantment with the cosmos. Although D. H. Lawrence's adolescent experience was as various as that of any youth, more than one of his biographers discussed those years almost wholly in terms of "the son and the lover," a young man torn by a protracted conflict of loyalties between his possessive mother and Jessie Chambers.

Sometimes the classic *in medias res* technique was used. The first chapter ("The Imperfect Triumph") of Symons' life of Carlyle described Jane Carlyle's sudden death in Hyde Park while her husband was in Scotland enjoying his inaugural as rector of Edinburgh University. By developing the irony of this coincidence, Symons indicated at once where the emphasis of his book would fall: it would be the story of a tempestuous marriage and its tragic end. Having intimated the dénouement, he then turned back to the origins of his mismated pair. Elsewhere, a single short scene, transferred from its chronological place, introduced a biography. Newton Arvin raised his curtain on the Wall Street law office of Melville's brothers, where an eccentric physician, having read the manuscript of *Typee,* urges Gansevoort Melville to take it to England for publication. A fateful decision is made, with the hero not even present: Melville's career as a published writer is about to begin.

Other kinds of opening, so unlike the cut-and-dried beginnings in conventional biography, proved equally effective. As Vincent Brome's life of Frank Harris opened, the ailing old reprobate, unrepentant after a career of shocking misconduct, was seen struggling, more or less, to put together a pot-boiling biography of Bernard Shaw. Harris' character was effectively established at the outset: if he was this bad so close (as he plainly was) to the end of his life, what was he like in his prime? Brome's book set out to tell a portion of the answer. Much earlier, Harris himself had opened a biography in a similarly provocative manner. His life of Oscar Wilde began with the trial—for libel, not a criminal cause as one might have expected—of Wilde's physician-father, who was accused of "violating," in his consulting room, the pretty young daughter of the professor of medical jurisprudence at Trinity College, Dublin. Apart from its obvious theatrical value, the scene had the double advantage of suggesting that any son of such a father was worth watching, and of foreshadowing the trials in which, thirty years later, Wilde himself would find his ruin. This in effect approached the frame technique, of enclosing a narrative between similar events.

Once in a while a biographer chose to view his hero's life from the initial retrospect of the man's funeral. Lewis Gibbs saw Sheridan's funeral as the long-delayed conclusion to an anticlimax: the dramatist-politician-theatrical manager's triple career had frayed out, many years before, into the debauchery of a disappointed man. Derek Hudson, writing the life of Lewis Carroll, began with the death announcement in *The Times*, the preparation of various tributes to "the author of *Alice*," the funeral, the distribution of his effects, and the spread of his posthumous fame; only in Chapter Two did he look in on the Cheshire rectory of the 1830's, where the happily proliferating Dodgsons, in due course, produced Charles.

A final opening technique often favored by biographers was the wide-sweeping panorama of scene and era that served as prelude to a birth—the "times" being described before the "life" began. John Buchan used the device successfully in his life of Scott, the first ten pages of which surveyed Edinburgh and Scotland as they were in the year of the novelist's birth. More obviously inspired by the motion picture was Amy Lowell's panorama of the housetops and streets of London in 1794, the camera eventually coming to dwell on St. George's Church, Hanover Square, where a wedding—of John Keats's prospective parents—was in progress.

This device, not alone among the techniques biographers learned from novel and cinema, quickly became banal. It was their glib employment, as much as the falsification of biographical fact, which marked the hundreds of "fictionized" literary biographies published to exploit the market in the decades after Strachey. These were the jauntily written, splashily jacketed books that used the central facts of a writer's life as the core around which was confected a romantic narrative, played by colorful characters who talked and thought in the manner familiar to readers of women's magazines. Because they are so vulnerable to laughter, it is tempting to devote more space to these books than, in fairly long perspective, they deserve. They were numerous, to be sure; and many of them made money for their authors. But since they belong to the history of popular literature as a cultural phenomenon rather than to that of biography as a serious literary art, they claim no larger attention in a study of this kind than do, say, run-of-the-mine circulating-library novels in a history of Victorian fiction. Each book had its brief day in the sun, but since its purpose was to purvey entertainment rather than historical truth, it contributed nothing to the progress of genuine literary biography.[5]

The prototype of the self-proclaimed biography that not only read like a novel but, for most purposes, was one, was André Maurois' *Ariel* (1923). This "life of Shelley," as the subtitle somewhat loosely described it, was presented largely in imaginary scenes and interior monologues, whose substance, if not the actual circumstances and phraseology, was sometimes derived from Shelley's letters and recorded conversation. The embellishments, however—the indulgent irony, the occasional sly innuendoes, the snappy sentences, the "poetic" touches—were Maurois' own. *Ariel* is well-nigh unreadable today; its portrayal of Shelley and his friends as a group of innocent and more than slightly silly children, and of the poet himself as an infant Don Quixote, is enough to offend even the most tolerant sensibilities. Maurois later publicly repented having taken a novelist's liberties with his subject, and in his later biographies, including a substantial *Byron,* he was more cautious in his use of sources. Though he did not forswear fictional techniques where they could be used without violence to historical truth, he never repeated the follies of his youth.

But *Ariel* had the same effect *Eminent Victorians* had: it attracted the flies to the feast. The standard defense of the biography that was neither wholly fiction nor wholly fact was that found in the "author's note" prefixed to the American Frances Winwar's first best seller, *Poor Splendid Wings* (1933): "This is not fictionized history or biography, though it read like a novel. . . . No statement is made, no scene depicted, that is not warranted by authoritative sources, nor thought process extended

[5] Beyond the fictionized biography lay the equally popular "biographical novel," which, making no pretense of adhering to history, simply derived some of its characters (sometimes renaming them) and the suggestion of plot from true biography. Among the authors transposed from fact into fiction have been Milton, Shakespeare, Poe, Dickens, Vaughan, Wordsworth, Lamb, Arnold, Burns, Whitman, Stevenson, Swift, Keats, Gissing, Byron, Vachel Lindsay, Herrick, Scott Fitzgerald, Katherine Mansfield, the Brontës, the Carlyles, Chatterton, and Donne. The distinction between "fictionized biography" and "biographical novel" is, of course, hazy; the assignment of a book to one category or the other depends in part on how freely the author admits that he (or, perhaps oftener, she) is writing fiction.

that is not implicit in some phase of the subject's work." The escape clause, of course, was contained in the final words. The external facts of the narrative could be verified easily enough from the list of books consulted that was appended, by way of credentials, to the text. (No matter if history was sometimes silently adjusted for the sake of a more consistent presentation of character, a smoother-flowing story, or a more dramatic effect.) But the sources seldom gave warrant for the extended scenes, complete with dialogue, that were the forte of the most popular fictionizers. Only a Fanny Burney, who kept her diaries as if they were installments of a never-ending domestic comedy, or a Boswell or a Byron, supplied scripts of whose circumstantial truth there could be little question. For every scene that could be derived in most or all its details from documentary evidence, a hundred had to be devised by the resourceful biographer, with perhaps no more than a few factual hints to go on. The conversations could be fashioned out of excerpts from letters, as they were in *Ariel* and, once in a while, in Strachey; but epistolary accents ring false when spoken, and the device was seldom anything but stagey. More often speeches were simply invented, the implicit rationale for doing so having been supplied long ago by no less honest a biographer than Izaak Walton: "In this Relation I have been so bold, as to paraphrase and say what I think he (whom I had the happiness to know well) would have said upon the same occasions." The modern romanticizing biographer could—and often did—claim that by his immersion in the records he too had known his subject well, albeit vicariously, and so could confidently infer what he would have said in a given set of circumstances. But the results were seldom convincing.

It was the same with "thought processes." Biographical practice had long approved the reconstruction of a man's mental life from the clues he had put down in letters and diaries, and from the refractions to be detected in the autobiographical passages of his formal literary work. With the coming of improved methods of psychological analysis, even cautious biographers felt justified in extending and enlarging upon the more or less fortuitous samplings of inner climate they found in their documents. But to more easygoing biographers the limitation of attributed thoughts to what was "implicit in some phase of the subject's work" was, in fact, no limitation at all, but a license hardly less ample than that which novelists enjoyed. By hooking these imagined thoughts into sequences, biographers sometimes approximated, in miniature, the currently much-admired technique of interior monologue. Thus was authorial omniscience carried to the final triumphant extreme: the biographer reported passages of discourse which had been wholly unheard by the person on whose mental premises it was said to have taken place. To represent these fluent fancies as true biography constituted, in many readers' minds, a willful breach of contract: the biographer's oath had been forgotten in the exuberance of his inventiveness.

· 6 ·

Enveloping all formal and technical devices, finally, and controlling his book's total effect, was the biographer's prose style. Carlyle's pronouncement in 1827, "a well-written Life is almost as rare as a well-spent one," was transmitted to a generation who knew not Carlyle by its paraphrase in the preface to *Eminent Victorians*. Few Victorian and Edwardian biographies had been distinguished for their style, partly, no doubt, because the notion of the biographer as mere compiler precluded the notion of the biographer as stylist. In the general reformation of biographical ideals that followed Strachey, it was agreed that the lives of men deserved to be written as well as any other kinds of narrative. No better statement of the case could have been found than Jeffrey's in the *Edinburgh Review* a century earlier—a year, indeed, before it printed Carlyle's complaint:

> We profess not quite to understand what is meant by the sober style of history. If the substance be conceived in the spirit of candour, calmness, and impartiality, we cannot but think that the more engaging and fascinating the manner can be made, the better —and really cannot comprehend that a history can be too delightful, too entertaining, or too brilliant, any more than too clear, too concise, or too true. To give it *all* these characters, *all* the resources of genius and eloquence may, we think, be lawfully and laudably

employed. . . . We *require* nothing more in a Judge than wisdom, learning, and integrity. But it is certainly an advantage that he should also be graceful and eloquent.

This was the program of the day for young biographers in revolt against the woolly dullness of most existing examples of their craft. Once Strachey had shown that biography could be written with color and verve, everybody wanted to write biography with color and verve. Unfortunately, many who tried their hand at the art had no model but Strachey; having discovered him, there seemed to be no point in looking further. But Strachey's coruscating style was, in the strictest sense, inimitable; any writer who aped it courted disaster. His archness, his questions that did not stay for an answer, his exclamations and ironies—these made the short-term fortune of many a biography in the 1920's, hungry as the public was for the Stracheyan manner even at remote second hand; but the brighter such biographies were, the sooner their light went out. Nothing dated a post-Strachey biography more quickly than its brittle attempts at liveliness. The few that survive do so in spite of that handicap; Harold Nicolson's *Byron: The Last Journey,* for example: "Leigh Hunt was Shelley's fault entirely: Shelley was like that, he let one in for things. One would just mention an idea, and expand it a little, and before one knew what had happened Shelley had shrilled off into another of his enthusiasms. That was the worst of Shelley: he could never see the difference between an idea and a proposal; obviously there was a very great difference."

In America, meanwhile, the ascendant dignity of biography as a genre not unworthy of one's most brilliant prose was signalized by Van Wyck Brooks's displays in his lives of Henry James and Emerson, books packed from cover to cover with an amazing stock of literary mannerisms—exclamations by the hundreds, rhetorical questions, sentences of authorial commentary lined up in antiphonal sequences, flights of the most contrived sort imaginable. To the seething texture thus produced, Brooks added many undesignated excerpts from James's and Emerson's own writings, relatively pale prose as originally written, but which somehow took on flamboyance by reflection.

Brooks's early style, whatever its excesses, could not be laid to

Strachey. Nor could some of the other errors of taste or judgment which followed the master. Nowhere in his books could be found any precedent for the manner of "Romer Wilson" (Florence Roma Muir Wilson O'Brien), the author of a frantically eccentric life of Emily Brontë (1928). This lady—who, by the way, listed among her "References" Michelangelo's "David," the complete works of Nietzsche and Dostoevsky, Joyce's *Ulysses,* and the later quartets of Beethoven—leaned heavily on the I-and-you manner of communication, pitched for the most part on the false-elegant level but often descending (to suit the phraseology to the case) into the chatty-chummy, with much reliance on drastically abbreviated sentences, paragraphs, and chapters. A respectable London firm published the book. Nor could Strachey be blamed, at a distance of twenty years, for the confidential style of Denis Mackail's life of Barrie, in which a substantial percentage of the syntactical units, presumably to add to the liveliness, were not even complete sentences.

Although the carnival spirit on the one hand and misguided artistic ambition on the other led to many stylistic abortions, they were at least proof that in the postwar era biographers were as much interested in cultivating prose as in combating prudery. Some critics feared that too pronounced an attention to style, especially as a determinant of tone, might interfere with the truth-revealing purpose of biography itself. "Attempts to be witty or profound," warned Newman Ivey White, "commonly warp the straight grain of truth and justice. Cleverness and brilliance usually score their points *for* the biographer and *against* his subject. The 'style' may indeed be the man, but it is too often not the man for whom the reader's interest has been engaged." In another vein, Humphry House deplored the distracting effect of Lord David Cecil's style in his *Two Quiet Lives* (Dorothy Osborne and Thomas Gray): "A marked and mannered style infects the whole treatment and sets up in the reader, unless he is on his guard, an attitude to the subject consonant with it. And the guarded reader has to look for Gray through the cobwebs. . . . Where the biographer has a mannered or highly personal style of his own, a new kind of unconscious and illegitimate selection occurs . . . and even in descriptive passages an alien rhythm and an alien style of vision may distort the mood and lineaments which the original documents reveal. . . . The last thing a biographer should express is himself; he cannot, of course, be wholly detached; but every sentence he writes should be an exercise in detachment, designed exactly to bring forward something other than himself."

The incongruence of the biographer's style and that of the author written about did, in fact, lead sometimes to the results House described. A daring alternative, seldom adopted and even more seldom successful, was for the biographer to adopt the style of his subject. Whether it was deliberate or simply the result of long association with the original, Aileen Pippett's sustained pastiche of Virginia Woolf's highly individual style was effective. It proved that a biographer could, through the device of a matching style, appear to merge his point of view with that of the author written about. This, the reader was invited to believe, was the way Virginia Woolf would have written a third-person autobiography. The success of large-scale pastiche, however, depends not only on the skill of the imitator but equally on the nature of the prose that is imitated. Madeleine B. Stern's biography of Louisa May Alcott, written for an adult audience in the style of *Little Women,* was an ill-advised experiment. Unlike Mrs. Pippett, Miss Stern adopted the persona of her heroine, professing to see everything, including interminable domestic detail, through her eyes. Unless one was willing to believe that an ironic intention lay behind it all, the lengthy masquerade in simple sentences, with the copious assistance of clichés and sentimentality, seemed a *tour de force* of dubious worth.

Such large-scale essays in ventriloquism were few. Whether or not they succeeded, there was much to admire in the English that biographers wrote after Strachey had freed the genre from the superstition of necessary prosiness and the genre had, in turn, been liberated from the brash cleverness of his imitators. Style was a means of conveying the biographer's own attitude: one thinks of the occasional wryness of Howard Mumford Jones's *The Harp That Once—*. It was a means of capturing the spirit of the subject: there comes to mind the artfully restrained liveliness of

Lodwick Hartley's life of Sterne. It afforded, in addition, a way of shifting tone, of implying changed attitudes or dramatic situations. In Marchette Chute's *Two Gentle Men* could be found a subtle discrimination of style that brought out the contrasting personalities of her subjects, George Herbert and Robert Herrick. Joyce Hemlow, similarly, adapted her style to the tone of Fanny Burney's adventures and of her records, treating early events as Fanny had treated them, in the spirit of light comedy, and later modulating to a sobriety appropriate to more serious, sometimes tragic, events.

To the intellectual stimulation and sharpened literary insights all good literary biographies offered, there sometimes was added the delight of prose as carefully wrought as any produced in the era. To take up a biography in the age after Strachey was often to take up a work of genuine literature, as full of sensitive art as a first-rate novel. Some biographers, at least, found it possible to deal as skillfully with words as they did with facts. Having taken their oath, they still could be artists.

CHAPTER XII

The Achievement of Literary Biography

T HESE thousands of biographies—books of every degree of accuracy, insight, and artistry—have had an incalculable effect upon our ways of regarding literature and the men and women who have made it. For one thing, today's image of every English or American author of consequence is primarily the accrued result of all the biographies that have been written about him, along, of course, with whatever volumes of his letters, journals, and reminiscences have been published. To a degree, depending on how brightly or dimly the creator shows through his creation, that image is also influenced by his works themselves. The self-revealing element in imaginative literature, however, is seldom literal or precise; because the writer presents himself in the distorting mirror of art, the reader seeking the man can only infer: he cannot *know*. It is therefore from biographies, which rely for the most part on historical evidence, that our conception of a writer as he actually lived is synthesized.

But what pertinence has biographical knowledge to a proper understanding of a writer's work? No sooner had the wave of literary life writing begun to swell, in the first decades of the nineteenth century, than protests were heard against the habit of confusing the poet and the poem and of neglecting the poem for the poet. Wordsworth's antibiographical dictum in 1816, that if poets' "works be good, they contain within themselves all that is necessary to their being comprehended and relished," was fol-

((401

lowed in 1832 by Carlyle's observation that "Even in the highest works of Art our interest, as the critics complain, is too apt to be strongly or even mainly of a Biographic sort." Although often restated in the next hundred years, the complaint became a major critical tenet only in the period from approximately 1915 to 1950, when some of the most influential critics maintained that a work of art is autonomous and complete in itself, and that any discussion of the author as a person is, for critical purposes, irrelevant and actually mischievous. But the authority of the so-called "intrinsicists" or "anti-biographists" in due course declined, and the case for biography as an instrument of interpretation is again being argued by critics who can by no stretch of terminology be called conservative or reactionary.

> There is no "work itself" [writes Leslie Fiedler], no independent formal entity which is its own sole context; the poem is the sum total of many contexts, all of which must be known to know it and evaluate it. "Only connect!" should be the motto of all critics and teachers—and the connective link between the poem on the page and most of its rewarding contexts is precisely—biography. The poet's life is the focusing glass through which pass the determinants of the shape of his work: the tradition available to him, his understanding of "kinds," the impact of special experiences (travel, love, etc.). But the poet's life is more than a burning-glass; with his work, it makes up his total meaning. . . . One of the essential functions of the poet is the assertion and creation of a personality, in a profounder sense than any non-artist can attain. We ask of the poet a definition of man, at once particular and abstract, stated and acted out. It is impossible to draw a line between the work the poet writes and the work he lives, between the life he lives, and the life he writes. And the agile critic, therefore, must be prepared to move constantly back and forth between life and poem, not in a pointless circle, but in a meaningful spiraling toward the absolute point.[1]

[1] Some will perhaps prefer Amy Lowell's statement of the case, uttered at the Brooklyn Institute in 1918, just as the intrinsicists were mustering their forces: "Criticism is not merely an interpretation of technique: it is a tracing of mental bias, a tracking of angles of thought to their starting points, a realization of the roots from which the flowers spring. . . . A knowledge of the man illumines his art if we mean by 'knowledge' a realization of his psychology and its shock against the world in which he lived. This in no way militates against the aesthetic consideration of his art *per se*, but leads in the end more directly towards it." (S. Foster Damon: *Amy Lowell* [Boston, 1935], p. 678.)

Whether or not biography and criticism should be linked, the inescapable fact is that they have been, ever since the beginning of the romantic era. In practice, biography has profoundly and continuously affected everyone's attitudes toward the literature he reads; toward, indeed, his very concept of the *institution* of literature.

For better or worse, literary history is the essence of innumerable biographies. To most people, it is a mélange of more or less vaguely remembered biographical headnotes in anthologies, history-of-literature textbooks that ticked off authors in chronological sequence, fly-specked portraits (the subjects usually bearded and standing on their dignity) on classroom walls, biographical anecdotes inserted in teachers' lectures to restore the drooping spirit, and romantic legends of the sort propagated by *The Barretts of Wimpole Street*. Despite the strenuous efforts made to direct attention to other valid interpretations of literary history (movements, schools, evolution of genres, the influence of the social and cultural environment—all of which look upon literature as the expression of a community of minds) the human being plainly prefers to think in terms of other individual human beings. Abstract explanations, such as those based on intellectual history and the expression of social tendencies, are seldom as congenial to the ordinary intelligence as pictures of people.

But although the psychology behind the phenomenon is easily understandable, the effects have not all been wholesome. There can be no question, for example, that the perennial interest in writers as people has resulted in far too much "criticism" devoting itself to the soul behind the masterpiece, to the neglect of the masterpiece itself. Moreover, throughout the nineteenth century and the earlier part of the twentieth there was a powerful tendency to commit one of the worst of all critical fallacies, the confusion of moral (biographical) and esthetic (critical) values: Good man, therefore good art; bad man, therefore bad art. The character of a writer, as described by biographers, illegitimately affected the response to his work: such was the man, such therefore must be his work. It is also true that the nature of his work influenced the biographers' conception of the person: such the

((403

work, such therefore must be the man. In many cases it is hard to decide which came first, the biographical or the critical misinterpretation; but the reciprocal connection between the two is unmistakable. The Victorians, taught to see literature and men through romantic spectacles, had a low opinion of Pope's poetry; so it was easy to accept the century-old biographical view that he was treacherous, vindictive, vain, waspish—a very dislikable man. On the other hand, the common-sense, prudential values Addison espoused in his essays made it plain to the Victorians that he was a man after their own heart, despite the biographical tradition, then still credited, that he was a hard drinker. The savagery and obscenity of some of Swift's work would have been enough, even without the ambiguity of his relations with two women, to disqualify him from admittance to the Victorian fireside. Such too was the fate of Fielding and Sterne, whose reputations as persons were inextricably bound up with the contemporary distaste for their robust works. It was left for succeeding generations to repair the damage by separating man from work and estimating each in terms of itself rather than of the other: a labor begun by Austin Dobson, for Fielding, and by Percy Fitzgerald, for Sterne.

Biographical accidents, such as the malign one that cast Fielding's fame into the hands of a succession of incompetent or downright hostile writers, beginning with Arthur Murphy, "a credulous blunderer of redundant imagination," were equally responsible for mistaken views of Shelley and Blake. In 1832 Thomas Jefferson Hogg wrote picturesquely and at great length about the poet's youth, when he had known him most intimately. The result was the proliferation of the legend of Shelley as an eccentric permanent adolescent, sailing paper boats on ponds, devouring Gothic novels, and rocking his rooms with explosive chemical experiments. It was this conception of Shelley as a person— strengthened by Matthew Arnold's unfortunately memorable description of him as "a beautiful and ineffectual angel, beating in the void his luminous wings in vain"—which for many decades governed the approach to his poetry. The legend has not even yet been wholly eradicated by the work of scholars intent on reminding us that Shelley grew into mature manhood, developed a tough intellect, and gave up his paper boats and Gothic novels. In similar fashion, the first large-scale life of William Blake, by Alexander Gilchrist (1863), which picked up and developed the many anecdotes about the poet-engraver that had already found their way into print,

> unconsciously helped to popularize Blake as a kind of Theophrastan character type: a lovable, absent-minded, enthusiastic artist, heroic in the sense of doing his work cheerfully and obstinately in the face of neglect, and preserving the peculiarly Victorian and English sense of the right of genius to harmless eccentricities. The biographical part of almost every general book on Blake since then has been mainly potted Gilchrist, and the biographical interest in Blake has been oppressively anecdotal. The consequences for Blake criticism have been disastrous, for the biographical picture thus dubiously highlighted becomes the basis for criticism. That is, the critic makes his value judgments on Blake's poetry in terms of what his biographical stereotype might have been expected to produce.

The history of English and American literary reputations abounds with such instances of biographical stereotypes shaping the reader's attitude toward what the writer wrote. Douglas Bush showed in 1946 how Ezra Pound, T. S. Eliot, and other modern critics used prejudices against Milton the man, some inherited from the previous century, "as a ready and easy way to establish a prejudice against his poetry. . . . The critic's conscious or unconscious endeavor has often been not to study the poem itself, but to fit the poem into his picture of the man."

The amount of mischief wrought by this confusion in the course of critical activity since 1800 is beyond reckoning. Yet it is surely balanced—many would believe outweighed—by the contribution which the wider and deeper knowledge of literary men's biographies has made toward the wider and deeper knowledge of their works. To specify is scarcely necessary: the observation applies to every English and American writer of the past two and a half centuries (as well as a few of earlier date) about whom enough information is extant to warrant interpreting a work in terms of the author's known character and experience.

((405

In particular, modern techniques of psychological analysis have made it possible to apply the data of an author's emotional life to a reading of his works. The exciting and profitable reexamination of Dickens' novels that has been a major accomplishment of English and American criticism in the past twenty-five years was set off by Edmund Wilson's essay "Dickens: The Two Scrooges" (first published in 1940), which found in a single fact, the bitterly attested psychological trauma Dickens suffered as a boy in a London bootblacking factory, a master key to the intentions of his art. Inspired by Wilson's example, numerous critics read with freshly opened eyes Dickens' letters and novels and found therein evidence of a complicated inner existence. Although, as usually happens in such instances, the search for hitherto unperceived depth and subtleties in Dickens' art sometimes outran the sanction both of biographical fact and of likelihood, no one who returns to his novels after reading his best recent critics can fail to profit by the brilliant new light the application of biographical data throws on them.

If, in addition, a man's literary production is to be considered not alone as a collection of individually interesting objects of art but also as the articulate emanation of a mind remarkable for moral strength or philosophical perception, biography often amplifies the effect the reader derives from the formal compositions. This point was made by Francis Jeffrey, writing in the *Edinburgh Review* as long ago as 1835. The biographies of "Philosophers and men of Genius and speculation—men, in short, who were, or ought to have been, authors . . . are truly to be regarded either as *supplements* to the works they have given to the world, or *substitutes* for those which they might have given. These are histories, not of men, but of minds." Jeffrey instanced, validly enough, Boswell's *Johnson*, "a work which . . . has not only made us a thousand times better acquainted with Johnson than all his publications put together, but has raised the standard of his intellectual character, and actually made discovery of large provinces in his understanding, of which scarcely an indication was to be found in his writings." Biography, besides clarifying the literary work itself, might open up contiguous realms of thought and feeling.

More generally, one can say that biography affords a means of enlarging the experience which literature itself affords. To the book, with whatever it contains by way of commentary on human life, it adds the maker, with whatever additional commentary the records of his private self provide. If the book, viewed from one angle, is a reflection of its writer's observation of, and participation in, the lot of mankind, then the relevant parts of his biography serve both as a torch, to illuminate further the content of the book, and as a magnifying glass by which it may be read more minutely.

· 2 ·

Literary biography has its historical as well as its critical uses. To examine its products in their chronological sequence is to gain valuable understanding of what a given figure meant to various epochs; for the reputed character and personality of an author go through the same transformations in the passage of the years after his death as do the interpretations of his works. If "Lycidas" has meant many different things in the course of its transmission from the mid-seventeenth century to the mid-twentieth, the accepted notion of Milton's character and deeds has gone through as many phases. And if, as Lionel Trilling and others have suggested, the poem as we have it today is the sum of all it has meant to successive generations of readers, so also is our conception of Milton the man the sum of the various Miltons who have been portrayed in biographies. Present-day opinion may, of course, emphasize certain aspects of poem or person at the expense of others that are currently held to be less relevant or less "true," but the image nevertheless contains, by a sort of retinal persistence, the residue of former notions.

Thus the history of literary biography, like that of criticism, records the process by which readers from era to era turn an object of literary interest—the received image of a poet, or his work itself—this way and that, each generation adopting the perspective and concentrating on the facets that are selected by its characteristic set of literary, intellectual, and ethical values. In so doing, it provides useful evidence of the communal mind and

((407

standards of every generation since the eighteenth century. A review of the biographies written of Thoreau since the 1880's, for example, offers a shorthand history of the altering opinions successive epochs have had of Thoreau's moral and social values. Apart from the way individual biographies of a given writer reflect current attitudes toward their subject's character and work—attitudes which are themselves determined by nonliterary preoccupations—the very abundance or conspicuous lack of lives of a figure in a certain era is itself a measure of critical fashion. The fact that Cowper and Goldsmith were among the most popular subjects of biographies in the first half of the nineteenth century, whereas no book-length biography of Donne appeared until 1899, is a significant illustration of the whirligig of taste.

Study of the "biographical tradition" of a given author often illustrates with extraordinary vividness the ironies of historical transmission. The circumstances that decide the form a writer assumes before later generations are frequently accidental, with no bearing on his true character or his literary achievement. The artistic or personal requirements of an early biographer may produce an image that proves as durable as it is false. Even before Thomas Jefferson Hogg set pen to paper, the popular image of Shelley was affected by Leigh Hunt's portraying him as a foil to Byron. In his anxiety to present Byron in as satanic a guise as possible (for the sake of venting his personal grievance against him), Hunt put Shelley in a strongly contrasting angelic role, "attractive and not a little pitiable, . . . a saintly consumptive, subject to spasmodic pains." Actually, Shelley was no more an angel than Byron was a devil, but it suited Hunt's artistic purpose to paint him thus. Wherever partisanship dominates biography, the delineation of subordinate figures is bound to be influenced by the biographer's attitude toward the central one—by, in other words, the requirements of casting. Although admittedly the ridiculous figure William Hayley has always cut in biography is supported by plenty of dispassionate evidence, the comic effect was heightened a century ago when Blake's biographer Gilchrist made Hayley "a sort of ludicrous Sancho Panza to the spiritual Quixote whose portrait he was drawing." Often wholly irrespective of facts, therefore, the influential early conception of a writer may be a by-product of another man's biography, and many years may be required to neutralize the fortuitous aspects of that conception and see him in the disinterested light of history rather than that of a biographical artist striving to make a point about someone else.

One also discovers that biographical reputation sometimes is at the mercy of—again, equally irrelevant—moral, religious, or political considerations. Prominent in the history of Milton's fame are Dr. Johnson's attack on him as a Puritan and an antimonarchist, and his elevation to hero rank by early nineteenth-century liberals who found in his political opinions the anticipation of their own—the latter a tendency which, by its necessary emphasis upon his prose writings rather than his poetry, fundamentally affected the nature of his literary fame. Cowper's reputation became the site of a long-drawn-out battle between Evangelicals on the one hand and proper Anglicans on the other, the issue being whether Cowper's madness had or had not been due to the hyperemotional religious atmosphere in which he lived. His cousin, Lady Hesketh, "persuaded," as she said, "that eternal praying was too much," selected Hayley to write Cowper's life from her anti-Evangelical standpoint; the Evangelicals heatedly replied, and the controversial framework was established for the thirty biographies of Cowper which the nineteenth century produced.

At the same time it shapes the public notion of a writer's character, literary biography also influences the popular attitude toward literary people in general. It helps determine how, in any era, the public will look upon literary artists as a class of people, and even, to some extent, how the public will regard literature itself. The intimate material—at first so novel, now so familiar—contained in the biographies of such men as Byron, Shelley, and Keats has been largely responsible for the enduring romantic stereotype of the poet as impractical, visionary, struggling against neglect, disheveled in his private affairs (with particular reference to women), a sensualist, and, in the rather unlikely event he has wealth, a sybarite: the poet in Browning's poem of whom it was rumored that

> he ate his supper in a room
> Blazing with lights, four Titians on the wall,
> And twenty naked girls to change his plate!

The weight of most biographical evidence may be against this treasured vulgar error, but so long as biographical popularizers ply their trade, the myths of the Ariels, the Weltschmerz-filled pilgrims of love and despair who made pageants of their bleeding hearts, and the frail youths who were killed by a stroke of the reviewer's pen will undoubtedly survive.

In literary biographies may be traced not only the evolving idea of the *genus* poet, but, more fundamentally, the changing social role of the writer, and therefore of literature—and even, by not too strenuous an extension, of art in general—since the Renaissance. "The Man-of-Letters," said Carlyle, "must be regarded as our most important modern person. He, such as he may be, is the soul of all. What he teaches, the whole world will do and make. The world's manner of dealing with him is the most significant feature of the world's general position. Looking well at his life, we may get a glance, as deep as is readily possible for us, into the life of those singular centuries which have produced him, in which we ourselves live and work." As we saw in Chapter One, literary biography could not exist until society was ready to recognize the special place of the literary artist in the total scheme of things, and ever since that first recognition, biography's altering attitudes and emphases have mirrored the frequent changes that have occurred in the relations between society and art.

Whatever its services to an enlarged comprehension of the human mind and the ways of society and culture, the primary importance of literary biography continues to lie in its quest for a deeper and more accurate understanding of the mind that produced a poem, a play, or a novel, and hence of the work itself. By continuing to seek new information and to reinterpret the old, by destroying legends and prejudices and misconceptions, by applying to the data of history the techniques of modern cultural and psychological analysis, the biographer strives for a fairer estimate of the author and his creation. In the nature of things, a complete and utterly just view can never be attained: the life records are never adequate, nor can the imaginative powers of even the most acute biographers supply any but, at best, plausible guesses where facts fail. But the very attempt is always worth while, for whenever the study of literary genetics succeeds in throwing even a tiny fresh beam upon a poem, we are by that much the richer.

The past, as reviewed in this book, has turned out to be prologue to a thriving present. Life writing is one branch of literature whose quality has conspicuously improved in our time. But impressive as the achievements of English and American literary biography have been, most notably in the past forty years, there is no danger that it will lack ambition in the foreseeable future. If a great deal has been done, a great deal more remains to be done. No truly "definitive," in the sense of final and unsurpassable, biography of any author exists. A book may contain all the facts that are recoverable, but the need for their reinterpretation continues. Every new biographer, if he is worth his salt, views his subject from a fresh vantage point. The file, so to speak, on an important literary figure is never closed.[2]

Furthermore, the advances that biography has made toward the ideal fusion of historical fact and informed imagination do not mean that perfection is anywhere in sight. Literary biography is still new enough as an art to be hospitable to experiment, and as a scholarly discipline it is malleable enough to be responsive to new intellectual tendencies as they appear. The materials are plentiful beyond our grandfathers' imagining; the methods for determining their significance are surer. Yet these very facts, so heartening in themselves, constitute a formidable challenge to the present-day biographer. Sheer bulk of information can be a handicap, for it can swallow up the essential in the irrelevant and the accidental. Sheer sophistication of method, such as is made possible by the great accretions in our knowledge of psychology and of cultural history, can be a snare, for there is always the danger of ingenuity outrunning common sense. The very novelty of the intellectual tools the biographer now has at his disposal can prove a curse, if

[2] This truth was illustrated by the appearance, in the autumn of 1963, of two excellent large-scale biographies of Keats. Although Keats had been well served by several previous biographers, critics agreed that both Aileen Ward and Walter J. Bate had important new things to say about him.

excitement over a new conception of a literary artist's life and character is not tempered by respect for the possible wisdom of an older one.

There have lately been signs that, faced with a plethora of data, the biographer is tempted to abdicate his role of shaping artist and resume, instead, the less demanding one of the compiler. Admirable though they are as giant accumulations of fact, books like Christopher Hassall's *Sir Edward Marsh*, Mark Schorer's *Sinclair Lewis,* and Barbara and Arthur Gelb's *Eugene O'Neill* are possible portents of a return to the *omnium gatherum* biography of the last century. Admittedly, these volumes present their subjects with far more perspective; they not only "let the man speak for himself" but add, before they are lost, the voices of everyone else who could speak about him. But the burden they place on the reader is no less heavy, and the artistic satisfaction they offer is almost as meager. At the same time, the comprehensive so-called "academic" biography of older figures, full of sternly tested information, meticulously documented, and characteristically avoiding both color and commitment, has flourished. It compels respect for its reliability and for the care with which its author has linked fact to fact through two or three long volumes; but it ordinarily lacks flavor and vivacity, the pervasive feeling (indispensable to a truly good biography) that it is the chronicle of a man who really lived. If the essence of a human being is missing from the very pages that in theory are dedicated to setting it forth, we are not much better off, apart from heightened confidence in the information received, than we were with the old multivolume compilation.

This is not to imply that the writing of literary biography has come to a crisis. It simply means that certain nonartistic ways of presenting biographical material still exist, as they will continue to do. But alongside the studiously undramatic writers of "source" biographies remain the biographers who inherit the conviction, never wholly abandoned though too often neglected in the many years since Johnson and Boswell wrote, that biography is both a demanding and a rewarding form of literary art. "There is no species of writing," observed Edmund Gosse more than sixty years ago, "which requires the exercise of a finer sense of proportion, of a keener appreciation of the relative value of things and men, or of a deeper sense of literary responsibility." To those who practice biography with that awareness, it seems to me, the future belongs. For out of that conviction are bound to be produced more books at least as good as the best that have been written since *Eminent Victorians* liberated the art from the crippling restraints of convention and timidity. They may well be even better, for the more difficult an art is to practice, the more splendid are its successes.

BIBLIOGRAPHICAL NOTES

✴

THE HISTORY of English biography from the beginnings down to the twentieth century has been traced by Waldo H. Dunn, *English Biography* (London, 1916) and Harold Nicolson, *The Development of English Biography* (London, 1927). Dunn's book is readable but superficial; Nicolson leans upon Dunn for his facts and suffers from the indiscriminate prejudice against all things Victorian that prevailed when the book was written. Edgar Johnson, *One Mighty Torrent: The Drama of Biography* (New York, 1937) is a generously proportioned and delightfully written appreciation of "personal literature" in general —not biography alone—which concentrates on the human subjects rather than on the development of the biographical art and its cultural matrix. John A. Garraty, *The Nature of Biography* (New York, 1957) touches on some passages in the history of English biography but does not attempt a coherent narrative.

PREFACE

Boswell's journal: *Boswell: the Ominous Years*, ed. Charles Ryskamp and Frederick A. Pottle (New York, 1963), p. 136.

Trilling's remark is in the introduction (p. viii) to his and Steven Marcus' abridgment of Ernest Jones's *The Life and Work of Sigmund Freud* (New York, 1961).

Yeats is quoted in Richard Ellmann, *Yeats: The Man and the Masks* (New York, 1948), p. 5.

Osbert Sitwell's observation is in *Noble Essences* (London, 1950), p. 3.

CHAPTER ONE

The earlier centuries of English biography have been covered more thoroughly by historians than has the period since Boswell. Donald A. Stauffer, *English Biography before 1700* (Cambridge, Mass., 1930) and the same author's *The Art of Biography in Eighteenth Century England* (2 vols., Princeton, 1941) are large-scale surveys. The earlier book is more critical in its orientation than the latter, which is handicapped by the sheer quantity of material to be covered and in addition lacks both a clear historical narrative and a coherent critical approach. (See severe reviews by René Wellek, *Modern Philology*, XXXIX [1942], 432–436, and Arthur Friedman, *Philological Quarterly*, XXI [1942], 193–195.) Vivian de Sola Pinto's anthology, *English Biography in the Seventeenth Century* (London, 1951), has an excellent prefatory essay (pp. 11–46) on the development of biography through the seventeenth century. Mark Longaker, *English Biography in the Eighteenth Century* (Philadelphia, 1931) is pedestrian, repetitious, and uninformative.

1. (pages 3–9)

Lounsbury on the Chaucer legend: *Studies in Chaucer* (New York, 1891), I, 143–144.

Wellek on the anonymity of early literature: *The Rise of English Literary History* (Chapel Hill, 1941), pp. 1–2. The entire book is valuable for an understanding of the climate in which literary biography began to develop.

2. (pages 9–19)

The books Heywood and Ralegh did not write: Alexander C. Judson, *The Life of Edmund Spenser* (Baltimore, 1945), p. 8.

A charming survey of the printed collections of literary biography that preceded Johnson's *Lives of the Poets* is Walter Raleigh, "Early Lives of the Poets," *Six Essays on Johnson* (Oxford, 1910), pp. 98–127.

3. (pages 19–29)

Walton and the "ideal character": Pinto, cited above, p. 35.

The most recent edition of Aubrey's *Brief Lives*, with a lengthy biographical introduction, is by Oliver Lawson Dick (London, 1949). A revealing examination of Aubrey's methods as he gathered and revised notes on a single figure, including type reproductions of the manuscript pages themselves, is found in *Early Lives of Milton*, ed. Helen Darbishire (London, 1932), pp. xxxiv–xxxviii, 1–15.

4. (pages 29–37)

The quotation on Curll: Raleigh, *Six Essays on Johnson*, p. 117.

Johnson's remark to Monboddo: Boswell, *Life of Johnson*, ed. George Birkbeck Hill, rev. L. F. Powell (Oxford, 1934–50), V, 79 (*Journal of a Tour to the Hebrides*).

5. (pages 37–45)

Johnson on Young's *Conjectures:* Boswell, *Life,* V, 269 (*Journal of a Tour to the Hebrides*).

Walpole's remarks are quoted from his *Life of the Reverend Mr. Thomas Baker* by way of Stauffer, *The Art of Biography in Eighteenth Century England,* I, 544. Sprat's are in his *Works of Abraham Cowley* (London, 1668), sig. e2ᵛ; Johnson's, in *The Idler,* No. 102.

Material on Sterne's contemporary fame is from Wilbur L. Cross, *The Life and Times of Laurence Sterne* (3rd ed., New Haven, 1929), with occasional supplementation from other sources. Bernard Barton's letter to Scott is cited in Wilfred Partington, *The Private Letter-Books of Sir Walter Scott* (New York, 1930), p. 320; the letter to Mark Twain in Albert Bigelow Paine, *Mark Twain: A Biography* (New York, 1912), II, 566. No doubt the fame of other authors has been measured in the same way.

William Jones's Milton pilgrimage: William Howitt, *Homes and Haunts of the Most Eminent British Poets* (New York, 1847), I, 86–89. The Welsh Addison-lover: Martha Winburn England, "The Grass Roots of Bardolatry," *Bulletin of the New York Public Library,* LXIII (1959), 124.

CHAPTER TWO

1. (pages 46–57)

Discussions of Johnson as a theorist and writer of biography include: Bergen Evans, "Dr. Johnson's Theory of Biography," *Review of English Studies,* X (1934), 301–310; Walter Raleigh, "Johnson's *Lives of the Poets,*" *Six Essays on Johnson,* pp. 128–176; J. Churton Collins, "Dr. Johnson's 'Lives of the Poets,'" *Quarterly Review,* CCVIII (1908), 72–97; Benjamin Boyce, "Johnson's *Life of Savage* and Its Literary Background," *Studies in Philology,* LIII (1956), 576–598; Frederick W. Hilles, "The Making of *The Life of Pope,*" *New Light on Dr. Johnson,* ed. Hilles (New Haven, 1959), pp. 257–284; and C. R. Tracy, "Johnson and the Art of Anecdote," *University of Toronto Quarterly,* XV (1945), 86–93.

Johnson's love of biography: Boswell, *Life of Johnson,* I, 425.

"No species of writing . . . ," "We are all prompted . . . ," "The business of a biographer . . . ," "More knowledge . . .": all quoted from *The Idler,* No. 60.

"Nobody can write . . .": Boswell, *Life,* II, 166.

"If nothing but the bright side . . .": *ibid.,* IV, 53.

Johnson's dictum in the Hebrides: *ibid.*, V, 240 (*Journal of a Tour to the Hebrides*). George III and Johnson: *ibid.*, II, 40.

Johnson's dilatoriness and haste: *ibid.*, IV, 34. "This is the work . . .": *ibid.*

Joseph Wood Krutch on Johnson and criticism: *Samuel Johnson* (New York, 1944), pp. 464–467.

2. (pages 58–66)

There is, of course, a large literature on Boswell as a biographer. Perhaps most directly relevant to this chapter is Geoffrey Scott, *The Making of the Life of Johnson* (Vol. VI of the privately printed edition of the Boswell papers from Malahide Castle), a well-documented analysis of Boswell's method of composition, which is now supplemented by the fresh information found in the editorial introductions to the various recently published volumes of his private journals.

"To write the Life . . .": Boswell, *Life*, I, 25. "In biography . . .": *ibid.*, I, 256.

Grub Street biographers: *ibid.*, IV, 34, note 5.

"Sorted till I was stupified": Scott, *The Making of the Life of Johnson*, p. 184.

"I am absolutely certain . . .": *Letters of James Boswell*, ed. Chauncey Brewster Tinker (Oxford, 1924), II, 344.

"an accumulation of intelligence . . ." and succeeding quotations: Boswell, *Life*, I, 29–30.

Boswell's running half over London: *ibid.*, I, 7.

"I profess to write . . .": *ibid.*, I, 30. Boswell and Hannah More: William Roberts, *Memoirs of the Life and Correspondence of Mrs. Hannah More* (2nd ed., London, 1834), I, 403.

"I cannot allow . . ." and Johnson and the dead cat: Boswell, *Life*, III, 190–191.

3. (pages 66–74)

Johnson's remark at Mrs. Garrick's: Boswell, *Life*, IV, 98.

CHAPTER THREE

1. (pages 77–90)

The *Penny Cyclopædia's* article on biography is at IV, 414–416. The other encyclopedia referred to is [Nicholson's] *British Encyclopedia* (London, 1809); the quotation is from the third American edition (Philadelphia, 1819), II, sig. Aa4ᵛ.

Carlyle on Boswell: *Fraser's Magazine*, V (1832), 387–389.

The Stanfield quotations are from his *Essay on the Study and Composition of Biography* (Sunderland, 1813), pp. vi, 224, 302.

Carlyle's dicta are found in his essay "On History" and his lecture on "The Hero as Divinity" (*Heroes and Hero-Worship*, I)—and, as was his habit, he repeated them elsewhere.

The material on positivism is drawn mainly from John Morley, "A New Calendar of Great Men," *Nineteenth Century*, XXXI (1892), 312–328, and *Macmillan's Magazine*, LXV (1892), 388–389. The Pre-Raphaelites' table of secular saints is reproduced, sometimes with slight differences, in most books dealing with Rossetti and his circle. The version given here is from William Holman Hunt, *Pre-Raphaelitism and the Pre-Raphaelite Brotherhood* (London, 1914), I, 111.

Stanfield on the sword of justice: *Essay*, p. 145. The Jeffrey quotation is from the *Edinburgh Review*, LXII (1835), 209.

Smiles: *Self-Help* (London, 1859), p. 5.

2. (pages 91–103)

Because Lockhart's *Scott* is available in many editions with different pagination, references will be made to chapter rather than to the location in a specific edition. The passage quoted from Scott's autobiography occurs in Chapter I; that preceding his letter to Buccleugh, in Chapter XXXIII.

Frederick Lawrence: *The Life of Henry Fielding* (London, 1855), p. v. "Barry Cornwall" (Bryan Waller Procter): *Charles Lamb: A Memoir* (London, 1866), pp. 231–234.

"So long as the poet . . .": M. H. Abrams, *The Mirror and the Lamp* (New York, 1953), p. 226. In the pages that follow I am much indebted to this indispensable book.

Browning's short so-called "Essay on Shelley" is found in most editions of his collected works.

Wordsworth's comment is in his *Letter to a Friend of Robert Burns* (1816), included in his *Prose Works*, ed. A. B. Grosart (London, 1876), II, 11. The *Cornhill Magazine* quotation is at XLVII (1883), 605.

"The widespread use of literature . . .": Abrams, *The Mirror and the Lamp*, p. 227.

"The largest mass of conjectural biography . . .": *ibid.*, p. 249.

Carlyle's dicta on men's lives as poems are found in his essays on Jean Paul Richter and elsewhere; Emerson's is in his essay "History."

Malone's observation is in "Some Account of the Life and Writings of Dryden" (*Critical and Miscellaneous Prose Works of John Dryden* [London, 1800], Vol. I, Part I), p. 469.

Hazlitt's (?) remark is in a review of Spence's *Anecdotes, Edin-*

burgh Review, XXXIII (1820), 303. The Moore sentence is from his *Letters and Journals of Lord Byron* (London, 1830), I, 200–201. The story about Taine and Tennyson is told by James Westfall Thompson and Bernard J. Holm, *History of Historical Writing* (New York, 1942), II, 451; I have not encountered it elsewhere. Its curious resemblance to the anecdote related by Dr. Johnson (note 9) renders it somewhat suspect.

Carlyle on biography illuminating both poet and poem: "Jean Paul Friedrich Richter," *Works* (Centenary ed., New York, 1896–1901), *Critical and Miscellaneous Essays,* II, 101. (First published in the *Foreign Review,* 1830.)

Jeffrey on criticism in biography: *Edinburgh Review,* LXII (1835), 207.

3. (pages 103–111)

The figures on poets' and other literary men's autobiographies are based on the subject index to William Matthews, *British Autobiographies* (Berkeley, Cal., 1955).

Stanfield on the function of the literary biographer: *Essay,* p. 320.

Currie's life of Burns (1800) was reprinted many times in the first half of the nineteenth century; the quotation here is from its appearance in an edition of Burns's works (Edinburgh, 1843), I, clvi. The quotations from Moore are from, respectively, his *Memoirs of the Life of the Right Honourable Richard Brinsley Sheridan* (2nd ed., London, 1825), I, 105, and his *Letters and Journals of Lord Byron,* I, 589. Scott's life of Dryden was included in his collected *Works of Dryden;* the quotations here are from the second edition (Edinburgh, 1821), I, 90.

Criticism of Moore's exhibiting chips from Sheridan's workshop: *Monthly Review,* 2nd ser., CVIII (1825), 150–151.

Scott and Goldsmith: *Lives of the Novelists* (Boston, 1826), II, 93–95.

The irrelevance of childhood trifles: Sir James Prior, *The Life of Oliver Goldsmith, M. B.* (London, 1837), I, 23.

CHAPTER FOUR

1. (pages 112–118)

The phrases from Raymond Williams are found in his *Culture and Society 1780–1950* (London, 1958), p. 32.

Howitt on pothouses, Burns, and Shelley: *Homes and Haunts of the*

Most Eminent British Poets, II, 113–115; I, 396–398, 509–513, respectively.

2. (pages 118–122)

James's remark on the honors and emoluments of the artist is in his preface to *The Tragic Muse.*

The Burns festivities: *Chronicle of the Hundredth Birthday of Robert Burns,* collected and edited by James Ballantine (Edinburgh, 1859), and *Memorial Catalogue of the Burns Exhibition 1896* (Glasgow, 1898).

Leigh Hunt's collection of locks of hair: Edmund Blunden, *Leigh Hunt: a Biography* (New York, 1930), pp. 368–373.

The Shelley shrine: Sylva Norman, *Flight of the Skylark* (Norman, Okla., 1954), p. 195.

Byron's dog: *Memoirs, Journal, and Correspondence of Thomas Moore,* ed. Lord John Russell (Boston, 1853), VI, 126.

3. (pages 122–132)

John Buchan's statement is in *Sir Walter Scott* (New York, 1932), p. 224.

The paragraphs on N. P. Willis are based on Henry A. Beers, *Nathaniel Parker Willis* (Boston, 1885); *Quarterly Review,* LIV (1835), 469 (italics in the original); *Fraser's Magazine,* XIII (1836), 195–203; and Harold H. Scudder, "Thackeray and N. P. Willis," *PMLA,* LVII (1942), 589–592.

4. (pages 132–136)

Yates's own comment on his interviews is in *Edmund Yates: His Recollections and Experiences* (London, 1884), II, 330–334.

Ouida and the press: Eileen Bigland, *"Ouida"* (London, 1950), pp. 42, 57, 59.

Hardy and the press: Florence Emily Hardy, *The Later Years of Thomas Hardy* (New York, 1930), pp. 112–113.

A. P. Watt and Bret Harte: George R. Stewart, Jr., *Bret Harte: Argonaut and Exile* (Boston, 1931), p. 302.

Meredith and interviews: Lionel Stevenson, "Meredith and the Interviewers," *Modern Philology,* LI (1953), 50–51, 63. Shaw's self-interviews: Archibald Henderson, *George Bernard Shaw: Man of the Century* (New York, 1956), p. 424, note 3.

The Dickens dinners: Edgar Johnson, *Charles Dickens: His Tragedy and Triumph* (New York, 1952), I, 339–341; II, 1074–1076.

Meredith's eightieth birthday: J. A. Hammerton, *George Meredith:*

His Life and Art in Anecdote and Criticism (Edinburgh, 1911), Chapter III. Kipling and the Pope: C. E. Carrington, *The Life of Rudyard Kipling* (New York, 1956), pp. 224–225.

5. (pages 136–145)

Dickens and his public: *The Letters of Charles Dickens,* ed. Walter Dexter (Bloomsbury, 1938), III, 12, 52.

Lamb and the London workman: *The Letters of Charles [and Mary] Lamb,* ed. E. V. Lucas (New Haven, 1935), II, 344–345. Moore and the loiterer: Howard Mumford Jones, *The Harp That Once—* (New York, 1937), pp. 312–313. Thackeray and the passersby: Gordon N. Ray, *Thackeray: The Age of Wisdom* (New York, 1958), p. 323. George Eliot's admirers: *The George Eliot Letters,* ed. Gordon S. Haight (New Haven, 1954–55), VI, 27–28, note. Dickens and the Liverpool cooper: *Letters,* III, 717.

Howitt and Coleridge: *Homes and Haunts,* II, 114–115. Dickens' Aberdeen fame: Johnson, *Charles Dickens,* II, 1062. Shaw's fame at Ayot St. Lawrence: Henderson, *Shaw,* p. 794.

Dallas on the hero: *The Gay Science* (London, 1866), II, 271–272.

CHAPTER FIVE

1. (pages 146–155)

Hayley's defense of eulogy: *The Life of Milton* (2nd ed., London, 1796), p. 213. Anna Seward's letter to Scott, dated March 26, 1806, is in Partington, *The Private Letter-Books of Sir Walter Scott,* p. 257; Scott's reply in *The Letters of Sir Walter Scott,* ed. H. J. C. Grierson (London, 1932–37), I, 180.

Dallas' observations: *The Gay Science,* II, 285–286, 298–299.

The Gosse quotation is from "The Custom of Biography," *Anglo-Saxon Review,* VIII (1901), 195.

Suppression of a Rossetti letter: *Some Reminiscences of William Michael Rossetti* (London, 1906), I, 259.

Milnes and Fanny Brawne: *Life, Letters, and Literary Remains, of John Keats* (London, 1848), I, 242–243. The reviews quoted are in the *Edinburgh Review,* CLXII (1885), 36, and the *Athenaeum,* No. 2625 (1878), 218.

Blackwood's position is asserted in "Modern Biography," LXV (1849), 222. Carlyle's famous protest was uttered in his article on Lockhart's *Scott* in the *Westminster Review,* XXVIII (1838), 299.

Morley's lament: *Voltaire* (London, 1913), p. 101 (first published in 1872).

2. (pages 155-163)

Moore's poem is quoted here by way of *Blackwood's Magazine,* XXIII (1828), 396-397.

Tennyson's poem, first printed in the *Examiner* for March 24, 1849, and included in all collected editions, is called "To——, After Reading a Life and Letters." "What business . . .": quoted in Hallam Tennyson, *Alfred, Lord Tennyson: A Memoir* (London, 1897), II, 165. Julia Cameron's report is in *The Autobiography of Henry Taylor* (London, 1885), II, 193.

Browning's "House" first appeared in *Pacchiarotto and How He Worked in Distemper* (London, 1876) and subsequently in his collected poems. The ensuing quotations from his letters are from *Dearest Isa: Robert Browning's Letters to Isabella Blagden,* ed. Edward C. McAleer (Austin, Texas, 1951), pp. 102, 149.

Tennyson and the old lady: *Memoir,* II, 301; Hallam Tennyson's comment, *ibid.,* I, 167. Browning's permission to print: *Letters of Robert Browning and Elizabeth Barrett Barrett* (New York, 1898), I, preface.

Mrs. Gisborne, the Swinburne holocausts, and the destruction of Jowett's papers: *The Swinburne Letters,* ed. Cecil Y. Lang (New Haven, 1959-62), II, 6; I, xxxv-xxxvii. Symonds' burning of correspondence: Horatio F. Brown, *John Addington Symonds: A Biography* (London, 1895), II, 171-174.

The fire at Gad's Hill: Johnson, *Charles Dickens,* II, 963. Edel on Henry James: *Literary Biography* (New York, 1959), p. 38. Hardy's fire: Richard Little Purdy, *Thomas Hardy: A Bibliographical Study* (New Haven, 1954), p. 266.

Byron falling on the Ostend chambermaid: *The Diary of Dr. John William Polidori 1816,* ed. William Michael Rossetti (London, 1911), pp. 11, 32-33.

3. (pages 163-174)

Leslie Stephen on the Browning love letters: *National Review,* XXXIII (1899), 407, 415. Dowden's remarks are from *Fragments from Old Letters, E[dward] D[owden] to E. D. W[est] 1869-1892* (1st ser., London, 1914), pp. 176-177.

Christopher Wordsworth's assertion is in his *Memoirs of William Wordsworth* (London, 1851), I, 89. The *Quarterly Review's* complaint: XCII (1852), 183.

Hayley on Cowper's madness: *The Life, and Posthumous Writings, of William Cowper, Esqr.* (new ed., Chichester, 1806), I, 34-35.

Talfourd's phrases are quoted from Percy Fitzgerald's conflation of Talfourd's two books on Lamb, *Memoirs of Charles Lamb* (London, 1892), pp. 47, 58, 119, 154. "Barry Cornwall's" are from his *Charles Lamb: A Memoir*, pp. 122-123, 162.

Lockhart's comments on Burns are in his *Life of Robert Burns* (Edinburgh, 1828), pp. 60-61; on Scott, in his *Memoir of Scott*, Chapter V.

Moore on Byron's "affairs of gallantry": *Letters and Journals of Lord Byron*, II, 51. *Fraser's* review of Moore is quoted from III (1831), 241.

Moore on Sheridan: *Memoirs of Sheridan*, II, 74, 174-175.

Mason's editorial misdeeds: *Correspondence of Thomas Gray*, ed. Paget Toynbee and Leonard Whibley (Oxford, 1935), I, xiv-xv; Edmund Gosse, *Thomas Gray* (London, 1882), p. 214. The rephrasing of Southey's indelicate metaphor: Partington, *The Private Letter-Books of Sir Walter Scott*, p. 77 and note. Cross's bowdlerization of George Eliot: *The George Eliot Letters*, ed. Haight, I, xiii-xvi. Her letter to a friend is in the same volume, p. 255. For a detailed analysis of the various motives that led Dickens' sister-in-law to exercise her editorial pen and scissors on his letters, see Arthur A. Adrian, *Georgina Hogarth and the Dickens Circle* (London, 1957), pp. 216-224.

4. (pages 174-180)

Contemporary opinion of Sir Percy Florence Shelley: Norman, *Flight of the Skylark*, pp. 215-217, 219. This book and Robert M. Smith *et al.*, *The Shelley Legend* (New York, 1945) contain the fullest accounts of Lady Shelley's exertions; neither is wholly free from bias.

Hogg's falsifications: Kenneth Neill Cameron, *Shelley and His Circle 1773-1822* (Cambridge, Mass., 1961), II, 668-670; Norman, *Flight of the Skylark*, pp. 197-200.

Shelley Memorials: Norman, *Flight of the Skylark*, p. 209.

Trelawny's remark is in *Letters of Edward John Trelawny*, ed. H. Buxton Forman (London, 1910), p. 233. Rossetti's letter to Garnett, dated June 11, 1869: *Letters About Shelley, Interchanged by Three Friends*, ed. R. S. Garnett (London, 1917), pp. 21-22.

Dowden's remark about the bishopric is in *Letters of Edward Dowden and His Correspondents* (London, 1914), p. 196. "I understand how they must feel . . .": *Letters About Shelley*, p. 116. "Oppressed by the duty . . .": *Fragments from Old Letters* (cited above, Section 3), p. 179. "I should like nothing worse . . .": *Letters About Shelley*, p. 118.

The quotations from *The Real Shelley* are from I, 12, 9, and 216 respectively; the epithets applied to its author, from Jeaffreson's *A Book of Recollections* (London, 1894), II, 155. The latter book recounts (II, 145–155) the whole squalid story of the writing of *The Real Shelley*.

CHAPTER SIX

1. (pages 181–186)

Carlyle's dicta on biography: "Rich as we are . . ." and "stone is laid . . .": from his essay on Richter, *Edinburgh Review*, XLVI (1827), 177, 178; "mere Indexes . . ." and "The truth is . . .": from his *Foreign Review* essay on Richter (1830), reprinted in *Critical and Miscellaneous Essays*, II, 101; "genuinely-good *Biographies* . . .": from "Biography," *Fraser's Magazine*, V (1832), 260.

2. (pages 186–190)

Gosse on the widow-biographer: "The Custom of Biography," *Anglo-Saxon Review*, VIII (1901), 205–206. Criticism of Mrs. Kingsley: *Blackwood's Magazine*, CXXI (1877), 184, and *Westminster Review*, CVII (1877), 384.

Christopher Wordsworth's qualifications: *Autobiography of Henry Taylor*, II, 58.

Thackeray's "forbidding" a biography: Malcolm Elwin, *Thackeray: A Personality* (London, 1932), p. 393.

Moore's remark to Rogers is quoted in H. M. Jones, *The Harp That Once—*, p. 270; Irving's letter to Moore in Stanley T. Williams, *The Life of Washington Irving* (New York, 1935), II, 18. Dowden's comments on his artistry are in *Fragments from Old Letters*, p. 161, and *Letters of Edward Dowden*, p. 164.

3. (pages 190–205)

Dryden on Plutarch: *Dryden's Works*, ed. Walter Scott and George Saintsbury (London, 1892), XVII, 62–63. Roger North on realism: *The Lives of the Right Hon. Francis North . . . , the Hon. Sir Dudley North, . . . and the Hon. and Rev. Dr. John North* (London, 1826), I, 154; his phrase "*copia* of matter" is *ibid.*, I, xiv.

Prior's comments are in his *Life of Goldsmith*, I, viii–ix; II, 158.

Moore on "a great mind in its undress": *Letters and Journals of Lord Byron*, I, 435.

Coleridge on addiction to minutiae: *The Friend* (London, 1850), II, 225.

Ruskin's remark on the confusion of epistolary talk with vital fact: *Praeterita*, in *Works*, ed. E. T. Cook and Alexander Wedderburn (London, 1903-12), XXXV, 124.

Mason's sentence is in his "Memoirs" of Gray, prefixed to *The Poems of Mr. Gray* (2nd ed., London, 1775), I, 401.

Hazlitt on the value of private letters: "Letters of Horace Walpole," *Edinburgh Review*, XXXI (1818), 83.

Johnson on Goldsmith: Boswell, *Life*, II, 237.

Currie's explanation is in his memoir of Burns, quoted here from the Edinburgh, 1843, edition of Burns's *Works*, I, clv.

Monckton Milnes: *Life of Keats*, I, xiii. The *Quarterly's* comment, not related to Milnes, is in CXIX (1866), 155.

Dr. Beattie on mosaicmaking: *Life and Letters of Thomas Campbell* (London, 1850), I, x.

Richard Cumberland's remarks on epistolary fiction are in his novel *Henry* (2nd ed., London, 1795), I, 204.

The wastebasket chapter referred to is in W. Carew Hazlitt, *Memoirs of William Hazlitt* (London, 1867), II, 1-10.

On Gray's editorial lapses, see above, notes to Chapter Five, Section 3. Lockhart's technique as editor of Scott documents is discussed by (among others) Davidson Cook, "Lockhart's Treatment of Scott's Letters," *Nineteenth Century*, CII (1927), 382-398, and Francis Russell Hart, "Proofreading Lockhart's *Scott*: The Dynamics of Biographical Reticence," *Studies in Bibliography*, XIV (1961), 3-22. For a rationalization of nineteenth-century biographers' freedom with their texts, see F. R. Hart, "Boswell and the Romantics: A Chapter in the History of Biographical Theory," *ELH*, XXVII (1960), especially p. 56 ff.

Moore to Murray: quoted in Jones, *The Harp That Once—*, p. 352.

Charles Whibley's assertion is in "The Limits of Biography," *Nineteenth Century*, XLI (1897), 435; Sidney Lee's in his lecture, "Principles of Biography" (1911), *Elizabethan and Other Essays* (Oxford, 1929), pp. 50-51.

James's statement of the artist's problem is in his preface to *Roderick Hudson*.

4. (pages 205-213)

The recommendation of Lucy Hutchinson is found in the editor's preface to her *Memoirs of the Life of Colonel Hutchinson* (3rd ed., London, 1810), I, xxviii. Irving's letter to Moore is quoted by Williams, *Life of Washington Irving*, II, 18. Carlyle's views are in his essay on "Biography," *Fraser's Magazine*, V (1835), 255, 257.

George Eliot's letter to Mrs. Gaskell: *The George Eliot Letters,* ed. Haight, II, 315.

Fitzjames Stephen's remark is quoted from his *Cambridge Essays* (1855) by Richard Stang, *The Theory of the Novel in England 1850–1870* (New York, 1959), p. 150. The unnamed critic next quoted was writing in the *North British Review,* XXIX (1858), 472.

The *Edinburgh Review's* comments on Mrs. Gaskell's *Charlotte Brontë* are in CVI (1857), 155.

The recommendation that novelists practice biography appeared in the *Athenaeum,* No. 2676 (1879), 177.

Lamb's objection to Godwin's *Chaucer* is in *Letters of Charles Lamb,* ed. Lucas, I, 361.

A large collection of reports of Byron's conversation is found in Ernest J. Lovell, Jr., *His Very Self and Voice* (New York, 1954). A similar collection relating to Coleridge is available in Richard W. Armour and Raymond F. Howes, *Coleridge the Talker* (Ithaca, N.Y., 1940).

The excerpts from Lockhart's *Scott* are from Chapters XVIII and XXXVIII, respectively.

5. (pages 213–218)

The comment on the title of Forster's *Goldsmith: Athenaeum,* No. 1069 (1848), 405.

The *Quarterly's* opinion of the *Goldsmith* is quoted from XCV (1854), 448.

Criticism of Fitzgerald's *Sterne: Blackwood's Magazine,* XCVII (1865), 541, 555.

The *Westminster Review* on Milnes's *Keats:* L (1849), 349.

6. (pages 218–222)

Godwin's strictures are in his *Life of Geoffrey Chaucer* (London, 1803), I, viii. Scott's criticism of the book is in the *Edinburgh Review,* III (1804), 439–440.

The characterization of Masson is quoted from an unnamed source in the *Spectator,* LIV (1881), 1609.

7. (pages 222–228)

Leslie Stephen on psychology in biography: *National Review,* XXII (1893), 181.

Moore on the same topic: *Letters and Journals of Lord Byron,* II, 782.

Carlyle: "Richter," *Critical and Miscellaneous Essays,* II, 101.

Lockhart on Burns's sentiments as a father: *Life of Burns,* pp. 60–61.

Morley's observation on the need for deeper psychological knowledge: *Rousseau* (London, 1886), I, 16 (first published in 1873).

8. (pages 228–232)

Malone's methods of biographical research are studied by James M. Osborn, *John Dryden: Some Biographical Facts and Problems* (New York, 1940), pp. 39–71. The quoted phrase is on p. 68.

Dickens on Forster as a biographer: *Letters,* ed. Dexter, II, 84.

CHAPTER SEVEN

1. (pages 233–242)

The *Saturday Review's* metaphors are at LV (1883), 502, and LVIII (1884), 598.

On the uproar over the publication of Keats's letters, see *The Letters of John Keats,* ed. Hyder E. Rollins (Cambridge, Mass., 1958), I, 4–6.

Benson's remark is in "On Undesirable Information," *Contemporary Review,* LXVIII (1895), 131–132. Yeats is quoted in Ellmann, *Yeats: The Man and the Masks,* p. 5.

Blackwood's law: LXV (1849), 222.

Henley's attack on Balfour's *Stevenson: Pall Mall Magazine,* XXV (1901), 505, 508. Colvin's censorship is described by Bradford A. Booth in the *Victorian Newsletter,* No. 8 (Autumn, 1955), p. 3. On the suppression of Clayton Hamilton's book see *A Stevenson Library . . . Formed by Edwin J. Beinecke,* ed. George L. McKay (New Haven, 1952), II, 542–543.

2. (pages 242–248)

Tennyson's lines are in "Locksley Hall Sixty Years After" (1886). Havelock Ellis' "Open Letter" appeared in his volume *Views and Reviews* (1st ser., London, 1932), pp. 86–99.

The sentence from Frederick Graves's "The Rakers": *Westminster Review,* CLXXVI (1911), 686.

Wells's protest was contained in a talk of 1911, printed in his *An Englishman Looks at the World* (London, 1914) and reprinted in *Henry James and H. G. Wells: A Record of Their Friendship,* ed. Leon Edel and Gordon N. Ray (Urbana, Ill., 1958), pp. 131–156. The quoted passage is on p. 153. Gosse's protest occurs in "The Ethics of Biography," *Cosmopolitan Magazine*, XXXV (1903), 317, 323.

Gosse and the Eumenides: *The Swinburne Letters*, ed. Lang, I, xlix. Gosse's letter to Baring: Evan Charteris, *The Life and Letters of Sir Edmund Gosse* (New York, 1931), p. 407.

Pound's review is in *Poetry: A Magazine of Verse*, XI (1918), 322–329. The quoted passage is on p. 322.

CHAPTER EIGHT

The history of biography in America has been surveyed in a small book, Dana Kinsman Merrill, *The Development of American Biography* (Portland, Maine, 1932), and a large one, Edward H. O'Neill, *A History of American Biography 1800–1935* (Philadelphia, 1935). Neither is very satisfactory.

1. (pages 249–260)

The Emerson quotations are from his *Journals*, ed. Edward Waldo Emerson and Waldo Emerson Forbes (Boston, 1909–14), V, 208; III, 440–441. Lowell's remark is in his *Letters*, ed. Charles Eliot Norton (New York, 1894), I, 90–91.

Southern Literary Messenger: XXXIII (1856), 283, 286.

Dennie's remark on authorship is paraphrased in Van Wyck Brooks, *The Times of Melville and Whitman* (New York, 1947), p. 476. Stephen Longfellow is quoted in Samuel Longfellow, *Life of Henry Wadsworth Longfellow* (Boston, 1886), I, 56.

Timrod is quoted by Brooks, *The Times of Melville and Whitman*, p. 53, note.

Irving's letter is in Pierre M. Irving, *The Life and Letters of Washington Irving* (New York, 1863–64), IV, 228–229.

Holden's Dollar Magazine: V (1850), 112.

Dickens on Thomas Powell: *Letters*, ed. Dexter, II, 181–183, 191, 193, 201. See also Wilfred Partington, "Should a Biographer Tell?" *Atlantic Monthly*, CLXXX (August, 1947), 56–63.

2. (pages 260–268)

Fields, Longfellow, and book promotion: William Charvat, "James T. Fields and the Beginnings of Book Promotion, 1840–1855," *Huntington Library Quarterly*, VIII (1944), 86.

W. M. Fullerton's article on Longfellow's study is reproduced in Samuel Longfellow, *Final Memorials of Henry Wadsworth Longfellow* (Boston, 1887), pp. 401–406.

Howells tells the story of Garfield's veranda in *Years of My Youth* (New York, 1916), pp. 204–205.

Bliss Perry on Whitman: *Walt Whitman* (Boston, 1906), p. 246. Whitman's remark is in Richard Maurice Bucke, *Walt Whitman* (Philadelphia, 1883), p. 8.

3. (pages 268–278)

Material on Griswold is from Arthur Hobson Quinn, *Edgar Allan Poe: A Critical Biography* (New York, 1941), Chapter XX.

Whittier's poem (quoted only in part) is "My Namesake," first published in *Harper's Weekly*, I (1857), 323.

On Pierre Irving and Richard Bentley, see the former's *Life and Letters of Irving*, IV, 337, 214–215.

Emerson and Miss Thoreau: F. B. Sanborn, *Henry D. Thoreau* (Boston, 1910), pp. 305–306 (first published in 1882).

The passages on nonresearch quoted from Woodberry's 1909 *Poe* are at I, vi and 102–103, note.

Bliss Perry on Whitman's social acceptability: *Whitman*, p. 123.

Woodberry on Poe's drinking and self-indulgence: *Edgar Allan Poe* (Boston, 1913), pp. 348, 350 (first published in 1885).

William Roscoe Thayer's judgment is in "Biography," *North American Review*, CLXXX (1905), 266.

CHAPTER NINE

1. (pages 281–289)

James L. Clifford, *Biography as an Art: Selected Criticism 1560–1960* (New York, 1962), p. 247, lists fourteen books and essays dealing with Strachey as a biographer. To these may be added:

Noel Annan, "Lytton Strachey and His Critics," *Listener*, XLI (1949), 848–849.

Edmund Gosse, "The Agony of the Victorian Age," *Some Diversions of a Man of Letters* (London, 1919), pp. 313–337.

J. K. Johnstone, *The Bloomsbury Group* (London, 1954), pp. 113–125, 267–319.

André Maurois, "Lytton Strachey," *Prophets and Poets* (New York, 1935), pp. 215–242.

Prince D. S. Mirsky, "Mr. Lytton Strachey," *London Mercury*, VIII (1923), 175–184.

F. A. Simpson, "Methods of History," *Spectator*, CLXXII (1944), 7–8.

There is an annotated bibliography of writings about Strachey, compiled by Martin Kallich, in *English Fiction in Transition,* V (1962), No. 3, pp. 1-77.

Kingsmill described his first encounter with *Eminent Victorians* in *The Progress of a Biographer* (London, 1949), pp. 4-7; Pearson, in *Thinking It Over* (London, 1938), pp. 203-204; Russell, in "Portraits from Memory: II," *Listener,* XLVIII (1952), 98.

E. M. Forster called Strachey's style "admirable" in the *Listener,* XLVIII (1952), 142.

Trevelyan's observation is quoted by André Maurois, *I Remember, I Remember* (New York, 1942), p. 194.

2. (pages 289-300)

Maurois' remark appears in his essay "The Modern Biographer," *Yale Review,* new ser., XVII (1928), 231; Virginia Woolf's in "The New Biography," *Granite and Rainbow* (New York, 1958), p. 151 (originally in the *New York Herald Tribune Books,* October 30, 1927).

Hesketh Pearson on the future of biography: *Ventilations: Being Biographical Asides* (Philadelphia, 1930), pp. 66, 68.

Gamaliel Bradford on "the new biography": letter of November 19, 1929, to George F. Bowerman, in *The Letters of Gamaliel Bradford 1918-1931,* ed. Van Wyck Brooks (Boston, 1934), p. 329.

Amy Lowell on the Freudian age: *Keats* (Boston, 1925), II, 57.

De Voto on debunking biography: "The Skeptical Biographer," *Harper's Magazine,* CLXVI (1933), 183.

Carswell on Scott: *Sir Walter: A Four-Part Study in Biography* (London, 1930), p. 161.

Gorman's book is *A Victorian American: Henry Wadsworth Longfellow* (New York, 1926).

Arvin's comments: *Hawthorne* (Boston, 1929), pp. 203-204. Thompson on Longfellow: *Young Longfellow (1807-1843)* (New York, 1938), p. xiii.

Katharine Anthony's dictum is in *Margaret Fuller: A Psychological Biography* (New York, 1920), pp. 57-58.

Frank Harris on the difficulty of biography: "The Art of Biography," *Confessional* (New York, 1930), p. 171.

CHAPTER TEN

There is an invaluable bibliography of twentieth-century criticism of biography in Clifford, *Biography as an Art,* pp. 241-248. (It should be borne in mind that this list does not include the books and articles represented in the anthology itself.) The following additional items are worth consulting:

St. John Adcock, "Much Ado About Biography," *Bookman* (London), LXXVI (1929), 108–110.

Percy H. Boynton, "Biography and the Personal Equation," *Some Contemporary Americans* (Chicago, 1924), pp. 242–264.

Oscar James Campbell, "The Biographical Approach to Literature," *English Journal* (College Edition), XXV (1936), 292–307.

John Galsworthy, *The Creation of Character in Literature* (Romanes Lecture, Oxford, 1931).

Humphry House, "The Present Art of Biography," *All in Due Time* (London, 1955), pp. 258–268.

Allen Johnson, "Tendencies of Recent American Biography," *Yale Review*, new ser., I (1912), 390–403.

Paul Murray Kendall, *The Art of Biography* (New York, 1965).

"On Reading Biographies," *Saturday Review of Literature*, VI (1929), 337, 340.

Peter Quennell, "The Mighty Dead," *The Sign of the Fish* (New York, 1960), pp. 150–173.

Gordon N. Ray, "The Undoctored Incident" (Founders Day Address, New York University, 1961; brochure issued by the university).

Mark Schorer, "The Burdens of Biography," *Michigan Quarterly Review*, I (1962), 249–258.

Stephen Spender, "How Much Should a Biographer Tell?" *Saturday Review*, XLVII (January 25, 1964), 16–19.

1. (pages 301–314)

MacCarthy's "Lytton Strachey and the Art of Biography" is reprinted in *Memories* (London, 1953), pp. 31–49. The sentence quoted is on p. 32.

Walter Bagehot's remark is in "The Character of Sir Robert Peel" (1856), reprinted in *Biographical Studies* (London, 1907), p. 1.

Leyda: *The Years and Hours of Emily Dickinson* (New Haven, 1960), I, xix.

The quotation from *Cakes and Ale* is from the Garden City, N. Y., edition (1930), p. 156.

A. C. Benson's view is expressed in "The Art of the Biographer," *Essays by Divers Hands* (Transactions of the Royal Society of Literature), new ser., VI (1926), pp. 140, 163. Nock's is in "The Purpose of Biography," *Atlantic Monthly*, CLXV (1940), 340–341.

The dramatic story of Mrs. Langley Moore's gaining access to the Wentworth and Lovelace papers in 1957 was told in a series of articles in the London *Sunday Times.* These were later gathered in a brochure, *The Great Byron Adventure,* by her American publishers, J. B. Lippincott Company.

The discovery of Dickens letters in a deedbox was described by K. J. Fielding, "New Letters from Charles Dickens to John Forster: How the Letters Were Found," *Boston University Studies in English,* II (1956), 140–141. On De Quincey and his creditors, see Horace A. Eaton, *Thomas De Quincey: A Biography* (New York, 1936), *passim.*

Books alluded to in the paragraphs on new information are Charles Tennyson, *Alfred Tennyson* (London, 1949); Leon Edel, *Henry James: The Untried Years* (Philadelphia, 1953) and *Henry James: The Middle Years* (Philadelphia, 1962); Iris Origo, *The Last Attachment* (New York, 1949); Admiral Sir William James, *John Ruskin and Effie Gray* (New York, 1947), and J. H. Whitehouse, *Vindication of Ruskin* (London, 1950). The fullest source of information on Dickens and Ellen Ternan, which reviews the gradual disclosure of the relationship in the years following 1934, is Ada Nisbet, *Dickens and Ellen Ternan* (Berkeley, Cal., 1952). Although most of the facts concerning Wilkie Collins' odd domestic arrangements were divulged in 1939—in Gladys Storey's *Dickens and Daughter* and C. K. Hyder, "Wilkie Collins and *The Woman in White*," *PMLA,* LIV, 297–303—they were first fitted into a book-length study by Kenneth Robinson (*Wilkie Collins: A Biography,* 1952).

2. (pages 314–329)

The paragraph on the unreliability of writers' autobiographical statements is based on Paine, *Mark Twain,* I, xix; Irving Howe, *Sherwood Anderson* (New York, 1951), pp. 18–24; Denis Mackail, *Barrie: The Story of J. M. B.* (London, 1941), pp. 5, 90–91; Joseph Hone, *The Life of George Moore* (New York, 1936), pp. 72–73, 187; Ellmann, *Yeats: The Man and the Masks,* pp. 2–4; Jocelyn Baines, *Joseph Conrad: A Critical Biography* (London, 1960), pp. 46–53; Henderson, *Shaw,* pp. 64–65; Hesketh Pearson, *G.B.S.: A Postscript* (New York, 1950), p. 19. There is a good general discussion of the problem of autobiographical statements in Roy Pascal, *Design and Truth in Autobiography* (London, 1960), Chapters V and XII.

Cecil's observation is in *Two Quiet Lives: Dorothy Osborne [and] Thomas Gray* (Indianapolis, 1948), pp. 109–110.

Lockhart on conversations and letters: *Memoir of Scott,* Chapter XLI; *Life of Burns,* pp. 260–261.

Randall Stewart's comments are in *Nathaniel Hawthorne: A Biography* (New Haven, 1948), p. 37.

On the "enormously varied and subtle" ways in which "the person affects and is revealed in his creations," see Patrick Cruttwell, "Makers and Persons," *Hudson Review*, XII (1959–60), 487–507.

Conrad's Marseilles period: Baines, *Conrad*, pp. 46–53 (the quotation is from p. 46).

Wolfe and Eliot on falsely attributed autobiography: Elizabeth Nowell, *Thomas Wolfe: A Biography* (New York, 1960), p. 11; Eliot, "Shakespeare and the Stoicism of Seneca," *Selected Essays* (3rd ed., London, 1961), p. 127.

Wilbur Cross's remark is in his *Life and Times of Laurence Sterne,* pp. xiv–xv.

The doubtful anecdotes referred to are examined in the following places: Maurice Johnson, "A Literary Chestnut: Dryden's 'Cousin Swift,'" *PMLA*, LXVII (1952), 1024–1034; R. W. Ketton-Cremer, *Thomas Gray: A Biography* (Cambridge, 1955), pp. 137–139; R. H. Super, "A Grain of Truth about Wordsworth and Browning, Landor and Swinburne," *Modern Language Notes*, LXVII (1952), 419–421.

Cross discusses the Sterne legends in his *Sterne*, pp. 487–489, 491–493. See also Lodwick Hartley, *This is Lorence* (Chapel Hill, 1943), pp. 270–272.

The main attempts to supply Emily Dickinson with one or more "lovers" have been Josephine Pollitt, *Emily Dickinson: The Human Background of Her Poetry* (New York, 1930); Genevieve Taggard, *The Life and Mind of Emily Dickinson* (New York, 1930); Rebecca Patterson, *The Riddle of Emily Dickinson* (Boston, 1951); and Millicent Todd Bingham, *Emily Dickinson: A Revelation* (New York, 1954). George Frisbie Whicher, *This Was a Poet: A Critical Biography of Emily Dickinson* (New York, 1939), Chapters V and VI and pp. 320–324, vigorously criticizes the arguments advanced on behalf of the various candidates down to that time. In his passages on these persons, Thomas H. Johnson, *Emily Dickinson: An Interpretive Biography* (Cambridge, Mass., 1955) offers the most sensible verdict on the whole matter.

Stanley Williams' canvassing of the Emily Foster "mystery" occurs in his *Irving*, I, 238–254; the quotation is on p. 250.

L. A. G. Strong's biography of Moore is *The Minstrel Boy* (London, 1937).

3. (pages 329–343)

Henry James on the Byron papers: John Buchan, *Pilgrim's Way* (Boston, 1940), p. 149.

Fraser's Magazine on the pose in letters: XLI (1850), 201.

The sanest recent treatments of psychoanalysis and literary biography are by Leon Edel, in Chapter V of his *Literary Biography* and in "The Biographer and Psycho-Analysis," reprinted in Clifford, *Biography as an Art*, pp. 226–239. A fairly full list of the books and articles that have examined literary biography from a psychoanalytic viewpoint is found in Section 1 of Norman Kiell, *Psychoanalysis, Psychology, and Literature: A Bibliography* (Madison, Wis., 1963).

Richard Aldington's remark is in his *Portrait of a Genius, But—* (London, 1950), p. 95.

"Psychoanalysis has made it increasingly apparent . . .": Ben Karpman, "Neurotic Traits of Jonathan Swift, as Revealed by 'Gulliver's Travels,'" *Psychoanalytic Review*, XXIX (1942), 26–27.

Krutch's diagnosis of Poe appeared in his *Edgar Allan Poe: A Study in Genius* (New York, 1926); Fagin's, in *The Histrionic Mr. Poe* (Baltimore, 1949). Mention should also be made of the Princess Marie Bonaparte's *Edgar Poe: étude psychoanalytique* (Paris, 1933)—one of the most enthusiastic ("fanatical" would doubtless be more accurate) of all such biographies. The quotation "Swift was a neurotic . . ." is from Karpman's article, just cited, p. 182. On Swift and Carroll, see Phyllis Greenacre, *Swift and Carroll: A Psychoanalytic Study of Two Lives* (New York, 1955). The analysis of Carlyle referred to is in James L. Halliday, *Mr. Carlyle, My Patient: A Psychosomatic Biography* (London, 1949). The theory of the Lambs' death wish is set forth in Katharine Anthony, *The Lambs* (New York, 1945). John Berryman attributes an Oedipus complex to Stephen Crane in his *Stephen Crane* (New York, 1950). Betty Miller's book is *Robert Browning: A Portrait* (New York, 1952).

Sackville-West on psychoanalysis: *Thomas De Quincey: His Life and Work* (New Haven, 1936), pp. 135–136. Jack Simmons on the same topic: *Southey* (New Haven, 1948), p. 214.

Howard M. Jones's criticism of psychoanalysis in biography: *The Theory of American Literature* (Ithaca, N.Y., 1948), p. 149.

Shaw on the fallacy of the "rigid single estimate": his "Postscript" to Frank Harris, *Bernard Shaw: An Unauthorized Biography Based on First Hand Information* (New York, 1931), p. 426.

Symons on the prevalence of anal sadism and the rarity of genius: *Thomas Carlyle: The Life and Ideas of a Prophet* (New York, 1952), p. 29.

4. (pages 344–350)

Carlyle on the individual man and his environment: "Burns," *Edinburgh Review*, XLVIII (1828), 269–270.

Zola (*Le Roman Expérimental,* Chapter II) is quoted by Miriam Allott, *Novelists on the Novel* (London, 1959), p. 303.

Lichfield and its effect on Johnson: James L. Clifford, *Young Sam Johnson* (New York, 1955), pp. 36–37.

Stanfield's words are in his *Essay on Biography,* p. 151; Sackville-West's in his *De Quincey,* p. 122.

Objectivity in biography: Alfred McKinley Terhune, *The Life of Edward FitzGerald* (New Haven, 1947), p. x.

Galsworthy's observations are in his *The Creation of Character in Literature,* pp. 8–9.

CHAPTER ELEVEN

1. (pages 351–360)

Virginia Woolf on biography as a craft: "The Art of Biography," *Atlantic Monthly,* CLXIII (1939), 506–510. The quotation is from pp. 509, 510.

Birrell on Marvell: *Andrew Marvell* (London, 1905), p. 2. Smithers on Addison: *The Life of Joseph Addison* (Oxford, 1954), p. v.

Shaw on Frank Harris: Vincent Brome, *Frank Harris* (London, 1959), p. 5.

Shaw on Wilde: Frank Harris, *Oscar Wilde: His Life & Confessions* (New York, 1930), p. 387. Furnas on Stevenson's life: *Voyage to Windward: The Life of Robert Louis Stevenson* (London, 1952), pp. 17–18.

The comments on Arnold Bennett's success story are from Reginald Pound, *Arnold Bennett: A Biography* (London, 1952), p. 290.

Carlyle on every man's life a poem: "Count Cagliostro," *Fraser's Magazine,* VIII (1833), 19. Wilbur Cross's remarks are in *The History of Henry Fielding* (New Haven, 1918), I, viii.

2. (pages 360–368)

The quotation from Harper's *William Wordsworth: His Life, Works, and Influence* (London, 1916), is taken from the Preface.

The watershed in Southey's life: Simmons, *Southey,* p. 109.

The watershed in Hunt's: Blunden, *Leigh Hunt,* p. 250.

Smithers on Addison: *Life of Addison,* pp. vi–vii.

3. (pages 368–382)

The book on Landor referred to is R. H. Super, *Walter Savage Landor: A Biography* (New York, 1954); the excerpts are from pp. 3 and 376.

The annals of Amy Lowell: S. Foster Damon, *Amy Lowell: A*

Chronicle with Extracts from Her Correspondence (Boston, 1935), pp. 365–366.

Bewley's review of Schorer's *Sinclair Lewis: Hudson Review*, XV (1962), 143–148. The quotation is from pp. 143, 147.

Henry James's comment on the novelist's search for "value" is in his preface to *The Spoils of Poynton.*

Peter Quennell on the multiple personalities of Byron: *The Sign of the Fish*, p. 162.

Shaw's remarks to Henderson are in the latter's *Shaw*, p. xxiv.

Frost to Cox: Elizabeth Shepley Sergeant, *Robert Frost: The Trial by Existence* (New York, 1960), p. 311.

Weber on the role of the literary biographer: *Hardy of Wessex: His Life and Literary Career* (New York, 1940), pp. v–vi.

4. (pages 382–390)

Stanfield's comment on "annalistic" biography is in his *Essay on Biography*, pp. 67–69.

Roger North's doctrine: *Lives* (cited in notes to Chapter Six, Section 3), I, 98–99.

Cantwell and Hawthorne's contemporaries: *Nathaniel Hawthorne: The American Years* (New York, 1948), p. x.

5. (pages 391–396)

Izaak Walton's remark is in the preface to his life of Dr. Sanderson.

For a demonstration of how vulnerable popularized biographies are to scholarly criticism, see Clifton J. Furness' review of Frances Winwar's *American Giant: Walt Whitman and His Times* in *American Literature*, XIII (1942), 423–432.

6. (pages 396–400)

Carlyle on "a well-written Life": "Richter," *Edinburgh Review*, XLVI (1827), 177. Jeffrey's comments are *ibid.*, XLV (1826), 47–48.

"Leigh Hunt was Shelley's fault entirely . . .": Nicolson, *Byron: The Last Journey* (London, 1924), p. 23.

Newman White on the style of biography: *Shelley* (New York, 1940), I, vii. Humphry House on the same topic: *All in Due Time*, pp. 265–267.

CHAPTER TWELVE

1. (pages 401–407)

Carlyle on overemphasis of biography: "Biography," *Fraser's Magazine*, V (1832), 254.

Fiedler's case for biography is in his "Archetype and Signature: A Study of the Relationship Between Biography and Poetry," *Sewanee Review*, LX (1952), 253–273. The quotation is from pp. 259–260. Another significant article illustrating contemporary critics' acceptance—sometimes reluctant—of biography as an adjunct to literary study is Walter J. Ong, "The Jinnee in the Well-Wrought Urn," *Essays in Criticism*, IV (1954), 309–320. Among the many other documents in the modern phase of the debate, the exchange between C. S. Lewis and E. M. W. Tillyard, "The Personal Heresy in Criticism," *Essays and Studies of the English Association*, 1934–36, is especially noteworthy.

The characterization of Arthur Murphy is Wilbur Cross's: *History of Henry Fielding*, III, 147. Cross (III, 125–150) has much to say of Murphy, none of it complimentary. See also Frederic T. Blanchard, *Fielding the Novelist: A Study in Historical Criticism* (New Haven, 1926), pp. 156–164. The comment on the unfortunate influence of Gilchrist on Blake criticism is by Northrop Frye, in *The English Romantic Poets and Essayists*, ed. C. W. Houtchens and L. W. Houtchens (New York, 1957), p. 7. Douglas Bush discusses the modern interpretation of Milton in "John Milton," *English Institute Essays 1946* (New York, 1947), pp. 5–19. Other essays in the same volume, devoted to "The Critical Significance of Biographical Evidence," are also germane to the topic of this chapter.

Jeffrey's remarks are in the *Edinburgh Review*, LXII (1835), 206–207.

2. (pages 407–413)

Shelley as a figure in Hunt's biography of Byron: Norman, *Flight of the Skylark*, pp. 86–87. Hayley as a figure in Gilchrist's *Blake:* Morchard Bishop, *Blake's Hayley* (London, 1951), p. 353.

On the controversial atmosphere of Cowper biography: Lodwick Hartley, "Cowper and the Evangelicals: Notes on Early Biographical Interpretations," *PMLA*, LXV (1950), 719–731.

Carlyle on the man of letters as "our most important modern person": *Heroes and Hero-Worship* ("The Hero as a Man of Letters").

Gosse's dictum on the difficulty of life writing: "The Custom of Biography," *Anglo-Saxon Review*, VIII (1901), 208.

INDEX

Italic numbers refer to pages on which the author concerned figures as the subject of biography. **Boldface** numbers indicate quotations dealing with biography.

A NOTE ON THE TYPE

THE TEXT of this book is set in *Caledonia,* a typeface designed by
by W(ILLIAM) A(DDISON) DWIGGINS for the Mergenthaler Linotype
Company in 1939. Dwiggins chose to call his new typeface Caledonia,
the Roman name for Scotland, because it was inspired by the Scotch
types cast about 1833 by Alexander Wilson & Son, Glasgow type
founders. However, there is a calligraphic quality about this face
that is totally lacking in the Wilson types. Dwiggins referred to an
even earlier typeface for this "liveliness of action"—one cut around
1790 by William Martin for the printer William Bulmer. Caledonia
has more weight than the Martin letters, and the bottom finishing
strokes (serifs) of the letters are cut straight across, without brackets,
to make sharp angles with the upright stems, thus giving a "modern
face" appearance.

W. A. Dwiggins (1880–1956) was born in Martinsville, Ohio,
and studied art in Chicago. In 1904 he moved to Hingham, Massachusetts, where he built a solid reputation as a designer of advertise-
ments and as a calligrapher. He began an association with the
Mergenthaler Linotype Company in 1929, and over the next twenty-
seven years designed a number of book types for that firm. Of especial
interest are the Metro series, Electra, Caledonia, Eldorado, and Falcon.
In 1930, Dwiggins first became interested in marionettes, and through
the years made many important contributions to the art of puppetry
and the design of marionettes.

Composed, printed, and bound by
The Haddon Craftsmen, Inc., Scranton, Pa.